Exploring Personhood

Exploring Personhood

An Introduction to the Philosophy of Human Nature

Joseph Torchia, O.P.

ROWMAN & LITTLEFIELD PUBLISHERS, INC.
Lanham • Boulder • New York • Toronto • Plymouth, UK

ROWMAN & LITTLEFIELD PUBLISHERS, INC.

Published in the United States of America
by Rowman & Littlefield Publishers, Inc.
A wholly owned subsidary of The Rowman & Littlefield Publishing Group, Inc.
4501 Forbes Boulevard, Suite 200, Lanham, Maryland 20706
www.rowmanlittlefield.com

Estover Road
Plymouth PL6 7PY
United Kingdom

Copyright © 2008 by Rowman & Littlefield Publishers, Inc.

British Library Cataloguing in Publication Information Available

Library of Congress Cataloging-in-Publication Data:

Torchia, Joseph, 1953–
  Exploring personhood : an introduction to the philosophy of human nature /
Joseph Torchia.
      p. cm.
  Includes bibliographical references and index.
  ISBN-13: 978-0-7425-4837-4 (cloth : alk. paper)
  ISBN-10: 0-7425-4837-6 (cloth : alk. paper)
  ISBN-13: 978-0-7425-4838-1 (pbk. : alk. paper)
  ISBN-10: 0-7425-4838-4 (pbk. : alk. paper)
  1. Persons. 2. Human behavior. I. Title.
  BD450.T645 2008
  128—dc22   2007016549

Printed in the United States of America

♾™ The paper used in this publication meets the minimum requirements of
American National Standard for Information Sciences—Permanence of Paper
for Printed Library Materials, ANSI/NISO Z39.48-1992.

To my parents, for the persons they are

Contents

Being and Substance/Substance and Change/Aristotle's Psychology/
Soul, Body, and the Separable Intellect

Preface

What does it mean to be a person? For some, posing such a question seems pointless; they assume they already know the answer, based on their knowledge of themselves and others. But the seeming obviousness of that answer can be deceptive. Assessing the meaning of personhood can be like looking into the Grand Canyon: while the observer gets a seemingly comprehensive bird's-eye view of the expanse, such a vantage point offers only the beginning of a prolonged journey of discovery that requires a deeper examination of the surrounding terrain and its underlying strata. Likewise, any attempt to define the meaning of the notion of the person opens a window to a vast horizon of inquiry that raises many additional questions on a variety of levels.

A POINT OF DEPARTURE

How do we begin so speculative an investigation? One possible avenue (albeit a preliminary one), I would suggest, lies in a pairing of two key questions. The central question, *What does it mean to be a person?* might initially be assessed in light of the more basic question, *What does it mean to be fully human?* Both questions, of course, can be approached from diverse standpoints—from the scientific to the religious to the philosophical. And any one of these perspectives involves further divisions reflecting the ideological or disciplinary backgrounds of the investigators.

Regardless of perspective, however, the fullness of our humanity points to the uniqueness of the human species as a whole. What, in fact, sets us apart from other living things? In this connection, the paleoanthropologist Ian Tattersall offers some thought-provoking observations.

> It is only with the arrival of Cro-Magnons in Europe that the archaeological record unequivocally declares that people of modern sensibility had arrived. Even the Neanderthals, complex and admirable as they might have been, were probably limited to an intuitive level of understanding of the world about them and there can be no doubt that they had quite sophisticated ways of communicating with each other. All this . . . was in every likelihood achieved in the absence of symbolic reasoning. The Neanderthals did not live, as we do, in a world of their own making, reconstructed in their minds, but in the world as nature presented itself to them.[1]

For Tattersall, then, the distinguishing mark of our humanness lies in the capacity for symbolic reasoning—the ability to reconstruct reality in our minds through the medium of thought and language. In fact, however, Tattersall's criterion of humanness represents another behavioral characteristic. From that standpoint, our uniqueness lies in what we are able to do or how we are able to behave, rather than in what we are by nature. But a consideration of what we are by nature is the very stuff of philosophical reflection. Accordingly, it takes us beyond the level of ordinary scientific discourse. This is not to deny that Tattersall's paleoanthropological viewpoint (or the viewpoint of any number of scientific practitioners) offers some valuable insights for our purposes. Yet any scientific discussion of what it means to be human reveals certain underlying presuppositions that ultimately trace their origin to that special mode of philosophical questioning appropriate to metaphysics, the science of being.

ontology.

FOCUS AND METHODOLOGY

In its broadest terms this volume explores the metaphysical underpinnings of theories of human nature, personhood, and the self, with a special attention to accounts of the relationship between soul and body (or alternatively, between mind and body). While such theories differ from thinker to thinker and tradition to tradition, the main philosophers considered in this work assess our humanness in terms of an immaterial principle (i.e., soul or mind) which transcends the limitations of the body and physiological processes. Indeed, even thinkers (e.g., Hume) who openly reject the notion of a soul or mind as something distinct from the body must still reckon with traditional metaphysical notions, even as they disavow them. In this respect, my investigation reflects philosophical anthropology on its ground floor, so to speak, on its most foundational level, with a focus on the basic constituents of the unified self.

This work is broad in scope, covering the Pre-Socratics to postmodernism, with an assessment of what transpired during the intervening 2,500 years. This volume is by no means an exhaustive history of the philosophical understanding of human nature, personhood, and the self. Rather, it uses the history of Western philosophy as the framework in which to explore critical problems pertinent to these three topics. Accordingly, the book is designed to meet the needs of a wide range of readers, from beginning students to those with a more sophisticated grasp of the issues.

Clearly, a work spanning two and a half millennia cannot satisfy everyone's expectations about which thinkers should be included. Indeed, an enterprise such as this can be as daunting as compiling a greatest hits anthology of popular music; inevitably someone's special favorite will be omitted. The thinkers and developments I have selected for inclusion represent what I consider some of the most important landmarks or nodal points along the way. Admittedly, two thinkers also happen to represent my own special favorites—Augustine and Aquinas.

The work is divided into four parts: part 1, "From *Psyche* to *Anthropos,*" traces the origins of a metaphysical account of the human person from the Pre-Socratics to Aristotle; part 2, "Human Nature and Personhood," explores the emergence of a full-fledged philosophy of the human person in two classical Christian thinkers, St. Augustine of Hippo and St. Thomas Aquinas; part 3, "Minds and Bodies," addresses the mind-body problem that emerges in Cartesian dualism and the subsequent critique of the notion of mind prominent in the empiricist tradition; part 4, "Humanity and Personhood," focuses on the postmodernist tradition, with a consideration of the relevance of personhood in current debates regarding bioethics and contemporary versions of the mind-body problem.

Each chapter can stand on its own, but collectively the chapters reveal a developing story that reflects a major preoccupation of the Western intellectual tradition—the attempt to come to terms with what defines us as human beings and how we understand ourselves as persons. In adopting this methodology, I intend to allow the history of philosophical anthropology to speak for itself, by telling this story in a real-time format—as it unfolds—and with a sensitivity to the development and refinement of key concepts. My interest in the emergence and evolution of basic anthropological notions is complemented by a critical analysis that isolates major themes and arguments, evaluates them in light of the influences that shaped them, and assesses their influence on subsequent trends. This evaluative dimension is most prominent in part 4, where I develop a critical response that has its roots in Aristotelianism and, in broader terms, in the Thomistic tradition of inquiry.

My historical treatment is organized on the basis of a series of anthro-pological models, each of which serves as the focus of a given chapter. By means of a commentary on seminal texts (e.g., Plato's *Phaedo*, Aristotle's *De Anima*, Aquinas's *Treatise on Man* in the *Summa Theologica*, Descartes' *Discourse on Method* and *Meditations*, Hume's *Treatise on Human Nature;* Ryle's *The Concept of Mind*), I offer the reader a perusal of some of the most significant developments in philosophical anthropology and thereby open a window into the process whereby Western thinkers made the tran-sition from (1) a preoccupation with humans in the most generic terms (i.e., as *anthropos* or *homo*) to (2) a recognition of our status as persons (i.e., beings that are individual, unique, and relational in our own right) to (3) the steady undermining of a metaphysical understanding of a unified, abiding self during the modern and contemporary periods. What stands out in this analysis is the extent to which different thinkers and periods bring to the fore and highlight diverse aspects of our humanness in either a constructive or critical fashion.

If the past is any indicator of future trends, then developments in tech-nology and science will continue to provide philosophers with new food for thought. Are all humans persons? Do humans acquire personhood, and can they lose it at some point in time as a result of neurological changes or cognitive impairment? For that matter, is personhood limited to the human species? Such questions assume a special poignancy at the beginning of the new millennium, as we confront the prospect of cloning, organ transplantation, and the capacity to prolong human life indefinitely by artificial means. Such developments (and the bioethical dilemmas they generate) invite a reassessment of our most fundamental anthropological presuppositions. In a very real sense, the story is by no means over; its telling is a work in progress.

ACKNOWLEDGMENTS

I thank Fordham University Press for permission to use the translations found in *An Aquinas Reader,* edited with an introduction by Mary T. Clark (New York: Fordham University Press, 2000). Select portions of chapters 5, 8, and 9 originally appeared in two of my previously published arti-cles: "Postmodernism and the Persistent Vegetative State," *National Catholic Bioethics Quarterly* (Summer 2002): 257–75; and "Incommensura-bility and Moral Conflicts: A Critical Assessment of the Response of Alas-dair C. MacIntyre," *Providence: Studies in Western Civilization* (Fall-Winter 2003): 40–68. I thank the editors of the *National Catholic Bioethics Quarterly* and *Providence: Studies in Western Civilization* for permission to use this material.

This book is the direct outgrowth of my course Philosophy of the Human Person, which I have taught at Providence College since 2001. Those classes provided veritable laboratory exercises for exploring the insights of the various thinkers discussed in this volume. In this respect, I cannot overlook the most important component of those exercises: my students who motivated me to grapple with those thinkers by providing a receptive audience committed to active learning. From this standpoint, they were my teachers as well. In broader terms, my interest in theories of human nature, personhood, and the self are rooted in my scholarship in later Greek and early medieval thought. These scholarly pursuits took a decisive turn as the result of two challenging ministries that placed my anthropological interests in a contemporary context: one involving advocacy on behalf of the mentally and physically disabled, and another in a hospice setting working with terminally ill patients. These pastoral experiences increasingly attuned me to the mystery inherent in human personhood, a mystery that by no means diminishes in mind-body impairment but is magnified and conveyed with greater clarity. My reflections in this vein found a nexus in my appointment as visiting research scholar at the Center for Clinical Bioethics at Georgetown University Medical Center in the summer of 1999, where I assessed the bioethical dimension of personhood, particularly as it pertains to end-of-life issues. In the process, my appreciation of the depth of our humanness and the profundity of personhood prompted a question that serves as a guiding motif in the present study: *What does it mean to be fully human, and what are the fundamental constituents of our personhood on its most foundational level?* This work provides an attempt to answer this question and, in so doing, to search for a metaphysical grounding of the self on which all parties can reach consensus. Only such a consensus (however tenuous at the outset) will free us from the seeming incommensurability of contemporary anthropological debates.

NOTE

1. Ian Tattersall, *Becoming Human: Evolution and Human Uniqueness* (New York: Harcourt, Brace, 1998), 229.

Introduction: Competing Anthropological Perspectives

The history of philosophical anthropology reveals the influence of two competing viewpoints about our human status that emerged at the beginning of the Western intellectual tradition and assumed varied forms over its long course. Roger Trigg describes the tension between these viewpoints and their accompanying presuppositions along these lines:

> If I think that humans are indeed a little lower than the angels, and may live beyond this life, then I shall view myself differently from the person who accepts that the species *Homo sapiens* is one animal species amongst many, characterized only by a particular evolutionary history. The tug between seeing humans as packages of genes, existing without purpose, and as the special creation of a loving God is the modern version of a perennial debate amongst philosophers. Is human life exclusively moulded by physical forces of which we may be totally unconscious?[1]

In broader philosophical terms, Trigg's characterization of these viewpoints can be conveniently described in terms of a conflict between the *teleological* and *mechanistic* perspectives. The former perspective endorses a metaphysical distinction between an immaterial mind and a material body. It likewise recognizes an order and a purposiveness in human existence by virtue of an appeal to something which transcends our physical being. The latter perspective ultimately reduces our mental life and decision-making capacity to no more than highly complex neurophysiological processes. In a contemporary context, this is tantamount to saying that there is no difference between mind and brain, or between thinking and brain-wave activity.

1

At the outset, an important qualification is in order. On the surface, it may appear that the teleological and mechanistic perspectives reflect an opposition between a philosophical interpretation of human nature and personhood (presupposing a spiritual dimension calling for a metaphysical explanation) and a scientific interpretation that is firmly grounded in an empirical analysis whose results are derived from verifiable data. But such a sharp distinction is too facile for our purposes; the lines simply cannot be so clearly drawn. In fact, the distinction between philosophical and scientific investigations pertinent to our humanness is frequently blurred.

Do scientific explanations about our status as humans ultimately depend on certain fundamental philosophical presuppositions? Or do philosophical accounts of our humanness find their inspiration, focus, and direction in scientific developments? Both questions seemingly admit of an affirmative response. On the one hand, scientists take for granted more philosophical notions regarding human nature or personhood than they may care to acknowledge. But by the same token, philosophical anthropology has consistently been driven by developments in empirical science and consequently prompted to address the probing questions it poses. When viewed from this standpoint, the teleological and mechanistic perspectives are competing outlooks that have offered mutual touchstones. In this respect, I propose the following question as a critical point of departure: *How is the tension between these perspectives evident in philosophical reflection on human nature, personhood, and the self from ancient times to the present?* While my primary concern lies in the emergence of an explicitly teleological understanding of these topics, this analysis unfolds with a continual attentiveness to the challenges posed by the mechanistic viewpoint, and its reductionist expressions over the centuries.

HUMAN NATURE AND PERSONHOOD

In the ebb and flow of philosophical anthropology, discussions of personhood frequently overlap with discussions about human nature. Scientists, however, freely talk about human beings and human nature without any explicit reference to persons. Although this omission may not have any practical bearing on the outcome or success of scientific research, a consideration of humans that does not appreciate their personal status can easily reduce us to so many biological entities, chemical aggregates, collections of neurons, or anonymous social units. Accordingly, this volume defends the somewhat controversial position (at least by contemporary standards) that humanness and personhood coincide (i.e., that every human being qualifies as a person in his or her own right). But I do not collapse the distinction between these notions. It is still important to distinguish the two from a conceptual standpoint.

In some cases, however, human nature and personhood are treated as wholly different categories; for example, various postmodernist thinkers sharply demarcate biological humanity and moral personhood. As a result, postmodernist philosophers like Michael Tooley, Roland Pucetti, and H. Tristram Engelhardt Jr. draw the conclusion that some human beings (e.g., those deprived of higher brain capacity) lack personhood, while some nonhumans (e.g., higher primates or hypothetical extraterrestrials) may well qualify as persons on the basis of certain behavioral characteristics.

Broadly speaking, human nature encompasses what all human beings share—a pattern or way of living comprising all of the traits (e.g., biological, emotional, rational) that set us apart from other living things. Accordingly, recognition of a "human nature" is tantamount to affirming that there is something distinctive about our humanness. The notion of human nature thus presupposes a common element which links every human (and manifests itself in the way we behave and respond to certain stimuli and situations), as well as something that distinguishes us from members of other living species.

But the claim that there is a set of universal human traits grounded in a stable, abiding "nature" which all humans share (simply by virtue of their humanity) is viewed with skepticism or even hostility by many contemporary thinkers. This critical attitude is aptly expressed by the evolutionary biologist Paul R. Ehrlich:

> What is human nature? For thousands of years, philosophers have discussed and debated that question. Underlying almost all those debates, however, has been a key shared assumption: that human nature is a unitary, unchanging thing. As the new millennium dawns, that assumption of a single, enduring nature remains widespread, but in my view it has become a major roadblock to understanding ourselves. "Human nature" as a singular concept embodies the erroneous notion that people possess a common set of rigid, genetically specified behavioral predilections that are unlikely to be altered by circumstances. Our better selves are seen to be in constant battle with a universal set of unchanging, primitive "drives," which frequently break through the veneer and create many of the most serious ills that afflict humanity.[2]

For these critics, definitions of human nature (and the proposal of some sine qua non of our humanity) are heavily laden with background assumptions or subjective biases about what it means to be human. Whose definition of human nature is the valid one? The history of Western thought includes a vast array of divergent and often conflicting opinions on this topic, leading one commentator to assert that "there can be no single, simple definition of human nature."[3] By the same token, the notion of a fixed human nature is perceived as antithetical to the freedom, spontaneity, and creative impulses that we perceive to be privileged assets. For the critics, then, those who endorse the notion of a universally shared and enduring human nature tacitly assume that we are locked into a standard mode of unalterable behavioral patterns.

If human nature pertains to what all humans have in common, personhood is inextricably linked with individuality, uniqueness, and an enduring self. Recognizing ourselves and others as "persons" acknowledges something that runs much deeper than what can be observed or tested. In contrast, many theorists (in the cognitive sciences, for example) confine their discussions of personhood exclusively to overt behavioral criteria rooted in empirically verifiable data.

This volume, in contrast, proceeds from the premise that designating a fellow human being as a person entails an implicit awareness of a dimension that always eludes our complete intellectual grasp and thus does not allow for reduction to another item of factual information. From this standpoint, the affirmation that one is a person is not the end product of some prolonged ratiocination process. Rather, it presupposes the kind of insight into the reality of others that can only grow out of true interpersonal relationships. In the final analysis, the search for the meaning of personhood is a person-to-person endeavor that fuses the intellectual and social dimensions of human existence. Accordingly, a suitable definition of something as profound as personhood cannot proceed from a mere catalog of the traits, characteristics, drives, and capacities that people tend to exhibit. Such a definition depends on an attunement to the inner life of oneself and others that reveals the depth of our being as humans.

TOWARD A METAPHYSICS OF PERSONHOOD

In its broadest terms, philosophy invites us to come to terms with the ultimate questions confronting us as humans—questions concerning self, world, and reality in general. A central concern of philosophy and philosophizing lies in subjecting our uncritical presuppositions about the way things are to critical evaluation. The very fact that we can raise these kinds of questions says something significant about us as humans and our need to clarify, to explain, and to know. When Socrates affirmed that the unexamined life is not worth living, he expressed a conviction that would define the intellectual tradition he inspired: questioning about what it means to be human is part and parcel of a complete and happy life.

philosophy : a concern for human happiness.

Closely connected with this critical task of philosophy is the search for a more comprehensive account of things. In contrast to other disciplines (which tend to a specialization and a compartmentalizing of knowledge), philosophers address issues that transcend disciplinary boundaries. This aspect of the philosophical enterprise assumes a special anthropological relevance. While other disciplines focus on particular facets of human existence, philosophy can approach it as an organic whole. In this respect, the luxury of philosophical questioning lies in the fact that its interests are necessarily broad in scope. For this reason, philosophical questions exhibit a multirelevance on at least two levels. On the one hand, they have important implications for manifold areas of inquiry; on the other, they hold significance for our entire vision of reality.

If metaphysics (as the investigation of the really real) represents the most fundamental branch of philosophical inquiry, then its mode of questioning is singularly suited to sounding the foundations of human personhood. But the metaphysical preoccupation with visions of reality, worldviews, or the "big picture" of things carries a certain limitation. While the answers that philosophers propose are outgrowths of reasoning and grounded in sense experience, they are not always verifiable (at least not by the standards of the empirical sciences). This is especially apparent in the context of philosophical discussions regarding the parameters of human personhood and the status of the soul or mind.

In actuality, however, many discussions of human personhood never come to terms with this deeper metaphysical dimension. The failure to do so is evident in treatments that confine themselves to epistemological criteria alone. For example, Ian Tattersall's appeal (as quoted in the preface, above) to our capacity for symbolic reasoning as the criterion of humanness raises a further question: *What supports this capacity on its most foundational level—the level of being?* Such a question assumes a distinctively metaphysical thrust because it addresses the ultimate cause of personhood. If such a cause exists, it serves as the principle responsible for integrating the diverse range of operations and capacities we display—not as members of the human species but as unique individuals.

A metaphysical account of the human person emerged on a gradual basis. It received its initial impetus from the ancient Greek philosophers, especially in that tradition of critical reflection beginning with Socrates (and the rich teleological perspective he promoted) and enriched by Plato and Aristotle. From the outset, Greek thinkers posited cognitive activities like reasoning and knowing as the mark of human beings, more precisely the rational soul. Later, thinkers in the Christian tradition recognized the uniqueness of each human as a person in his or her own right. By drawing on their belief in a personal Creator (and the accompanying belief that humans were created in God's image and likeness), Christian thinkers radically redefined what it means to be fully human. In this respect, the challenge of twenty-first-century debates about what it means to be a person lies in the need to retrieve a sense of the richness of that notion in the face of an increasing deemphasis of the intrinsic value of human life in general.

A GENERAL OVERVIEW: CONTENT AND APPROACH

Philosophical anthropology is deeply rooted in the Western intellectual tradition. Accordingly, part 1 traces the growth and maturation of such foundational concepts as soul and mind from the dawn of that tradition. This period encompasses the emergence of a comprehensive theory of human nature and the beginnings of sustained critical reflection on the relationship between soul or mind and body. It opens the way, in turn, to a refined understanding of personhood under the influence of Christian thought during the Middle Ages.

Chapter 1, "In the Beginning: Defining Some Key Issues," offers a broad survey of major Pre-Socratic philosophers of the sixth and fifth centuries before Christ. While these thinkers are not usually considered in light of their contributions to philosophical anthropology, a reading of the surviving evidence (fragmentary as it is) introduces some of the key concepts, themes, and arguments that dominate its history. In these cosmological deliberations, we can discern the origins of the mind/body problem that constitutes such an important feature of later anthropological speculation. Although the Pre-Socratic philosophers reveal a wide range of positions, they share a common commitment to the search for a basis of intelligibility in the broadest metaphysical sense. The Pre-Socratic tradition thus lays the groundwork for an explicit statement regarding the teleological perspective in Plato, with his emphasis on the difference between physical causes and the ultimate causes that make physical causality possible. But this position could neither stand on its own nor meet the challenges of mechanism without a metaphysics both broad and technical enough to acknowledge the existence of immaterial reality.

Chapter 2, "Plato: The Primacy of Soul," considers the emergence of a psychological theory of human nature that is inextricably bound up with the philosophy of mind. Plato (428/7 to 348/7 B.C.) unequivocally claims that mind (more specifically, the soul) is completely incorporeal and stands in a special relationship with a higher conceptual realm that can be approached through reasoning alone. Plato's deliberations on the soul and the soul-body relationship reflect the overall humanistic emphasis that characterizes the next great transition in the Western intellectual tra-

Substance = 'Really Real'

dition. In this respect, however, Plato transformed Socrates's educational program (and its attempt to restore the integrity of moral discourse) into a comprehensive vision of reality centering on the Forms, as the ultimate foundations of the really and truly real.

By virtue of his dualism, Plato relegated the body (along with emotions and desires) to an inferior status. In the course of his philosophical development, however, he would moderate this dualism and broaden his psychology to allow for an emotional and appetitive dimension in the life of the soul. But he never relinquished his commitment to rationality and our capacity to think as the distinguishing feature of our humanness. It was left to his student Aristotle (384–322 B.C.) to develop a psychology that reflects our experience of psychosomatic unity and the role of the senses in knowing truth. Chapter 3, "The Human Composite," considers this Aristotelian contribution and its explicit emphasis on the substantial unity of soul and body.

Aristotle followed Plato in positing form as the object of knowledge and the perfection of a given thing. But he departs from Plato in his teaching that form is immanent in the substantial realities accessible to us through the senses. In Aristotelian terms, substance is the paradigmatic example of the really real. Accordingly, Aristotle's philosophy of nature (and its analysis of moving, changing substances) provides the general framework in which he discusses the human soul and life in general.

One of the great legacies of the Classical ideal of human nature lies in the idea of a parallelism between the way we think and act and the way things are. This metaphysical kinship between human nature and the really real provides the basis for an understanding of what contributes to our fulfillment as rational beings. But what is the role of the individual in this anthropological model? In their preoccupation with the nature or essence of things, Plato and Aristotle fail to address the uniqueness of each and every human being. It is only in the Christian intellectual tradition that the individual qua individual becomes the focus of anthropological speculation.

By drawing on their belief in a personal Creator God, Christian thinkers radically redefined the parameters of philosophical anthropology and, by implication, the Classical understanding of what it means to be fully human. In part 2, we consider the emergence of viable theories of personhood in two key contributors to these developments: Augustine of Hippo (chapter 4, "A Harmonious Union") and Thomas Aquinas (chapter 5, "A Subsistent Individual"). In their own lives, Augustine and Aquinas confronted radical strains of dualistic anthropologies (Manichaeism in the case of Augustine and Albigensianism in the case of Aquinas) that downgraded matter and bodily existence in favor of the soul. Each sought a balanced theory of our humanness that accounts for the unity of soul and body. In the process, they strove for a middle ground between an excessive spiritualism, which defines us in terms of the soul alone, or a thoroughgoing materialism, which defines us in purely physicalistic terms.

Augustine and Aquinas thus stand firmly in the line of ancient and medieval thinkers who uphold the teleological perspective in opposition to both materialism (which reduces the really real to matter and corporeal things) and extreme dualism (which defines reality in terms of two distinct principles in perpetual conflict with each other). In so doing, they envision a moral cosmos in which humans possess an appropriate role and function conducive to the realization of their proper good. While this vision of things shares much in common with what we find in the Greek philosophical tradition, it also reflects the Judeo-Christian belief in a free creation by a good and loving Creator.

From the Christian perspective represented by Augustine and Aquinas, the human person constitutes a unified but relational being to its core—the vital center of a multidimensional reality encompassing psychological, physical, and ultimately ontological levels of explanation. In historical terms, this model of the person provides something of a paradigm for assessing what preceded and what followed. On the one hand, it represents a synthesis and refinement of anthropological speculation spanning the ancient Greek and medieval Christian eras; on the other hand, it provides an ideal of psychosomatic unity that serves as a standard for assessing subsequent developments. In part 3, we address modern challenges to this ideal, with the emergence of the mind-body problem and the difficulties it generates for coming to terms with the integrated experience of mental and physical activity that characterizes our sense of self. At this juncture, the tension between the teleological and mechanistic perspectives intensified with the growth of a new scientific outlook and its reaction against an Aristotelian worldview and Christian theological presuppositions about the nature of reality and our place in that overall scheme.

If the new science offered an accurate explanation of things, then how would one uphold a commitment to an immaterial soul or mind that is immune to the limitations of natural processes? In modern philosophical circles, we encounter two dominant responses to this question. The first attempts to reconcile theistic and scientific accounts of human nature on the basis of a pronounced dualism between mind and body. This is the response of René Descartes (1596–1650), the focus of chapter 6, "The Ghost in the Machine." The second response rejects any reference to an immaterial principle and endorses a thoroughgoing materialism that defines humans and personhood in a manner consistent with the methodology of natural science. This is the response exemplified by David Hume (1711–1776), the focus of chapter 7, "A Bundle of Perceptions."

As a Christian believer who was also a thoroughgoing rationalist, Descartes saw the only hope for upholding the integrity, freedom, and immortality of the soul in its separation from the body. By confining what is essentially human to the soul alone (or, more precisely, to the mind), he sought a demarcation of that privileged sphere of our humanness. In a manner consistent with his dualism, any claim to individuality or personhood is rooted in the mind. When Descartes states "I think; therefore I am," he affirms that he is a thinking substance whose nature is to think. Thinking is proper to us as humans and constitutes our defining activity; it belongs to us essentially. Conversely, everything connected with the body and sense experience is extrinsic to our essential nature. For Descartes, there is nothing about the body that measures up to the rigid criteria of his method and its demand that we only accept those truths we grasp clearly and distinctly as such.

By treating us on the basis of such disparate accounts (i.e., a mind-based/teleological one and a body-based/mechanistic one), Descartes lays the groundwork for a psychological materialism that dispenses with an immaterial dimension. Why not bypass any discussion of mind as an immaterial principle and confine one's analysis of human nature to what is empirically verifiable? This was Hume's strategy, the key representative of the other facet of modern philosophy: British empiricism. While Descartes reflects the mathematical orientation of the new science (with its focus on deduction and a priori standards of truth), Hume exemplifies its commitment to the experimental method (with its emphasis on induction and the gathering of empirical evidence in expanding our knowledge of the world). In this respect, Hume's brand of empirical psychology was an outgrowth of a mitigated skepticism that calls into question any unsubstantiated theories regarding the soul or self—that is, theories not grounded in the publicly verifiable data of sense experience.

Hume's critique of these fundamental metaphysical and anthropological presuppositions sets the tone for a distinctively empiricist approach to human nature and personal identity that anticipates the philosophical behavioralism of the twentieth century. This school of thought rejects a metaphysical dualism between mind and body and thereby reduces talk of mental activity to a physical level. The dominant trend here is the attempt to define our humanness (and ultimately our personhood) on the basis of overt behavioral characteristics alone, rather than an immaterial nature (whether designated as "mind" or "soul"). In a contemporary context, then, scientists and philosophers increasingly transfer what was once attributed to the mind to the brain and neurophysiological activity.

Part 4 addresses a new brand of dualism that is a salient feature of postmodernist anthropology: the distinction between biological humanity and moral personhood. Is every human being a person simply by virtue

Empiricists : brain = mind

of his or her humanity? This question assumes a special relevance at the beginning of the present century. The claim that every human being qualifies as a person by nature presupposes certain metaphysical notions (e.g., the soul or a stable personal identity over time) that do not find widespread endorsement in a pluralistic culture that calls into question the objectivity of truth and knowledge claims.

In lieu of firm metaphysical criteria for accounts of human nature and personhood, postmodernist thinkers look to behavioral characteristics supporting a sense of self that allows us to enter and sustain moral relationships. In postmodernist terms, the most fundamental and irreducible of these traits is a conscious awareness of oneself and one's environment. From this standpoint, only personhood guarantees membership in a moral community of free agents possessing rights and the competence to exercise responsibilities on behalf of themselves and others.

Chapter 8, "Postmodernism: Humans, Persons, and Nonpersons," considers the consciousness criterion of personhood and the extent to which it shapes contemporary anthropological discussions. If personhood is defined on the basis of such factors as the quality of conscious life and decision-making capacity, then it becomes an attribute that extends beyond the basic biological requirements for membership in the human species. And if personhood depends primarily on conscious awareness, then the ultimate ground of personhood is not an immaterial mind but the brain. Conversely, the loss of consciousness and moral autonomy is viewed as coinciding with a loss of personal status and accompanying rights.

In the absence of any overarching metaphysical principles that command a universal consensus, we confront a seemingly unresolvable conflict between classical and contemporary accounts of personhood. Indeed, the challenge of postmodernism for those who support traditional interpretations of human nature, personhood, and the self lies in the attempt to uphold our intrinsic value and dignity over against those who reject the very notion of an immaterial soul or mind. In the face of this dilemma, we are left with an impasse between those who would define us exclusively on the basis of overt traits and those committed to a metaphysics of the person rooted in the facts of being. How can such an apparent incommensurability be overcome? In the intellectual project of Alasdair C. MacIntyre, we encounter what amounts to a compelling program for retrieving this metaphysical dimension in a contemporary setting.

According to MacIntyre's diagnosis, only a teleological understanding of human nature and the virtuous life rooted in the Aristotelian/Thomistic tradition of inquiry allows us to come to terms with the current disintegration of moral discourse. For him, this situation reveals the importance of recovering a genuine sense of a human *telos* as the basis for our vision of happiness. From this standpoint, human life must be interpreted as a coherent narrative directed toward the realization of our final end as humans beings.

MacIntyre's overall strategy provides a segue for chapter 9, "Our Interpersonal Journey," and my crafting of a viable alternative to postmodernist interpretations of personhood (and by implication to the materialistic assumption that mind coincides exclusively with the brain). Such an alternative appeals to a spiritual dimension of our humanness that does justice to the scope and extent of human thought, the integrity of free will, and most significantly our capacity to love in a selfless manner. But it does so in a way that addresses the challenge of contemporary scientific developments. If materialism is correct, then perhaps we are so many animals, albeit highly sophisticated ones. As I perceive it, then, the critical question amounts to this: *Can a purely reductionist account of human nature and personhood explain everything we are capable of doing in cognitive, volitional, and affective terms?* In responding to this question, I ground my deliberations in that experience of psychosomatic unity that manifests itself in our day-to-day activities.

In contrast to anthropological theories prominent in modern philosophy and its aftermath, Thomism offers an account of personhood that is firmly grounded on metaphysical principles instrumental in making sense of reality. In this context, personhood is not a matter of arbitrary interpretation, whereby a person is whatever we judge it to be. Nor is personhood definable on the basis of behavioral characteristics alone. Rather, its ultimate explanation is found in the act of being appropriate to individuals possessing a rational nature.

Indeed, the term "human being" is imbued with a distinctively ontological import. But we can use it in such a casual manner as to lose sight of this dimension. In my reckoning, "human being" is correlative with "being human," the mode of existence appropriate to persons as dynamic centers in their own right who participate in human nature even as they transcend it in their uniqueness. This touches on the mystery inherent in our way of being, a mystery that can only be revealed and appreciated by entering into the experience of the other through the intimacy of interpersonal relationships. In the face of such a penetrating mystery, a metaphysical explanation alone suffices, since this type of account attunes us to the luminosity of an inner life that always eludes attempts at complete empirical analysis.

The book concludes with an epilogue, "In Search of an Irreducible Self," that assesses contemporary theories of mind and consciousness in light of current research in artificial and animal intelligence. But whatever the success of science in accounting for what we do and what we are about on a purely empirical basis, those who reject an immaterial soul or mind must still reckon with the implications of that rejection and the vacuum it leaves in coming to terms with an understanding of the unity of the self. We all have a vested interest in this issue, despite contentions that we stand to lose very little by discarding the spiritual or immaterial dimension in human existence.[4]

The attempt to comprehend and define what is essentially human is an attempt to ascertain our distinctiveness in the midst of an ever-changing world. If there is no substantive metaphysical difference between soul or mind and body, then claims regarding our special status as rational beings with an inviolable spiritual dimension (along with the assumption that we are free, morally responsible agents) becomes a moot point. In twenty-first-century terms, the challenge has been framed along the following lines:

> Consciousness, cognition, and volition are perfectly natural capacities of fully embodied creatures engaged in complex commerce with the natural and social environments. Humans possess no special capacities, no extra ingredients, that could conceivably do the work of the mind, the soul, or free will as traditionally conceived.[5]

Despite claims to the contrary, there is evidence of an increasing attentiveness among researchers in the cognitive sciences and neurosciences to the spirituality inherent in our humanness and the indefatigable resistance of the human phenomenon to a thoroughgoing materialistic explanation. In this context, the biblical assertion that *there is nothing new under the sun* finds ready support in current attempts to uphold the causal role of the mind in a manner that would be highly amenable to an Aristotelian or a Thomist. Contemporary theorists discover that their talk about mind does not necessarily commit them to the drawbacks of Cartesian dualism and its assumption of an impassable gulf between mind and body. We instead encounter a renewed emphasis on a psychosomatic unity rooted in the interaction of spirit and matter on the most fundamental levels. In the face of reductionist attempts to show that our minds are "nothing but" the brain and its processes, or that we are "no more than" complex animals, the time is ripe for a reaffirmation of all we truly are.

DISCUSSION QUESTIONS

1. Define the difference between the teleological and mechanistic perspectives, and explain how these diverse perspectives offer competing explanations of what it means to be human.
2. How do the notions of "human nature" and "personhood" differ? Do these notions overlap or coincide? Assess the contention that every human being is a person.

3. How does a metaphysical account of human nature and personhood go beyond a materialistic or naturalistic account? What does a metaphysical account presuppose about what is essential to being human?

NOTES

1. Roger Trigg, *Ideas of Human Nature: An Historical Introduction*, 2nd ed. (Oxford: Blackwell, 2000), 1.

2. Paul R. Ehrlich, *Human Natures, Genes, Cultures, and the Human Prospect* (Harmondsworth, U.K.: Penguin, 2000), ix.

3. Trigg, *Ideas of Human Nature*, 1.

4. Owen Flanagan, *The Problem of the Soul: Two Visions of the Mind and How to Reconcile Them* (New York: Basic, 2002), xii, frames the question in these terms: "Can we do without the cluster of concepts that are central to the humanistic image in its present form—the soul and its suite—and still retain some or most of what these concepts were designed to do?" Flanagan would reply in the affirmative, arguing that while "there are no souls or nonphysical minds, no immutable selves, . . . no such thing as free will, there are still, at the end of the day, persons."

5. Flanagan, *Problem of the Soul*, xii.

I

FROM *PSYCHE*
TO *ANTHROPOS*

Salient Points of Chpt. 1:

- Ignition of Western philo. is the desire for an ultimate causal explanation.
- Pre-Socratics are teleological or mechanistic
  (cause distinct from nature) (cause w/in nature)

  <u>Relevant to anthro</u> b/c: People are microcosms of the macro-cosm: an order in the uni. is reflected in the ordering & purpose of humans.

  - there is no ultimate purpose to human life. based on an ordering of the uni.

<u>Anaximander</u> posits ἀπειρον as extra-material cause - big break!

may fave: <u>Heraclitus</u> - metaphysics of <u>becoming</u>. posited λογὸs, which orders & directs the constant change in the uni.

<u>Parmenides</u> - metaphysics of being. Monistic - v. Vedic in his take.

<u>Empedocles</u> - cyclical conflict btwn Love & Strife - relevant in the passive mindset that Good & Bad trade off about 50-50.

astro-nomer <u>Anaxagoras</u> - Principle of Mind directing the uni. sez he's ground for challenging the mechanistic.

<u>Pythagoreans</u> - Mystical Math. Introduce ethics to their speculation.

1

In the Beginning:
Defining Some Key Issues

The quest for intelligibility was a dominant concern of the Greek philosophical tradition. This preoccupation found expression in a fundamental metaphysical question: *How do many things arise from one?* The problem of the one and the many may be said to lie at the heart of all metaphysical inquiry. This question seeks a means of coming to terms with the multiplicity and diversity of the world of sense experience by means of some unifying principle. But such an investigation (and the philosophical responses it yields) presupposes that reality is not merely a continuous flow of events and perceptions. Rather, it assumes that what is real is only rendered intelligible, meaningful, and coherent in light of some ultimate causal explanation.

The Pre-Socratic thinkers of the sixth and fifth centuries before Christ actively searched for just such an explanatory principle. While their principal focus was the natural world, the responses they formulated set the tone for later anthropological reflections as well. The search for causal explanation on this fundamental level, I submit, is the beginning of all metaphysical speculation into human nature. By implication, a perusal of this seminal period may serve as a touchstone for defining significant issues and problems punctuating the history of philosophical anthropology.

For all practical purposes, the Pre-Socratic thinkers introduced a conflict that permeates the history of philosophical anthropology. The lines were increasingly drawn between a teleological and a mechanistic perspective: the view that reality is explicable only by recourse to something outside nature that renders it orderly and purposeful versus the view that the world can be explained on the basis of natural processes and observable

[handwritten annotations: people as miniatures of the P.P. — Jane's idea that the soul/body connect is also a mystery to contemplate... Plato.]

causes that are operative in the natural environment. These positions, of
course, have direct anthropological correlates: on the one hand, the view
that humans possess something that allows them to be microcosms of a
greater whole, incorporating a *telos* within their nature consistent with the
order and purposefulness of the macrocosm, and on the other hand, the
notion that humans (like everything else) are no more than the result of
an arbitrary, chance intersection of material elements.

In subsequent chapters, we will confront this tension in a variety of historical settings. Each of the thinkers we encounter in this volume faced a
challenge that remains fairly constant: how do we reconcile our uniqueness and moral sensibility as humans (along with the freedom it presupposes) with accounts that would reduce us to physical entities? This problem, which becomes acute in the modern period and beyond, emerged at
the dawn of the Greek philosophical tradition. Indeed, the key anthropological issues that philosophers addressed over the following two millennia grew out of the Ionian physicists' scientific speculation and the refinement of this mode of questioning by later generations of thinkers
comprising the Pre-Socratic period. But what follows makes no claim to
being a detailed treatment of this early period. It merely attempts to highlight some nodal points exhibiting a clear metaphysical relevance for later
reflection on the meaning of human nature, personhood, and the self.

At this early period, clear demarcations between philosophy and science or between metaphysical and empirical modes of investigation were
nonexistent. The thinkers considered in this chapter scrutinized the totality of things on the basis of sense experience and rational inquiry. In this
connection, the intellectual historian W. C. K. Guthrie astutely observed
that philosophies are "the reaction of a certain temperament to the external world as it presents itself . . . influenced . . . by reflections on the remains of previous thinkers."[1] In my estimation, the most significant (and
most overlooked) factor in Guthrie's classic equation may lie in temperament, a somewhat nebulous notion encompassing the whole range of uncritical (and largely unconscious) presuppositions which enter into the
thought world of any thinker.

From Guthrie's standpoint, differing temperaments among philosophers give rise to not only different philosophical content but different
kinds of answers as well. For him, the most fundamental division between philosophical outlooks exists between materialists and teleologists—
that is, between philosophies of matter and form, respectively.

The two types may be clearly discerned among the ancient Greeks. Some defined things with reference to their matter, or, as the Greeks also called it, "the
out-of-which." Others saw the essential in purpose or function, with which
they included form, for . . . structure subserves function and is dependent on

[handwritten annotation at bottom: Kuhn/Popper & philo. of science?]

Teleological: Matter defines a thing
Mechanistic: Form defines a thing.

it. The desk has the shape it has because of the purpose it has to serve. A shuttle is so shaped because it has to perform a certain function for the weaver.[2]

At the very outset of the tradition, then, we discern the emergence of two perspectives that would become central features of philosophical anthropology. The preference for a matter-based anthropology or a form-based one has a direct bearing on how we understand human nature, indeed, how we understand ourselves in relation to reality at large. A material starting point in one's metaphysical deliberations tends toward a view of humans as part and parcel of the material universe. A preoccupation with form and function is conducive to the teleological conviction that there is an order, purposefulness, and intelligibility inherent in reality and human nature. While the Pre-Socratic philosophers can all be labeled as "materialists" (by virtue of their general assumption that the really real is definable on the basis of aspects of the physical universe), we can still distinguish those who endorse such a teleological vision from those who view reality in the mechanistic language of chance and indeterminacy.

THE TRANSITION FROM MYTH TO REASON

One of the major breakthroughs in the history of Western thought emerged in the sixth century before Christ. This great shift in consciousness is traditionally localized on the Ionian peninsula on the eastern edge of the Mediterranean. Ionia had been colonized by settlers from the Greek mainland in response to pressures from the north. There were three successive waves of invasions (and correlative migrations) into the Aegean area between 3000 and 1000 B.C. The final incursion was the Dorian invasion (between 1200 and 1000 B.C.), which initiated a kind of dark age in the Greek world. In the face of these upheavals, however, life on the Ionian peninsula remained relatively secure. Such an environment abetted the growth of an energetic and affluent merchant class whose wealth allowed sufficient leisure time to engage in artistic and other creative pursuits. But the most significant and lasting of these activities was philosophy, the love and pursuit of wisdom for its own sake.

These Ionian thinkers studied geology, observed the stars and planetary movements, suggested primitive theories of evolution, and worked out the basic elements of plane geometry centuries before Euclid.[3] Their scientific inquiry stimulated broader philosophical questioning as well. On the basis of what is readily observable in nature, the early natural philosophers looked for the fundamental explanation for everything that exists. Implicit in this observation and analysis of nature, we find a sensitivity toward two central problems of Western metaphysics: the relationship between unity and plurality and between stability and change.

Could the same be said about us?

Although the Ionians engaged in rational inquiry, their thought exhibits continuity with the mythical accounts of their cultural tradition. By and large, the early expression of philosophical concepts was based in mythical representation, which accepts an account on its own terms, without rational scrutiny or critical assessment. But this is not to suggest that myth involves nothing more than a simplistic response to one's environment. Instead, myth offers a powerful vehicle for transmitting profound truths pertinent to a people's understanding of its origins, way of life, and foundational beliefs. Myth provides a means of expressing what is otherwise inexpressible through ordinary discourse.

Because mythical accounts are ahistorical and atemporal, they transcend the need for considerations of proof or disproof, verifiability or nonverifiability, accuracy or inaccuracy. Accordingly, we must overcome our tendency to relegate such stories to the status of entertaining but naive fables. Indeed, the crucial point of intersection uniting the goals of myth, philosophy, and science lies in the attempt to make sense of our world. From this standpoint, myth carries a profound explanatory power that enables it to say something significant about humanity to all people at all times.

The explanatory power of myth is prominent in Hesiod's *Theogony* (c. 776 B.C.), which represents an ambitious attempt to treat the traditional gods and goddesses in a somewhat systematic fashion. Hesiod, however, attempted to order the customary accounts of not only the deities but the world itself in light of a divine hierarchy. Accordingly, he provides the foundation for a primitive cosmogony in its own right. If there is a locus classicus of such a program in the *Theogony*, it may exist in the following passage:

> Verily first of all did Chaos come into being, and then Gaia, a firm seat of all things. . . . and misty Tartarus and Eros. . . . Erebos and black Night came into being, . . . and from Night . . . Aither and Day . . . and Earth . . . brought forth starry Ouranos . . . to be a firm seat for the blessed gods forever, . . . and having lain with Ouranos she bore Okeanos, and Koios and Krios and Hyperion and Iapetos.[4]

Hesiod's depiction of the origin of the cosmos and its forces is notable for two reasons. First, it is grounded in the uncritical language of myth and characterized by a personification of natural phenomena. Second, Hesiod's purpose in using such language and motifs places him closely in touch with the goals of the Pre-Socratic thinkers of the following century. Hesiod, like his more rationally inclined Ionian successors, sought a comprehensive vision of the world as a whole, against the background of an account of its orderly process of emergence. Hesiod's attempt to achieve a systematization of the ancient creation myths seems to reflect what has been characterized as a "quasi-rationalistic" view of the world.[5]

Hesiod's systematic bent dispels any notion that he represents an outlook diametrically opposed to the philosophical spirit of a later generation. In fact, he exhibits the same cosmic awareness that characterizes the Greek intellectual tradition as a whole. For this reason, some designate him the "first Pre-Socratic philosopher."[6] But the vast distance between Hesiod and the Ionian thinkers underscores the great transformation in Greek society from the ninth centuries to the sixth centuries B.C.

Hesiod's painstaking assignment of cosmic powers and roles to specific gods and goddesses opened the way for more explicit philosophical attempts to penetrate the ultimate causes of things in terms of abstract, wholly impersonal principles. But this positive attitude toward the cosmos as an orderly, hospitable realm was offset by a pessimistic one concerning humans and their place in nature. In the Homeric writings and early poets (and later in the tragedies of Euripides, Sophocles, and Aeschylus) humans are depicted as pawns in a game with no discernible ground rules. This trend reflected a preoccupation with the vagaries and uncertainty of human existence. In this context, the greatest sin was an impious attempt to overstep the boundaries assigned to us in seizing the prerogative reserved to the divinities. In the face of their uneasy relationship with gods and nature alike, the only recourse left to humans was a courageous resignation to the inexorable dictates of fate and cosmic necessity. From this standpoint, the rational perspective associated with the philosophers can be viewed as a reaction against a sense of passivity in the face of forces exceeding our control.

[margin note: fatalism in tragedy]

While Hesiod and Homer inhabited a world shaped by tradition and the oral transmission of legends, the Pre-Socratic philosophers reflect a mind-set that tried to free itself from the uncritical beliefs of the past and forge an understanding of reality grounded on observation and the data of sense experience.[7] Still, the implementation of such a rational, scientific program should not be viewed as a radical break with everything that came before. Indeed, it displays a clear continuity with that past; like the early poets, the Pre-Socratic philosophers exhibit a marked preoccupation with the search for origins and explanation, along with the conviction that the universe is permeated with the divine.

By the same token, the philosophers also demonstrate a tendency to transfer their analysis of causality from a divine plane to an increasingly materialistic one. From their standpoint, the reason why things act or behave as they do is less explicable on the basis of divine decree than by the natural elements and physical processes. While such a shift from the religious to the naturalistic could be viewed as liberating, it also placed a burden on humans to shape their own destiny in a hostile environment. As Wallace Stevens puts it, "To see the gods dispelled in mid-air and dissolve like clouds is one of the great human experiences, . . . and yet it left us . . . feeling dispossessed and alone in solitude."[8]

[handwritten note: the alienization that stems from demythologizing]

THE MILESIAN RESPONSE

The earliest Pre-Socratic philosophers are identified with the Ionian city of Miletus, a thriving commercial center. Collectively, these Milesian thinkers were motivated by their interest in a stable principle of unity underlying the manifold of appearances accessible through the direct observation of the world. Their methodology was largely empirical and inductive; each chose one of the four commonly recognized elements (earth, air, fire, and water) and posited it as the primal substance that all things share in common. From their standpoint, this common material principle constitutes the ultimate cause from which everything proceeds and, conversely, the end to which everything is reducible. Such a direct encounter with the natural world assumed a marked theological and metaphysical character. Although they retained the old conviction that nature is infused with the divine, their goal was nothing less than determining the ultimate source and explanation of reality as a whole.[9] In this connection, these early thinkers developed what amounts to a cosmic psychology, positing *psyche* or 'soul' as a divine principle that permeates and animates the natural world. In this way, they put new rationalistic use to an old anthropological notion. In fact, the Homeric tradition never referred to *psyche* as a constituent of living beings. When it uses the term, it tends to do so in reference to the disembodied status of the dead. In E. R. Dodds's succinct assessment, "It is well known that Homer appears to credit man with a *psyche* only after death, or when he is in the act of fainting or dying or is threatened with death: the only recorded function of the *psyche* in relation to the living man is to leave him."[10]

In keeping with the Milesian program, Thales (c. 640–562 B.C.), the earliest of these natural philosophers, proposed water as the source and principle of all things. While Thales' choice of water as the primal reality is explicable on the basis of ordinary observation (e.g., water is necessary for sustaining life, assuming various forms throughout nature), he could also draw on the mythical tradition and the rich religious symbolism surrounding this particular element. Aristotle assesses the agenda of the Milesians in general (and specifically Thales) in these terms:

> Most of the first philosophers thought that principles in the form of matter were the only principles of all things . . . but Thales, the founder of this type of philosophy, says that it is water . . . perhaps taking this supposition from seeing the nurture of all things to be moist.[11]

Thales' search for the primal reality or "stuff" of the universe was tantamount to a search for the cause that explains how material things move themselves, on the basis of their ensoulment. According to Aristotle, Thales interpreted soul as something kinetic, since he imparted *psyche* to a magnet by virtue of its power of attraction.[12] For theorists like Thales, natural phenomena such as magnets, the surging sea, and the rushing wind underscored animation by such a divine principle. In this respect, Aristotle numbered Thales among philosophers who believed that soul was intermingled with the universe and thus "that all things are full of gods."[13] On its most fundamental level, Thales viewed the universe as both vital and dynamic.

Almost from the outset, however, such speculation regarding the basic constituent of the universe confronted a problem of major philosophical import. This problem emerges against the background of the Milesians' overall agenda. By asking what all things share in common, these thinkers were looking for something that remains stable in the face of change and offers a means of making sense of natural processes. But implicit in this methodology (as exemplified by Thales) lies a serious pitfall. If all things are ultimately derived from and reducible to one thing, then how do we account for attributes contrary to this primal element? If, for example, all things are water, how do we explain such observable phenomena as fire, heat, and dryness?

Anaximander (c. 611–546 B.C.), in contrast to Thales (who stressed the unity of all things in one abiding principle), viewed the universe as comprising opposites: hot/fire, cold/air, wet/water, dryness/earth. Accordingly, he rejected Thales' selection of a single element as the ultimate explanatory principle. In trying to come to terms with the multiplicity of opposites, Anaximander sought a principle which provides a balance of contrary forces. On the basis of Simplicius's testimony, he designated this principle the *apeiron*—one, moving, and infinite.[14]

For Anaximander, the *apeiron* constituted the regulative cause of the cosmos responsible for bringing conflicting opposites into a state of harmony and equilibrium. From this standpoint, only a principle that is wholly indeterminate and spatially unbounded allows for indestructibility in the midst of an eternal process of generation and movement.[15] Because the *apeiron* is no one element, it transcends the material world it orders. In Aristotle's reckoning, this principle is divine since it possesses the earmarks of divinity—namely, immortality and indestructibility.[16] And as Aristotle further observed, only the infinite character of this principle prevents it from dominating all the other elements comprising the observable world.[17]

Anaximander's notion of the *apeiron* represented a significant leap in the history of Western metaphysics. Its brilliance lies in the recognition that what governs the many must be distinct from what it governs. As Simplicius observes, "Anaximander made the primal reality something other than the four elements which change into each other."[18] But for all its metaphysical profundity, such an insight did not immediately take root. The immediate successor of Anaximander, Anaximenes (c. 550–446

Anax's big contribution: governing principle is distinct from what it governs.

B.C.), adhered to the basic methodology of Thales, positing the material element of air as the primal stuff of all things. In this regard, however, Anaximenes sought a compromise between the positions of Thales and Anaximander. While he endorsed Thales' materialistic physics, air presents itself as more indeterminate and amorphous than earth, fire, or even water. Conversely, Anaximenes could not accept Anaximander's complete departure from nature and its essential constituents in positing the *apeiron*. From Anaximenes' perspective, air not only occupies a middle position between celestial fire and terrestrial moisture but also seems transformable into any number of qualities and things through the processes of condensation and rarefaction.[19] Like his Milesian predecessors, Anaximenes divinized his primal reality. But divinity is not here understood in static terms as an immutable substance. Like Thales' water and Anaximander's *apeiron*, air assumes a kinetic character as a psychic principle of perpetual movement. On the basis of Aetius's testimony, however, Axaximenes also attempts to link soul with the very constitution of human nature, as the air which holds us together, just as the wind embraces the entire world.[20]

Milesian speculation bequeathed an important legacy to subsequent metaphysical reflection. On the one hand, these theorists recognized the need for a principle of unity as a means of integrating and rendering intelligible the diverse phenomena of sense experience. But this commitment to a substantial reality that endures in the face of change required refinement. In this respect, an important qualification is in order: when these thinkers refer to the primal element as a "soul," they understand soul as a power of self-movement rather than an immutable substance in its own right. And while each Milesian addressed the perennial problems of the one and the many and of change and stability, only Anaximander recognized the importance of a primal reality generic enough to account for the conflicting attributes nature continually exhibits. It was left to the next generation of Pre-Socratics to sustain the metaphysical momentum that Anaximander initiated.

need for a substance that is steady & beyond all the permutations.

TWO METAPHYSICAL RESPONSES

As we have seen, the Milesian physicists attempted to explain the really real in terms of a single element that unifies the disparate features of the universe. From their standpoint, intelligibility is a matter of reducing multiplicity and change to one unifying principle. Two thinkers offered more explicit metaphysical commentaries on the nature of things in light of general characteristics of reality as a whole. The responses they developed, however, represent diametrically opposing views as to what constitutes the really real and how it is to be understood. In so doing, they anticipated two distinct perspectives which loom large in later developments in philosophical anthropology: empiricism and rationalism.

Heraclitus (c. 504–456 B.C.), who hailed from Ephesus (a flourishing city just north of Miletus), focused primarily on the phenomenon of change. For him, observation discloses the fact that the world exhibits continual upheavals and tensions between opposites and that all things are generated by strife and necessity.[21] If any stability is apparent in the midst of such ceaseless flux, it lies in the constancy of change itself. The famous Heraclitean epigram "No man steps twice in the same river" points to his central assumption: life and the world are in a constant process of becoming that does not allow for stability or sameness from moment to moment.[22]

But this is not to say that Heraclitus viewed change as wholly chaotic or haphazard. Indeed, there is a great difference between mere becoming and an orderly process of becoming. For Heraclitus, the crucial problem lies in determining what accounts for such coherent transitions from one state of affairs to another. In the absence of a principle of stability inherent in a world characterized by ongoing change, he sought a higher rational principle or *logos* external to the world itself. On the one hand, the *logos* constitutes a cause of cosmic unity; on the other hand, it balances all of the opposing forces operative in reality. According to Heraclitus's formulation, we find a unity in the midst of plurality and a plurality in the midst of unity.[23]

By positing the *logos* as the cause of orderly change, Heraclitus reflects the influence of Anaximander and his notion of the *apeiron* as the indeterminate regulative principle. For Heraclitus, however, the *logos* is imbued with a divine character of its own and encompasses the divine law immanent in the matter it dynamically charges with intelligibility. In the face of unending change and the conflict of opposites, the *logos* remains wholly immutable. But it brings what is in a state of tension into balance and equilibrium. In this way, Heraclitus introduces a cosmic vision into the mainstream of Greek philosophical thinking—a rational, Mind-governed universe. For if reality is governed by Mind, then reality shares in and reflects this higher intellect.

Although Heraclitus's attribution of coherent change to the operation of the *logos* represents a major metaphysical advance, he still displays a crucial kinship with his Milesian predecessors. In keeping with their overall approach, he posited one of the material elements as the primal reality. But unlike them, Heraclitus's choice of fire reflects a focus on process and the dynamic character of the cosmos. Heraclitus thus found what he called "the hidden attunement of the universe" in the conflagration lying at the very center of things.[24] If fire is the all-pervasive element in Heraclitus's reckoning, then the soul must also be viewed as made of fire. This

(Coherent ordering of change)

materialistic psychology is emphasized in testimony from Stobaeus, who attributes to Heraclitus the teaching that "a dry soul is wisest and best," since becoming water is destructive to the soul.[25] For this reason, we observe some ambiguity in Heraclitus's psychology. On the one hand, soul's fiery nature binds it up with natural processes; on the other hand, Heraclitus lends soul an intellectual character, implicitly linking it with the operation of mind and the maintenance of ethical conduct. Indeed, if a dry (i.e., fiery) soul is conducive to what is best in us, then a moist soul contributes to dissolute living. Accordingly, Heraclitus derides the moist soul by likening it to a drunken youth who stumbles around with no sense of direction.[26]

In the interplay of fire's upward and downward movements (whereby it intensifies and diminishes, respectively), Heraclitus perceived the basis of the balance between such opposites as dryness and moisture, strife and concord, plurality and unity. While he viewed reality in terms of perpetual strife, he nonetheless perceived a fundamental unity inherent in this flux.[27] In one brilliant move, then, he elevated the philosophical discussion of change to a higher metaphysical plane. While the Milesians had grappled with the relationship between change and stability, it was Heraclitus who underscored the importance of a principle of rationality as a means of explaining intelligible process on a universal scale. An important dimension of Heraclitus's overall response lies in his recognition of the scope and extent of change and the tremendous diversity it promotes in the natural environment. In this respect, he grounded his metaphysics firmly in the world of sense experience and focused exclusively on the fact of becoming. This is why Heraclitus's thought (fragmentary as it is) contains a clear strain of skepticism that called into question what the senses disclose. Thus, if becoming is viewed as the chief characteristic of the really real, any stability, sameness, or substantiality we perceive is no more than illusion.[28] In Heraclitean terms, then, sense experience generates the false belief in a permanence which simply does not exist in the face of perpetual movement.

In contrast to Heraclitus's focus on the phenomenon of becoming, Parmenides of Elea (c. 504–456 B.C.) introduced a new dualistic orientation into this extended metaphysical discussion. Like Heraclitus, Parmenides questions the veracity of sense experience. But Parmenides' brand of skepticism drew him to radically different conclusions. While Heraclitus denied stability in the face of process (other than the dynamic, mercurial element of fire), Parmenidean skepticism grew out of a deep conviction that decisively shaped his entire philosophical perspective. Parmenides, in effect, denied the reality of change in all its forms. This thesis can be summed up in the comprehensive formula that "Being is and cannot not-be." For him, being alone exists, and that which truly is must be one, immutable, continuous, and indivisible, like a sphere whose points are all equidistant from their center.[29] On the basis of this fundamental presupposition, he relegated a world exhibiting motion, change, and plurality to the status of mere illusion. Because his metaphysical vision could not admit negation or nonbeing on any level (including empty space), he rejected the possibility of becoming on any level as well. In a manner consistent with his formula that "Being is and cannot not be," then, Parmenides held that being arises neither out of being (since it already exists) nor out of nonbeing (because nothing can generate something).[30]

Parmenides was the rationalist metaphysician par excellence. Indeed, the tension between being and becoming which dominates his thought is rooted in a parallel one between reasoning and sense experience. This latter tension finds expression in the diametrically opposed paths of inquiry at the center of Parmenides' rationalism: the Way of Truth and the Way of Opinion.[31] The Way of Truth is the path of reasoning, the only means of arriving at an understanding of being, the really and truly real in the most literal, all-encompassing terms. The Way of Opinion, on the other hand, is the path of sense experience, the means to a mutable and wholly uncertain (and thus unknowable) world. But implicit in this distinction was an important value judgment on Parmenides' part; the Way of Opinion opens us to error precisely because it promotes the false assumption that substantial reality is grasped on the basis of what the senses disclose.

Parmenides' metaphysics introduces various dichotomies into the Pre-Socratic tradition that would exert a profound influence on subsequent developments in Hellenic thought: the dichotomy between being and nonbeing (and, by implication, becoming), the dichotomy between reality and appearance, the dichotomy between reasoning and sense experience. From the standpoint of Eleatic thinking, the conclusions of reasoning must be deemed more true (and more consistent with what is the case) than those derived from the testimony of the senses. For Parmenides and his disciples, this holds true even if the conclusions based on logic and reasoning contradict what immediately appears to be the case through sense experience.

Parmenides' thoroughgoing rationalism was inextricably bound up with a monism which acknowledges being alone and reduces all things to a static, unchanging unity.[32] In this respect, he reflects the influence of Xenophanes of Colophon (c. 540 B.C.), a relentless critic of the traditional Greek conceptions of the divinities.

Homer and Hesiod have attributed to the gods everything that is a shame and reproach among men, stealing and committing adultery and deceiving each other. But if cattle and horses or lions had hands, or were able to draw with their hands, . . . horses would draw the forms of the gods like horses, and cattle like cattle, and they would make their bodies such as they each had themselves.[33]

Xenophanes, in effect, wished to replace a pantheon founded on myth with a rational theology centering on a single, supreme godhead that is immutable and is the prime mover of all things.[34] Thus his critique of the often crude anthropomorphism inherent in his own religious tradition was complemented by his efforts as a constructive theologian. Such a critical program in theology finds its philosophical parallel in Parmenides' distinction between the paths of reasoning and sense experience. Just as Xenophanes reduced the beliefs prominent in popular piety to the status of fanciful (and even dangerous) mythmaking, his disciple Parmenides reduced everything derived from the senses to the status of illusion. Both thinkers established a fault line between everyday conceptions of things (either the gods or reality) and a more astute rational grasp of the really real that is reserved for the few.

For this reason, the importance of Xenophanes in the Greek intellectual tradition cannot be discounted. His indictment of anthropomorphic depictions of the gods and goddesses and his search for an alternate critical approach to theology reflect that overall transition from myth to reason which characterizes the Pre-Socratic period as a whole. Xenophanes represents the beginning of a tension between popular religious conceptions and a rational approach to religion (and, by extension, to the entire universe) that reached its boiling point in the age of Socrates and decisively shaped subsequent theological and philosophical developments. In succeeding centuries, Greek intellectuals found it increasingly difficult to harmonize traditional religious explanations with the probing causal analysis advanced by the new critical theologians, philosophers, and natural scientists. These thinkers increasingly separated the gods and goddesses depicted by Homer and Hesiod from the impersonal principles they viewed as ultimately responsible for the way things are.

THE MOVE TOWARD RECONCILIATION

Heraclitus and Parmenides developed radically divergent visions of reality that reflected different metaphysical emphases. Heraclitus was preoccupied with process and fluidity, while Parmenides was interested in the stability of being. Such conflicting perspectives reflect an exclusionary focus which confined them to one specific aspect of the world of experience. Indeed, reality does exhibit both sameness and change, oneness and plurality. The challenge for metaphysicians (at this early stage and thereafter) lies in forging a comprehensive explanation as to how things remain the same even as they undergo change on a variety of levels. The Pre-Socratic successors of Heraclitus and Parmenides addressed this problem and, in so doing, attempted to reconcile their seemingly irreconcilable accounts of the really real.

Still, this commitment to reconciliation must be qualified. These thinkers display a decidedly Heraclitean bent in their desire to explain things in a manner consistent with the data of sense experience. Their appeal to being (that which is) presupposes that being and intelligibility only emerge in the context of a pluralistic universe of many beings. If these so-called pluralists reflect a Parmenidean stance, it lies in their rejection of absolute nonbeing on the level of becoming. From their standpoint, change is only intelligible because it involves the separation and mixing of immutable principles.

Empedocles of Acragas (c. 444 B.C.) held that true being is constituted by the four basic elements or roots *(stoicheia)* of things: earth, air, fire, and water.[35] While these constants never change in themselves, they are arranged in different combinations to form the things and phenomena all around us. In Empedoclean terms, each element is viewed as eternal, homogeneous, and unchangeable; but each is divisible and capable of movement. Everything arises from the union, separation, and proportioning of these root elements. But this can only be accomplished by two active powers. For Empedocles, Love and Strife act as motive forces in generating cosmic activity: Love produces unity by drawing things together; Strife produces plurality and separates what was formerly united. Love and Strife acquire an alternate dominance over each other in an eternal cyclic process.[36]

In anthropological terms, Empedocles' physical theory provides the basis of a materialistic understanding of human nature. Along with the Milesian philosophers and Heraclitus, Empedocles perceived a kinship between nature and psychology. For him, activities like thought and the feelings of pleasure or sorrow are explicable by means of the configuring of the root elements. In a manner consistent with ancient physiological presuppositions, he posits the heart and the flow of blood as the center of intellectual activity in humans.[37]

Empedocles' appeal to overarching, external principles of motion, change, and alteration of opposite states of being gave way to a more explicit noetic emphasis in Anaxagoras of Clazomenae (c. 534–462 B.C.). Anaxagoras taught that orderly movement must proceed from the influence of a universal Mind or cosmic Intellect *(nous)*. Like Heraclitus, he endorsed the notion of a rationally governed universe but rejected Empedocles' reliance on the four elements. In his estimation, that kind of explanatory account failed to come to terms with the qualitative differences between things. For him, being is understood in terms of a vast amount of infinitely divisible and infinitesimally small seeds *(spermata)*.[38]

If Anaxagoras went beyond the materialism of Empedocles, he also supplanted the Milesian notion of self-moving material principles with his theory of a Mind-directed universe. Empedocles had already tended in that direction by virtue of his incorporation of Love and Strife into his overall cosmological account. But Anaxagoras's distinction between Mind and the matter it governs represents an important watershed in Pre-Socratic philosophy that served as a vital inspiration for later developments.

> All other things have a portion of everything, but Mind is infinite and self-ruled and is mixed with nothing but is all alone by itself, . . . and Mind controls all things, both the greater and the smaller, that have life.[39]

Mind is not personal.

This is not to say that Anaxagoras freed himself from the limitations of a materialistic outlook. He still conceived Mind as wholly immanent in the world and bound up with natural processes.[40] But the insight that the universe depends on a principle of Intelligence (and thereby exhibits rationality and purposefulness) was a crucial feature of the teleological perspective that decisively shaped the cosmologies of Plato (with his account of the creative activity of the Demiurge) and Aristotle (whose god assumes the character of pure, self-thinking Thought). From this standpoint, Anaxagoras provides a key referent for challenges to an exclusively mechanistic theory of the universe and, by extension, of human beings.

Pre-Socratic philosophy offers a continual study in contrasts: thinkers and their schools moved from monism to pluralism; allegiances shifted from a thoroughgoing commitment to rationalism (and a distrust of sense experience) to a radical empiricism; mind-based explanations competed with purely naturalistic ones. In keeping with this general trend, the next group of Pre-Socratics viewed the universe in a manner starkly at odds with what we find in Anaxagoras. These so-called atomists advanced a wholly mechanistic perspective that resembles the cosmological theory of Empedocles.

Like Empedocles, the atomists attempted to come to terms with qualitative differences on the basis of the essential constituents of things. But while Empedocles focused on the elements, Leucippus of Miletus (c. 430 B.C.) and Democritus of Abdera (c. 494–404 B.C.) postulated infinitesimally small particles or atoms (*atomoi*) as the building blocks of the real.[41] Both Empedocles and the atomists thus exhibit a Parmenidean orientation: elements and atoms represent unchanging constants in the midst of change. But the atomists also departed from Empedocles and Parmenides in significant ways. In contrast to Empedocles, they had no place for external forces like Love and Strife. From their standpoint, the *atomoi* are self-moved, and things are no more than the products of a chance intersection or arbitrary combining of solid, unified, complete particles.

Atomists bring The Void into the picture.

The atomists departed from Parmenides by introducing the void into their scheme. For them, only the void allows for that infinite, unbounded space in which the *atomoi* assume the diverse arrangements that constitute the things of our experience.[42] Qualitative differences like hard or soft, sweet or bitter find their concrete explanation on the basis of the relative density or compactness of these indivisible particles. For the atomists, such adjectives are no more than a matter of opinion and convention.[43] Thus atomism provided another source of skeptical thinking that filtered its way through Greek intellectual life in many different contexts. Indeed, the epistemological thesis that the world and its things are not exactly as they appear through the agency of sense experience is conducive to doubting the veracity of truth claims across the board, so to speak, from a metaphysical to a moral to a religious level.

The radical materialism and indeterminism inherent in atomist metaphysics has clear anthropological implications. The atomists depict the soul (like everything else in the universe) as an aggregate of particles. In this respect, they follow Heraclitus in positing fire as the soul's underlying element. More specifically, Aristotle testifies that Democritus taught that the soul and mind are composed of spherical atoms, as is fire.[44] If this is the case, however, then any appeal to a purposeful human existence becomes a moot point. Human destiny, in effect, is rendered as random as the universe as a whole, and soul is depicted in purely physicalistic terms.

THE PYTHAGOREAN CONTRIBUTION

Surveys of Pre-Socratic thought usually proceed in chronological terms. For purposes of this chapter, however, I have elected to depart from that approach by postponing my treatment of the Pythagoreans to the end of this survey for two reasons. First, there is a continuity that runs through the speculation of the Milesians, Heraclitus, Parmenides, and the pluralists as all of these thinkers were preoccupied with the problem of the one and the many, as well as the phenomenon of change. Accordingly, I wished to preserve the unity of their questions and responses for the reader's benefit. My second reason is that Pythagorean speculation represents something of a distinctive viewpoint. For its practitioners, cosmology assumed an explicit anthropological focus in connection with such issues as the relationship between the soul and the body, and the foundation of ethical living.

The Pythagorean school was founded by Pythagoras (c. 569–494 B.C.), who was born on the island of Samos (near Asia Minor) and later settled in Croton, a Greek colony on the southern Italian peninsula. Pythagoreanism represents a highly eclectic blend of metaphysical, religious, and mystical elements. But its most salient feature lies in a mathematical interpretation of concrete reality. Its adherents applied numerical principles to nature and sought to make sense of the world within a mathematical framework. Their speculation had a pointed ethical orientation that emphasized ritual purification, asceticism, silence, and reverence for music.[45] In this regard, the Pythagoreans described the relation between things in terms of the same proportion governing musical harmony and the numerical expression of the intervals between the notes of the lyre.

Just as pitch was found to depend on the length of the strings, musical harmony was found to be determined by mathematical proportions, whereby the chief musical intervals are expressible by means of simple ratios between the first four integers (octave, 2:1; fifth, 3:3; fourth, 4:3). This numerical understanding of music extended to the broader metaphysical interpretation of reality as a whole. From this perspective, the universe was conceived as a great musical scale, whose space was marked off by the commonly accepted ten astronomical bodies.[46]

The mathematical account of universal harmony (and the perception of a relationship between number and physical space) decisively shaped the Pythagorean view of things (e.g., physical realities were expressed by 4, lines by 2, plane surfaces by 3, and solids again by 4).[47] On an anthropological level, the mathematical interpretation of universal harmony was combined with an analysis of human conduct in terms of the antithesis between the Limit and the Unlimited. The Pythagoreans thus forged a new brand of dualism that was highly compatible with the mathematical thrust of their metaphysical speculation. For them, such contrary principles are reflected in a variety of opposites inherent in reality, ranging from numerical distinctions between odd and even or unity and plurality, to geometrical distinctions between straight and curved or square and oblong, to the biological distinction between male and female, to the physical distinction between rest and motion, to the key ethical distinction between good and evil.[48]

The Pythagorean depiction of the good life as subject to Limit (and the wicked life as displaying the characteristics of the Unlimited) was consistent with a conviction that the universe reveals structure and order by virtue of its numerical determination and boundedness.[49] Conversely, evil was linked with what is indeterminate and amorphous. From this perspective, what is lacking in numerical determination and boundaries is tantamount to unintelligible chaos. For the Pythagoreans, such a moral outlook reflected the metaphysical intuition that all things are reducible to number and that number constitutes their very nature. This dualism between observable realities and the numerical principles that govern and define them found its anthropological counterpart in the dualism between form and matter and, more specifically, between soul and body. In this context, a kinship was perceived between order on an individual level and a broader cosmic one. Accordingly, the good and happy life requires a harmonization of one's desires and drives in a manner consistent with the harmony of the entire universe and the dictates of the gods.[50]

This parallelism between the microcosmic and the macrocosmic became a hallmark of Greek ethical theory. It rested on the assumption that moral goodness reflects the beauty, balance, and symmetry inherent in the nature of things. In this respect, the Pythagorean ideal blended metaphysical and mathematical speculation, ethical and aesthetic reflection into a highly optimistic vision of the really real. While the Pythagoreans were pluralists at heart, their pluralism was shaped by a firm belief that the physical world needs regulation by higher principles that impart it (and the humans that inhabit it) with a basis of intelligibility and coherence. On a human level, the higher principle in question is the soul, the source of life and the basis of a uniquely human range of activities and functions.[51]

In keeping with their spiritualistic and dualistic emphasis, the Pythagoreans thus rooted the essence of our humanness in the soul. Their conviction that the soul is immortal (and thus akin to the divine) was closely linked with their religious belief in the soul's transmigration from one body to another. This cycle of rebirth (and the meting out of punishments according to the bodily life to which the soul is consigned in a given incarnation) is geared to moral improvement and the soul's ultimate liberation from corporal limitations. In the final analysis, the Pythagorean understanding of human destiny paralleled a vision of cosmic order. From this standpoint, the happy life amounts to becoming a moral cosmos in one's own right, so that the various aspects of human nature are harmonized for the goodness of the whole.

THE BROADER ANTHROPOLOGICAL SIGNIFICANCE OF IT ALL

The Pre-Socratic thinkers represent the beginning of Western philosophical speculation about human nature. They also laid the metaphysical groundwork for later theories of personhood and the self. At this early period, psychological reflection on the life and activity of the soul is rooted in accounts of reality as a whole. Some of these accounts are consistent with the materialism of their proponents; others suggest the origin of a teleological understanding of things that points to the need for causal principles transcending the very world they render intelligible.

In the final analysis, this seminal period of Greek philosophy yielded a set of diametrically opposed viewpoints that required reconciliation. Reality simply does not present itself to us in terms of a set of either/or alternatives. Is the really real in constant process, or is it an immutable nexus of being? Are all things ultimately reducible to a single material element or to some indefinite principle encompassing each and every material element? Is the world one and unified or pluralistic and diversified? In actuality, an adequate grasp of reality demands an attunement to all of these characteristics of what exists in the broadest sense of the term. By extension, the subsequent history of philosophical anthropology reveals an ongoing struggle to come to grips with the same conflicts operative in human existence that the Pre-Socratics discerned throughout the universe.

The quest for a viable theory of personal identity, then, may be viewed as a variant of the Pre-Socratic interest in a unifying principle or general characteristic of things that allows for a comprehensive explanation of the entire universe. As we have seen, the response to this problem reveals a marked evolution, ranging from the naive materialism of the Ionian physicists to the more abstract metaphysical responses of Heraclitus, Parmenides, and the pluralists, to the quasi-mystical worldview of the Pythagoreans. In the course of this development, we ascertain a key conviction that weaves its way through Pre-Socratic thinking—namely, that an adequate explanation of a changing world requires a cause that stands apart from the world's constituents. From Anaximander's *apeiron*, to Heraclitus's *logos*, to Empedocles' Love and Strife, to Anaxagoras's Mind, to the Pythagorean focus on the soul, we observe consistent appeals to something external to the matter that these principles endow with intelligibility.

While the Pre-Socratic philosophers were bound by the limitations of metaphysical materialism, some key representatives (e.g., Heraclitus and Anaxagoras) introduced a teleological orientation that stands opposed to the explicitly mechanistic outlook of the atomists. The Pythagoreans exemplify that orientation. Their psychology correlated with their mathematical interpretation of the universe and their intuition of a harmonious arrangement of its diverse components. Since they viewed humans as microcosms of reality as a whole, they perceived the same dichotomies in us as in the larger world we inhabit. Accordingly, their understanding of what it means to be human emerges against the background of a series of polarities between unity and plurality, being and becoming, stability and change, order and chaos, Limit and Unlimited, form and matter. Pythagoreanism thus reflects the tensions that permeate Pre-Socratic treatments of reality and, more specifically, human existence.

By virtue of their emphasis on the primacy of the soul, the Pythagoreans (through the influence of Orphism) introduced a pronounced dualism into the mainstream of philosophical anthropology. This dualism relegates the body (and bodily life in general) to a subordinate status. While other Pre-Socratic thinkers or schools distinguished between mind and

Modernity — Monistic?

matter, the Pythagoreans placed this dichotomy at the heart of their theory of human nature. As the form of the body, the soul was viewed as the cause of everything about us that is peculiarly human, most notably our ability to reason. The body, in turn, was considered a negative influence on the life of the soul. This pessimistic attitude toward the body (reflecting the Orphic presupposition that the body is the soul's prison or tomb) represents a marked departure from the traditional understanding of humans in unitary terms.[52] From this standpoint, the body is viewed as no more than a faint image of the true human being.

Pyth ↓ Plat

The Pythagorean emphasis on the primacy of the soul over the body (and reasoning over sense experience) would exert a profound impact on Plato's psychology and the dualism that dominates Western anthropological assumptions. This dualistic model is closely aligned with the teleological perspective and its appeal to an immaterial principle that accounts for the independence, spontaneity, and creativity of human thought, the freedom of the will, and the integrity of the self. But positing the essence of humanness in the soul and rationality carried a certain price that haunts the subsequent tradition of philosophical inquiry in this vein. If soul and body represent different kinds of reality, then we are hard-pressed to explain their interaction. The problem can be framed in terms of a question: how does an immaterial principle influence the physical apparatus of the body, and how does bodily experience impinge on that principle? The dualistic model must always confront this question.

Accordingly, the challenge of explaining psychosomatic unity is a challenge of bridging the gap between two fundamental dimensions of our humanness—that is, between soul and body (in ancient and medieval philosophy), or between mind and body (in modern philosophy), or between mind and brain (in a contemporary context). Contemporary thinkers collapse the distinction between mind and body or, more precisely, between mind and brain. According to William R. Uttal, this trend reveals a definite move toward a monistic model that reduces all mental activity to neurophysiological processes.

> In the case of modern science, the fundamental philosophy has been monist rather than dualist expressing the axiomatic assumption that there is only one level of reality and that all mental processes are nothing more or less than manifestations or processes of the activities of the brain.[53]

DISCUSSION QUESTIONS

1. How did the Pre-Socratic philosophers tend to respond to the metaphysical problem of change, and how does this particular problem

highlight the difficulty of explaining the continuity of personal identity over a lifetime?

2. To what extent does Heraclitus's notion of the *logos* (Law/Reason) and Anaxagoras's notion of *nous* (Mind) suggest a teleological perspective?

3. What are the implications of the atomists' assumption that the universe is the product of a chance intersection or arbitrary combining of material particles for an understanding of our humanness?

4. How do Pre-Socratic accounts of the soul reflect the growing tension in ancient Greek culture between a rationalistic approach to the divine and popular religious conceptions?

5. How did the Pythagoreans' mathematical interpretation of reality shape their interpretation of the relationship between the soul and the body?

NOTES

There is little evidence as to what the Pre-Socratics actually taught, and their doctrines must be reconstructed from fragments of their writings or sayings. These sentiments are frequently quoted by later ancient thinkers and writers. Several significant sources provide direct quotes from the Pre-Socratic thinkers: Diogenes Laertius (c. A.D. 250), in his *Lives and Opinions of Famous Philosophers*; Plutarch (c. A.D. 46–120), in his *Moralia*; Sextus Empiricus (c. A.D. 200) in *Adversos mathematicos* and *Pyrrhrroneioi hypotyposes;* Simplicius (A.D. sixth century), in *De anima*, in *Aristotelis de caelo commentarii*, and *in Aristotelis de physica commentarii*; Clement of Alexandria (c. A.D. 150–217), in the *Protrepticus* and *Stromateis*; Hippolytus of Rome (c. A.D. 225), in his *Refutation of Heresies*; and Johannes Stobaeus (c. A.D. 500), in the *Anthologium*. Another group of sources does not directly quote the Pre-Socratics but offers testimony to what they taught: Plato, who comments on their teachings throughout his dialogues; Aristotle, who provides a complete survey of the teachings of his philosophical predecessors in the first book of the *Metaphysics*; and Theophrastus, whose *Opinions of the Physicists* provides a history of Greek philosophy from Thales to Plato as a defense of Aristotelian philosophy.

Several early- to mid-twentieth-century sources provide classic collections and commentaries relating to Pre-Socratic thought: Hermann Diels, *Die Fragmente der Vorsocratiker*, ed. Walter Kranz (Berlin, 1934–1935); Kathleen Freeman, *The Pre-Socratic Philosophers: A Companion to Diels'* Die Fragmente der Vorsokratiker (Oxford: Blackwell, 1953); Milton Nahm, *Selections from Early Greek Philosophy* (New York: Appleton-Century Crofts, 1935).

For purposes of this introduction, all references to Pre-Socratic sources are drawn from G. S. Kirk, J. E. Raven, and M. Schofield, *The Presocratic Philosophers*, 2nd ed. (Cambridge: Cambridge University Press, 1983), hereafter referred to as KRSch; and Kathleen Freeman, *Ancilla to the Pre-Socratic Philosophers: A Complete Translation of the Fragments in Diels'* Die Fragmente der Vorsokratiker (Cambridge: Harvard University Press, 1971), hereafter referred to as Ancilla.

1. W. C. K. Guthrie, *The Greek Philosophers from Thales to Aristotle* (New York: Harper Torchbooks, 1975), 19.

2. Guthrie, *Greek Philosophers*, 21.

3. Cyril E. Robinson, *History of Greece* (London: Crowell, 1929), 23.

4. Hesiod, *Theogony* 116 (KRSch, 35).

5. KRSch, 34.

6. KRSch, 73.

7. KRSch, 73–74.

8. Wallace Stevens, *Opus Posthumous* (New York: Knopf, 1957), 206–7.

9. George F. McLean and Patrick J. Aspell, *Ancient Western Philosophy: The Hellenic Emergence* (New York: Appleton-Century Crofts, 1974), 24.

10. E. R. Dodds, *The Greeks and the Irrational* (Berkeley: University of California Press, 1973), 15–16.

11. Aristotle, *Meta.* A3, 983b6 (KRSch, 89).

12. Aristotle, *de an.* A5, 411a7 (KRSch, 95).

13. Aristotle, *de an.* A2, 405a19 (KrSch, 95).

14. Simplicius, in *Phys.* 24, 13; DK 12 A9 (KRSch, 106–7).

15. Eduard Zeller, *Outlines of the History of Greek Philosophy* (New York: Dover, 1980), 26.

16. Aristotle, *Phys.* G4, 203b7 (KrSch, 115).

17. Aristotle, *Phys.* G4, 203b15 (KRSch, 113).

18. Simplicius, in *Phys.* 24, 21 (KRSch, 129).

19. Theophrastus, *ap.* Simplicium in *Phys.* 24, 26 (KRSch, 145).

20. Aetius I, 3, 4 (KRSch, 158).

21. Fr. 80, Origen, *c. Celsum* VI, 42 (KRSch, 193).

22. Plato, *Cratylus* 402A (KRSch, 195). Cf. Fr. 12, Arius Didymus *ap.* Eusebium P.E. XV, 20 + fr. 91, Plutarch de *E* 18, 392B (KRSch, 195).

23. George F. McLean and Patrick J. Aspell, *Ancient Western Philosophy: The Hellenic Emergence* (New York: Appleton Century Crofts, 171), 46. Cf. Fr. 50, Hippolytus, *Ref.* IX, 9, 1 (KRSch, 187): "Listening not to me but to the Logos it is wise to agree that all things are one."

24. Frederick W. Copleston, *A History of Philosophy*, vol. 1, pt. 1 (Garden City, N.Y.: Image, 1962), 58. Cf. Fr. 30, Clement of Alexandria, *Stromateis* V, 104, 1 (KRSch, 198): "This world-order . . . did none of gods or men make, but it always was and is and shall be: an everliving fire, kindling in measures and going out in measures."

25. Fr. 118, Stobaeus *Anth.* III, 5, 8 (KRSch, 203).

26. Fr. 117, Stobaeus *Anth.* III, 5, 7 (KRSch, 203).

27. Emile Brehier, *The History of Philosophy: The Hellenic Age*, trans. Joseph Thomas (Chicago: University of Chicago Press, 1963), 49.

28. Zeller, *History of Greek Philosophy*, 51.

29. Zeller, *History of Greek Philosophy*, 49–50.

30. Fr. 6, Simplicius, *in Phys.* 86, 27–28; 117, 4–13 (KRSch, 247).

31. Fr. 1, Sextus, *adv. math.* VII, 3; Simplicius, *de caelo* 557, 25ff. (KRSch, 243). Cf. Fr. 2, Proclus, *in Tim.* I, 345, 18; Simplicius *in Phys.* 116, 28, lines 3–8 (KRSch, 245).

32. Fr. 8, 1–4 (Simplicius, *in Phys.* 78, 5; 145, 1), Fr. 8, 22–25 (Simplicius, *in Phys.* 144, 29), Fr. 8, 26–31 (Simplicius, *in Phys.* 145, 27), KRSch, 248, 250–251.

33. Fr. 11 (Sextus, *adv. math.* IX, 193), Fr. 14 (Clement of Alexandria, *Stromateis* V, 109, 2), Fr. 16 (Clement of Alexandria, *Stromateis* VII, 22, 1), Fr. 15 (Clement of Alexandria, *Stromateis* V, 109, 3), KRSch, 168–169.

34. Fr. 23 (Clement of Alexandria, *Stromateis* V, 109, 1); Fr. 25–26 (Simplicius, *in Phys.* 23, 11 and 23, 20), KRSch, 169–70. Cf. Aristotle, *Meta.* A5, 986b21 (KRSch, 171).

35. Brehier, *History of Philosophy*, 60.

36. Fr. 17, 1–13, Simplicius, *in Phys.* 158, 1 (KRSch, 287).

37. Fr. 105 (Ancilla, 63).

38. Fr. 4, Simplicius, *in Phys.* 34, 29 (KRSch, 369).

39. Fr. 12, Simplicius, *in Phys.* 164, 24, 156, 13 (KRSch, 363).

40. Fr. 14 (Ancilla, 85).

41. Aristotle, *Phys.* A3, 187a1, DK 29A22 (KRSch, 407).

42. Simplicius, *de caelo* 242, 21 (KRSch, 426).

43. Democritus Fr. 9, Sextus, *adv. math.* vii, 135 (KRSch, 410).

44. Aristotle, *de an.* A2, 405a11 (KRSch, 427 and 427 n. 1).

45. Copleston, *History of Philosophy*, 47, 49.

46. In *de caelo* B9, 290b12, DK 58B35 (KRSch, 345), Aristotle criticizes the Pythagorean notion of the universal harmony as yielding the so-called music of the spheres.

47. McLean and Aspell, *Ancient Western Philosophy*, 38. The motion of heavenly bodies was observed to be repeatable in numerical intervals of time. In this connection, the number ten (the decad) assumed a special significance, since it was viewed as the most perfect number, embracing within itself the whole nature of numbers. And because ten is the sum of the initial four integers, it was believed to contain the secret of the musical scale. Cf. Fr. 4, Stobaeus, *Anth.* I, 21, 7d (KRSch, 326). For Aristotle's testimony to this aspect of Pythagorean teaching, see his *Meta.* A5, 985b23, DK 58B4–5 (KRSch, 329).

48. Aristotle (*Meta.* A5, 986a22, DK 58B5 [KRSch, 338]) delineates Pythagoras's table of opposites.

49. Fr. 1, Diogenes Laertius VIII, 85 (KRSch, 325).

50. Iamblichus, *Vita Pythagorae* 137, DK 58D2 (KRSch, 348–49).

51. Aristotle, *de an.* A4, 407b27, DK 44A23 (KRSch, 346).

52. For a lucid summary of how Orphism entered the Greek philosophical mainstream, see Zeller, *History of Greek Philosophy*, 14–16. According to Zeller's analysis, the cult of Dionysius was linked with the Thracian bard Orpheus. The cult held that Dionysius (in the form of an ox) had been devoured by the Titans, who were in turn burned by Zeus, who made humans from the ashes of the Titans. In the context of this cultic belief, humans assume a dual nature, combining a Titanic dimension (rooted in the mortal body) and a divine Dionysiac dimension (the basis of the immortal soul). The Orphics likewise believed that the soul was imprisoned in the body as a penal measure for some transgression committed in a previous existence. A component of this punishment is a cycle of rebirths in successive bodies geared to purification and eventual salvation.

53. William R. Uttal, *Neural Theories of Mind: Why the Mind-Brain Problem May Never Be Solved* (Mahwah, N.J.: Erlbaum, 2005), 5.

2

Plato: The Primacy of Soul

"The safest generalization of the European philosophical tradition," wrote Alfred North Whitehead, "is that it consists of a series of footnotes to Plato."[1] Whitehead by no means overstates Plato's importance regarding subsequent philosophical developments. Plato, however, also provides a key referent against which earlier speculation can be measured. While the early cosmologists and metaphysicians directed themselves largely to an analysis of nature and the material world, Plato's concerns are grounded in human affairs and the ethical issues they generate. But Plato's concern with human endeavor extended much farther than a preoccupation with moral questions. His account of human nature is intimately connected with his psychology and with the metaphysical dualism that psychology presupposes. In this respect, Plato's psychology must be approached on the basis of the most literal sense of that term—that is, a study of the soul in its own right. This intellectualist and spiritualistic emphasis, in turn, decisively shaped his attitude toward the body and sense experience.

THE SHIFT TOWARD HUMANISM

The history of Western philosophy presents itself as a series of transitions or decisive turns in outlook, focus, and methodology. Along with the Sophists and his teacher Socrates, Plato was instrumental in effecting the great shift toward humanism that represents the second phase of Greek philosophical development. The first great transition, as we have seen, signaled the movement from mythical, cosmogonical accounts to increasingly rational and naturalistic attempts at explaining the universe. But implicit in this transition (and the prolonged course of development it assumed) were the seeds of its eventual supplantation. By the time the atomists emerged, Pre-Socratic philosophy had become far too abstract to suit people's concrete needs. The general perception was that philosophy and its practitioners were woefully detached from the fundamental problems confronting human beings. To a great extent, atomism exemplified a growing tendency to introduce a fault line between the world as it presents itself to us on a commonsense basis and the world as it was understood by the philosophers themselves—that is, in terms of suprasensible, nonverifiable concepts and principles.

[margin note: lack of ethics]

This cleavage between the perspective of the philosopher as natural scientist and that of the proverbial man in the street promoted a spirit of skepticism that assumed a dual thrust: first, a skepticism toward the testimony of sense experience and, second, a skepticism toward the philosophical enterprise itself, especially in respect to its metaphysical dimension. Skepticism was already deeply ingrained in a rationalistic outlook that rejected an uncritical acceptance of myth and devalued traditional religious conceptions of the divine. In this respect, Xenophanes' critique of the anthropomorphic tendency of his own tradition (and his emphasis on the subjective depictions of the gods and goddesses) encouraged a widespread questioning of the divine origin of law or *nomos* itself. This theological critical stance was reinforced by the Pre-Socratics' search for causal explanations on a purely naturalistic plane.

THE SOPHISTIC LEGACY

The historian Herodotus provides ample evidence of Greek encounters with the diverse customs and institutions operative in the larger world. Such cross-cultural contacts lent support to the philosophical and theological strains of skepticism engendered by the Pre-Socratics. In this connection, the Sophists (itinerant teachers who traveled about Greece offering what amounted to a liberal arts education) promoted a growing conviction in the variable character of laws, moral principles, and religious beliefs. For them, cultural relativism provided ample justification for moral relativism. Moral inquiry was reduced to a matter of cultural anthropology and an investigation of how people live. From their standpoint, the morality of a given practice or activity was no more than a matter of interpretation and common acceptability. *— Epicureans*

This position carried significant metaphysical and epistemological implications. Such a relativistic perspective seriously challenged the notion

[margin note: conflation of cultural relativism w/ moral relativism.]

of a universally valid, abiding truth. Correlatively, it posed a threat to the very possibility of knowledge. Indeed, one cannot really claim to know in the absence of a stable truth to be known. When the Sophist Protagoras proclaimed that "man is the measure of all things," his message was clear: the ultimate standard of moral valuation is a human, not a divine, one. For this reason, sophistic relativism is bound up with a spirit of egoism and its assumption that moral judgments are based on considerations of practical expediency alone. For the Sophists, the ability to make the better case for one's position was the paramount concern (not the objective truth or falsehood of a proposition). It is significant, then, that they were renowned for their skill as teachers of rhetoric, the art of persuasive speaking.

In fifth-century Athens (the intellectual center of Greece), the flourishing democratic ideal created a demand for individuals with the intelligence and ability to assume positions of leadership. Over the previous two centuries, the Greek world had rejected kings in favor of aristocracies and then gravitated toward an oligarchic pattern of governance that exalted wealth over noble birth.[2] Around 508 B.C., Athens had become a thoroughgoing democracy. The opening of new possibilities for political ascendancy made the skills that the Sophists purveyed highly desirable assets. In this respect, the Sophists radically redefined the traditional notion of virtue and deeply ingrained presuppositions as to what constitutes the good life.

The English word "virtue" does not do justice to the richness inherent in its Greek counterpart, *arete*. In its broadest terms, *arete* refers to excellence or skill at performing a specific function. Statesmen or warriors or craftsmen all could be said to possess an *arete* pertinent to their particular skills. In a stratified culture characterized by well-defined social and occupational roles, discernment of one's *arete* is fairly straightforward. But in the absence of traditional structures which assign people their identities and tasks in life, determinations of "excellence" become somewhat nebulous.

The rise of democracy opened the field considerably to those with the acumen, will, and determination to succeed. Such a situation was amenable to the sophistic assumption that virtue consists of a teachable set of skills for use in the public forum. Hadot sums up this understanding of virtue:

> Thus, *arete* conceived as competence intended to enable young people to play a role in the city, could now be the object of an apprenticeship, so long as the student had the right natural aptitudes and practiced hard enough"[3]

The Sophists contributed to this great democratization process. In the context of their own time, the means to success was no longer noble birth, special gifts, or feats of courage but the practical ability to navigate the turbulent waters of public life.

In the period after the Persian Wars, Athens had assumed the preeminent position among Greek city-states in wealth, power, and influence. But the rise of the Athenian empire led to rampant materialism and an erosion of traditional values. The devastating effects of the Peloponnesian War (431–404 B.C.) accelerated these developments. By the final decades of the fifth century, Athens was a generational battleground. Young people (whose role models were their sophistic teachers) found themselves in conflict with an older generation committed to the ancestral virtues and age-old religious and patriotic ideals.[4]

The entire Greek world exhibited a struggle between competing factions and interest groups. The vibrant life of the *polis* was enervated as the democratic ideal gave way to governance by demagogues and tyrants. The Greek historian Thucydides assessed this state of affairs on the eve of the Peloponnesian War:

> Revolutions broke out in city after city and new extravagances of revolutionary zeal, expressed by an elaboration in the methods of seizing power and unheard-of atrocities in revenge. To fit in with the change of events, words too had to change their usual meanings.[5]

The Sophists thus acted as the philosophical spokesmen of their age, inculcating the very traits that Thucydides bemoaned, since cultivation of language for achieving one's own ends was a crucial component of the Sophists' educational program. In a manner consistent with their relativism, the Sophists reduced the meaning of moral terms to a purely subjective status. But this rejection of the isomorphism between language and objective reality pointed to a broader rejection of metaphysical and moral foundations. The time was ripe for resuscitating a commitment to objective values. The man who set himself to this enormous task was Socrates (469–399 B.C.).

ENTER SOCRATES

Socrates transformed Western thought. The fact that everything preceding him is designated as "pre-Socratic" attests to his importance as a man and thinker. Still, Socrates' contribution to the nature of philosophical inquiry was intimately linked with the rise of Sophism. While he wished to fill the moral void characterizing his own cultural milieu, he did so in the context of the shift toward humanism that the Sophists abetted. Socrates may never have emerged without the challenge posed by the Sophists,

since the Socratic approach to moral inquiry found its dialectical foil in
the relativism which Sophism promoted.

In the final analysis, the real division between Socrates and his sophistic opponents is reflected in their divergent views concerning the virtuous
life. There is a great difference between practical knowledge or know-how
and the wisdom that penetrates the ultimate causes of things. Socrates
carried out this educational project by prompting his hearers to self-
knowledge. He conceived his task as attempting to bring to birth a critical self-scrutiny in his interlocutors. Socrates' way of teaching was based
on the same art of dialectic that the Sophists had introduced as a debating
device. But Socrates transformed the approach to such an extent that it
rightfully bears his name. This Socratic method entailed a grueling cross-
examination of Socrates' fellow citizens (especially politicians and ora-
tors). In the able hands of its master practitioner, dialectic became a vehicle for discerning what is true and consistent with the soul's good. This
presupposes the ability of each individual to find the truth independently.

For Socrates, dialectic was directed toward the grasp of those constants
which render the vast multiplicity of human opinions intelligible and
meaningful. In the context of his dialectical encounters (as depicted in
Plato's early dialogues), we observe him leading his opponents from a
narrow, parochial understanding of traditional virtues (e.g., piety, justice,
and courage) to universal definitions that speak to all people at all times.
In Socratic terms, then, the life of wisdom is by no means a matter of abstract speculation. Socrates was firm in the conviction that practical moral
living must be based on unshakeable constants such as the good, the true,
and the beautiful and shaped by unchangeable transcendental values. He
thereby redefined the very meaning of *arete* as a way of knowing. By
equating virtue with knowledge, Socrates underscores the fact that any
virtuous activity presupposes a cognitive dimension.

Universalizing virtues

Socrates' concern, however, was not merely the excellence of specific
acts or even specific ways of life; he was concerned with nothing less than
the good of human life in general. In this respect, Socrates held that the
right knowledge of what to do in a given situation will be translated into
right action. From this standpoint, one is considered morally good only
insofar as one possesses an intellectual grasp of the good.[6] This is the antithesis of mere conjecture about what is right and the erroneous opinions
based on sense experience alone.

The fact that Socrates represents the pivotal figure in the great shift toward humanism is not disputed. The challenge lies in reconstructing his
ideas on the basis of what others say about him. The major exponent of
Socrates' teaching (aside from such commentators as Aristophanes,
Xenophon, and Aristotle) was his disciple Plato (428/7 to 348/7 B.C.),[7] for
whom Socrates provided the very embodiment of a life dedicated to the

love of wisdom. So great was Socrates' influence on Plato that the latter thinker developed a new genre of philosophical writing to express his teacher's unique way of philosophizing. This genre is the Socratic dialogue, an extended conversation between Socrates and his interlocutors on a wide range of topics and problems.

SOCRATES AND PLATO

Plato attempted to translate Socrates' pedagogical ideals into a comprehensive vision of reality that could reestablish the foundations of the life of the *polis*. Socrates convinced Plato that shifting human opinions must be anchored on stable and invariable norms of judgment grasped on the basis of reasoning alone. Socrates' moral stance, his role as a teacher, and his overall character held a tremendous appeal for the young Plato. Plato remained a member of Socrates' inner circle of followers until Socrates died in 399 B.C.

As portrayed by Plato, Socrates emerges as a relentless questioner. The Socratic method elicits opinions from those questioned and then scrutinizes and refutes them in light of mutually accepted principles. An important component of the method is the assumption that ignorance is a vital stage in arriving at a knowledge claim. Socrates showed his interlocutors that they were actually ignorant of what they assumed they already knew. Ultimately this cooperative endeavor (involving a give-and-take between the questioner and the one questioned) was geared to discovering the most universal definitions possible. It rejected definitions or theories reflecting no more than the individual interpretations or personal preferences of their exponents.

Socrates' dialectical approach (which presupposes that truth can be attained when opposing viewpoints confront one another) provided the model of philosophizing for Plato and, by extension, for the subsequent intellectual tradition he so decisively shaped. Plato fully absorbed the Socratic conviction that the reasoning activity of the human soul is the means to the comprehension of truth. Like his mentor, Plato was convinced that truth is the best antidote for the moral corrosiveness posed by the dissolution of Athenian values. Knowledge can only be founded on the universal concepts that dialectic yields. For Plato, those concepts give expression to the Forms, the ultimate constituents of the really real.

But if the Forms provide the objective content of the concepts we use in making sense of things, then the intelligibility of things depends on a transcendent thought world. For Plato and Socrates alike, the soul provides the nexus between this suprasensible world of Forms and humans. In this connection, Plato adapted Orphic and Pythagorean teaching that the soul is a divine principle which imparts us with a claim to the incorruptibility and immortality of the gods. This thesis presupposes a dualism between soul and body: the soul is destined to rule a corruptible body that undermines the soul's moral integrity and intellectual acuity.

Plato's psychology developed over the course of his writings, but its basic tenets remained relatively stable. While his later works offer a more sophisticated treatment of the range of psychic activities attributable to humans, his commitment to the primacy of the soul never wavered. This theme assumes special prominence in Plato's *Phaedo* (c. 380 B.C.), a dialogue written at the beginning of the period reflecting his maturation as a thinker. By virtue of its wide-ranging character and depth of analysis, the *Phaedo* serves as an ideal critical touchstone for assessing Plato's philosophical anthropology and its careful intertwining of Socratic themes with Plato's epistemological and metaphysical perspective.

In its broadest terms, the *Phaedo* specifies the criteria of true knowledge and the foundations on which any claim to genuine knowing must rest. In so doing, it underscores the basic tenets of Plato's anthropology: we are fundamentally our souls, and bodily life must always assume a subordinate (and even an inferior) status in relation to the soul and its reasoning capacity. In this respect, Plato's anthropology amounts to a psychology in its most literal terms: a study of the life and fate of the soul.

THE PSYCHOLOGY OF THE *PHAEDO*

The fact that Plato begins the *Phaedo* by referring to a myth is a matter of no small philosophical importance. This point of departure says something significant about his own culture and his role within that cultural framework. Plato stands in continuity with the spirit of rationalism that had its beginnings in Ionian speculation and found a specific humanistic focus in the life and teaching of Socrates. But this is not to say that Plato completely abandoned the mythical vehicle. In a number of dialogues, he incorporates mythical motifs and imagery, ranging from discussions of the origins of the cosmos in the *Timaeus*, to allegories intended to penetrate certain truths about human nature and the ascent to knowledge (as in the ring of Gyges story and Allegory of the Cave in the *Republic*), to quasi-religious treatments of the prospect of an afterlife in the *Phaedo*. In each case, the crucial consideration is Plato's conscious control of myth.

From this standpoint, Plato's reference to the account of Theseus and the Minotaur at the very outset of the *Phaedo* can be somewhat deceptive. It ostensibly reports the reason why Socrates' death has been postponed. On a deeper level, however, it underscores the influence that myth continued to exert on most Greeks (including the intellectually astute Athenians).

In Athens religion was inextricably bound up with every facet of private and public life. Because religion permeated the popular consciousness, it also played a role in determining the fate of its most enlightened citizen.

What amounts to a passing allusion to a myth at the beginning of the dialogue sets the tone for what follows. In the course of this penetrating investigation into the nature and destiny of the human soul, Plato repeatedly refers to popular conceptions of these topics as key counterpoints in developing his own philosophical position. The *Phaedo* concludes with an extended deliberation on the soul's fate that reveals how Plato uses myth in dealing with issues that do not allow for easy verification or precise explanation. Such an account frees Plato from the need to prove things that simply transcend the parameters of philosophical argumentation.

THE PHILOSOPHICAL WAY OF LIFE

The discussion proceeds from Echecrates' query about Socrates' final days.[8] We are immediately informed that there was a delay between Socrates' sentencing and his death because executions were prohibited during the annual mission to the shrine of Apollo, in commemoration of Theseus slaying the Minotaur and rescuing seven young men and women from sacrifice. In response to Echecrates' request, Phaedo stresses Socrates' general equanimity in the face of death.

Socrates' calm demeanor prompts mixed emotions among his visitors. Phaedo acknowledges "an unaccustomed mixture of pleasure and pain," pain because of Socrates' impending departure but pleasure at the prospect of his happiness in the life to come. Reflection on the simultaneity of pleasure and pain provides an interesting segue for Socrates' observations as to how great discomfort can give way to great satisfaction. While pleasure and pain are viewed as opposites, these feelings are frequently related, so that a man who "pursues either is generally compelled to take the other."[9] Socrates' remarks amount to a wry commentary on the ambiguities inherent in human existence, or at least that phase of human existence while the soul is attached to the body. In metaphorical terms, the "bonds" which cause Socrates' pain pertain to the body itself and its capacity to trouble the soul, until those corporeal bonds are shed at death.

In a manner consistent with Socrates' commitment to "practice the art of philosophy," he now invites Evenus (a Sophist) to follow him. This advice is a source of some consternation among Socrates' hearers: does he encourage Evenus to follow him literally, in the sense of taking his own life? Cebes perceives a paradox in Socrates' invitation: "Why do you say . . . that a man ought not to take his own life but that the philosopher will be ready to follow the dying?"[10] Cebes' riveting question prompts Socrates to

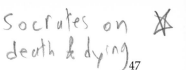

justify his stance. But in broader terms, it serves as the point of entry for Socrates' deliberation on his understanding of death and its relation to the philosophical way of life. If Socrates does not resent the prospect of death under the present circumstances, it is because he expects something better to come.

> I ought to be grieved at death, if I were not persuaded in the first place that I am going to other gods who are wise and good . . . and . . . to men departed, better than those whom I leave behind; and therefore I do not grieve as I might have done, for I have good hope that there is yet something remaining for the dead, and as has been said of old, some far better thing for the good than for the evil.[11]

In the final analysis, Socrates looks forward to death because of his confidence that a future awaits us after death and his assumption that the souls of good people will enjoy a better future than the souls of the wicked.

Socrates' belief in the human capacity to survive physical death (and the sense of cosmic justice underlying this optimism) underscores a Pythagorean strain of thinking that subtly weaves its way through the dialogue. This Pythagorean dimension is most evident in the next phase of the discussion, as Socrates argues for the reasonableness of confronting his death in a spirit of joy.[12] This argument reflects his special understanding of the goal of philosophy, when practiced in the proper manner. When viewed in this light, Socrates' invitation to Evenus to "follow him" with due haste amounts to a challenge to embrace the same philosophical art that he has embraced and train for dying and death. Socrates thus presents the love of wisdom as a life-and-death commitment, not merely a profession. Accordingly, his equanimity in his death cell is understandable and reasonable: how could one who has devoted his life to a philosophical training for death balk at the critical moment? Socrates' credibility as a thinker and a human being are on the proverbial firing line. "It would be strange indeed," he observes, "if they were eager for this all their lives and then resent it when what they have wanted and practiced for a long time comes upon them."[13]

In Socrates' reckoning what constitutes death? Stated simply, death is a mutual separation of the soul from the body, and the body from the soul.[14] This operative definition (a definition which everyone present in the cell endorses) has a direct link with Socrates' understanding of philosophy as a training or preparation for dying. From this standpoint, the true philosopher is one who frees the soul from an association with the body as much as possible.[15] Socrates paints a stark picture of the philosophical life consistent with the Pythagorean emphasis on ritual purification, bodily discipline, moderation, and a general abstinence from physical pleasures. But Socrates by no means confines his understanding of the philosophical way of life to this ascetic ideal. If he did, he would offer no more than his Pythagorean predecessors and contemporaries in their own vision of the philosopher's art. What sets Socrates' interpretation apart lies in the refined epistemological deliberations in which he now engages.

> What again shall we say of the actual acquirement of knowledge? Is the body . . . a hinderer or a helper? I mean . . . have sight and hearing any truth in them? Are they not, as the poets are always telling us, inaccurate witnesses?[16]

Suddenly the discussion assumes a new slant: by calling into question the veracity of sense experience, Plato's "Socrates" introduces a dichotomy between the way of opinion and the way of knowledge. The former is the way of the body, while the latter is the province of the soul. If the senses are a source of deception, when and how does the soul grasp truth? In Platonic terms, reasoning is most effective when the soul works on its own, without the intrusion of the senses and without the distraction of external influences such as pleasure or pain. In order for reason to flourish, the soul must be "by itself, taking leave of the body and as far as possible having no contact or association with it in its search for reality."[17] And because the soul of the true philosopher has the greatest aversion to the body, it detaches itself from bodily life, seeking its own mode of existence. Can't this just be moderate?

Socrates' stipulation that the soul reasons best when it has as little contact with the body as possible is crucial. This provides Plato's point of departure for introducing his theory of Forms. But he leads us into this metaphysical realm gradually. Indeed, his initial reference to the Forms is so understated as to escape notice. But he now lays the groundwork for what becomes the foundation of his arguments in favor of the soul's immortality. At this stage, his primary concern lies in establishing the kind of reality which constitutes the proper focus of the soul's attention. "Is there or is there not," Socrates queries, "an absolute Justice . . . and an absolute Beauty and absolute Good?"[18] Once Simmias acknowledges the existence of universals, he admits they can never be grasped by means of the senses.

> Did you ever reach them with any . . . bodily sense? And I speak not of these alone, but of absolute greatness, and health, and strength, and of the essence or true nature of everything.[19]

The objects of reasoning, then, are the essential realities that find expression in the universal concepts we take for granted in understanding our world. This is the sphere of pure thought, the sphere reserved for the soul alone. But such a grasp of true reality is by no means instantaneous. Socrates stresses that any grasp of the real requires an effort to separate

✻ A relevant question in light of synthesesia, Helen Keller, brain trauma, etc.

ourselves from "eyes and ears and . . . the whole body, these being . . . distracting elements."[20] Yet how can we engage in reasoning without bodily contact or reliance on sense experience? The implication is that we can only attain this goal once we die, when the soul is completely separated from the body and its negative impact. In this respect, however, Socrates' depiction of the philosophical way of life as a training for death reveals an intriguing ambiguity. On the surface, it appears that he is speaking in literal terms, about that moment of death when the soul and the body are actually separated. But at this juncture of the dialogue, Socrates is as concerned with the soul's integrity in the present life as he is with the soul's future destiny. Accordingly, the claim that philosophy is a training or preparation for death must encompass the philosopher's activity *here and now*, when soul and body are unavoidably associated with each other. For Socrates, the philosophical way of life must entail an existential commitment that radically shapes and defines the quality of our choices on an immediate basis. This is precisely what accounts for his sense of mission and is the reason he now finds himself in a prison cell awaiting death.

Paradoxically, the philosopher must live as if the soul and body were already separated in fact. This is qualified by Plato's use of the phrase "the least possible." The philosopher must strive for detachment from the body in a manner consistent with what is practically feasible and expedient in our embodied state.

Asceticism

> In this present life . . . we make the nearest approach to knowledge when we have the least possible . . . communion with the body . . . but keep ourselves pure until the hour when God . . . is pleased to release us.[21]

Socrates does not conceive this purification process as an isolated enterprise. Those who live the philosophical life (i.e., those willing to die to the body) open themselves to the company of like-minded people.[22] Collectively, those who live this way can expect a comparable destiny in the future.

In this opening part of the dialogue, Socrates establishes a key aspect of his extended argument for the soul's immortality. This argument hinges on a proper understanding of the meaning of philosophy as a way of dying.

> What is purification but the separation of the soul from the body, . . . the habit of the soul gathering and collecting herself into herself from all sides out of the body, the dwelling in her own place alone . . . as far as she can?"[23]

The purified soul is a soul intact, a soul that concentrates its energies on what is essential and forfeits all spurious claims to truth. Conversely, excessive contact with the body results in a distention or "spreading thin" of the soul's reasoning powers. Those who practice philosophy in the *so Pauline.*

right way, then, will not resent the prospect of death when it manifests it-self and will fear it least of all people. This is because the lover of wisdom loves the soul, not the body. In this context, Socrates draws on the bacchic teaching that those who enter the underworld in a purified state "will dwell with the gods."[24]

ARGUMENTS FOR THE SOUL'S IMMORTALITY

Socrates' references to the mystery religions help translate his philosoph-ical position into a popular idiom to which people can easily relate. The mystery cults were fast becoming the religious outlet of the masses of peo-ple craving assurance of the soul's survival and the prospect of reward in the afterlife. Cebes' response to Socrates' remarks underscores this desire:

> In what concerns the soul, men are apt to be incredulous; they fear that when she has left the body her place may be nowhere and that on that day of death she may perish and come to an end, . . . dispersed like smoke or air and in her flight vanishing away into nothingness.[25]

But it is just such individuals that Socrates wants to convince. As Cebes observes, the belief that the soul can survive the body's death "requires a great deal of argument and many proofs."[26] Accordingly, Socrates crafts his first argument for the soul's continued existence independently of the body. His touchstone is not one of the "mysteries," however, but a vague "ancient theory" founded on the premise that things come to be on the ba-sis of the generation of opposites. "If it be true that the living come from the dead, then our souls must exist in the other world; for if not, how could they have been born again?"[27]

From this standpoint, life gives way to death and death to life, just as sleep gives way to wakefulness and wakefulness to sleep. This alternating movement presupposes a perpetual process whereby one condition or mode of being generates its antithesis, and vice versa. For those who sup-port this particular theory, the very existence of the world and living things attests to that ongoing cycle: "If all things which partook of life were to die, and after they were dead remained in the form of death, and did not come to life again, all would at last die, and nothing would be alive."[28]

But how persuasive is this argument? In the final analysis, it rests on two unprovable assumptions: first, that nature exhibits an eternal "turn of the wheel," so to speak, whereby one state of affairs is generated out of its contrary; second, that human existence and the fate of the soul can be understood on the basis of this naturalistic analog. In anthropological terms, the argument also presupposes a belief in the soul's transmigration or cycle of rebirths from one embodiment to another. As it stands, then, the argument from opposites seems neither sound nor convincing. At the very least, however, Socrates has broached the issue of the soul's immortality against the background of an established theory that offers a rational approach to something that most people accept as a matter of untested belief.

Socrates now introduces his key argument for the soul's immortality in response to Cebes' reference to "Socrates' favorite doctrine," that learning is a matter of recollecting.[29] In the sharp epistemological turn the dialogue now takes, Socrates assesses the question of the soul's immortality on the basis of its capacity to grasp truths inaccessible to us through sense experience or any bodily input. The ensuing line of argumentation builds on the notion of learning as a "recollection," and the assumption of "a previous time in which we have learned that which we now recollect."[30] But it also builds on Socrates' conviction that the proper mode of questioning can elicit correct responses even from those who do not possess an explicit grasp of the subject matter at the outset.[31]

In what sense is knowledge an exercise in recollection? Socrates addresses this question by investigating ordinary experiences of recollection. What immediately stands out in these cases is the difference between a direct encounter with things on a sensory level and their calling to mind of realities not immediately present to us.

> Whether a person who, having seen or heard or in any way perceived anything, knows not only that but has a conception of something else which is the subject, not of the same but of some other kind of knowledge, may not be fairly said to recollect that of which he has the conception?[32]

Socrates draws an interesting connection here between recollection and forgetfulness; indeed, remembrance is particularly poignant when something calls to mind things we have apparently forgotten. In all of these instances, however, recollection can be prompted by things that are either similar or dissimilar to each other. In this respect, the critical issue concerns the extent to which we discern a disparity between what we actually perceive and what we recollect. At this point in the dialogue, the reader's acquaintance with Plato's theory of Forms is taken for granted. This theory, as we have seen, rests on the dichotomy between a changing world of sense experience and an immutable realm of purely intelligible realities expressed through universal concepts.

We readily assume, for example, that we can judge things as "equal" in relation to each other on the basis of their appearance, as when we compare the size of two sticks or two pieces of chalk. But where do we acquire our knowledge of the Form or essence of Equality, the standard whereby we judge things to be equal or unequal? Comparative value judgments regarding things that appear more or less "equal" presuppose a wholly abstract concept. From Socrates' standpoint, our ability to differentiate between equal things and Equality itself presupposes some prior grasp of the latter notion; sense experience can never yield our knowledge of a comprehensive criterion by which we judge things as "equal" or "unequal." The things we grasp through the senses merely prompt us to recollect a notion to which our minds are somehow already attuned.

By the same token, the things we designate as "equal" in height, length, or shape may not appear so to everyone. Such assessments are highly variable and open to conflicting interpretations. But this is clearly not the case in respect to our grasp of the Form of Equality: it is what it is and nothing else; it admits neither deficiency nor any suggestion of inequality. In this case, then, Socrates draws the following conclusion:

> Before we began to see or hear or perceive in any way, we must have had a knowledge of absolute equality, or we could not have referred to that standard the equals which are derived from the senses? For to that they all aspire, and of that they fall short.[33]

Socrates now extends this argument to the Forms of all those universal concepts that provide the core of our comparative value judgments. If we cannot arrive at these kinds of truths on an inductive basis (through our perception of individual instances of these notions), Socrates concludes that we must have acquired this knowledge in a prenatal state and that our souls existed apart from the bodies they assumed.[34] But since knowledge presupposes an ability to render an account or *logos* of what we profess to know (as the justification of true belief), this epistemological criterion is somewhat problematic.

The fact that few of Socrates' contemporaries could do this calls into question the capacity to know in this life. Simmias bemoans that after Socrates dies, "there will no longer be any one alive who is able to give an account of them and, thereby, justify their own knowledge claims."[35] The recollection motif, however, provides a means of addressing this dilemma. As described by Socrates, knowing in this life assumes the character of a gradual but prolonged dialectical process of learning. This ideal of active learning is consistent with the thrust of the Socratic method and its emphasis on each individual's capacity to discern the truth under the guidance of the proper questioner. Accordingly, any knowledge that humans hope to achieve at the present time is the outgrowth of a dynamic act of ongoing intellectual growth.

Socrates thus grounds his argument for the soul's independence from the body in the human capacity to judge in light of universal (and wholly unobservable) conceptual models like the Equal, the Beautiful, the Good, and the Just. But in so doing, he draws on a religious theory of the soul's preexistence and its transmigration from one bodily existence to another. Whether Socrates and Plato actually accepted this theory or merely incorporated it as another "likely story" of the soul's origins for the benefit of their audience is a matter of conjecture. A literal reading might take Socrates' words at face value and assume that the argument from recollection presupposes a belief in the soul's preexistence (and its acquisition of knowledge in some prior life). Or we might focus on what the argument says about the way in which the mind grasps truths *here and now*, even as our souls are bound up with our bodies. The crucial consideration here is not any argumentation on behalf of the soul's existence before our birth. Rather, it concerns our capacity to know what modern philosophers characterize as a priori truths (i.e., truths which the mind understands independently of sense experience or sensory verification).

From this perspective, the success of Socrates' argument from recollection does not necessarily require a personal belief in the soul's previous existence or a cycle of rebirths in order to be persuasive. What it does require, however, is a convincing demonstration that the soul has a life of its own, separate from the body, corporeal desires, and physical needs. As Socrates stresses at the conclusion of this phase of the discussion, the soul is attuned to a level of reality for which it possesses a metaphysical and epistemological affinity. Accordingly, his conviction in the soul's ongoing existence "apart from the body" (even while it is conjoined with a body) is closely aligned with his teaching that universal concepts refer to things which are objectively real in their own right. If these realities do not exist, Socrates observes, "there would be no force in the argument."[36]

But a persuasive argument in favor of the soul's independence of the body (or its preexistence) does not really demonstrate that the soul will survive the body's death. This is precisely the objection that Simmias now raises, as he speaks on behalf of that "opinion of the majority" which he and Cebes represent: "Why after having entered in and gone out again may she not herself be destroyed and come to an end?"[37] Implicit in this objection, however, lies a commitment to a materialism which equates the soul with the body, along with the corruptibility of corporeal reality. Socrates is quick to perceive the deeper implications of Simmias's critique. Accordingly, he now focuses on the realities that are susceptible to dissolution and scattering. By extension, he deliberates on the respective natures of body and soul, and the differences between these classes of things.

THE NATURE OF SOUL AND BODY

As Socrates has already suggested, there is a generic difference between body and soul that runs to their very nature. Earlier in the dialogue, he defined this difference largely in epistemological terms, in conjunction with the soul's capacity to grasp unchanging, universal truths (as opposed to the sense experience of changing particulars). Now he delineates this difference on the basis of a metaphysical distinction between things of a composite nature (i.e., those things composed of parts) and noncomposites. What is the crux of this distinction? As defined by Socrates, it lies primarily in mutability—susceptibility to change. The composite is "always changing and never the same," while the noncomposite is "the same and unchanging."[38]

We are surrounded by things continually subject to change. But what of the noncomposites? When and how do we experience these realities? Since the Forms themselves constitute the ultimate criteria for things of a noncomposite nature, such things are accessible through reasoning alone. "Each of them always what they are," Socrates asserts, "the same simple self-existent and unchanging forms, not admitting of variation at all . . . in any way . . . at any time."[39] The immutable Forms, then, stand in sharp contrast to the things of ordinary experience, which never remain the same, either in themselves or in relation to one another. This contrast is as sharp as the difference between the soul and the body.

Proceeding from the premise that "like grasps what is like," Socrates affirms the soul's kinship with the Forms and, conversely, the body's affinity with perishable things. This is the basis of a dualistic anthropology that decisively shapes Plato's overall understanding of the soul-body relationship. In the ensuing discussion, he depicts this relationship as one of tension and conflict. If the soul is akin to the unchanging Forms (and by implication to what is divine), its contact with a mutable, mortal, and corruptible body can only yield negative effects on its life and powers.

> When using the body as an instrument of perception . . . the soul . . . is then dragged by the body into the region of the changeable, and wanders and is confused . . . like a drunkard, when she touches change.[40]

From this dualistic perspective, the soul must detach itself from reliance on sense experience, the gateway to changing things of a composite, corruptible nature. But promoting the life of the soul is concomitant with cultivating the love of wisdom—that is, practicing philosophy in the right way. By virtue of its inherent affinity with the Forms, Socrates imparts a divine character to the soul, along with attributes traditionally associated with the gods. "The soul is in the very likeness of the divine," he asserts, "immortal, intellectual, uniform, indissoluble, and unchangeable."[41]

soul is divine.

Socrates perceives a hierarchical relationship between the soul, which is ordained to govern the body, and the body to be governed. The extent to which the soul maintains this regulative status has a bearing on its fate after death. The soul's destiny is a direct outgrowth of its attitude toward the body in the present life. For this reason, those who practice philosophy in the right way actively prepare their souls for a future in "the company of the gods."[42] By dying to the body and its range of affectivities, the soul purifies itself of corporeal attachments and any evils attendant upon human existence. In Socratic terms, the soul of the philosopher shuns everything that renders it corporeal. For those who "materialize" their souls by an inordinate involvement with bodily life, however, Socrates envisions a frustrating cycle of rebirths (again drawing on the transmigration motif) that can only diminish their integrity and efficacy.

> The soul which has been polluted, and is impure at the time of her departure, and is the companion and servant of the body always, . . . do you suppose that such a soul will depart pure and unalloyed?"[43]

But is Socrates' apparent invective directed toward the body per se or to the distorted picture of true reality that immersion in the body promotes? The extreme asceticism and dualism of Socrates' remarks need to be assessed in light of a greater concern: the common human assumption that we are no more than our bodies and that our physical desires define the parameters of our value system. Socrates, of course, now has a personal stake in this particular issue. If the majority opinion is true, then his own willingness to die, and his very anticipation of a happy future life, is a pointless gesture.

TWO EPIPHENOMENALIST THEORIES

Simmias and Cebes provide immediate touchstones for such a popular viewpoint and the general tendency to reduce the soul to a physical plane. In this respect, both endorse the epiphenomenalist position that the soul either depends on the body for its continuing existence or that mental life is explicable solely on the basis of physiological processes. Simmias and Cebes now express versions of this position in questioning the persuasiveness of Socrates' argument from recollection. While they agree that the argument establishes the soul's preexistence, they are not entirely convinced that it proves its survival after the body's dissolution. Each, in turn, casts Socrates' argument in terms of the materialistic presupposition that the soul is viewed as no more than an extension of the body.

Simmias begins the questioning along clear Pythagorean lines. For him, what Socrates contends is comparable to claiming that the soul is like an invisible harmony responsible for attuning the body (likened to the strings of a lyre). In Simmias's portrayal of Socrates' argument, the soul (i.e., the harmony) must continue to exist after the mortal body (i.e., the strings) ceases to exist, merely because the harmony is akin to the divine and hence indestructible. Socrates postpones his response until he hears Cebes' objection.

Cebes echoes Simmias's sentiments, but with a slant that incorporates elements of transmigration theory. Cebes construes Socrates' argument this way: if the body remains present after death and the soul is deemed more excellent than the body, it is reasonable to assume that the greater part of us will endure if the weaker endures. In support of this "version," Cebes proposes an image: since the cloak survives after the death of an old man, the man must still exist, since he is greater than a cloak.[44] From Cebes' perspective, this contention is untenable, since it merely demonstrates that the old man (i.e., the soul) has worn out many cloaks (i.e., bodies) over his lifetime. But it fails to demonstrate that the soul will survive in perpetuity. Indeed, survival for a long time does not ensure survival in an absolute sense. Likewise, durability does not necessarily ensure immortality. In this way, Cebes construes Socrates' position as endorsing a prolonged series of rebirths that will eventually cease after the soul leaves the last body in this cycle.

Socrates' response to both Simmias and Cebes builds on their mutual acceptance of the thesis that learning is a matter of recollection and that the soul exists on its own, even before embodiment. On the basis of this joint admission, however, he fastens upon an inconsistency implicit in Simmias's depiction of the soul as a harmony of bodily parts. How can Simmias uphold the soul's preexistence of the body if he assumes that the soul constitutes a harmony or attunement of its parts? "Harmony is not like the soul," Socrates admonishes, "but . . . made last of all and perishes first."[45]

Indeed, a harmony cannot exist before the parts. Simmias readily concedes Socrates' point and arrives at a decisive conclusion: that which harmonizes composite things is not really different from what it harmonizes.[46] If the soul is a harmony of the body, then it can never qualify as a true governing principle in its own right. Rather, it only exists for the sake of the body it serves. A harmony, then, cannot act as a genuine cause of bodily movement. By the same token, such a psychic theory fails to do justice to the complexity inherent in human behavior. If the soul were exclusively a harmony, how could we account for the degrees of goodness we observe in people or the emotional upheavals they experience?[47] From Socrates' standpoint, the exact opposite is the case: the soul directs and frequently challenges corporeal drives. No mere harmony could fulfill such a regulative role, especially as the soul sometimes opposes the affections of the body.[48]

Together, Simmias and Cebes question whether Socrates has demonstrated no more than the soul's capacity to last for a long time, rather than its true immortality. Perhaps its association with the body was merely "a sort of disease which is the beginning of dissolution."[49] Socrates' reply is wholly consistent with his earlier contention that soul and body constitute different kinds of reality. In this particular objection, he discerns an important philosophical problem that touches on the very cause of generation and destruction. Accordingly, the distinction between noncomposite and composite things finds a new focus in the causal analysis which dominates the final part of the dialogue.

MIND AND CAUSALITY

Socrates' discussion of generation and destruction prompts some preliminary autobiographical reflection. He recounts his early interest in natural science and the opportunity it offered for grasping "the causes of things and why a thing is and is created or destroyed."[50] In the course of this investigation, he became acquainted with the philosophy of Anaxagoras and his teaching that Mind acts as the directing principle of the universe. Socrates was drawn to this account and its emphasis on the ordering of things to their best end.

> If mind is the disposer, mind will dispose all for the best and put each particular in the best place, . . . and . . . if any one desired to find out the cause of the generation or destruction or existence of anything, he must find out what . . . was best for that thing.[51]

Socrates initially perceived Anaxgoras as a kindred spirit who could enlighten him about the ultimate causes of things. But as he delved deeper into Anaxagoras's philosophy, this hope was dashed. From Socrates' perspective, Anaxagoras failed to exploit the powerful notion of a Mind-governed universe in any comprehensive way. Rather than appealing to this intelligible principle, he continued to posit material elements as causes, in the manner of his predecessors. In this respect, Socrates distinguishes between causes of a purely empirical nature from the true causes of things. While the former category of cause is responsible for *how* an activity or process occurs, only a true cause accounts for *why* it does so. This distinction assumes a profound existential import in light of Socrates' own situation.

In this context, a penetrating question emerges: how do we account for the fact that Socrates now finds himself sitting in a death cell? On one level, we could explain his presence there exclusively on the basis of physiological factors, such as the arrangement of his bones, sinews, muscles, and limbs.[52] But this would merely scratch the surface of causal explanation, at least for the radical choice that Socrates has made. The real *reason why* he finds himself awaiting death has little to do with the physical act of sitting there; what it really concerns is his decision that this is the best course of action. Such a free decision presupposes a value judgment on his part that transcends the causal influences operative in the natural world and, by implication, in the functioning of the human body. Thus the fact that Socrates is now awaiting death can only be explained on the basis of an intellectual choice which represents the most excellent option open to him.[53]

This causal analysis opens the way for Socrates' interpretation of the dynamics of human action in terms of higher intelligible principles. His commitment to the "true causes" of things dovetails with the theory of Forms and the dualism between material and immaterial reality it presupposes. In a very real sense, however, this dualistic outlook is but a variant of Socrates' juxtaposing of the philosopher's life with the lives of the vast majority of people. Indeed, the very ability to appreciate what Socrates says about genuine causes demands a capacity to look beyond the immediately observable world, on both a scientific and a moral level. Socrates himself bears this out; his willingness to die for an ideal flies in the face of the value system of most of his contemporaries.

Socrates' disavowal of natural science (and its commitment to causal explanations based on visible things alone) thus coincides with his focus on the Forms as the ultimate causes of observable reality and, more specifically, the life of the body. In this respect, he now affirms that his arguments for the soul's immortality depend on the existence of the Forms themselves. "Grant me this," he pleads, "and I hope to be able to show you the nature of the cause and to prove the immortality of the soul."[54] What ensues, then, consists of a final demonstration of the soul's imperishability. The argument turns on the relationship between the Forms and the things of our experience. Socrates somewhat tentatively describes this relationship as involving a "participation" of the manifold in higher intelligible principles.

THE FORMS AS CAUSES

On the one hand, Socrates points out that things acquire their names by "sharing" or "participating" in the universal concepts that express the Forms. For example, things are only designated as "beautiful" in relation to the Beautiful Itself, or "equal" in relation to the Equal Itself. In this way, the empirical manifold assumes its cognitive significance by virtue of some common ground of meaning. But if Socrates confined his analysis to this dimension of the participation relationship, the Forms would assume no more than semantic significance. For his purposes, it is crucial to uphold their grounding in reality. For this reason, he imparts a causal significance to the Forms that renders them responsible for the way things are, just as by the Form of Beauty "all beautiful things become beautiful."[55]

The causal role of the Forms in making things what they are correlates with their integrity as realities in their own right; a Form is what it is and nothing else. In a manner consistent with the Law of Noncontradiction, Socrates affirms that "these essential opposites will never admit of generation into or out of one another."[56] The somewhat labored discussion which follows underscores a vital point: the Forms are mutually exclusive—by definition, by meaning, and on the basis of their causal efficacy. Thus what is responsible for causing one state of affairs cannot be responsible for causing its antithesis.[57]

Socrates has already established that a noncomposite reality like the soul is immune to the corruption associated with composite things like the body. At this juncture, however, he also draws on the common understanding of *psyche* as a life principle. But as we have seen, his major challenge throughout the dialogue was not necessarily a demonstration that the soul is responsible for life. The real bone of contention between Socrates and his skeptical interlocutors was whether the soul ultimately survives the body's death (or more precisely the last body it animates before its own annihilation). Accordingly, the theory of Forms now places his previous arguments for the soul's immortality on a firmer metaphysical foundation. The tacit assumption here is that the soul constitutes the Form of life in which the body shares. But in that case, the soul can never admit its opposite—death. If the soul is the Form of life and its activities, it can neither die nor undergo physical corruption.

> If the immortal is also imperishable, the soul when attacked by death cannot perish; the soul will not admit of death, or ever be dead, any more than three or the odd number will admit of the even or fire, or the heat in the fire, of the cold.[58]

Socrates' discussion of the soul has come full circle. What he earlier designated as a noncomposite reality oriented toward the immutable truth of the Forms is now explicitly designated as deathless by its very nature. If death accrues to humans, it can only proceed from the composite nature of the corruptible body. For all practical purposes, however, this is where Socrates' philosophizing about the soul's destiny comes to an end. In the elaborate myth of the soul's fate which concludes the dialogue, he situates this extended rational demonstration within a traditional religious framework.

CONCLUDING MYTH

This concluding myth offers a likely account of what happens to us (more precisely, to the authentic part of us) after our bodies die. Socrates himself disclaims any appeal to objective truth about these matters. "No sensible man would insist that these things are as I have described them," he acknowledges.[59] Instead, he undertakes a "noble risk" by believing in something that is worthy of our credence. For him, a belief in the soul's future destiny not only provides solace to someone facing death but also shapes the moral quality of one's life before death.

In moral terms, a commitment to the soul's immortality raises the stakes of human existence considerably. As Socrates asserts, if the soul is immortal, "it requires our care not only for the time we call our life but for the sake of all time."[60] From this standpoint, what happens to the soul after death matters in a way that is not feasible for one committed to a materialistic or epiphenomenalistic psychology. Once again, Socrates draws on transmigration theory as a means of fleshing out his account of the soul's prospect for reward or punishment in the afterlife. Overall, his discussion of the fate of pure and impure souls mirrors his earlier assessment of the respective fates of those devoted to the philosophical way of life and those not so inclined. Ultimately, the place suited to the soul of the true philosopher is the realm of the Forms, the realm of pure thought. Accordingly, Socrates depicts the final destiny of the good soul as a disembodied state, free of the cares and influences of bodily existence.

This elaborate myth of the soul's future destiny implicitly renders an alternate vision of reality and our place in it. Plato challenges the uncritical assumption that the visible world and variable opinions provide the definitive way of viewing things, from our human nature to our capacity to discern a higher standard of truth. Throughout this discussion, Plato emphasizes the significance of proper order in a manner consistent with the dictates of the classic Hellenic ideal of justice (*dike*) in its cosmic sense. In this teleological scheme, everything has its appropriate place and function, including the human soul. Properly ordered, human souls exhibit the operation of reason, which contributes to the realization of a uniquely human *arete* that finds its flourishing in the life of the intellect. The soul committed to living a moral life is thus a cosmos in microcosm, a mirror of the totality of things. This is why Plato depicts the wise and orderly soul as already aware of its surroundings; it is right at home, in the place where it is best suited. The pure soul, he now assures us, "finds fellow travelers and gods to guide it, and each of them dwells in a place suited to it."[61] What is absent here is any reference to the capriciousness or licentiousness of the gods and goddesses. Rather, Plato stresses that our future destiny is in the hands of good divinities that give the worthy soul its appropriate recompense.

THE BROADER ANTHROPOLOGICAL DIMENSION

What does the *Phaedo* disclose regarding the general thrust of Plato's anthropology? Strikingly, he intertwines Socrates' arguments for the soul's immortality with a discussion of the theory of the Forms. Each stage of the discussion introduces a different dimension of this metaphysical theory. Socrates establishes that the soul can grasp truth on its own, without any reliance on the body and sense experience. But this theme emerges in a somewhat roundabout fashion, as an outgrowth of Socrates' discussion of the philosophical way of life and the need to purify the soul from corporeal influences. This is why he designates philosophy (as the love of wisdom in the fullest sense), as a training for death. Since philosophy promotes detachment from bodily life, it offers its practitioners an excellent preparation for the soul's ultimate separation from the body at the point of physical death.

Thus Socrates' poignant reflections on the meaning of his philosophical vocation (along with its implications for his fate at the hands of his fellow Athenians) serves as the backdrop for exploring the nature and destiny of the soul. By extension, however, it invites us to enter into the activity of the true philosopher as well and thereby engage in dialectical pursuits conducive to raising our consciousness to abstract conceptual levels. Socrates' very portrayal of the philosophical endeavor says something significant about the independent status of the soul: the soul only grasps truth through reasoning, when it is most aloof from the body.

From a Platonic perspective, then, the knowledge of true reality proceeds from thought alone. In this respect, Plato presents himself as a thoroughgoing rationalist completely at ease with the mind-set of Parmenides and the general outlook of the Pythagoreans. On the one hand, Plato endorses Parmenides' distinction between reasoning (as the means to truth) and sense experience (the basis of error and illusion). On the other hand, Plato incorporates and refines the Pythagorean dimension of Socrates' teaching into his own metaphysical vision. Plato conceives the philosophical way of life as a prolonged exercise in self-discipline and purification. His linking of this effort to cultivating the soul's powers of concentration finds a special outlet in his theory of Forms, which elevates the objects of knowledge to a divine plane.

When Plato posits a kinship between the soul and the Forms, the implication is clear: the soul is best attuned to universal, immutable truth. In other words, the soul is most at home when removed from the body. As Socrates asserts early in the *Phaedo*, the philosopher's goal is "the habit of the soul gathering and collecting herself into herself from all sides out of the body . . . dwelling in her own place alone."[62] The soul's entry into the realm of wisdom (the goal of the philosophical way of life) presupposes that the soul strives for this end without any corporeal intrusions. To be

Contradiction of solitary, detached ideal of the soul w/ the practice of philosophy in a social, dialogic setting.

true to itself and its intrinsic nature, the soul must restrict its attention to what is similarly immutable and everlasting.

But is this ideal of wisdom adequate for Plato (or Socrates)? The salient message, it seems, is that the philosopher aspires to a solitary, spiritual mode of existence. Such an ideal, however, clearly goes against the grain of both thinkers' conceptions of the philosophical enterprise itself. Indeed, the very implementation of the Socratic method presupposes a social dimension inherent in the very act of philosophizing. Does not Socrates anticipate joining the company of good gods and good men (*Phaedo* 63b–c) after he dies the philosopher's death? For thinkers so deeply committed to the life of the *polis* (and the rich opportunities it offered for intellectual interchange and enrichment), the afterlife that the *Phaedo* envisions for the soul of the true philosopher seems somewhat deflating.

The goal to which Socrates aspires is distinctively asocial: the purified soul will ultimately lose itself in an unimpeded contemplation of the Forms. But how will it do so? The fact that Plato resorts to the language and imagery of myth in discussing the soul's afterlife underscores his reluctance to address this issue with any rational or scientific precision. But by the same token, the conclusion of the *Phaedo* prompts a valid philosophical question: will the soul that survives the body's death be the soul of Socrates (or Plato, or you, or me, for that matter) or merely some abstract spiritual principle, emptied of all vestiges of a concrete human personality? While the *Phaedo* envisions a destiny for individual souls based on the quality of their embodied existence, it never moves beyond understanding human immortality in terms of "types" of souls. Thus the good souls of philosophers will enjoy a fellowship with the gods, while the wicked souls of carnal-oriented individuals will be trapped in a cycle of rebirths.

But what is Plato's explanation for the individuality of each and every soul and more precisely each and every individual human being? While he affirms that the soul takes its previous "education and upbringing" into the afterlife, it is not clear what constitutes the basis of this immortality or what really endures after death. Indeed, recognition of the soul's immortality is not the same as a theory of personal immortality involving the continuing existence of a truly individual self. In the final analysis, Plato's rejection of the significance of the body and its contribution to personality does not adequately account for what it means to be fully human, now or in the life to come.

While the psychology of the *Phaedo* is soul centered, Plato's theory of knowledge implicitly recognizes the role of sense experience. The entire recollection argument presupposes our ability to distinguish between individual instances of things arrived at through the senses and a conceptual grasp of the universals operative in comparative judgments of a

Recollection theory presupposes distinction 'twixt indiv. things & universals.

quantitative and qualitative character. While Plato would vehemently deny that knowledge is grounded on changing particulars accessible through the senses, he would still be obliged to affirm that knowledge at least begins on a sensory level, with the immediate data derived from the world around us. From this standpoint, he would have to acknowledge some contribution by the body and its sensory apparatus in the mind's movement toward knowledge, and in the dialectical process which abets this cognitive ascent. For this reason, dismissing the body as no more than an impediment to the soul's intellectual and moral progress is far too facile.

But by the same token, the rather unitary interpretation of the soul that emerges in the *Phaedo* is far too facile to account for the varieties of psychic experience inherent in our humanness. A major component of Plato's overall argument for the soul's immortality, as already noted, rested on the notion that the soul or mind is wholly distinct from the body *by its very nature*. In this respect, the *Phaedo* isolates the distinguishing feature of the soul in its simplicity as a noncomposite, immutable, and incorruptible reality. But such a uniform understanding of the soul imposes severe restrictions on its range of operations. The *Phaedo*, in fact, largely confines its psychological analysis to the soul's intellectual activity.

But despite this unequivocal intellectualist emphasis, the dialogue reveals some awareness of conflicts in our psychological constitution. In rebutting the epiphenomenalist theory that the soul is a harmony, Socrates contends that the soul could never oppose or even challenge physical desires if it were no more than a harmony or attunement of bodily parts (*Phaedo* 94c). Although the Plato of the *Phaedo* at least recognizes an emotional dimension inherent in human nature, he viewed it as no more than an outgrowth of the dualistic struggle between soul and body. In this respect, the soul is the principle of rational governance which directs and controls any upheavals prompted by the corporeal side of our humanness.

THE PSYCHOLOGY OF THE *REPUBLIC*

The rather narrow psychology that dominates the *Phaedo* would be refined in subsequent dialogues. By the time he completed the *Republic*, Plato had transformed his rigidly dualistic analysis of the mind-body relationship into a tripartite theory of the soul and its functions. What was formerly seen as a conflict between the soul (or mind) and the body is now viewed along the lines of an inner tension between three distinct orientations within a unified self. From this latter perspective, the soul is no longer viewed as a simple, monolithic whole but as a whole comprised of the rational, spirited, and appetitive parts.

But how do these "parts" of the soul stand in relation to one another? In the *Republic*, Plato addresses this issue on the basis of a political analog between the just society and the just individual. Where justice is operative, each part (whether in respect to the society or the individual) exhibits an ordering so that each performs its appropriate task without encroaching on the sphere reserved for the others.

> The just man does not permit the several elements within him to interfere with one another or any of them to do the work of others: he sets in order his own inner life, and is his own master and his own law, and at peace with himself; and when he has bound together the three principles within him . . . and is no longer many, but has become one entirely temperate and perfectly adjusted nature, then he proceeds to act.[63]

In this key passage, Plato conceives the good life in hierarchical terms as a harmonizing of the soul's various elements. In this context, the rational part of the soul assumes the same role of governing principle so prominent in the earlier *Phaedo*. The spirited part, in turn, is deemed superior (or nobler than) the appetitive, as the seat of the most basic physical desires.

> When the whole soul follows the philosophical principle, and there is no division, the several parts are just, and do each of them their own business, and enjoy severally the best and truest pleasures of which they are capable.[64]

Whereas the *Phaedo* discussed the soul in terms of its reasoning power alone, the psychology of the *Republic* allows for a broader understanding of the soul's range of experiences. Accordingly, Plato also speaks in terms of pleasures appropriate to each part of the soul, including its highest, rational principle.[65] This is quite an advance over the *Phaedo*. But it merely brings to the fore what was already implicit in Socrates' deliberations in that earlier dialogue. What is lacking in the *Phaedo* is an explicit attempt to come to terms with the varieties of pleasure inherent in human existence and thereby integrate them into the soul's very life. In the *Republic*, however, Plato takes the passions and desires (and their accompanying pleasures) that he formerly relegated to the corporeal sphere and allocates them to different psychic levels. Clearly, some pleasures must be deemed better than others. For this reason, pleasures proper to the spirited and appetitive parts of the soul are less noble than those reserved for the rational. As the proper governing principle of the soul as a whole, the rational part sets the tone for what occurs on lower psychic levels.

In the absence of this crucial regulative function, the individual self would be subject to all the whims and vagaries of its lesser drives. Accordingly, in the good life pleasures are ordered in a way that allows each part to function and flourish by each doing its "own business."[66] But they can only do so under the guidance of reason. The psychology of the *Republic* thereby invests our affectivity with significant status. From this standpoint, it is as legitimate to recognize the satisfaction that proceeds from intellectual pursuits as it is to acknowledge those proceeding from emotional and corporeal gratification. Did not Socrates himself exhibit a passion for truth and a love of philosophy? His willingness to die for his beliefs, and ultimately for the sake of a philosophical ideal, was by no means the response of a disembodied soul devoid of feeling; it was the outgrowth of a conscious decision by a multidimensional individual. Socrates' cultivation of the life of the soul was not merely subordinating the inclinations and needs of his body to the control of reason. According to the more technical psychology of the *Republic*, such action is the mark of a well-ordered soul which is able to channel its passions and desires toward the best ends for humans.

CONCLUSION

While the psychology of the *Republic* and subsequent dialogues like the *Timaeus* seem a giant step removed from the *Phaedo*, how much really changed? Although Plato refined his understanding of the dynamics of human action, he remained committed to the soul's superiority over the body, as well as the superiority of the soul's rational part over its lower parts. This hierarchical emphasis has an important bearing on his theory of the soul's immortality. If he viewed the soul as immortal, it was only in respect to its rational part.[67] This remained a central tenet of his psychology from his earliest to his later writings. Since the irrational parts of the soul are closely connected with the body, they are designated as mortal and perishable. In this respect, the *Timaeus* distinguishes between the immortal, rational soul (localized in the head) and a mortal soul that is further divided into superior and inferior parts.[68]

But such a division of the soul's intrinsic unity raises nettling questions that cut across the lines separating the periods in which Plato's psychology developed and matured: what part of us achieves immortality from Plato's perspective? If only the rational part of the soul has a claim to exist after the body's death, what is the foundation of its uniqueness, in the absence of any specific features derived from the body and from the lower, mortal parts of the soul? In the final analysis, the later Plato leaves us with the same dilemma that the *Phaedo* generates: an immortal, rational mind is simply not the same thing as an immortal *person*, with all the rich individuating features and traits that personhood encompasses. It would be left to a subsequent thinker, with a rather different metaphysics at his disposal, to provide a more persuasive philosophical explanation of the phenomenon of psychosomatic unity and the basis of individuality in human beings. Accordingly, we now turn our attention to Aristotle.

DISCUSSION QUESTIONS

1. What is the significance of the Sophist Protagoras's teaching that "man is the measure of all things"?
2. Why was Plato's interpretation of the philosophical way of life as a "training for death" a crucial component of his commitment to the soul's immortality?
3. Explain why (in Plato's *Phaedo*) Socrates was disappointed with Anaxagoras's notion of *nous* (Mind) and how Socrates' understanding of the soul provides a means of accounting for the motivations of human actions (including his decision to die for his philosophical ideals).
4. Explain the significance of Plato's interpretation of the soul as the Form of life in human beings and why the Forms provide the "true causes" of things.
5. In Platonic terms, why does our ability to discern universal truths affirm the soul's independence from the body?

NOTES

Quotations from Plato's *Phaedo, Republic,* and *Timaeus* are drawn from Benjamin Jowett, *The Dialogues of Plato*, vols. 1–2 (New York: Random House, 1937).

1. Alfred North Whitehead, *Process and Reality* (New York: Free Press, 1979), 39.
2. Chester G. Starr, *The Ancient Greeks* (New York: Oxford University Press, 1971), 45–46.
3. Pierre Hadot, *What Is Ancient Philosophy?*, trans. Michael Chase (Cambridge: Belknap Press, Harvard University Press, 2002), 14.
4. Hadot, *What Is Ancient Philosophy?*, 145.
5. Thucydides, *History of the Peloponnesian War*, bk. 3 (82), trans. Rex Warner (London: Penguin, 1972), 242.
6. George F. McLean and Patrick J. Aspell, *Ancient Western Philosophy: The Hellenic Emergence* (New York: Appleton Century Crofts, 1971), 107.
7. Any treatment of the relationship between Plato and Socrates must address the so-called Socratic problem: since Socrates wrote nothing, to what extent does Plato provide an accurate presentation of his teachings? In this respect, a distinction can rightfully be made between the "historical" Socrates and the Socrates of Plato's dialogues. But to what extent do these dimensions of Socrates the man coincide, and to what extent do they differ? While the sum and substance of Plato's

depiction of Socrates' final hours in the *Phaedo* is probably an accurate portrayal of what Socrates said, Plato admits that he was not actually present at Socrates' death (*Phaedo* 59b). While he could have easily learned what occurred from others, we must not lose sight of the fact that Plato wrote this dialogue from his own philosophical perspective, delineating his metaphysical and moral vision. For stylistic purposes, I generally refer to the insights contained in the dialogue as those of Socrates. But the reader must be attuned to the fact that the words of Socrates are very much those of Plato. Accordingly, we should avoid the natural tendency to view this as a verbatim, blow-by-blow report of what transpired in Socrates' death cell.

8. In addition to Echecrates, Plato lists the following people as present in the cell on Socrates' final day (*Phaedo* 59 b–c): Phaedo, Apollodorus, Critoboulos and his father (Crito), Hermogenes, Epigenes, Aeschines, Antisthenes, Ctesippus of Paene, Menexenus, Simmias from Thebes, Cebes, Phaidondes, and Euclides and Terpsion from Megara (along with several anonymous individuals).

9. *Phaedo* 60b.

10. *Phaedo* 61d.

11. *Phaedo* 63b–c.

12. Socrates tips his hand in this direction (61d) when he queries Cebes and Simmias about their acquaintance with a Pythagorean named Philolaus. The implication is that they would have heard the things Socrates now relates from this practitioner of the philosophical art.

13. *Phaedo* 64a.

14. *Phaedo* 64c.

15. *Phaedo* 64e–65a.

16. *Phaedo* 65a–b.

17. *Phaedo* 65c.

18. *Phaedo* 65d.

19. *Phaedo* 65d–e.

20. *Phaedo* 65e–66a.

21. *Phaedo* 67a.

22. *Phaedo* 67a.

23. *Phaedo* 67c–d.

24. *Phaedo* 69c.

25. *Phaedo* 69e–70a.

26. *Phaedo* 70b.

27. *Phaedo* 70c–d.

28. *Phaedo* 72a–b.

29. *Phaedo* 72e.

30. *Phaedo* 72e.

31. Cf. *Meno* 80e–86c, for Plato's seminal illustration of recollection in the context of Socrates' encounter with a slave and his effort to "teach" the slave to demonstrate a geometrical theorem simply by posing questions.

32. *Phaedo* 73c–d.

33. *Phaedo* 75b.

34. *Phaedo* 76c.

35. *Phaedo* 76b.

36. *Phaedo* 76e.
37. *Phaedo* 77b.
38. *Phaedo* 76c.
39. *Phaedo* 78d.
40. *Phaedo* 79c.
41. *Phaedo* 80a.
42. *Phaedo* 82b.
43. *Phaedo* 81b.
44. *Phaedo* 87b–c.
45. *Phaedo* 92b–c.
46. *Phaedo* 92e.
47. *Phaedo* 94e.
48. *Phaedo* 94b.
49. *Phaedo* 95d.
50. *Phaedo* 96a.
51. *Phaedo* 97c–d.
52. *Phaedo* 98c–d.
53. *Phaedo* 99a.
54. *Phaedo* 100b.
55. *Phaedo* 100d–e.
56. *Phaedo* 103c.

57. Socrates resorts to challenging quantitative and numerical analogs for purposes of illustration (*Phaedo* 101a–105b). In these distinctions between "tall" and "short," "oddness" and evenness," Socrates wishes to stress the mutual exclusivity of opposites and, by implication, the distinctness of each Form. In the case of a person who is described as "taller" than someone and "shorter" than someone else at the same time, such comparative judgments refer to a standard which is distinct from the people under scrutiny. While the same individual can be described in contradictory terms as both "tall" and "short" (depending on conflicting interpretations), the standard whereby we judge them as such can never admit of its opposite. Socrates carries this contention a bit further. Not only do opposites not admit each other, but even things which contain opposites (even if they are not necessarily opposites in relation to each other) do not admit each other. From this standpoint, he considers the number three as distinct from the number two, by virtue of the fact that odd numbers and even numbers are mutually exclusive. Even if something is not in strict opposition to something else, it may still not admit it. Thus the Form of the number three not only encompasses "threeness" but oddness as well.

58. *Phaedo* 106b.
59. *Phaedo* 114d.
60. *Phaedo* 107c.
61. *Phaedo* 108c.
62. *Phaedo* 67c–d.
63. *Republic* IV, 443.

64. *Republic* IX, 586–587. Cf. *Phaedrus* 246, for Plato's discussion of the tripartite division of the soul in terms of a charioteer and his horses. In this analog, the char-

ioteer symbolizes reason, and the horses represent the spirited and appetitive parts of the soul.

65. *Republic* IX, 580.

66. *Republic* IX, 586–587.

67. *Timaeus* 69:

Now of the divine, he himself was the creator, but the creation of the mortal he committed to his offspring. And they, imitating him, received from him the immortal principle of the soul; and around this they proceeded to fashion a mortal body and made it to be the vehicle of the soul and constructed within the body a soul of another nature which was mortal, subject to terrible and irresistible affections; . . . these they mingled with irrational sense and with all-daring love according to necessary laws, and so framed man.

68. *Timaeus* 69–70.

Hylomorphism—"Substances = forms inhering in matter"

Matter — that out of which a thing is made.
a word is 'made' out of letters;
i'm made out of cells.

Form — Actuality — Essence — Functions

For humans, soul makes us alive (form).
Body is our material (matter).

3

Aristotle:
The Human Composite

In Raphael's fresco *The School of Athens,* Plato and Aristotle occupy center stage: Plato points upward as Aristotle extends his arm outward, his palm facing the ground. These gestures tell us something significant about the philosophers' divergent visions of reality. Plato's metaphysics, as we have seen, opened a wide gulf between the conceptual realm of transcendent Forms or Ideas and everyday experience. In contrast, Aristotle rooted the formal principle in the objects of sense perception, lending them intelligibility and knowability in their own right. By directing metaphysical inquiry to the empirical world, he focused his scientific method on what is immediately accessible to us through the five senses.

Methodologically, Aristotle proceeded directly from the data of sense experience. On the basis of this data, he attempted to discover the principles from which things derive their meaning and intelligibility.[1] In this way, he fell into that great speculative tradition initiated by the Pre-Socratic thinkers who set themselves to the task of investigating nature and physical processes. But by the same token, Aristotle is firmly committed to the teleological brand of metaphysical speculation that came to fruition in Socrates and Plato, and their common commitment to isolating the ultimate causes of things. As Aristotle states, "It is plain that philosophic wisdom is scientific knowledge, combined with intuitive reason, of the things that are highest by nature."[2]

ARISTOTLE'S BACKGROUND AND DEVELOPMENT

Aristotle (384–322 B.C.) was born in Stagira on the Chalcidic peninsula, the son of a prominent physician in residence at the Macedonian court. Aristotle traveled extensively throughout his life, which gave him ample opportunity to cultivate his keen observational powers and skill at penetrating the complexities of nature. At the age of seventeen, he settled in Athens and became a student at Plato's Academy, marking the beginning of a twenty-year association. After Plato's death, Aristotle distanced himself from Plato's academic successors and founded his Lyceum (around 329 B.C.), a name derived from a public park in Athens.[3] Its members became known as Peripatetics, an appellation possibly derived from the covered walk *(peripatos)* at this site.

In philosophical and personal terms, Aristotle was a man of praxis. Indeed, the same thinker who extolled the godlike character of the contemplative life assumed a markedly different disposition than Socrates when Athenians charged him also with impiety. While Socrates perceived his philosophical vocation as demanding nothing less than death in the face of this charge, Aristotle pursued an alternate course of action. "I wish to prevent the Athenians from committing a second sin against philosophy," he supposedly said, and then went into voluntary exile. This anecdote tells us less about the quality of his commitment to the love of wisdom than about his pragmatism as a thinker and a man. From this standpoint, Raphael's artistic depiction of Aristotle is most apt. Aristotle redirects our attention to the realm of common sense; his speculative interests lie in what is tangible and immediate. By recognizing the sense world as the locus of the really real, he did nothing less than restore its metaphysical integrity.

The development of Aristotle's thought reflects his phases of intellectual maturation. It was not until the 1920s, however, that this evolutionary dimension of his philosophy was fully recognized. In a landmark study, Werner Jaeger presented a chronology of Aristotle's growth as a philosopher.[4] His development can be divided into three major periods. The first encompasses Aristotle's years as Plato's student, when he concurred with Plato's central doctrines; the second comprises the time when Aristotle broke with the Academy and began to forge his own insights; the final and most significant phase of his life unfolded after his return to Athens, when he founded the Lyceum and formulated the sum and substance of his metaphysical approach. The body of Aristotle's writings *(Corpus Aristotelicum)* is immense, reflecting these various developmental stages.[5]

Handwritten annotations (top):
Art = all productive forms of human knowing.
↳ Useful b/c it provides insight into the reason why things exist.

THEORETICAL KNOWLEDGE AND WISDOM

"All humans," Aristotle said, "desire to know by nature."[6] For him, the desire for knowledge is fundamental to us as human beings. Accordingly, he delineated the various levels on which this desire manifests itself. The most basic level of knowing is sensation, a faculty shared by animals as well. Likewise, knowledge is acquired through the experience of individual things and the memories of those experiences. But in addition to these abilities, Aristotle focuses on the human ability to engage in artistic and rational pursuits. By "art," Aristotle refers to all productive forms of human knowing; by means of art, we are able to formulate one universal judgment or theory about an entire class or group of objects.[7] Accordingly, Aristotle perceived the chief characteristic of art as providing insight into the reason why things exist as they do.[8] Artists are deemed wiser than master workers or manual laborers because they not only act but possess the underlying theory or rationale which enables them to appreciate causes and to teach what they know. This is the mark of wisdom, an attunement to the first causes and underlying principles of things.[9]

THE NATURE OF WISDOM AND CAUSALITY

Aristotle explains the causes of things on the basis of an anthropological model of the wise man. The wise man knows about everything that is possible to be known (although not necessarily in detail); the wise man is capable of learning difficult things, is more exact about things, and is able to teach their underlying causes.[10] In this respect, the wise man possesses universal knowledge; such knowledge is hardest to attain, since its subject matter (i.e., universal concepts) is far removed from sense experience. The most precise sciences, then, examine the first causes that Aristotle considers most knowable. From them, and by reason of them, things come to be known. Accordingly, Aristotle reasons that there must be a science that directs itself to an inquiry into the causes of first principles of all things.[11]

Aristotle's focus on causality prompts him to investigate the speculations of his philosophical predecessors. These earlier philosophers, he maintains, were motivated by a sense of wonder and a desire to know for the sake of knowing, rather than by purely utilitarian goals.[12] But thinkers like Thales, Anaximenes, Heraclitus, and Empedocles confined their analysis to what Aristotle designates the material and efficient causes of things—their material composition and source of generation and change.

Handwritten annotations (bottom):
Wise man: - knows everything (in general)
- capable of complex learning
- Is exact
- Can teach causes.

Handwritten annotation (right margin): natural science.

Because they failed to account for the formal cause (the essence or nature of a thing) and the final cause (the end, good, or purpose of a thing), they lacked a genuine scientific grasp of the nature of causality. Aristotle thus looked to empirical investigation as a means of penetrating the ultimate causes of reality. This scientific approach was guided by the teleological perspective that emerged in the Pre-Socratic tradition and was refined in the moral speculation of Socrates and Plato. Thinkers of this stamp perceive a kinship between form and function; how something is structured or organized dictates what it does or how it behaves. Reality is intelligible in respect to its ends, since the end, goal, or purpose of a thing or action determines its perfection.

ARISTOTLE AND PLATO

Aristotle was one of the greatest Platonists. He internalized key Platonic convictions that shaped and defined the parameters of his own thinking, from the earliest to the latest stages of his intellectual development. For Plato and Aristotle alike, the ultimate object of knowledge is the formal cause responsible for the intelligibility and coherence we observe in the world of sense experience. From this standpoint, the world is only meaningful in light of certain unchanging principles which all things of a given class or kind share in common. Although Aristotle agreed with his teacher that truth must be universal in scope, unchanging, and based on a stable and abiding formal principle, he disagreed with Plato's grounding of the Forms in a transcendent conceptual realm. "How," Aristotle queries, "could the Ideas being the substances of things exist apart?"[13]

Aristotle's chief criticism of Plato's theory of Forms thus focuses on his separating the Forms from the concrete world of sense experience. From Aristotle's perspective, this amounts to a superfluous duplication of entities. "For to each thing," he observes, "there answers an entity which has the same name and exists apart from the substances."[14] Plato's theory of Forms thus undermines the very things which should rightfully command our attention. By relegating them to mere images of the Forms in which they share, Plato lends them a subordinate and (by implication) an inferior status. Likewise, the Forms' very transcendence obviates their role in the movement or change of material objects.[15]

BEING AND SUBSTANCE

In contrast to Plato, Aristotle posits a substantial form immanent in the world of sense experience. Accordingly, the really real can only be found

predications

substance

Matter: Individual based on accidents,
Form: Definite kind of individual/
substance

Aristotle   175

in individual things or substances: what a thing is substantially cannot exist apart from the thing itself.[16] This thesis is wholly consistent with Aristotle's understanding of the goal of metaphysical inquiry. Metaphysics, he contends, is directed toward the investigation of being as being and its natural attributes.[17] In contrast to the other sciences, which merely treat some aspect of being, metaphysics treats being in its most universal, comprehensive sense. Metaphysics addresses things insofar as they are or exist. In Aristotelian terms, the ultimate referent for being is the individual thing or substance, that which exists in its primary sense.[18] For this reason, substance constitutes the appropriate point of departure for all metaphysical inquiry. According to Aristotle, discussion of a given thing's existence revolves around considerations of it as a substance, whether we focus on its affections, the changes directed toward it, an undermining of its qualities, its generation, or merely something relative to it.[19]

Aristotle broadly defines substance as what is neither predicable of something nor a property. The chief sense of Aristotelian substance, then, is the notion of an underlying substratum of which everything else is predicated but which is not itself predicated of anything else.[20] While the individual thing is a substance, the universal form makes it a substance of a particular kind. In this respect, the formal element (e.g., man) makes the thing a definite kind of individual or instance; matter (e.g., Socrates), on the other hand, is the principle of individuation by virtue of its range of properties or accidents. While Socrates can die and cease to exist as an individual man, the universal form "man" persists.

SUBSTANCE AND CHANGE

As we saw in chapter 1, the Pre-Socratic philosophers were concerned with analyzing the phenomenon of change. They were preoccupied with a problem that is crucial in making sense of our world and ourselves—how to account for stability in the midst of ongoing cosmic processes. The Parmenidean response imparted a special urgency to this question, since Parmenides reduced change to the status of illusion: if Being *is and cannot not be*, then reality can only be an immutable whole that allows for no possibility of becoming. Aristotle's metaphysics of substantial reality provided a means of addressing this very dilemma: incorporating the further metaphysical distinction between potency and act. In Aristotelian terms, change involves a movement or transition from a potential to an actual state of affairs. This transition presupposes the continuity provided by matter, the underlying substrate of change. One who learns to play a musical instrument, for example, is indeed the same individual, but that individual acquires a skill not possessed before. A substance undergoes change because it has the potential to be altered in some way or to become something else altogether. As Aristotle puts it, a statue of Hermes is potentially in the block of wood.[21]

Aristotle's ability to distinguish a potential and an actual state of being (in relation to the same thing or same state of affairs at least) permitted him to address the problem of change in a manner that had eluded the Pre-Socratics. For them, change involved an either/or proposition; for example, a thing is either dry or moist, and what is dry must be wholly distinct from what is moist. But the fact that a single thing can be both dry *and* moist (albeit at different points in time) requires a metaphysical explanation of change that allows for understanding how a dry thing can become moist while remaining what it is. Aristotle, in effect, redefined change in terms of a developmental process of becoming in relation to an enduring substance.

Still, a thing can only become what it is capable of becoming. This capacity is rooted in form, which determines its potentiality for fuller development. A small seed has the potential to become a large oak tree because that is the proper end of its natural process of growth and maturation. While some potentialities (like growth) are purely natural, however, others are acquired through practice and experience.[22] Actuality, however, is always prior to potency. While childhood is temporally prior to adulthood (since the child precedes the adult in time), adulthood is logically prior to childhood, since it constitutes the goal toward which human development aspires. In this respect, Aristotle views the actuality of a thing as the end or final cause *(telos)* of what formerly existed in a potential state.

Thus actuality is the complete realization of a given thing's capabilities. In this we see a clear indication of Aristotle's continuing allegiance to Platonic teaching. Like Plato, he assumed that something in a state of becoming can only be understood or rendered intelligible in light of a higher ideal or standard. Accordingly, Aristotle defines things in relation to what they are fully capable of becoming. In this respect, the formal cause (what something is) is inextricably connected with the final cause (the ultimate end or purpose).

Aristotle's metaphysical analysis of change provides the framework in which he investigates the natural world, more specifically, natural bodies that are alive. Aristotle's philosophy of nature encompasses an investigation of material things which undergo change or engage in movement. In the case of living things, soul constitutes the actualizing principle which provides the perfection of a body that possesses the potential for life. Just as all natural motion tends toward its proper end, the changes initiated in bodies by their appropriate souls bring them to the full realization of their capabilities. Form and finality are intimately related. Accordingly, soul is the formal principle of natural living bodies which it directs toward their true *telos*.

Since everything which moves and undergoes change requires an act responsible for initiating these processes, Aristotle reasons that the entire universe requires some ultimate principle of actuality. In its absence, we would be bound to posit a cause for every being and event, ad infinitum. Lest we fall into an infinite regress of caused causes and moved movers, we are led to affirm the necessity of an eternal, immovable substance. While not moving itself or subject to change, this substance must be capable of causing motion and change on every level. As pure act, it has no potentiality; it neither changes nor moves.[23] Accordingly, Aristotle's Prime Mover (the god of his universe) is the end toward which all action tends, as the ultimate object of desire. The Prime Mover thus attracts everything to itself by virtue of an eternal self-contemplation of itself alone, the most excellent object of thought.[24] In this respect, Aristotle's universe is distinctively teleological in orientation: everything tends in a rational manner toward this final divine cause, as pure self-thinking Thought. "The final cause, then, produces motion as being loved," Aristotle asserts, "but all other things move by being moved."[25]

ARISTOTLE'S PSYCHOLOGY

Aristotle's critique of Plato's theory of Forms is reflected in his anthropological outlook and the psychology it presupposes. Just as Aristotle could not accept the claim that the Forms transcend the very things they invest with intelligibility, he likewise could not endorse the contention that humans are no more than souls which use bodies as tools or instruments. If there is one dimension of Aristotle's philosophy that underscores his own growth as a thinker, it lies in this area. Aristotle began his intellectual career deeply rooted in the Platonic perspective. The *Phaedo* served as the ultimate philosophical touchstone for his early psychology. In this regard, Aristotle's *Eudemus* closely followed the early Plato in emphasizing the soul's immortality and complete independence of the body (except for the penal condition proceeding from its embodiment). Over the next three decades, however, Aristotle would forge a psychological theory that represents a clear break from Platonism, in a manner consistent with the overall evolution of his thinking.[26] This theory found its mature expression in the *De Anima* (c. 322 B.C.).

The *De Anima* develops a theory of the soul-body relation based on the fundamental premise that the soul is the substantial form and perfection of a body possessing the potentiality for its actualizing powers. In contrast to the highly personal tone of Plato's *Phaedo*, the *De Anima* is written in the voice of the detached scientific practitioner. At the outset, Aristotle defines the problems and issues under scrutiny and offers an elaborate survey of the psychological theories of his predecessors. On the basis of this historical grounding, Aristotle formulates a psychological account that preserves the independence and integrity of the soul, even as it emphasizes the soul's inextricable union with the body and its sophisticated biological apparatus. Aristotle's comprehensive treatment includes not only the human soul and human life but living things in general. Accordingly, Aristotle situates his analysis of the human *psyche* within the broader context of a psychic hierarchy, along with the full range of psychic powers that life encompasses.

Scope of the *De Anima*

In keeping with the scientific character of his treatment, Aristotle begins by defining the scope of the overall investigation. At the outset, he offers an epistemological rationale for the importance of this type of inquiry. If knowledge is something we deem valuable, then a study of the soul must surely rank among the highest kinds of knowledge.[27] From Aristotle's standpoint, such a study offers the opportunity for a fuller grasp of the truth, precisely because the soul constitutes the first principle among living things. But he recognizes the difficulty of this endeavor. "To attain any assured knowledge about the soul," Aristotle acknowledges, "is one of the most difficult things in the world."[28] This understatement provides a convenient point of departure for delineating the key issues and problems at the heart of Aristotle's psychological deliberations. In fact, the task at hand would be futile without a methodology precise enough to address specific types of things but broad enough to treat reality in general. Accordingly, Aristotle views his investigation into the soul as sharing much in common with the scientific investigation of any substance whatsoever.

In Aristotelian terms, scientific investigations are primarily concerned with the "whatness" of things. The starting point of any inquiry will differ according to the subject matter at hand. In this respect, Aristotle's initial concern lies in delineating the focus of a given inquiry. He stresses the importance of distinguishing the substantial reality under scrutiny from its accidental properties.[29] In this context, any accidents or properties of the soul must be assessed on the basis of what the soul *is by its very nature*. This order of procedure is crucial. In its absence, one could easily confuse a definition of the soul with a description of behavioral characteristics. From this standpoint, things are defined primarily in terms of what they are substantially and then on the basis of what they do or what they are capable of doing. This is not to say that the soul's operations are not consistent with its nature but does affirm Aristotle's commitment to the primacy of substance in discussions of things that are living. Accordingly, he roots the starting point of any demonstration in the question, What is it?[30]

Aristotle's initial consideration of the difference between a substance and its categories assumes a distinct psychological focus in a series of hypothetical questions. Their complexity underscores the difficulties surrounding investigations into the soul. Is the substance of the soul an active principle, or is it one of those things in a potential state? Is the soul a simple or a composite reality? Are all souls the same, or do they differ in regard to species or genus? If the soul is composed of parts, should it be first assessed as a whole or in terms of its parts? By the same token, should the soul's parts or functions (e.g., intellect or thought, respectively) be examined at the outset? If the functions merit a priority of interest, should their objects (e.g., the contents of thought) be considered before the functions (e.g., thought or thinking)? Does the soul admit of a comprehensive account applicable to all living things, or does each living thing require a separate psychic explanation? This final question touches on a vital issue. As Aristotle observes, most people confine their conception of soul to humans alone. The goal of the *De Anima*, however, is nothing less than a psychological theory broad enough to encompass life forms in general.

Aristotle's preliminary survey concludes with a consideration of the origin of the soul's affections. This topic is intimately connected with his understanding of the relationship between the soul and the body. The pivotal question can be framed in this manner: are the soul's affections part and parcel of the soul itself, or are they bound up exclusively with the body? While some of the soul's affections clearly overlap with bodily life (e.g., desire, anger, or perception), an activity like thinking is clearly the mark of the soul itself. Yet Aristotle acknowledges that thinking requires the faculty of imagination and the data of sense experience. This emphasis on the complementarity of soul and body underscores a concern that dominates the *De Anima*.

From Aristotle's standpoint, the delineation of affections appropriate to the soul or body (or to soul and body alike) serves to reveal affections *peculiar to the soul alone*. Indeed, only an isolation of such privileged psychic features provides adequate grounds for affirming the soul's separability (and thus its independence) from the body. If such a feature cannot be isolated, then the soul's affections are inseparable from the body and thus mere outgrowths of physiological processes. Aristotle finds ready support for such a thesis in our own experience. Indeed, many of the soul's affections are closely intertwined with physical experiences. Aristotle surveys the evidence for this grounding of psychic responses in the body along these lines:

> It seems that all the affections of soul involve a body-passion, gentleness, fear, pity, courage, joy, loving, and hating; in all these there is a concurrent affection of the body. From all this it is obvious that the affections of the soul are . . . formulable essences.[31]

This observation provides a segue for examining two different ways of defining the soul's affections. These approaches, however, reflect distinct metaphysical stances concerning the soul's very nature. In this connection, Aristotle contrasts the positions of the natural philosopher or physicist and that of the dialectician. The former position confines its analysis to the empirical world and observable, efficient causes; the latter is receptive to formal and final causes. Accordingly, the response to a question like, What is anger? reflects a definite theoretical commitment to one of these stances.

> A physicist would define an affection of soul differently from a dialectician; the latter would define . . . anger as the appetite for returning pain for pain, or something like that, while the former would define it as a boiling of the blood or warm substance surrounding the heart.[32]

The physicist, then, is preoccupied with an explanation grounded in matter, while the dialectician focuses on form and purposefulness. Although Aristotle offers no definitive teaching regarding the province of these diverse perspectives in the nebulous remarks that follow, he stresses that the form and purpose of a thing always have a material referent. By the same token, even a natural philosopher must come to terms with such teleological considerations as form and purpose. The issue that remains unresolved at this point concerns the separability of the soul, or some affections of the soul which remain independent of the body. The dilemma Aristotle now confronts is a direct outgrowth of his hylomorphism and its assumption that the really real is only found in substantial things composed of form and matter.

Aristotle on His Predecessors

After defining the scope of his psychological investigation, Aristotle surveys the theories of his philosophical predecessors.[33] In so doing, he gleans what he discerns as sensible proposals regarding the soul's nature from those he considers flawed or erroneous. What is the difference between things which possess a soul and those which do not? For Aristotle, the mark of things ensouled is an ability to initiate movement and to perceive.[34] However, he observes that these features were generally recognized as the soul's chief attributes by earlier thinkers as well. Aristotle first addresses the common assumption that the soul is numbered among those things that are moved. As we saw in chapter 1, the notion of the self-moving soul figures prominently in early Greek accounts of the cosmos and natural phenomena such as magnetic force and the rushing of the winds. Such a belief is evident in the speculation of both the atomists and the Pythagoreans: if the soul is the principle through which all other things are moved (and movement is the most salient characteristic of soul), then the soul's movement must proceed from the soul itself. This contention, Aristotle asserts, rests on the thesis that something moves another only if it is itself moved.[35] In this respect, he discerns a certain trend among his predecessors that touches on the criteria just proposed for ensouled realities: those who consider the ensouled reality in regard to its motion assume it is the cause of motion; those who consider the ensouled in terms of perception and knowledge connect soul with the first principles of things.[36] Aristotle bemoans the fact that the latter group espouses a materialistic understanding of psychic principles. He specifically cites Empedocles, who taught that the soul is a composite of all the elements or, conversely, each element is an instance of soul.[37]

Critically speaking, then, the initial thrust of Aristotle's survey centers on the notion that the soul is the cause of its own movement. He rejects that position, arguing that the soul must be viewed in spatial terms if the cause of its motion belongs to it by its very nature. If the soul itself is identified with movement, then the soul is localized in space and thus movable by force.[38] By extension, Aristotle observes that some thinkers depict the soul as moving the body in the same manner as it is self-moved. He links this theory with Democritus, in whom he finds a similarity with the poet Philippus's claim that Daedalus made a statue of Aphrodite move by filling it with molten metal.[39] From Aristotle's standpoint, Democritan atomism rests on the same premise, namely, that perpetually mobile atoms are responsible for moving the body by virtue of their own internal movement.

In contrast to such blatant materialists, Aristotle finds a notable exception in Anaxagoras. On one level, Anaxagoras displays a kinship with the atomist Democritus in his view of the soul as a source of movement, in a manner consistent with his claim that mind is responsible for moving the universe.[40] But unlike those who collapsed the distinction between soul and mind, Aristotle contends that Anaxagoras posited mind as the cause of good action and right thinking.[41] From this standpoint, Anaxagoras imparted to mind a distinctively intellectual role. This set him apart from those who view the soul as capable of cognition as either composed of the elements or identified with a given element.

Anaxagoras seems to distinguish between soul and mind, but in practice he treats them as a single substance, except that it is mind that he specially posits as the principle of all things; at any rate he says that mind alone of all . . . is simple, unmixed, and pure; . . . he alone says that mind is impassable and has nothing in common with anything else.[42]

Aristotle's recognition of Anaxagoras's ambiguity regarding the character of the soul and its cognitive capacity is reminiscent of Socrates' autobiographical reflections in Plato's *Phaedo*.[43] While Socrates was initially drawn to Anaxagoras's theory of a mind-governed universe, he became disillusioned with his failure to exploit this notion in positing an ultimate causal principle of material processes. But despite this lack of precision, Aristotle considers Anaxagoras as presenting a clear challenge to the dominant Pre-Socratic model of cognition as "like by like," a model that reduces the soul to the very things it knows.

If the soul moves the body, then Aristotle explains such an influence on the basis of choice and intellectual motivation. The intellect is "one and continuous in the sense in which . . . thinking is so," he contends, "and thinking is identical with the thoughts which are its parts."[44] In this respect, thinking is viewed as diametrically opposed to quantitative determinations of any kind. But what still needs to be explained is the soul's relationship with the body, or the means whereby soul and body exert a mutual influence, so that "one acts and the other is acted upon, the one moves and the other is moved."[45] In this respect, Aristotle acknowledges that his predecessors recognized the interaction between the psychic and corporeal, but they made no attempt to specify the reason for this union or the conditions which render it possible. Anticipating a key feature of his own psychology, Aristotle stresses the importance of each soul attending to the kind of body for which it is suited.

The second phase of Aristotle's critical survey of his predecessors focuses on the Pythagorean theory that the soul is a harmony of those opposites comprising the body. Like Plato before him, he rejects any such interpretation. For Aristotle, the term "harmony" assumes two connotations in this context: first, the notion of a composition of the quantities in things that move and occupy spatial positions; second, the notion of the ratio of ingredients constituting a mixture.[46] From his standpoint, neither sense of "harmony" applies to the soul.

The complexity of bodily parts (and the variety of their composition) raises the question of *which parts* does the soul harmonize? The implication of such a thesis, Aristotle contends, is that many souls will be involved in the life of a body composed of the mixtures of elements, each of which requires a separate harmonizing principle of its own.[47] But what of the suggestion that the soul defined as a harmony is in motion? In this case, Aristotle specifically addresses the claim that the soul's experience of emotions presupposes movement on its part." Indeed, the claim that the soul is sad, happy, cheerful, or fearful (or alternately that the soul becomes angry, perceives, or thinks) can easily suggest that it is moved.[48] Aristotle, however, reduces this apparent difficulty to semantics. Instead of asserting, for example, that it is the soul which suffers or enjoys, he enjoins us to focus on the soul's causative role in relation to the body (and conversely, the body's influence on the soul).

> Better to avoid saying that the soul pities or learns or thinks and rather to say that it is the man who does this with his soul. What we mean is not that the movement is in the soul but that sometimes it terminates in the soul and sometimes starts from it.[49]

But in this vein, Aristotle's interest in the close relationship between soul and body prompts a more challenging question: to what extent does the soul's union with the body render it perishable? This could easily be assumed to coincide with the aging process.[50] However, Aristotle localizes the defects of age in the body rather than the soul. Just as an elderly man would see in the manner of a young one if he still had the eyes of youth, the soul would think with clarity through the instrumentality of a sound body.[51]

At this early juncture, Aristotle thus broaches a topic which assumes increasing importance throughout the *De Anima*, namely, the necessity of the soul's imperishability in relation to the body. "The mind," he asserts, "seems to be an independent substance implanted within the soul and to be incapable of being destroyed."[52] In this respect, he entertains the possibility that the soul or mind is not only wholly unaffected by the body's input but akin to the divine. Accordingly, he distinguishes the activities of the soul itself from those parallel activities which he designates as affections of the body.

> In old age the activity of mind or intellectual apprehension declines only through the decay of some other inward part; mind itself is impassable. Thinking, loving, and hating are affections not of mind but of that which has mind, so far as it has it. That is why memory and love cease; they were activities not of mind but of the composite which has perished; mind is, no doubt, something more divine and impassable.[53]

S. Lewis cribbed this.

At the conclusion of this critical survey, Aristotle introduces a key feature of his psychological theory. The soul, he informs us, comprises a range of operations that include cognition, perception, and belief states; appetite and desire; and locomotion, growth, flourishing, and decay.[54] But in the face of this assertion, another penetrating question emerges: are

3 levels of substance: III Composite - Natural Bodies
II Form - Structure - Order - Intelligibility
I Matter - Cause/Substrate

84   Chapter 3

these activities the province of the whole soul, or is each operation allocated to a different part? Aristotle quickly dismisses any suggestion regarding "parts" of the soul. In the face of such a claim, we must still establish an integrating principle responsible for unifying and coordinating the diverse faculties we exhibit as human beings.

"If its nature admits of its being divided," Aristotle queries, "what can it be that holds the parts together?"[55] For him, the only acceptable response is that the soul fulfills this role. But such an affirmation obviates further inquiry concerning a plurality of operations and powers. Indeed, if the soul did have parts, we would still be bound to investigate what conjoins these components and so on, ad infinitem. The consequence would be an endless regress of psychic principles enlisted to account for the unity of the parts. The only reasonable alternative, Aristotle argues, is the positing of a single soul. "Why," he proposes, "not at once admit that 'the soul' is one?"[56]

The Soul as Substantial Form

As dictated by his overall metaphysical outlook, Aristotle's in-depth treatment of the soul (beginning at book 2) proceeds from a discussion of the soul as substance. Broadly speaking, the notion of substance provides Aristotle's ultimate referent for discussion of the really real. In more concrete terms, a substance refers to any real thing whatsoever. At the outset, Aristotle considers three perspectives from which substance can be analyzed. They point directly to his hylomorphism and its emphasis on the relationship between form and matter among natural bodies.[57] On its most basic level, substance can be considered in terms of matter; sensible substances all have a material substrate or material cause. Likewise, substance can be considered in terms of form, the basis of a thing's definition and the principle which imparts to it structure, order, and intelligibility. Finally, substance encompasses the composite of form and matter. In this third sense, natural bodies have a special claim to substantiality. Indeed, natural bodies are substances in the way that substance in general constitutes a composite of form and matter.

But some natural bodies happen to be living things. For Aristotle, as we have seen, the criterion of living things (and the means of differentiating living from nonliving ones) is the presence of soul. In these terms, the soul is the form of a body that serves as the matter or potentiality for its actualization. Accordingly, Aristotle defines the soul as "the actuality of a body that has life potentially."[58] In keeping with his hylomorphism, he affirms an inextricable relationship between soul and body. While he denies that the soul is a kind of body, he also declines to consider it without a body. "While it cannot be a body," he contends, "it is in a body and a body of a definite kind."[59] Herein lies a major difference between the psychological accounts of Aristotle and Plato. Plato was content to define human nature chiefly in terms of the life of the soul. But Aristotle's metaphysics requires an explicit recognition of the body's contribution to our humanness. Aristotle's overt commitment to the psychosomatic unity of the human being presupposes that we are neither souls nor bodies alone but composites of soul and body together.

If the body stands in a relationship of potentiality to the soul, then the body's ongoing receptivity to what the soul offers its recipient is underscored. In this respect, the claim that "the body has life potentially" implies that the bodily matter which soul informs (and thereby animates) provides a suitable apparatus or instrumentality. Accordingly, the potentiality for life presupposes that soul and body are already conjoined in the composite living being. The soul is suited to be the form of a body; the body, in turn, has a receptivity to ensoulment. For this reason, Aristotle stresses that only a body that is ensouled can be said to be alive, even potentially.[60] In the absence of a soul, the body would fail to qualify as a living body or as human in any genuine sense.

This stage of Aristotle's psychological analysis, however, is not confined to human life. Rather, it offers a comprehensive statement regarding the parameters of life in general. The soul's status as "the first actuality" of the body is highlighted by means of two key analogs.[61] Consider, for example, an ax. In order to be an ax, the tool must assume a specific form which allows it to function effectively as a cutting implement. So, if an ax were a natural body, Aristotle suggests, its soul would reside in whatever constitutes its being an ax. Strictly speaking, however, the soul is only fitted for a natural body that possesses a principle of movement and rest. Accordingly, Aristotle proposes an organic analog, based on a part of the human body. If an eye, for example, were an animal, its soul would reside in the power of sight, and the eye itself would constitute its matter. But if it lacked the power of vision, the eye could only be designated as such in metaphorical terms, in the manner of the glass eye in a statue. Aristotle thus uses these analogs to underscore the inseparability of soul and body, form and matter, respectively. He no more questions the unity of form and matter in a single reality than he doubts whether the wax and the imprint it bears qualify as one integral thing.[62] For this reason Aristotle cautions against questioning whether soul and body constitute one reality.

The Psychic Hierarchy

Aristotle's avowed goal in the *De Anima* is to formulate a comprehensive theory of soul which can explain *all living things* through the empirical observation of their activities. Subsequently he identifies three kinds of soul

distinguishable on the basis of the powers they offer bodies with the potential to implement them. The kind of soul that a living body possesses
(whether it be the body of a plant, animal, or human) manifests itself in
its vital operations. From this psychological perspective, what a living
thing can do (and indeed does) points to the kind of soul which actualizes
its potential. Accordingly, Aristotle envisions a gradation of psychic kinds
(and their corresponding powers) in which more primitive manifestations
of life are subsumed by superior ones.[63] In the context of this ascending
series, animals are "virtually" plants, and humans are "virtually" animals
and plants alike. In its broadest terms, then, Aristotle designates the soul
as the principle of the nutritive (or vegetative), sensitive, and rational (or
intellective) powers or faculties.[64] Each faculty, in turn, finds its psychic
counterpart in a specific kind of soul (plant, animal, or human souls, respectively). Plants, for example, are capable of movement connected with
nourishment, growth, decay, and reproduction; animals of sense appetites, sense perception, and movement from place to place; and humans
of rational knowing and willing.[65]

    In Aristotelian terms, the ability to be nourished not only constitutes the
most basic vital activity but the power that all living things share. Aristotle characterizes the nutritive faculty as "the most primitive and widely
distributed power of soul, in virtue of which all are said to have life."[66] At
each level of the psychic hierarchy, the vegetative soul serves as the active
principle responsible for coordinating the movements and changes instrumental in sustaining living things. In this respect, the vegetative soul
assumes a direct role in reproduction, the activity in which Aristotle discerns the universal aspiration to share in what is eternal and divine
through the perpetuation of the species.[67]

    While all living things enjoy the powers associated with the vegetative
soul, higher life forms possess powers consistent with their more sophisticated bodily organs. Living things qualify as animals if they are
equipped with sense perception.[68] Aristotle views the sense of touch as
the most rudimentary way of perceiving. Touch is present in animals that
lack the other senses, but it constitutes (at least from Aristotle's standpoint) the condition for all other sensation.[69] At this point, the significance
of a hierarchical interpretation of psychic experience is readily apparent:
this interpretation depicts animals as *virtually* possessing the powers of
plants, but in a loftier way. Indeed, the ability to perceive enhances a more
fundamental psychic activity like nourishing, since animals have the advantage of perceiving the food they ingest.[70]

    In keeping with this hierarchical model, sense perception involves a
process of assimilation analogous to what occurs in nourishment. In both
cases, the body receives something external to itself. In the act of nourishing, the body appropriates the substance of food and transforms it (by

means of its psychic principle) into its own substance. But sense perception likewise involves a transference and transformation, yet of a wholly different character. The difference lies in how the sense organs internalize the objects of perception. Clearly the eye does not literally absorb the object it sees. What carries over from the external world into the sense organ is form. By a "sense" is meant what has the power of receiving into itself the sensible forms of things without the matter.[71]

In Aristotelian terms, the sense organ receives form in the manner that wax bears the impression of a signet ring without absorbing the metal which constitutes the ring. As Aristotle observes, "What produces the impression is a signet ring without the iron or gold, but its particular constitution makes no difference."[72] In this way, the perceiver becomes one with the perceived, albeit at an ontological distance. The sensible form, in effect, serves as an analog or a similitude of the material object which mirrors what is found in the world of sense experience. This is a hallmark of Aristotle's epistemological realism that rests on the assumption of an isomorphism between perceiver and what exists in the world independently of the perceiving subject. In this respect, we encounter a close kinship between Aristotle's accounts of sense perception and knowledge.

For Aristotle, both perception and knowledge presuppose a grasp of form. But while perception involves the grasp of the sensible form of particular things, knowledge culminates in the apprehension of universal intelligible forms or concepts.[73] Accordingly, the act of knowing is never confined to any specific object; since the contents of knowledge are universal in scope, the knower is not restricted to any one thing. It is possible to think and know truth without relying on external objects at all. Perception, then, involves an encounter between the perceiver and a sense object appropriate to a given sense organ. But this is an activity of the animal soul and is shared by animals and humans. Aristotle, however, attributes knowledge and understanding to the rational soul alone. In this highest of psychic principles, he finds the cause of the intellective faculty distinctive to humans.

Because humans occupy the summit of Aristotle's psychic hierarchy, they incorporate all of the operations found on lower levels, through the wide-ranging powers of the rational soul. Like plants, humans are capable of nourishment, growth, and reproduction; like animals, humans engage in sense perception and exhibit sense appetites and are capable of moving from place to place. The rational soul, however, puts a uniquely human stamp on all of these activities, as a result of the more sophisticated bodily apparatus that humans possess. By the same token, the conscious awareness that accompanies rationality intensifies the experience of lower psychic powers. But since those powers are inextricably bound up with the body, Aristotle believes that they perish along with the body as well. He is emphatic, however, in affirming that the highest part of the rational soul (i.e., the intellect) must be separable from the body.

For Aristotle, the capacity for knowledge demands the separability of the intellect. This is not to say that the intellect does not rely on the bodily senses in acquiring knowledge. Indeed, one of the salient features of Aristotle's epistemology is a recognition that sense experience provides the raw data of concept formation and, by implication, the beginning of knowledge. "No one can learn or understand anything in the absence of sense," he teaches, "and when the mind is actively aware of anything it is necessarily aware of it along with an image."[74]

By the same token, the intellect cannot be bound up with the body if it is to exercise its unique capacity to think everything which is thinkable. Aristotle thus opposes any suggestion that the intellect is somehow "mixed" with the body. In that case, it would be reduced to some specific physical quality requiring an organ comparable to those instrumental in sense perception. The fact that the intellect is not identified with the body or any bodily parts lends it the potential to be all things. In contrast to the bodily senses (whose ability to perceive deteriorates when exposed to such stimuli as extremely loud noise or intensely bright light), intellect never wears out through too much thinking.[75] Because it is incorporeal in nature, it cannot exhaust its cognitive powers. But Aristotle makes a key distinction between two powers of intellect or, more precisely, intellect at its highest, noetic level.

> Since in every class of things, as in nature as a whole, we find two factors . . . a matter which is potentially all the particulars included in that class (and) a cause . . . that makes them all, these distinct elements must likewise be found within the soul.[76]

Aristotle, then, distinguishes a passive intellect with the potential to become all things (through its reception of forms) and an active intellect responsible for discerning or abstracting intelligible forms from their material embodiment. In this respect, the active intellect is the principle which renders knowledge possible.

> Mind is what it is by virtue of becoming all things, while there is another which is what it is by virtue of making all things: this is a sort of positive state like light; for in a sense light makes potential colours into actual colours. Mind in this sense is separable, impassible, unmixed, since it is in its essential nature activity.[77]

The distinction between the active and passive intellects requires qualification. Aristotle is not concerned with establishing the temporal priority of one over the other, as if the active intellect had to discern form before presenting it to its passive counterpart. Rather, the cognitive process presupposes the active discernment of intelligibility and a receptivity to form. From this standpoint, the intellect must be more than a "blank slate" with an unlimited capacity to know; it also requires a principle responsible for the activities of knowing and understanding. What does this say about us as "knowers"? Aristotle's theory of the active intellect underscores the fact that cognition involves more than gathering information. The mind must recognize truth for what it is and make a judgment about what is the case in an objective order of being.

SOUL, BODY, AND THE SEPARABLE INTELLECT

In contrast to the excessive spiritualism and intellectualism inherent in the Platonic anthropology, Aristotle develops a theory of psychosomatic unity which addresses the mental and physical dimensions of our humanity. From this standpoint, humans are neither souls nor bodies alone but composites of soul and body together. Aristotle's view of what it means to be human also presupposes a sophisticated psychology that situates us within the broader framework of all living things. The fact that Aristotle's psychology is so firmly grounded in the biological facts of life in the concrete affords it an impressive comprehensiveness of coverage. Accordingly, any discussion of the human soul stands in continuity with an analysis of life forms in general. In this respect, Aristotle treats humans as the highest manifestation of life, the summit of an ascending hierarchy of souls exhibiting increasingly complex powers and operations.

Aristotle's psychic hierarchy underscores the entelechism that posits the soul as the form of a body with the potential for life. At each stage of the psychic hierarchy he envisions, Aristotle aligns a different soul with a bodily counterpart capable of receiving and implementing that soul's actualizing power. But his entelechism also presents a challenge to his interpretation of the human soul as the principle or cause of the body's life and range of operations. This causative role presupposes a measure of independence from the body the soul informs. However, some of the soul's affections (e.g., desire or anger) clearly overlap with bodily life. But according to Aristotle, even thinking (the privileged sphere of the rational soul) involves the body, drawing on the imagination and sense experience for its data. While such a close alliance between soul and body offers a compelling basis for affirming the wholeness of our humanity, it also generates an acute problem regarding the ultimate separability of the intellect (the highest part of the rational soul) from bodily life. How separable (and imperishable) is the soul which constitutes the body's formal principle (or at least the human soul at its highest level of activity)? Aristotle is firm in his conviction that the intellect is wholly separable from the body. For him, the soul demonstrates its separability when it engages in uniquely human activities—knowing and understanding.

In the *Nicomachean Ethics*, Aristotle expounds upon the life of the intellect in a more explicit manner than we find at *De Anima* III.5. In the *Nicomachean Ethics*, he exalts the intellectual way of life as that which is most conducive to human happiness, precisely because it is most appropriate to human nature.

> That which is best and most pleasant for each creature is that which is proper to the nature of each; accordingly the life of the intellect is the best and the pleasantest life for man, inasmuch as the intellect more than anything else is man; therefore this life will be the happiest.[78]

Despite his emphasis on the composite character of human nature, Aristotle's attitude toward the intellect reveals the extent to which he remained attached to fundamental Platonic presuppositions. In keeping with his lingering Platonic allegiance, Aristotle believed that our goal as humans is to become as godlike as possible. How is this accomplished? Humans imitate the divine by doing what the divine does.

> The activity of god, which is transcendent in blessedness, is the activity of contemplation; and therefore among human activities that which is most akin to the divine activity of contemplation will be the greatest source of happiness.[79]

While Aristotle clearly affirms that at least the active intellect is separate, unaffected, and unmixed in relation to the body, his theory of its separate status is still a matter of speculation. The following passage from the third book of the *De Anima* has prompted much debate over the centuries:

> It is in its separate state that the intellect is just that which it is, and it is this alone that is immortal and eternal, though we have no memory, as the separate intellect is unaffected, while the intellect that is affected is perishable, and in any case thinks nothing about the other.[80]

How is the collective "we" in the foregoing quote to be construed? Does it imply that humans somehow share an active intellect in common? For that matter, does Aristotle provide sufficient grounds for affirming that each of us possesses an active intellect appropriate to us as the individuals we are? Such a consideration is crucial, since it has a direct bearing on the foundation of human personhood. If each of us does not possess an active dimension of mind that is our own, then what about us is truly unique, aside from physical appearance? If the active intellect alone is separable from the body, then this principle offers the only prospect for the endurance of the individual self. The issue, then, is not the imperishability of the intellect but its mode of existence apart from the body. In Aristotelian terms, however, any discussion of an intellect detached from a corporeal referent is extremely problematic. Indeed, Aristotle's biological concerns permeate his entire psychological perspective. Although he stressed the higher intellect's separability from the body and its influences, the dominant part of his psychological deliberations concern the manifestation of psychic powers in an empirical context. In the final analysis, his real interest as an empirical psychologist lies in the embodied soul (and how our humanness manifests itself in the soul-body composite).

So,,, there's on enduring "collective" mind?

CONCLUSION

Is it fair to demand of Aristotle more than his theory of human nature offers or more than he wished to offer regarding what it means to be human? In this respect, we must resist the temptation to impose certain expectations on Aristotle's psychology rooted in a Christian perspective, rather than a classical Hellenic one. The question of immortality is a case in point.[81] From a Christian standpoint, immortality coincides with the endurance of a personal self after the body's death. Aristotle, however, emphasized the perpetuation of the human species rather than the survival of its individual members qua individuals. Accordingly, the question as to whether each of us possesses an active intellect in our own right did not assume the urgency it would for later generations of thinkers.

Aristotle's psychology exhibits an ascending hierarchy of souls. A salient feature of this psychological theory lies in its recognition that lower psychic levels provide the foundation for higher ones and the more complex bodies that accompany them. But higher psychic levels do not merely depend on what is lower in the scale of living things. Rather, they exhibit a tendency toward fulfillment, in a manner consistent with the striving of all living things to be what they are in the fullest sense. This teleological orientation reveals a universal aspiration among life forms toward that perfection found in the divine. Even plants reveal such an aspiration in the act of reproducing, since this is the means of immortalizing their species. On the human level, Aristotle views the intellectual life as encompassing the noblest activity of the rational soul.

Like Plato before him, Aristotle linked human happiness with the contemplative activity that opens us to a theoretical wisdom of the ultimate causes of things. But by the same token, Aristotle developed what amounts to a this-worldly understanding of the good life. Accordingly, his anthropology reflects an extremely positive attitude toward the sociopolitical dimension of human existence. "Man is by nature a political animal," Aristotle asserts, "and he who by nature and not by mere accident is without a state is either a bad man or above humanity . . . compared to an isolated piece at draughts."[82] Aristotle is a thinker at home in the world, and his philosophy is firmly grounded in what is empirically observable. In keeping with this empirical focus, he viewed the body and sense experience as indispensable components of our humanness. For him, our spiritual and physical dimensions are inextricably conjoined: humans are composite realities of soul and body, mind and matter. Accordingly, Aristotle could never depict us as souls confined to a corporeal prison.

But in Aristotelian terms, humans are not only understood as composites of form and matter. By virtue of his distinction between act and potency, Aristotle infused human existence with a dynamic character. The model human that he envisioned is capable of a range of psychic operations encompassing the actualizing powers of the soul and the rich potentiality that the body offers. Over a lifetime, each individual engages in various degrees of becoming en route to the achievement of our final end as humans. Aristotle was as much an intellectualist as Plato in his focus on the life of contemplation as the mark of our full humanity. But the relationship between the intellect (the means to contemplation) and the body is tenuous at best. Aristotle leaves us with a nagging dilemma: either the human soul perishes along with the body, or the intellect (the defining component of our humanness) survives in some disembodied state. In any case, Aristotle's anthropology poses the same problem that looms large in Plato. For Aristotle and Plato alike, the only basis of human individuality is found in the attributes and traits associated with a perishable body. Aristotle makes a notable advance over Plato's dualistic anthropology in forging a unitary conception of human nature. But he falls short of developing a viable theory of personhood that explains the uniqueness of each individual human being in terms of the intellect as well as the body. Thinkers in the Christian tradition would grapple with this very challenge.

DISCUSSION QUESTIONS

1. Explain Aristotle's teaching that "the soul is the substantial form of a body with the potential for life."
2. What does Aristotle mean by the claim that animals are "virtually" plants and that humans are "virtually" animals and plants alike?
3. A central problem in Aristotle's *De Anima* concerns the separability of the soul from the body. Why is this problem especially acute in light of Aristotle's teaching regarding the soul-body relationship?

4. What is the difference between the active and the passive intellect in Aristotle's psychology?
5. In Aristotle's psychic hierarchy, why can we view diverse activities like nutrition, sensation, and knowledge in analogous terms?

NOTES

Aristotle quotations are drawn from the following translations: for the *De Anima*, J. A. Smith, in *The Basic Works of Aristotle*, ed. with an introduction by Richard McKeon (New York: Random House, 1941); for the *Metaphysics*, W. D. Ross, in *The Basic Works of Aristotle*, ed. with an introduction by Richard McKeon (New York: Random House, 1941); for the *Nicomachean Ethics*, H. Rackham, in the Loeb Classical Library (Cambridge: Harvard University Press; London: William Heinemann, 1968); for the *Politics*, Benjamin Jowett, in *The Basic Works of Aristotle*, ed. with an introduction by Richard McKeon (New York: Random House, 1941).

1. *Nicomachean Ethics* VI, 3 (1139b).
2. *Nicomachean Ethics* VI, 7 (1141a).
3. *New Catholic Encyclopedia* (Washington, D.C.: Catholic University of America Press, 1967), 1:809, s.v., "Aristotle," by J. Owens.
4. Werner Jaeger, *Aristotle: Fundamentals of the History of His Development*, trans. R. Robinson (Oxford: Clarendon, 1948).
5. The *Corpus Aristotelicum* is immense. Many works are lost and are known only by title. A great number, however, are extant and are divided into dialogues, treatises, and collections. The dialogues were written in the spirit of Plato and exhibit a general agreement with Platonic teaching. These include *On Rhetoric, Eudemus (On the Soul), Protrepticus (Exhortation to Philosophy), On Pleasure, On Friendship, Politics, On Justice, On the Good, On Ideas,* and *On Philosophy.* The treatises span Aristotle's three developmental phases and include the *Categories, On Interpretation, Prior and Posterior Analytics, Topics, Physics, On the Heavens, On Generation and Corruption, Metaphysics, Nicomachean Ethics, Eudemean Ethics, Politics,* and *On the Soul (De Anima).* The factual collections encompass compilations of data on a wide range of topics, based on research into nature and animal life.
6. *Metaphysics* I, 1 (980a).
7. *Metaphysics* I, 1 (981a).
8. *Metaphysics* I, 1 (981a–b).
9. *Metaphysics* I, 1 (981a–982b).
10. *Metaphysics* I, 1 (982a).
11. *Metaphysics* I, 2 (982b).
12. *Metaphysics* I, 2 (982b).
13. *Metaphysics* I, 9 (991b).
14. *Metaphysics* I, 9 (990b).
15. *Metaphysics* I, 9 (991a).
16. *Metaphysics* I, 9 (991b).
17. *Metaphysics* IV, 1 (1003a).

18. *Metaphysics* VII, 1 (1028a).

19. *Metaphysics* IV, 2 (1003b).

20. *Metaphysics* VII, 3 (1028b–1029a).

21. *Metaphysics* IX, 6 (1048a).

22. *Metaphysics* IX, 5 (1047b).

23. *Metaphysics* XII, 6 (1071b).

24. *Metaphysics* XII, 9 (1074b).

25. *Metaphysics* XII, 7 (1072a).

26. As recognized by such twentieth-century scholars as Jaeger (see note 4 above for reference) and F. J. Nuyens, *L'Evolution de la psychologie d'Aristote* (Louvain, 1948), who applied Jaeger's thesis of a genetic development in Aristotle specifically to his psychological theory.

27. *De Anima* I, 1 (402a).

28. *De Anima* I, 1 (402a).

29. Such accidents are attributed to substances by means of the categories, the ways in which we speak of substances and make predications of them. Aristotle specifies nine categories (see *Categories* IV): quantity, quality, relation, place, time, position, state, action, and affection.

30. *De Anima* I, 1 (402b).

31. *De Anima* I, 1 (403a).

32. *De Anima* I, 1 (403b).

33. This statement requires some qualification. The survey which Aristotle provides is heavily laden with his own interpretation of what his predecessors actually taught. Accordingly, the survey reflects an Aristotelian stance.

34. *De Anima* I, 2 (403b).

35. *De Anima* I, 2 (403b).

36. *De Anima* I, 2 (404b).

37. *De Anima* I, 2 (404b).

38. *De Anima* I, 3 (406a).

39. *De Anima* I, 3 (406b).

40. *De Anima* I, 2 (404a).

41. *De Anima* I, 2 (404a).

42. *De Anima* I, 2 (405b).

43. Cf. *Phaedo* 96a–100e.

44. *De Anima* I, 3 (406b).

45. *De Anima* I, 4 (407b).

46. *De Anima* I, 4 (408a).

47. *De Anima* I, 4 (408a).

48. *De Anima* I, 4 (405b).

49. *De Anima* I, 4 (405b).

50. *De Anima* I, 4 (408b).

51. *De Anima* I, 4 (408b).

52. *De Anima* I, 4 (408b).

53. *De Anima* I, 4 (408b).

54. *De Anima* I, 5 (411a).

55. *De Anima* I, 5 (411a).

56. *De Anima* I, 5 (411b).

57. *De Anima* II, 1 (412a).
58. *De Anima* II, 1 (412a).
59. *De Anima* II, 2 (414a).
60. *De Anima* II, 1 (412b).
61. *De Anima* II, 1 (412b).
62. *De Anima* II, 1 (412b).
63. *De Anima* II, 3 (414b).
64. *De Anima* II, 2 (413b).
65. *De Anima* II, 3 (414a–414b; 415a). By way of analogy, Aristotle in *De Anima* II, 3 (414b) describes the relation between lower and higher psychic levels in terms of the relation between geometrical figures: "The situation with the figures is similar to that with the things that have soul, the earlier member of the series always being present in the later in both cases, the triangle for instance in the square and the nutritive faculty in the perceptive."
66. *De Anima* II, 4 (415a).
67. *De Anima* II, 4 (415a).
68. *De Anima* II, 2 (413b).
69. *De Anima* II, 3 (414b).
70. *De Anima* II, 3 (414b).
71. *De Anima* II, 12 (424a).
72. *De Anima* II, 12 (424a).
73. *De Anima* II, 5 (417b).
74. *De Anima* III, 8 (431b).
75. *De Anima* III, 4 (429a).
76. *De Anima* III, 5 (430a).
77. *De Anima* III, 5 (430a).
78. *Nicomachean Ethics* X, 7, 9.
79. *Nicomachean Ethics* X, 8, 7.
80. *De Anima* III, 5 (430a). For a lucid treatment of the main lines of this debate from antiquity to the late Middle Ages, see the introduction in Hugh Lawson-Tancred, trans., *De Anima* (London: Penguin, 1986), 100–1.
81. Lawson-Tancred, trans., *De Anima*, 93–94:

Aristotle himself was not directly concerned with the possibility of the survival after death by the human soul, and this issue makes no impact whatever on the *De Anima*. To scrutinize the work, therefore, for hints it might offer to a controversy to which its author was not party, and which he might indeed not fully have understood, can surely be characterized as perversity, and we need not be surprised if such an approach leads rather to rhetoric than to insight.

82. *Politics* I, 2 (1253a).

II

HUMAN NATURE
AND PERSONHOOD

Big Ideas:

- Augustine is strongly influenced by a collection of Neoplatonic texts (Plotinus esp.) that locates the true person — while a unity of body & soul — in the 'middle ground' between higher (spiritual) and lower (corporeal) planes of existence.

- Has a breakthrough into personality from his understanding of the relational nature of the Trinity — love is the move.

4

St. Augustine:
A Harmonious Union

"What," asked the Church Father Tertullian (c. A.D. 160–230), "has Athens to do with Jerusalem?"[1] The object of Tertullian's invective was Greek philosophy. His provocative question challenged any attempt to come to terms with matters of faith by means of dialectical tools derived from pagan thought. In broader terms, however, it reflects a certain tension among the Fathers (and within the Christian tradition as a whole) between an approach to the faith based on a strict literalist interpretation of Scripture and one open to the resources of secular wisdom, especially philosophical reasoning. Tertullian's viewpoint was representative of the minority opinion among early Christian intellectuals. The initial centuries of Christianity disclose an increasing reliance on the ideas and arguments of classical Greek philosophers (as well as Hellenistic thinkers of late antiquity) as a means of understanding the contents of faith and defining its fundamental doctrines.

One of the most fertile areas for this blending of faith and reason is found in speculation regarding the creation of humans and their relation to God. During the patristic era, theology and philosophy combined to yield a new model of what it means to be human, a model inspired by the scriptural teaching of a free creation by a loving, personal Creator of true individuals in his own image and likeness. Such an endeavor reflects an adaptation of philosophical insights in the service of theology. But herein lies a problem that points to a crucial disparity between Greek and biblical ways of thinking that engenders a special problem for a Christian anthropology.

THE CHALLENGE OF CHRISTIAN ANTHROPOLOGY

The dichotomies between soul and body, spirit and matter, are largely alien to the creation accounts of the Old Testament tradition, where God creates the whole human being. In the words of Genesis 2:7, "The Lord God formed man from the dust of the ground and breathed into his nostrils the breath of life, and man became a living being." This emphasis on human unity carries over into the New Testament as well. Indeed, Christ's redemptive activity was directed toward the fullness of the individual, not toward soul or body in isolation from each other. But a reading of the New Testament can easily produce evidence in support of the primacy of the soul over the body. In Matthew's Gospel, Christ teaches, "Do not be afraid of those who kill the body but cannot kill the soul" (10:28), and "The spirit is willing but the flesh is weak" (26:41). Likewise, the Pauline corpus introduces a polarity between the life of the spirit and the life of the flesh consistent with a dualistic mentality.[2]

These teachings must be balanced against those which extol the value of the human body as the temple of the Holy Spirit and a member of Christ himself.[3] But while the New Testament tradition reflects a clear commitment to a unitary conception of human nature, it also displays a distinct spiritualistic emphasis. For this reason, a Christian anthropology must come to terms with a challenge: if such an account is to remain true to its scriptural sources, it must do justice to our spiritual and bodily dimensions alike. But how is the relationship between these dimensions to be defined? This question might be reframed in these terms: how do we explain our humanity in such a way that acknowledges the dignity of the body, while recognizing that we are more than bodily beings, with the hope of a life after the body's death? Too much emphasis on the spiritual aspect of human existence undermines the importance and worth of the body, but too much emphasis on the body reduces us to no more than perishable things. A Christian account of our humanness bears the special burden of navigating between two worlds, so to speak, and thereby upholding the unity of the whole person.

The following statement from the Second Vatican Council provides an illuminating referent for this emphasis on a unitary conception of human nature:

> Man, though made of body and soul, is a unity. Through his very bodily condition he sums up the elements of the material world. For this reason man may not despise his bodily life. Rather he is obliged to regard his body as good and to hold it in honor since God has created it and will raise it up on the last day.4

The foregoing quote expresses the ideal attitude toward the relationship between the inner and outer dimensions of human existence that any Christian anthropology can endorse. On the surface, then, it would appear that Aristotle's composite theory could have served Christian purposes from the outset. But this was not the case. In the early tradition (i.e., the patristic era), the writings of Nemesius of Emesa fostered and solidified an anti-Aristotelian bias. Nemesius's highly influential *On the Nature of Man* (composed in the final decade of the fourth century) promoted a positive attitude toward a Platonic account of the soul-body relationship and correspondingly undermined Aristotle's credibility.[5] In Etienne Gilson's assessment, "A severe criticism of Aristotle's definition left behind by Nemesius . . . had a deep and lasting influence on the history of the controversy."[6]

Overall, Nemesius endorses the basic Platonic dichotomy of soul and body and the presupposition that the soul uses the body as its tool. "There is general consent that the soul deserves more regard than the body, and that the body is only an instrument employed by the soul."[7] But as composites of soul and body humans are also the point of contact between the spiritual and corporeal dimensions of reality.

> Man's being is on the boundary between the intelligible order and the phenomenal order. As touching his body and its faculties, he is on a par with the irrational animate and with the inanimate creatures. As touching his rational faculties he claims kinship with incorporeal beings.[8]

From Nemesius's standpoint, the unity of soul and body in humans reflects the larger unity of the universe as a whole. Humans exemplify this unity in their very being. "God created both an intelligible and a phenomenal order and required some one creature to link these two together that the entire universe should form one agreeable unity, unbroken by internal incoherences."[9] Nemesius closely aligns this Neoplatonic motif with a theme derived from the Stoicism of Posidonius. In this respect, he depicts humans as microcosms of the whole, or more precisely, "the world in little" (*mikros kosmos*).[10] As such, they occupy the summit of a universe exhibiting a gradation of perfections, so that what is lower is subservient in rank to what is higher and more sophisticated in the scale of being.

Nemesius's view of humans as the culmination of the created order is consistent with teaching in Genesis that man was created last, as the end to which the world's entire development is oriented and subordinated. But by the same token, it displays an affinity with Aristotle's entelechism and the assumption that what is higher in an ascending order of living things draws on and perfects what is found on lower levels. In point of fact, however, Nemesius explicitly rejects Aristotle's theory of the soul as the body's entelechy, on the grounds that the soul "must be something that seeks a perfection of its own, apart from the body."[11] Nemesius in effect contends that Aristotle denied that the soul is a self-subsisting thing in its own right, reducing it to a bodily component. Whether his critique is aimed at the *De Anima* or some Neoplatonic commentary on Aristotle is a matter of scholarly conjecture.[12]

In any case, Nemesius raised suspicion regarding Aristotle's commitment to the soul's immortality and the survival of the self after the body's death. While Aristotle upheld the separability of the intellect from the body, the degree to which he endorsed personal immortality is open to question. Plato, on the other hand, made a persuasive case for the soul's immortality, even if his conception of immortality was confined to the soul alone (rather than encompassing the composite human being). For Christians, Plato's arguments for the soul's survival lent support to their belief in its imperishability and supernatural destiny.

Despite his downgrading of bodily existence (and his failure to account for the unity of soul and body), then, it was largely Plato (and Plato's Neoplatonic successors) who provided anthropological touchstones for early Christian thinkers.[13] One of the most ambitious efforts in this vein is found in the writings of St. Augustine of Hippo (A.D. 354–430). Augustine serves as a vital bridge between pagan and Christian thought and in broader terms between ancient and medieval philosophy. He also shows the usefulness (as well as the limitations) of Greek philosophy for Christian anthropological purposes.

Augustine provided an extremely powerful statement on what it means to be human. He attempted to navigate between different worlds on two significant levels: on the one hand, by reconciling the contents of faith with the resources of reason; on the other hand, by steering a middle course between the life of the soul and the life of the body. In the process, he demonstrated the extent to which the Christian perspective can contribute to an understanding of us as truly personal beings intermediate between the realms of spirit and matter.

AUGUSTINE'S PERSONAL EXPERIENCE

"Man is a mighty abyss," wrote Augustine, "whose very hairs you have numbered."[14] This intensity in Augustine's anthropological deliberations readily engages our attention. Augustine's struggle to understand humanity is very much our own. Each of us has a vested interest in grasping what makes us unique, despite the fact that a firm resolution to this question continually eludes our grasp. The problem is even more acute in our own age, when science offers the real possibility of developing an exhaustive explanation of human nature on purely empirical grounds. Augustine was no stranger to the complexity of this problem and harbored no illusions about the prospects of an easy solution. In the same passage of the *Confessions* just quoted, he further laments that "man's hairs are easier to count than his affections and the movements of his heart."[15] Augustine's personal experience provided the raw data for his wide-ranging anthropological investigations. This extended analysis, however, proceeded from his preoccupation with a question that shaped and defined his early journey of faith: whence comes evil? In attempting to answer this question, Augustine experimented with various philosophical and theological perspectives. The reasons for this excursus were many and varied, and a detailed commentary on Augustine's preconversion experience is beyond the scope of this study. For our purposes, however, it suffices to focus briefly on his nine-year association with Manichaeism and its influence on his intellectual and spiritual development.

MANICHAEISM AND THE PROBLEM OF EVIL

A question often raised in respect to Augustine's early life is how anyone so intelligent and critical could have embraced Manichaeism at all. One factor that was highly instrumental in his gravitation toward this eclectic amalgam of Christianity, Judaism, and Zoroastrianism was the materialism that had influenced so much of his attitude toward the Bible. Like many of his contemporaries, the young Augustine was an uncritical materialist who assumed that anything which exists (including God) must be of a mutable and corruptible nature. For this reason, Augustine could only conceive of God in bodily terms and on a more personal level, in purely anthropomorphic ones.

Augustine's materialism made him receptive to the radical dualism of Manichaeism. The Manichaeans defined reality in terms of the conflicting principles of Light and Darkness, Good and Evil. This conflict translated into a sharp dichotomy in human nature between spirit and matter, the *loci* of the particles of Light and Darkness, respectively. For the Manichaeans, humans are caught in a kind of crossfire between these warring principles. For the Manichaeans, salvation consisted in the liberation of the soul from the body, accompanied by the freeing of the particles of Light from their imprisonment in matter. An implication of this dualistic materialism was the belief that evil is a substantial reality that even renders God vulnerable to its corruptive influence. Conversely, the Manichaeans taught that God is a great material mass diffused through infinite space.

Augustine's break with Manichaeism and his eventual conversion to Christianity involved two significant developments. On the one hand, he

acquired a new way of understanding Scripture through the preaching of
Ambrose, the Catholic bishop of Milan.[16] On the other hand, his celebrated encounter with the "books of the Platonists" *(libri platonicorum)* introduced him to a new vision of reality.[17] As twentieth-century scholarship has disclosed, these writings were not those of Plato but of a later
generation of Platonists, the Neoplatonists. Accordingly, the *libri platonicorum* might have encompassed writings by Plotinus, the major exponent
of Neoplatonism (A.D. 204–270), his disciple Porphyry, or, alternatively, a
compilation of the writings of both thinkers. The authorship of this corpus, in fact, has been the focus of a prolonged debate.[18] By and large, however, we can safely say that the major thrust of Augustine's anthropology
(and his theory of reality in general) bears a distinctive Plotinian imprint.
For this reason, I confine my discussion of Augustine's Neoplatonic influence chiefly to Plotinus's *Enneads,* while acknowledging the possibility
of his indebtedness to other Neoplatonists (as well as various thinkers, including Cicero and the Stoics, Origen, Tertullian, Ambrose, and Marius
Victorinus, to name but a few).

But debates regarding its authorship notwithstanding, one thing is certain: the *libri platonicorum* exerted an incalculable influence on Augustine's entire outlook. In addition to what Ambrose taught him, they provided him with a sharper intellectual lens through which he could
interpret the Bible and come to terms with the theological and philosophical problems that had posed a stumbling block to his own spiritual
progress. Augustine's attempts to sound the depths of the mystery inherent in human existence thus reveal something of a dual allegiance. As a
Christian, he wished to remain faithful to scriptural teaching and the importance it afforded the body as well as the soul. But by the same token,
his discussions of human nature were decisively shaped by the insights,
motifs, and arguments he derived from Neoplatonism. And this lent his
anthropology a distinct spiritualistic and intellectualist emphasis.

AUGUSTINE'S NEOPLATONIC LENS

First and foremost, Neoplatonism allowed Augustine to appreciate the
possibility of immaterial reality. This perspective had a profound effect on
his understanding of God and, by extension, created being in general. On
the one hand, it afforded him a means of defining the divine nature in
purely spiritual terms as the highest, immutable Good. Once he was free
of the limitations of materialism, Augustine could see that God's infinite-
ness consists in an unlimited power, rather than in some quantitative or
spatial immensity. On the other hand, Neoplatonism imparted a sense of
the inherent goodness of all things. The realization that everything which

God creates reflects the goodness of its creator provided a basis for overcoming the radical dualism that Augustine had formerly endorsed as a Manichaean.

Augustine's preoccupation with the origin of evil reflects a concern that is a direct outgrowth of Christian belief, namely, whether God's role as creator renders him ultimately responsible for evil. The Manichaeans (like all extreme dualists) attempted to explain away this problem by imputing evil to a principle other than God. But in so doing, they subjected even God to its encroachments. In Neoplatonism, Augustine found a means of preserving not only the integrity of God but of created reality as well. From this standpoint, evil does not exist as a substantial reality in its own right but in a negative sense, as a privation, deficiency, or corruption of created goods. If evil only manifests itself in relation to the good, then the notion of an absolute or substantial evil is a contradiction in terms. Indeed, if something were evil by nature it simply could not exist.[19]

The Neoplatonic interpretation of evil in negative terms presupposes an understanding of reality in which all things assume their appropriate place, in a manner consistent with a Classical ideal of cosmic order. In Augustine's Christian recasting of this ideal, everything which God creates is good but arranged in a hierarchical scheme extending from God to corporeal natures. In this context, things exhibit varying degrees of excellence according to their position in that framework.[20] For this reason, any defects they might exhibit must be considered against the background of their participation in the goodness and beauty of the whole. In contrast to the mutability and perfection of God, creatures are finite and hence mutable and contingent to the very core of their being.

Plotinus viewed the really real in terms of a vast system in which what is lower participates in what is higher, inauthentic reality sharing in the authentic. The Plotinian universe encompasses what can be depicted as a vertical hierarchy of three levels or hypostases: the One (the ultimate source of all things), *nous* or Intellect (the repository of the Forms, the principles of intelligibility), and Soul (the principle of life). The One gives rise to what is ontologically lower by virtue of an eternal process of emanation of its power and a diffusion of its goodness. The outward movement of emanation is complemented by an ascending movement whereby all things return to their source. Soul occupies a special position in this model, sharing in the higher noetic world of Intellect and communicating this intelligibility to lesser reality. Humans occupy the hinterland of being, sharing in the aspect of Soul that animates the material world. In this respect, they stand on the periphery between being and nonbeing, between the eternal realm of contemplation and a temporal world that bears but a faint imprint of the higher intelligible order.

We find the most explicit anthropological statement by Plotinus regarding the relationship between soul and body in a late treatise, *Ennead* I.1(53), "The Animate and the Man." Plotinus devotes this treatise to a discussion of the nature of personal identity. In general terms, he closely follows Plato in affirming the primacy of the soul in humans. But his emphasis on the unity of soul and body imparts a distinctive Aristotelian character to his anthropology. His point of departure in *Ennead* I.1 is an assessment of Aristotle's treatment of the soul-body relationship in the *De Anima* (I.4). In this respect, his special concern lies in determining the basis of certain affections and experiences (e.g., pleasure and distress, fear and courage, desire and aversion): do they exist in the soul alone, in the soul as using the body, or in something else that draws soul and body together?[21] Likewise, how are reasoning and intellective acts related to the affections and sense experience? Such questions prompt him to consider the nature of the soul and whether a distinction can be made between Soul itself (i.e., as Universal Soul) and individual souls (i.e., your soul and mine). If such a distinction is valid, Plotinus contends, then the soul in man is some sort of composite (and thus a recipient), and all affections and experiences have a psychic basis.[22]

But Plotinus is careful not to collapse the distinction between individual souls and Soul in a universal sense. In that case, our soul would be so immersed in the Ideal realm that it would be rendered completely impassive to any activities that it imparts to the body.[23] Accordingly, a new question must be addressed: how could the soul lend itself to any admixture of its powers with the corporeal? This amounts to inquiring about the soul's relation to the body and the sense in which the soul can be designated as "in" the body.[24] The soul and body together constitute one reality—the "animate organism." Although he recognizes their close relation, Plotinus explicitly rejects the portrayal of the body as no more than a passive tool at the soul's disposal.

> If soul uses body as a tool it does not have to admit the affections which come through the body; craftsmen are not affected by the affections of their tools.[25]

Plotinus goes beyond Plato in recognizing a point of contact between psychic and corporeal experience, thus anticipating Augustine's struggle in a pagan Neoplatonic context. Both thinkers were committed to the substantial unity of the human being even as they upheld the primacy of the soul. As Plotinus contends, "It is from the combination of body and soul that the 'complete living creature' takes its name."[26] The soul, however, is the essence of the human being. And, if the compound of soul and body constitutes an animate being (or alternatively "the living creature"), it does so by virtue of the soul's presence.[27]

Plotinus designates the soul itself as divine. His final words (as quoted by his disciple Porphyry) provide an illuminating commentary on his conception of the proper destiny of the human soul, the basis of our authentic self: "Try to bring back the god in you to the divine in the All!"[28] This assertion expresses the aspiration at the heart of the mystical side of Plotinian thought: to achieve union with the One, the wellspring of all things and the end toward which everything tends. In an earlier treatise (i.e., *Ennead* III.8[30]), Plotinus identifies our authentic self as humans with the intelligible world, even if our lower self is bound up with the vicissitudes of corporeal existence. "The first part of soul . . . that which is above and always filled and illuminated by the reality above, remains There; but another part goes forth . . . for actuality reaches everything, and there is no point where it fails."[29]

By virtue of its exalted status, this higher level of soul is immune to negative bodily experiences and free of any moral culpability for wrongdoing. Plotinus attributes such evils exclusively to "the living being, the joint entity."[30] But to what extent does his dichotomy between a higher Soul and a lower soul destroy the very unity of the self he wishes to uphold? Indeed, the same thinker who contends that "we must certainly consider soul as being in body" sharply distinguishes what belongs to the "joint entity" (the composite of soul and body in the living being) from what is proper to the soul alone. For him, then, what pertains to the composite concerns the body, the source of any changes, turmoil, or affections experienced by us as a "joint entity."[31]

Plotinus's real concern here lies in maintaining the unity and separability of the soul from the body. A problem with this particular interpretation is that it detaches our authentic self from the body that constitutes one of its integral parts. In this regard, a more satisfactory psychic theory can be derived from a series of Plotinian passages that depict the soul as occupying a kind of middle rank between higher and lower orders of reality. What lies in the middle, however, is not only the soul but our entire self, or what Plotinus describes collectively as the "we": "It is we ourselves who reason, and we ourselves make the acts of intelligence in discursive reasoning; for this is what we ourselves are."[32]

This "upward" or "downward" orientation assumes an ethical significance in the context of Plotinus's metaphysical vision of reality as a whole. Because the soul is positioned in the middle, it has the freedom to shift its contemplative gaze from one level of reality to another. Its orientation thus establishes the moral quality of one's life.[33] From this standpoint, one can be in touch with the realm of true being even while the soul is attached to a body. Conversely, the soul can become so preoccupied with changing corporeal images that it all but forfeits its divine status. In any case, the crucial factor lies in its focus, regardless of embodiment.

In Plotinian terms, we become what we make the object of our attention. "When good people are in this state their life is increased," Plotinus
teaches, "not split out into perception, but gathered together in one in itself."[34] But this requires sufficient intellectual discipline (through the
philosophical way of life) and moral purification (through the practice of
virtue). Moral living coincides with the cultivation of the life of the mind.
Plotinus takes for granted that the truly wise individual is also a good
one—an individual grounded in the world of Intellect.[35]

Plotinus's defining of the moral life in terms of this contemplative ideal
also establishes the soul's proper disposition toward the world at large.
While his metaphysics dictates that what is other than the One must always be inferior to its source (and that the "farther" removed from the
One in ontological terms, the greater the inferiority), it also depicts the
world and the body as images of what is greater. Granted, Plotinus can exhibit ambivalence toward corporeal things. His remarks from his treatise
On Beauty provide a case in point, comparing the soul involved with the
body (and with matter in general) to unrefined gold.[36]

But the *Enneads* are also rich in praise for a visible world that points to
a higher intelligible beauty and majesty. The Plotinian universe constitutes a vast participation scheme in which lesser degrees of reality reflect
the One's infinite goodness and beauty. While an image is inferior to the
original, it still retains something of what it imitates. "If there is another
universe better than this one," Plotinus maintains, "then what is this
one?"[37]

The *Enneads* exhibit a tension similar to what we encounter in Plato—
that is, between a pessimistic view of the body (as reflected in the *Phaedo*
and *Phaedrus*) and an optimistic stance toward the material world (as reflected in the *Timaeus*). This tension assumes a distinct anthropological focus in Plotinus, who oscillates between a disdain of bodily existence and
an exaltation of its capacity to reveal being in its most authentic sense. To
a great extent, such a tension carries over into the thought of Augustine,
whose creative adaptation of Plotinus shaped the character of his Christian anthropology. For Augustine, however, the stakes are much higher. As
a Christian philosopher, he represents a tradition that values the body not
merely as an image of higher intelligible reality but as the result of the creative activity of a personal and loving God.

AUGUSTINE'S DEFINITIONS OF *HOMO*

Augustine's anthropological discussions reflect an ongoing commitment
to the notion of the human being as a unity of soul and body. This attachment to a Neoplatonic perspective led him to define humans chiefly in

terms of the soul and, by implication, to emphasize the superiority of the soul over the body. An excellent point of departure for assessing the main lines of Augustine's Christian anthropology is found in a work written shortly after his conversion to Christianity, the *De Moribus Ecclesiae Catholicae et de Moribus Manichaeorum* (*The Catholic and Manichaean Ways of Life*, composed between A.D. 388 and 390). One is immediately struck by the tentative nature of his deliberations. In his response to the question What is man?, Augustine explores alternative ways of understanding the human phenomenon. While he stresses that soul and body are essential components of human nature, he wrestles with the problem as to what constitutes the human being as such.

> What do we call man, then? Is he soul or body like a centaur or two horses harnessed together? Or shall we call him the body alone in the service of a governing soul, or shall we say that man is nothing but the soul, inasmuch as it rules the body?[38]

As Augustine recognizes, this dilemma will not be easily resolved. In a great understatement of the enormity of the task at hand, he bemoans the fact that "even if its solution were simple, it would require a lengthy explanation involving an expense of time and labor."[39] The crux of the problem seems to lie in the distinction between soul and body. In our own day-to-day experience, we do not (unless otherwise prompted to do so) make fine distinctions between our mental and physical life, or between our minds and our bodies. Practically speaking, we all implicitly endorse what amounts to a unitary conception of human nature. In this respect, both soul and body have an equal claim to our humanity. As Augustine himself observes, "although they are two things it might happen that one of these would be looked upon and spoken of as man."[40]

Consequently the *De Moribus* discloses at least a provisional endorsement of the unity of the self. Yet in that same work, Augustine proffers the following comprehensive definition: "man as he appears to us is a rational soul, making use of a mortal and earthly body."[41] Clearly Augustine was torn in two directions: the direction of the Christian theologian, on the one hand, and that of the Christian Neoplatonic philosopher on the other. But even as he upholds the primacy of the soul over a body it uses as its instrumentality, he recognizes that Christian charity is directed toward the good of a being encompassing soul and body alike.

Still, the early Augustine displayed an ongoing bias in favor of the soul, not just in keeping with his Neoplatonic allegiance, but with the promptings of Scripture as well. In one of his initial anthropological formulations, he defined the soul (in a manner reminiscent of the language of Plato's *Phaedo*) as "a certain kind of substance sharing in reason, fitted to rule the body."[42] At this stage of his intellectual evolution, he was firm in the conviction that the essence of our humanness cannot be found in something as mutable and unstable as the body. For this reason, he stresses that the soul is completely different from the body in nature and closest to God among created things.[43]

If the soul (as the essence of the human being) has any claim to imperishability and immortality, it must be radically different from (and independent of) a perishable corporeal nature. But while Augustine's teaching concerning the soul reveals an allegiance to Platonic and Neoplatonic sentiments, his teaching regarding the body is still unmistakably Christian. As he consistently affirms, an emphasis on the primacy of the soul need not demand negativity toward the body. In his estimation, such an attitude is the mark of human vanity, not the truth that proceeds from God.[44] In the context of his antidualistic agenda, those beset with such vanity are readily apparent—his former Manichaean associates.

But it is one matter to acknowledge the importance of soul and body alike; it is quite another to formulate a viable anthropological theory that upholds their unity. Augustine's most explicit articulation of what amounts to a composite model of human nature emerges in the *De Civitate Dei* (*City of God*). In a passage which represents his mature outlook regarding the relation between soul and body, Augustine still places a higher value on the soul, but only in view of its contributions to the life of the whole being. "Man is not a body alone nor a soul alone," he contends. "He is composed of both soul and body."[45]

If Augustine had assimilated the writings of Aristotle rather than those of the Platonists, he could have dispensed with references to the body as "the inferior part of man" and treated it in more positive terms as the potentiality for the soul's actualizing power. For better or worse, however, his Christian anthropology developed within a Neoplatonic framework. Consequently Augustine attempted to uphold the substantial unity of human beings, but he was hard-pressed to do so with the conceptual tools at his disposal.[46] In this regard, even his emphasis on the substantial unity of humans always presupposes a commitment to the superiority of soul over the body. But by the same token, the later Augustine would adopt a critical stance toward his philosophical sources.

> The Platonists are not so foolish as the Manichaeans; for they do not detest earthly bodies as the natural substance of evil. Nonetheless, they hold that souls are so influenced by earthly limbs and dying members that they derive from them their unwholesome desires and fears and joys and sorrows.[47]

In Augustinian terms, then, human nature presupposes a "harmonious union" of the inner man of the spirit and the outer man of the flesh. This technical formulation emerges in Augustine's first scriptural commentary, the *De Genesi contra Manichaeos* (*On Genesis against the Manichaeans*), a work which combines the allegorical method of interpretation with a Christian Neoplatonic reading of the sacred text. In the teaching that "God formed man from the clay of the ground" (Gen. 2:7), Augustine discerns a reference to the creation of the whole person as the conjoining of soul and body. In his rendering of this teaching, however, "clay" or "mud" (according to the wording of an alternate translation) provides the material out of which God forms man. By means of this image, Augustine underscores what is crucial to his exegesis of the passage: the human composite is the product of a union of two distinct substances (i.e., earth and water).

> If we understand man in this place as made from body and soul, that mixture bears the name of mud with good reason. For, as water gathers, glues, and holds earth together when by its mixture it makes mud, so the soul by vivifying that matter of the soul forms it into a harmonious unity and does not allow it to fall into dissolution.[48]

AUGUSTINE ON THE PERSON

Augustine's characterization of the relationship between soul and body as a "harmonious union" represents his response to what constitutes the special problem inherent in his Christian anthropology: if we are essentially souls that use bodies (as his definitions maintain), how are they united? More precisely, how do two different natures come together in one individual being? Augustine found a convenient device for dealing with this dilemma in the Neoplatonic theory of "a union without confusion," a notion whose source is traceable to Porphyry's *Quaestiones Commixtae*.[49] For the Neoplatonists, this theory provided a more sophisticated means of describing the union of soul and body than Stoicism offered. The Stoics proposed two possibilities for explaining the soul's relationship with the body: a mere juxtaposing of different substances or a crude mixing, whereby the distinct substances of soul and body become a completely different one. The theory of "a union without confusion" allows for a third possibility—a conjoining of soul and body in such a way as to maintain the integrity of each.

Christian theologians used this Neoplatonic motif as a means of elucidating how disparate divine and human natures were united in the single person of Christ. In this respect, Nemesius's *On the Nature of Man* reflects thinkers (including Augustine) who came to terms with the hypostatic union of the Incarnation on the basis of the unity of the human self. Indeed, Nemesius perceived as much of a mystery in the unity of soul and body in human nature as he did in the union of the Divine Word with the fullness of Christ's humanity.[50] On the anthropological side, Nemesius frames the problem in this manner:

> How is it possible for body to be united to soul without losing corporeity, or how is it possible for soul (being incorporeal and self-subsistent) to be joined to body, and become part of a living creature, still keeping distinct and uncorrupted its own entity?[51]

Nemesius rejects the Stoic options for explaining the soul-body relation: soul and body cannot be "mixed," since such a haphazard union would destroy both natures (just as mixing water and wine yields neither pure water nor undiluted wine). Likewise, soul and body cannot be "juxtaposed," since "only that part of the body would be alive that was in proximity to the soul" (and any part of the body not in contact with the soul would be lifeless).[52] But Nemesius is equally cautious about the contention that soul and body are "united," if union presupposes a mutual change and destruction of the respective natures. If the soul is united to the body, it can only be by means of a "union without confusion," whereby soul retains its incorporeality even as it constitutes a single subject in conjunction with the body. "The union of soul and body involves no confusion of one with the other," he contends, "so that the more spiritual being is not impaired by the inferior being, but the latter only is profited by the more spiritual."[53]

Like Nemesius, Augustine discerned a parallel between the unity of the human person (as a composite of body and soul) and the unity of divinity and humanity in the person of Christ. His clearest articulation of this relationship is found in a letter he wrote to Volusianum in A.D. 412. In it he draws an analogy between the way the human soul uses the body in a single human person to form a human being and the way God uses human nature in a single person to form Christ.

> In the former person there is a mingling of soul and body; in the latter Person there is a mingling of God and man. Therefore, the person of man is a mingling of soul and body, but the Person of Christ is a mingling of God and man.[54]

This interplay of Christology and philosophical anthropology illustrates the extent to which Augustine recognized the compatibility of theology and philosophy, faith and reason. In both contexts, he employs the notion of a "union without confusion" in explaining how different natures can be united in one individual. He viewed both types of union as deeply enshrouded in mystery. Augustine, however, contends that the union of the Word of God and a soul conjoined to a body in Christ is more credible than the more familiar union of body and soul in human beings. "For this reason," he contends, "it ought to be easier to believe in the intermingling of the Word of God and a soul than of a soul and a body."[55]

Christological speculation had an immense impact on Augustine's understanding of humans in personalist terms. The early Augustine, as we have seen, confined his definitions of man *(homo)* to the unity which holds between soul and body. The mature Augustine, however, introduces the term *persona* into his anthropological lexicon. At that later juncture, he came to see that the composite unity of soul and body constitutes not only the human being but an individual person *(persona)* in his or her own right. This is more than a matter of incorporating a new vocabulary. Rather, it underscores a transition from a preoccupation with what we all share in common to a recognition of the uniqueness of each and every human being. Augustine's ability to designate us as persons points to a richer grasp of what it means to be fully human. This achievement, it seems reasonable to assume, was the fruit of deep theological reflection on Christ's personhood. In a very real sense, Augustine's understanding of the person of Christ as a dynamic center of divine and human attributes provided the vital touchstone for coming to terms with the unity of the human self.

But Christ's designation as a "person" assumes both a Christological and a Trinitarian connotation. Christ's person is the nexus of what is proper to God and humans, the point of contact between his divinity and humanity. Augustine affirms the unity of Christ's personhood on the basis of an anthropological analog of the soul-body relation. "Just as you, one human being, are soul and flesh," he writes, "so too He, one Christ is God and man."[56] In this respect, human persons can be viewed as images of Christ, the divine mediator who was himself fully human, and the exemplar of the best that humanity can be.

In broader Trinitarian terms, however, Christ is also the Second Person of a Trinity of divine persons encompassing God as Father, Son, and Holy Spirit. Once again, Augustine treats humans as images of a divine prototype. As one commentator has observed, "the nature of a human person is relevant only as an image of the divine trinity."[57] For Augustine, humans bear the imprint of God's triune nature primarily in their intellects, the highest part of their rational nature.

> Any single man, who is not called the image of God in terms of everything that belongs to his nature but only in terms of his mind is one person and is the image of the trinity in his mind. But that trinity he is the image of is nothing but wholly and simple trinity . . . three persons of one being, not, like any single man, just one person.[58]

Yet, for all his commitment to an intellectualist interpretation of human nature, Augustine saw us as fundamentally relational beings. This interpretation found its theological referent in the relations constituting the divine persons of the Trinity.[59] In this respect, Augustine's theory of

Trinitarian relations represents an attempt to explain how one indivisible Godhead can be approached as Father, Son, and Holy Spirit. In this way, the question as to whether the person of Christ allows for an interchange of predicates appropriate to his divine and human natures finds a Trinitarian parallel in the question as to whether divine properties are applicable to God as Father, Son, and Holy Spirit.

This Trinitarian question assumed prominence during the final phase of the Arian controversy. For the late ("Homoian") Arians, the claim that the persons of the Trinity were one and equal was tantamount to denying their individual integrity. The Arian bishop Maximinus stated the case in this way: "But you say that the Father and the Son are one. Say of the Son what belongs to the Father; call the Son unbegotten, call Him unborn, say that no one has ever seen Him or can see Him."[60] Augustine's classic response to this challenge is found in his monumental treatise the *De Trinitate* (*On the Trinity*). In it, he distinguishes between absolute predicates pertaining to the divine nature itself (e.g., "good," "simple," "immutable") and relative predicates which pertain to relationships within the Trinity. While absolute predicates can be applied freely to the Father, Son, and Holy Spirit (because they refer to the nature of God as God), relative predicates refer to properties or attributes proper to each Person.

From this standpoint, whatever we say of Father, Son, and Holy Spirit as individuals can also be said of the others as well. As Augustine says, "They are not called these things substance-wise, but relation-wise."[61] In Augustinian terms, the Trinity is relational at its very heart. By extension, human personhood is fully realized only by patterning our own relationships after the divine relations, and the mutual love which binds together the Persons of the Trinity as one. "We are bidden to imitate this mutuality," he affirms, "both with reference to God and to each other."[62] Such a Trinitarian model of relationality is reflected in the capacity of free, rational agents to love in a completely gratuitous manner. In this respect, Robert Lauder contends that Augustine considered the Trinity the most perfect expression of personal love on a human level.[63]

THE SUBJECTIVE EGO

If Augustine's Christology was conducive to an appreciation of the unity of the human person, his Trinitarian theology inspired his vision of humans as originating in the creative activity of God and finding their completion in a contemplative union with their creator. For Augustine, however, the religious quest is no solitary endeavor but assumes a significant social dimension. This is most evident in his great spiritual autobiography, the *Confessions*. Augustine frequently charts his spiritual progress on

the basis of crucial encounters with people who stimulated his awareness
of God and the extent of his intellectual and moral error. But the *Confessions* also reveal Augustine's commitment to the bonds of friendship. His
very ability to forge such meaningful relationships presupposes the integrity of the self. In Lauder's reckoning, the *Confessions* "presents us with
a theory of self as a dynamic center of activity, unfolding and developing
by experiences and contacts with other selves."[64]

Augustine's recognition of the relational character of the human person
thus presupposes a recognition of the subjective ego. Indeed, we can only
relate to others in an interpersonal manner if there is something substantial about our self that we can share with them. The fact that Augustine
composed the *Confessions* in the first person not only attests to this subjective point of departure but invests his investigation with a riveting
honesty. "You stood me face to face with myself," he prays, "so that I
might see how foul I was."[65] The ego, in effect, serves as Augustine's continual touchstone for assessing interpersonal relationships with God and
neighbor alike. The philosophical significance of his affirmation of the ego
is most clearly evident in his discussions of the freedom of the will.

Augustine's focus on the will as the basis of personal moral accountability was intimately connected with his rejection of Manichaean dualism.
Just as this perspective attempted to absolve God from responsibility for
the cause of evil (by positing a principle of evil), it also absolved humans
from responsibility for their deeds by attributing the cause of sin to an evil
mind. Augustine's break with the Manichaeans coincided with his gradual acceptance of his own freedom. "I was absolutely certain that when I
willed a thing or refused to will it," he asserts, "it was I alone who willed
or refused to will."[66] But by the same token, he also marveled at the extent
to which he found himself controlled by the dictates of that same will.
Such a paradoxical control by a power that seems so completely one's
own generated what he perceived as a "great struggle in my inner house"
rooted in a divided will between opposing moral alternatives.[67]

For Augustine, such inner conflict proceeds from the fact that one human being can be pulled in many different directions simultaneously. But
in the midst of this internal upheaval, he discerned a single, abiding nature. In rebutting the Manichaean teaching that the divided will corre-
sponds to a good mind and an evil mind in the same individual, Augustine proffers the following argument: "If there were as many contrary
natures as there are conflicting wills, there will now be not only two natures, but many of them."[68] In response, Augustine upholds the integrity
of the self as the ultimate referent for praise or blame. "It was I myself,"
he confesses, "who willed to serve God or who did not so will."[69]

While Augustine's focus on the mind as the bearer of God's image reflects a distinct intellectualist emphasis, his anthropology also recognizes

the contribution of the body to our dignity as humans. In the final analysis, the whole person (as the harmonious union of soul and body in one being) stands in relation to God as a rational creature. In a manner consistent with his allegorical method of exegesis, Augustine finds the concrete symbol for this exalted status in our upright posture.

> What is the basis of man's greater dignity except that he was created in the image of God not in his body but in his intellect? And yet he does have in his body also a characteristic that is a sign of this dignity insofar as he has been made to stand. Man's body, then, is appropriate for his rational nature, because he stands, able to look up to heaven and gaze upon the higher regions in the corporeal world.[70]

MORAL AND COSMIC ORDER

In Augustinian terms, to be a human person is to participate in a vast community of being, extending from God to corporeal natures. Augustine's localization of the human soul in the middle of things reflects his appropriation of the Plotinian notion of the soul's midrank status. His creative adaptation of this motif assumes a prominent role in his Christian Neoplatonic interpretation of Genesis. In this exegetical context, Augustine discerns the scriptural symbol for the soul's intermediate position between spiritual and corporeal reality in the tree of life described in Genesis 3:3.

> The tree of life planted in the middle of paradise signifies the wisdom by which the soul should understand that it is ordered in a certain middle range of things. Thus, though it has all corporeal nature subject to itself, it still understands that the nature of God is above it.[71]

Augustine's anthropology thus presupposes a hierarchical understanding of a universal order of creation. "Man is a mean between beasts and angels," he says, "the beast an irrational and mortal animal, the angel a rational and immortal one, and man is between them."[72] More precisely, Augustine posits the human soul (finite but immortal) between God (the fullness of being) and corporeal natures (finite and perishable). This hierarchical arrangement is reflected in the life of every human. From Augustine's standpoint, we are the beings in whom the realms of spirit and matter overlap. While humans possess an immortal soul, they exhibit (like creatures in general) an ontological instability rooted in their causal dependence on God and the mutability proceeding from their creaturely status. Such mutability underscores the tendency toward nonbeing that characterizes finite things in general. "They are because they are from you," Augustine reasons, "they are not, since they are not what you are."[73]

On a human level, this susceptibility to change is by no means confined to the body. The soul also changes, through conflicting movements of the will. For Augustine, the human will finds its fullest expression in those loves which bind us to the objects of our desire on a truly personal basis. From this standpoint, a good and moral life is one which mirrors the order of reality in regard to what we love and how we pursue those ends. Augustine envisions a moral cosmos in which humans (like everything else) assume their proper place and function. Humans are well ordered when reason controls the body and its manifold desires—that is, when what is less perfect is subject to what is more perfect.[74]

Augustine's affirmation of the primacy of reason shapes his overall attitude toward created goods. When he prays at the opening of his *Confessions* (I, 1) that "our heart is restless until it rests in you," he acknowledges God as our ultimate end, since God alone can satisfy the deepest cravings within the human spirit. Mutable realities, on the other hand, are incapable of fulfilling us in any lasting sense. In this respect, the life of virtue amounts to a rightly ordered love whereby one loves created goods in the right way, attuned to the dictates of a divinely established order. What is more excellent in the hierarchy of creation must govern what is less so.[75] Conversely, moral evil (i.e., moral disorder) arises as a result of a misplaced love that elevates the things we should rightfully govern and use for the sake of a higher good to the status of ends in themselves. For this reason, corporeal things must be used for the good of the body, the body must be used for the good of the soul, and the soul or mind must be enjoyed in relation to God.[76]

CONCLUSION

Augustine's understanding of human personhood reflects a uniquely Christian perspective, but one decisively influenced by a Neoplatonic vision of reality. However, we must not overlook the impact of his Manichaean experience on the evolution of his thinking, including his anthropological theory. Augustine's intellectual outlook matured in the course of the doctrinal controversies which prompted him to clarify his own position on a wide range of topics. His anti-Manichaean polemic shaped various aspects of his philosophy and theology, including his account of creation and his response to the problem of evil. More specifically, it strengthened his conviction in the unity of the person.

The fact that Augustine had formerly endorsed a radically dualistic interpretation of human nature at least partially explains the vehemence with which he came to uphold the wholeness of our humanity, as a union *what about Pauline?*

of soul and body. Another explanation, of course, lies in his commitment to Christian teaching, and its recognition of the goodness of the body as well as the soul. But by the same token, Augustine's definitions of man would always emphasize the primacy of the soul over the body, in a manner consistent with his allegiance to Neoplatonic (and in a broader sense to Platonic) ways of thinking.

A salient feature of Augustine's anthropology is the presupposition that what is essentially human must transcend the transitory character of corporeal reality, along with the human body itself. While Augustine was committed to a unitary conception of human nature, he nonetheless defined the human being as a soul which uses a body. His reading of the "books of the Platonists" intensified his ongoing commitment to the cultivation of the life of the mind. Augustine's attribution of a divine character to the soul or mind thus reflects a metaphysical presupposition on his part that put him in direct continuity with thinkers from Parmenides and the Eleatics to Socrates, Plato, and the Neoplatonists. In this respect, Augustine equates the really and truly real with what is immaterial and unchanging. This conviction is evident in the degree to which he emphasizes the superiority of the soul and reasoning over the body and sense experience (even as he acknowledges the body's created goodness).

In Augustinian terms, soul and body are distinct realities. Still, they are by no means diametrically opposed, as the Manichaeans taught. Rather, soul and body constitute a harmonious union. In this regard, Augustine drew on the Neoplatonic notion of the soul's midrank between higher and lower reality and adapted it in the interests of his Christian anthropology. If the soul is the essence of our humanness, then we as humans have an affinity for two complementary worlds: the inner world of the mind and the outer world of sense experience. From this standpoint, both soul and body contribute to the rich multidimensional being that is the human person.

In fact, however, Augustine's recognition of humans as "persons" emerged on a gradual basis. The early Augustine was preoccupied with defining "man" (*homo*) in the broadest sense. But there is a great difference between an account of human beings as members or expressions of the human species and one that addresses their personhood. Every human being (according to Augustine's response to the question, What is man?) is a composite of soul and body. But only a person qualifies as a true individual. If a personalist transition can be detected in Augustine's thinking, it was greatly inspired by his Christological speculation. In the doctrine of hypostatic union of divinity and humanity in the person of Christ, he found the paradigm of the unity of soul and body in the human person. By virtue of this technical innovation, Augustine rendered explicit what was formerly only implicit in his anthropology: that each and every

homo vs. persona

human being is a unique individual, with a rational intellect capable of discerning truth and a rational will capable of free, morally responsible decisions.

From Augustine's Christian perspective, human individuality points to a special relationship with God as personal creator. In this respect, Augustine links the scriptural teaching that God created humans in God's own image with his Trinitarian theology and its model of divine love. This synthesis imparted a relational dimension to Augustine's understanding of human personhood: as images of God, we are called to imitate the love which lies at the heart of the Trinity. This ideal raises the bar of human affectivity to a higher plane. Animals can exhibit patterns of social organization and cooperative behavior. But humans have the capacity to love in a selfless manner. The ability to do so, however, presupposes an integrated self that can recognize the other as a being worthy of respect and the dignity of personhood in God's own image.

Augustine's anthropology also reflects an all-encompassing vision of things in which humans (like everything else) have their appropriate function. In this scheme, moral order complements cosmic order, since the good life requires an adherence to a hierarchical arrangement in which humans are subordinated to God and placed over corporeal natures for their organization and governance. Stated in other terms, moral living is a condition which reflects a proper relationship between the parts and a greater whole—that is, the totality of creation which has its beginning and end in God. Augustine's cosmic vision is thus fundamentally a teleological one. The good human life is conducive to the realization of our proper end as humans. For Augustine, we reveal our distinctively human character primarily in the way we think. But we also reveal it in our acts of willing, those free choices which shape the moral quality of our lives and solidify our relationships with God and our fellow humans.

If Augustine makes a decisive contribution to a philosophy of the human person, it lies in the degree to which he treats our minds and wills as components of a unified self that remains intact throughout the many changes, crises, successes, and disappointments that punctuate anyone's life history. Despite his emphasis on the wholeness of our personhood, however, his anthropology was decidedly intellectualist in its orientation. In keeping with his Christian Neoplatonic bent, he posited the mind as the bearer of God's image and the essence of our nature. The real lacuna here lies in an apparent failure to link this rich understanding of the person as a dynamic center of rationality and affectivity with a viable explanation of each person's individuality. But if this was a failing on Augustine's part, it was ultimately rooted in his essentialist metaphysics, an interpretation of the really real that emphasized universal natures over individual beings. The next millennium would open the way to a Christian anthropology that drew on the more versatile metaphysics of Aristotle and the possibilities it offered for an account of persons as unique and subsistent individuals in our own right.

DISCUSSION QUESTIONS

1. How did Neoplatonism provide Augustine with a means of challenging the radical dualism of Manichaeism (especially in regard to its interpretation of evil)?
2. What is the significance of Plotinus's designation of the human being as "the animate organism" or "living creature" for his interpretation of psychosomatic unity?
3. Why did the later Augustine criticize his earlier commitment to a Neoplatonic model of the relationship between soul and body (the "inner" and "outer" dimensions of human nature, respectively)?
4. What theological influences were operative in Augustine's designation of the human person as fundamentally "relational"?
5. How is Augustine's hierarchical understanding of creation reflected in his theory of the soul as occupying a middle rank between spiritual and corporeal reality?

NOTES

This chapter relies on the following translations (listed in order of appearance): Nemesius of Emesa, *On the Nature of Man,* trans. William Telfer, Library of Christian Classics, vol. 4 (Philadelphia: Westminster, 1955); Augustine, *Confessions,* trans. John K. Ryan (New York: Image/Doubleday, 1960); Plotinus, *Enneads,* trans. A. H. Armstrong, Loeb Classical Library (Cambridge: Harvard University Press; London: William Heinemann, 1978); Augustine, *The Catholic and Manichaean Ways of Life,* trans. Donald A. Gallagher and Idella Gallagher, Fathers of the Church 56 (Washington, D.C.: Catholic University of America Press, 1966); *The Magnitude of the Soul,* trans. John J. McMahon, The Fathers of the Church 2 (New York: CIMA Publishing, 1947); *City of God,* trans. Henry Bettenson (Harmondsworth, U.K.: Penguin, 1972); *On Genesis,* trans. Roland J. Teske, The Fathers of the Church 84 (Washington, D.C.: Catholic University of America Press, 1991); *Letter 137, To Volusian,* trans. Wilfrid Parsons, The Fathers of the Church 20 (New York: Fathers of the Church, 1953); *Sermon 174,* trans. Edmund Hill, *Sermons* III/5, The Works of Saint Augustine (New Rochelle, N.Y.: New City, 1992); *The Trinity,* trans. Edmund Hill, The Works of Saint Augustine, I/5 (Brooklyn, N.Y.: New City, 1991); *Arianism and Other Heresies,* trans. Roland J. Teske, The Works of Saint Augustine, I/18 (Hyde Park, N.Y.: New City, 1995).

1. Tertullian, *De Praescriptione Haereticorum* vii.
2. Cf. Romans 8.
3. 1 Corinthians 6:15.
4. *Gaudium et Spes* 14, 1.
5. Johannes Quasten, *Patrology* (Allen, Tex.: Christian Classics, 1995), 3:352. Quasten (353) bases this date on various factors, including: Nemesius refers to Eunomius and Apollinaris of Laodicea as contemporaries, he provides no indication that Origen had been formerly condemned, and he offers no references to Nestorius, Eutyches, and Pelagius.
6. Etienne Gilson, *The Spirit of Medieval Philosophy* (New York: Scribner's, 1936), 175. Nemesius's *On the Nature of Man* enjoyed a wide readership throughout the Middle Ages. In this connection, however, it was mistakenly attributed to Gregory of Nyssa and confused with Gregory's *On the Making of Man* (*De hominis opificio*).
7. *On the Nature of Man* I, 1.
8. *On the Nature of Man* I, 1.
9. *On the Nature of Man* I, 4.
10. *On the Nature of Man* I, 10.
11. *On the Nature of Man* II, 16. According to Nemesius's rendering of Aristotle (*On the Nature of Man* II, 11), the soul "is the fundamental energy possessed by a physical organic body, giving it the power to live."
12. In this vein, William Tefler (in his commentary on Nemesius's *On the Nature of Man*, II, 11, Library of Christian Classics, 4:261) offers the following assessment:

> In fact, Nemesius' own doctrine of the soul might fairly be characterized as Aristotelian. In any case, it would be unlike Nemesius, with his apologetic aim, to air a novel and unfavorable interpretation of the great philosopher, likely to rouse the opposition of his readers. We may assume that the view which he expresses was current in the Syria of his day, and we may go on to father it upon the Neo-Platonic school. Putting these facts together, we may conclude that Nemesius . . . had before his mind some recent Neo-Platonic commentary on the work of Aristotle's *On the Soul*.

13. In this connection, Stoicism also provided a philosophical touchstone for early Christian thinkers, especially in an ethical context. For a broad survey of its influence, see M. Spanneut, *Le Stoicisme des Peres de l'Eglise de Clement d'Alexandrie* (Paris, 1969).
14. *Confessions* IV, 14(21).
15. Confessions IV, 14(21).
16. *Confessions* V, 14(24). Ambrose introduced Augustine to the allegorical method of scriptural exegesis and its presupposition that the sacred text is the bearer of deeper spiritual truths which lay concealed beneath its many allegories and images.
17. *Confessions* VII, 9(13), where Augustine refers to his introduction to "certain books of the Platonists that had been translated out of Greek into Latin."
18. In the midst of this debate, we can discern a plausible hypothesis in support of the claim that the *libri platonicorum* largely encompassed the works of Plotinus, and that Plotinus's *Enneads* provide the key philosophical framework in which Augustine developed a uniquely Christian vision of reality. Early attempts to

establish parallels between Plotinus and Augustine include M. N. Bouillet, *Les Enneades de Plotin*, 3 vols. (Paris, 1857–1861); L. Grandgeorge, *Saint Augustine et le Neoplatonisme* (Paris, 1896); Prosper Alfaric, *L'Evolution intellectuelle de Saint Augustin* (Paris, 1918); Charles Boyer, *Christianisme et neoplatonisme dans la formation de Saint Augustin* (Rome, 1923); Jens Norregaard, *Augustins Bekehrung* (Tübingen, 1923). Robert J. O'Connell's many publications provide compelling evidence for the plausibility of this hypothesis. See O'Connell, *St. Augustine's Early Theory of Man, A.D. 386–391* (Cambridge: Harvard University Press, 1969); *St. Augustine's Confessions: The Odyssey of Soul* (Cambridge: Harvard University Press, 1969); *Art and Christian Intelligence in St. Augustine* (Cambridge: Harvard University Press, 1978); *The Origin of the Soul in St. Augustine's Later Works* (New York: Fordham University Press, 1987).

19. *Confessions* VII, 12(18).
20. *Confessions* VII, 13(19).
21. *Ennead* I.1(53).1.
22. *Ennead* I.1(53).2.
23. *Ennead* I.1(53).2.
24. *Ennead* I.1(53).3.
25. *Ennead* I.1(53).3.
26. *Ennead* I.1(53).3. Cf. Plato, *Phaedrus* 246C5.
27. *Ennead* I.1(53).7.
28. Porphyry, *Life of Plotinus* 2, 25–27.
29. *Ennead* III.8(30).5.
30. *Ennead* I.1(53).9.
31. *Ennead* I.1(53).9.
32. *Ennead* V.3(49).3.
33. *Ennead* II.9(33).2.
34. *Ennead* I.4(46).10.
35. *Ennead* VI.7(38).36.
36. *Ennead* I.6(1).5.
37. *Ennead* II.9(33).8.
38. *De moribus* I, 4(6).
39. *De moribus* I, 4(6).
40. *De moribus* I, 4(6).
41. *De moribus* I, 27(52).
42. *De Quantitate Animae* 13, 22.
43. *De Quantitate Animae* 34, 77.
44. *De Civitate Dei* 14, 5.
45. *De Civitate Dei* 13, 24.
46. R. A. Markus, in "Marius Victorinus and Augustine," pt. 5 of *The Cambridge History of Later Greek and Early Medieval Philosophy*, ed. A. H. Armstrong (Cambridge: Cambridge University Press, 1970), 357, acknowledges the studies of E. L. Fortin, *Christianisme et culture philosophique au cinquieme siecle* (Paris, 1959); H. Dorrie, *Porphyrios' "Symmikta Zetemata"* (Munich, 1959); and J. Pepin, "Une nouvelle source de St. Augustin," *R. Et. anc.* 66 (1964): 53–107 in support of the thesis that

"Augustine owed not only his difficulties but also his manner of solving them to the philosophical framework he adopted."

47. *De Civitate Dei* 14, 5.

48. *De Genesi contra Manichaeos* II, 7(9).

49. According to Markus, "Marius Victorinus and Augustine," 358, "Augustine . . . availed himself of a current philosophical theory for the purposes of Christological debate: he never seems to have doubted its adequacy for formulating the mode of union of soul and body in man." According to I. P. Sheldon-Williams, "The Greek Platonist Tradition from the Cappodocians to Maximus and Eriugena," pt. 6 of *The Cambridge History of Later Greek and Early Medieval Philosophy* (Cambridge: Cambridge University Press, 1970), 489, "This is suggested in Porphyry's *Quaestiones commixtae,* where he may be recording Plotinus's explanation of the association of body and soul, which in turn may have been learnt from Ammonius Saccas."

50. *On the Nature of Man* III, 22: "The Word mingles with body and soul, and yet remains unmixed, unconfused, uncorrupted, untransformed, not sharing their passivity but only their activity, not perishing with them, nor changing as they change."

51. *On the Nature of Man* III, 20.

52. *On the Nature of Man* III, 20.

53. *On the Nature of Man* III, 22.

54. *Letter* 137, 11. Augustine's use of the term *persona* in a Christological and an anthropological context must be appreciated against the background of its theological and philosophical evolution. In this connection, Kenneth L. Schmitz, "The Geography of the Human Person," *Communio* (Spring 1986): 27–48, offers an excellent survey of the history of this term, tracing it into the Christian tradition, in which he discerns its special appropriateness for application to God and the Divine Persons.

55. *Letter* 137, 11.

56. *Sermon* 174, 2. Cf. *Commentary on St. John's Gospel* 19, 5(2).

57. A. C. Lloyd, "On Augustine's Concept of a Person," in *Augustine: A Collection of Critical Essays,* ed. R. A. Markus (Garden City, N.Y.: Anchor Books/Doubleday, 1972), 191.

58. *De Trinitate* XV, 2(11). Still, Augustine is rather conservative about applying the term "person" to members of the Trinity, viewing this usage as a concession to the demands of linguistic expediency.

59. Perry J. Cahall, "Saint Augustine on Marriage and the Trinity," *Josephinum Journal of Theology* n.s. (Winter-Spring 2004): 89:

In his *De Trinitate* Augustine posits a relational quality of personhood, both human and divine, which enables human beings to understand how we ought to relate to each other in our most intimate of relationships. Augustine's concept of the relational quality of human personhood is analogous to his conception of the relations that are the divine persons of the Trinity.

60. *Collatio cum Maximino Arianorum Episcopo* 13: PL 42, 719.

61. *De Trinitate* V, 5(6).

62. *De Trinitate* VI, 1(7).

63. Robert E. Lauder, "Augustine: Illumination, Mysticism, and Person," in *Collectanea Augustinian, Augustina: Mystic and Mystagogue*, ed. Frederick Van Fleteren, Joseph C. Schnaubelt, and Joseph Reino (New York: Lang, 1994), 190:

> The most perfect expression of personal love is the Trinity. Each person is distinct yet each is identical with the divine nature. There is absolute unity and yet distinction, unity of nature and distinction of persons. The Trinity is the ideal of all personal existence: to be fully oneself, but only in dependence upon and in adherence to, another in the communion of unity,

citing Paul Henry, *Saint Augustine on Personality* (New York: Macmillan, 1960), 10. This formulation contains Augustine's doctrine of person.

64. Lauder, "Augustine: Illumination, Mysticism, and Person," 190.

65. *Confessions* VIII, 7(16).

66. *Confessions* VII, 3(5).

67. *Confessions* VIII, 8(19).

68. *Confessions* VIII, 10(23).

69. *Confessions* VIII, 10(22).

70. *De Genesi ad Litteram* VI, 12(22).

71. *De Genesi contra Manichaeos* II, 9(12).

72. *De Civitate Dei* IX, 13(3).

73. *Confessions* VII, 7(7).

74. *De libero arbitrio* I, 8(18).

75. *De Civitate Dei* XV, 22.

76. Augustine's definition of virtue as a "rightly ordered love" in the *De Civitate Dei* (XV, 22) is complemented by his distinction between the "use" *(uti)* and "enjoyment" *(frui)* of goods. This distinction provides a means of clarifying the human will's proper attitude toward created things. According to Augustine (*De Doctrina Christiana* I, 4, 4), only God can be enjoyed or loved as an absolute end; corporeal things must be used as a means to lasting happiness. From this standpoint, the good and moral life amounts to enjoying what ought to be enjoyed and using what ought to be used in a manner consistent with a rightly ordered love that "neither loves what he ought not, nor fails to love what he should" (*De Doctrina Christiana* I, 27–28).

5

St. Thomas Aquinas:
A Subsistent Individual

After celebrating mass on the Feast of St. Nicholas in the year 1273, Thomas Aquinas suspended his usual routine of writing and dictation. On that day, for all practical purposes, his life's work came to an end. As he confided to his *socius*, Reginald of Piperno, "I can write no more. All that I have written seems nothing but straw compared to what I have seen and what has been revealed to me."[1] So began his slow but steady withdrawal from worldly cares which culminated in his death the following March.

But how is his cryptic utterance to be construed, especially from one so deeply committed to the written word and intellectual pursuits? Was Thomas commenting on the futility of human efforts in the face of our supernatural destiny? Or was he exhausted by ceaseless work and ongoing controversy? These are reasonable assumptions. But in a very real sense, Aquinas's pronouncement serves as a fitting epitaph for a life devoted to the search for God and the investigation of things divine. Fitting indeed that the final chapter of his life consisted in a gradual absorption into the same mystery that was the focal point of all his speculative endeavors. Yet Aquinas's words to Reginald were by no means a devaluing of his vast literary output. Rather, they only underscored a fundamental tenet of the theological method he defined and honed to a fine art: that human reasoning, however penetrating, however efficacious in discerning truth, must ultimately give way to the higher Truth that proceeds from God alone. This centeredness on God permeates Aquinas's thought and the comprehensive vision of reality he forged through a remarkable synthesis of Christian doctrine and Aristotelianism.

A TEACHER'S LIFE

Aquinas was born at the castle of Roccasecca in the kingdom of Naples between 1224 and 1226.[2] After early studies at the Benedictine abbey of Monte Cassino, he enrolled at the University of Naples, where he was first exposed to the study of Aristotle. This put him on the cutting edge of theological and philosophical developments, in the wake of the rediscovery and gradual assimilation of Aristotle's physical, metaphysical, and ethical writings during the twelfth and thirteenth centuries.[3] At Naples Aquinas also became acquainted with the Dominicans, joining the Order of Friars Preachers in 1243 or 1244.

Aquinas's Dominican vocation would shape the great intellectual project that culminated in his monumental but unfinished *Summa Theologica.* His work with Albert the Great (at both Paris and Cologne) refined his grasp of Aristotle and profoundly influenced his development as a theologian and philosopher. Subsequently he devoted his life to an intense regimen of scholarship, writing, and teaching. After returning to Paris (where he eventually became professor of theology at the university), Thomas lectured extensively on both Scripture and Peter Lombard's *Sententia.* Paris was also the locus of his disputes with the secularists, the medieval Augustinians, and the Latin Averroists. His final years saw his return to Naples, where he established a House of Studies. En route to the Second Council of Lyon, he died on March 7, 1274, at the Cistercian monastery of Fossanuova.

Aquinas's writings reveal a passion for penetrating things in their full existential reality. He was also driven by a desire to impart what he knew and, conversely, to dispel error. He did this with a unique ability to grasp the viewpoint and mind-set of learner and adversary alike. This was a thinker who could enter into a variety of outlooks with a spirit of creativity and imagination. In the process, he adapted and reconciled traditions that others perceived as wholly irreconcilable (or, in contemporary parlance, incommensurable). His versatility and openness to truth (wherever it can be found) make him and his vision of reality perennially relevant.

AQUINAS ON *SACRA DOCTRINA*

One of the great intellectual legacies of Aquinas proceeds from his distinction between truths derived from divine revelation and those attained by the natural resources of the human intellect. By virtue of his formal distinctions between philosophy and theology (the expressions of faith and reason, respectively), he developed a self-supporting system of thought capable of engaging a wide range of intellectual perspectives by appealing to truths on which rational beings find mutual agreement. According to Aquinas, reason can indeed arrive at conclusions about God and divine matters independently of the influence of any religious tradition or divine revelation. As he affirms in the *Summa Theologica*, "the existence of God and other like truths about God, which can be known by natural reason, are not articles of faith but are preambles to the articles; for faith presupposes natural knowledge."[4]

But Aquinas also stresses that any knowledge of God based exclusively on the resources of human reason must be severely circumscribed.

> To know that God exists in a general and confused way is implanted in us by nature, inasmuch as God is man's beatitude. This, however, is not to know absolutely that God exists; just as to know that someone is approaching is not the same as to know that Peter is approaching.[5]

What, then, is the means of bridging the gap between a "general and confused" knowledge provided by natural reason and the "precise and clear" knowledge derived from a special revelation necessary for realizing our final end as humans? For Aquinas, this can only be accomplished by a sacred science *(sacra doctrina)* which allows for a knowledge of God in a manner that is both authoritative and conducive to a sense of certitude.

Aquinas by no means confines *sacra doctrina* to theological teachings impossible to establish on rational grounds. Rather, human salvation requires that "certain truths which exceed human reason should be made known by Divine revelation, . . . even those truths about God which human reason could have discovered."[6] His affirmation of the necessity of *sacra doctrina*, then, is correlative with a recognition of the limits of philosophical reasoning. Aquinas even extends this requirement to truths concerning God which reason is capable of discovering on its own.

In the final analysis, divine truths must be taught by divine revelation to ensure that our end as humans is rendered secure. Accordingly, Aquinas concludes that "it was necessary that there should be a sacred science *(sacra doctrina)* learned through revelation, besides philosophical science built up by reason."[7] Reason can indeed enhance faith as a means of explicating its contents, as a preparation for belief, or as a dialectical tool for refuting errors. Aquinas stresses that we use everything in our natural power to attain that perfection consisting in union with God.[8] But while he appeals to that natural reason "to which all are forced to give their assent," he also stresses that "in divine matters, reason has its failings."[9]

Accordingly, *Summa Theologica* (the ultimate touchstone for his discussions of the relation between faith and reason) is at base a theological endeavor. As one writer observes,

> In this compendium of theology everything is theological, even the philosophical reasoning that makes up such a large part of it. The water of

philosophy and the other secular disciplines it contains has been changed into the wine of theology.[10]

The structure of Aquinas's monumental *Summa Theologica* reflects his conception of the structure of reality as a whole. This great speculative endeavor proceeds from God to the act of creation and creatures (with a concentration on human beings) and follows humans in their return to God through moral and religious life. Aquinas thus envisions reality in terms of two complementary movements: an outgoing *(exitus)* from God and a return *(redditus)* to God, as the final end and perfection of all things. If Aquinas conceives of reality in dynamic terms, then God provides the ultimate actualizing principle. In Peter Kreeft's analogy,

> God is the ontological heart that pumps the blood of being through the arteries of creation into the body of the universe, which wears a human face, and receives it back through the veins of man's life of love and will.[11]

For this very reason, any attempt to penetrate the richness of Aquinas's anthropology must address how humans stand in relation to their creator and how they exist within the larger scheme of creation. This vision of reality presupposes a metaphysics grounded on an understanding of being as a dynamic act. As a point of departure, let us consider the main lines of that metaphysics.

A METAPHYSICS OF *ESSE*

In keeping with his commitment to Aristotelianism as his principal philosophical touchstone, Aquinas begins his metaphysical inquiry on the level of sense experience, with what is immediately accessible on a concrete level. On the basis of this empirical starting point with changing particulars, he proceeds to universal truths concerning being in general. Like Aristotle, Aquinas views substance as the irreducible referent for discussions of the really real. He likewise incorporates Aristotle's distinctions between substance and accident, form and matter, act and potency into his analysis of substantial realities. But he enriches these distinctions by means of one he considers implicit in revelation: the distinction between essence and existence—between *what a thing is* and *the fact of its being.* While Aristotle's metaphysics was preoccupied with the intelligibility of things (as revealed in form), Aquinas raised the bar of metaphysical inquiry to a new existential plane. For him, the crucial issue was not merely what things are, but why they exist at all.

In Aquinas's reckoning, Plato and Aristotle represent a watershed—a recognition of universal causes from which everything came into existence. But such a recognition is rooted in the discovery of the universality of being. From this standpoint, the claim that being is common to many distinct things presupposes that their being proceeds from the action of a cause different from themselves.[12] This contention points to Aquinas's understanding of reality in terms of a vast participation system, in which things depending on something else for their existence require a being which exists perfectly—that is, as pure act.

> There is a being that is its own being; and this comes from the fact that a being that is pure act without any composition is required. And so all other beings that are not their own being but have being by participation must proceed from that one being.[13]

A being which is pure act is a simple substance that admits no distinction between its essence (i.e., its whatness or quiddity) and the fact of its existence. As pure act, no addition can be made to its nature, since it is perfect without qualification and thus possesses perfection in the fullest manner.[14] Only such a simple being provides a means of overcoming an endless regress of causal dependence in finite things.

> Because everything that exists through another is led back to that which exists through itself as to its first cause, there must be one thing which is the cause of existence in all things because it alone is the act-of-being; otherwise there would be an infinite series of causes.[15]

The Judeo-Christian belief in God as supreme creator (or in Aristotelian terms, the efficient cause) of everything other than himself offered Aquinas an ultimate standard for explaining things in their broadest metaphysical terms. In the scriptural identification of God as I Am Who Am (Exodus 3:14), Aquinas (like other Christian thinkers) discerned a profound metaphysical import. From this standpoint, God's nature is to exist, and his essence and existence coincide. Unlike his Christian predecessors (e.g., Augustine), however, Aquinas did not designate God by means of the substantive *essentia* but by *esse*, the infinitive of the verb "to be." God is the act of being whereby finite beings exist (and continue in existence).[16]

Being is predicated of God *essentially*; being is predicated of creatures *by participation*, since they do not exist by their very nature. By extension, any perfections possessed by creatures are possessed by participation in a perfection that God is essentially.[17] In contrast to the simplicity of the divine nature (as pure *esse*), finite things are composed in two senses: first, on the basis of form and matter (i.e., their essence or what they are) and, second, on the basis of essence and existence (i.e., something which exists). In Thomistic terms, composition on both levels is found in things in a potential state.[18] On the one hand, Aquinas follows Aristotle in linking potency with matter and its capacity for formation. On the other hand, however, Aquinas binds potency inextricably to essence: since being always pertains to some thing or *ens*, its essence or nature limits and defines its being in a manner consistent with what it happens to be.

> *Esse* belongs to an utterly different order from that of essence and . . . therefore, existence is determined by something other, not as potentiality is determined by act but rather as act is determined by potentiality, and it is in this way that this existence differs from that existence, for it is the existence of this or that nature.[19]

An individual being exists to the extent that it participates in being itself *(Ipsum Esse)*. For Aquinas, things are differentiated from one another on the basis of diverse natures, not existence; conversely, different things receive existence in proportion to their natures.[20] Indeed, a rock and a human being both exist. But if human existence can be said to be richer than the existence of a rock, it is because the human being enjoys a greater aptitude for participation in *esse*. Accordingly, what is limited by the parameters of a specific essence shares in an unlimited act of existence.[21] Aquinas thereby blends the new wine of his understanding of *esse* into the framework of an Aristotelian metaphysics which had largely confined the act/potency distinction to an analysis of motion and change. In so doing, he imparts a dynamism to the notion of being that was heretofore lacking in earlier essentialist ontologies.

In Aquinas's theory of participation, what receives its being from another stands in a potential state to receive its act of being. Things are actualized or brought into being to the extent that they participate in God as the pure act of self-subsistent *esse (Ipsum Esse Subsistens)*.[22] The act of *esse*, however, participates in nothing at all, since such a reality has no potentiality whatsoever. Accordingly, God transcends any classifications that would confine God to one particular kind of existence. "What I mean by existence *(esse)* is the most perfect of all," Aquinas affirms, "and this is apparent from the fact that actuality is always more perfect than potentiality."[23]

By way of illustration, Aquinas draws on a classic Aristotelian analog: since God is self-subsisting *esse*, he lacks no perfection of being, just as something hot would possess the full perfection of heat if that heat were self-subsisting.[24] If genuine perfection presupposes something existent (rather than merely conceptual), then the supremely existent reality possesses the totality of perfections. In this respect, Aquinas (following Pseudo-Dionysius) holds that the perfections of all things preexist in God in a more excellent way.[25]

Aquinas closely links God's unqualified perfection with his role as efficient, creative cause of everything other than himself. This position draws on Aristotle's teaching (*Metaphysics* ii) that the maximum in any genus is the cause of everything in that genus.[26] God is the supreme creator of the totality of finite being, and that creaturely dependence is absolute. "At the same moment as He gives existence (*esse*)," Aquinas contends, "God makes that which receives existence."[27] If existence is always attributed to an *existent nature,* then creation encompasses both the existence and essence of a given reality.

> Since existence is attributed to the quiddity (essence), not only the existence but the very quiddity is said to be created, since it is nothing before having existence, except perhaps in the Creator's intellect, where it is not a creature but the creative essence itself.[28]

HUMAN BEINGS, BEING HUMAN

Aquinas's anthropology exhibits a skillful synthesis of insights drawn from the Bible, the teaching tradition of the Church, and explanatory principles derived from Aristotle's metaphysics, as well as Platonism, Augustinianism, and the various channels through which these sources were communicated. From this standpoint, Aquinas's anthropology is as much an amalgam of philosophical and theological reflection as other aspects of his exposition of *sacra doctrina*. Indeed, clear-cut classifications about what is exclusively philosophical or theological in his thinking miss a vital point about his overall methodology. He develops a comprehensive account of what it means to be fully human, but in a way firmly grounded in revelation, and wholly conversant with the main currents of secular wisdom. Aquinas's theories of human nature and personhood, then, are a hybrid of philosophy and theology.

Aquinas, in effect, steers a middle course between the extremes of his predecessors and contemporaries in recognizing the complementarity of soul and body—the spiritual and corporeal dimensions of human existence, respectively. In keeping with the general thrust of Pauline anthropology, Aquinas stresses a unitary conception of our humanity. On the basis of the hylomorphism he inherited from Aristotle and adapted in a Christian context, he defines humans as composites of the formal principles of the soul and the material substrate of the body. The soul is thus conjoined with the body in an inextricable union comprising one substantial reality.

But Aquinas's refined anthropological model was not merely the product of synthesizing what he found in his intellectual predecessors and his own religious tradition. It also presupposes a new metaphysical vision. This vision, as we have seen, rests on an explanation of the really real which focuses upon being or existence *(esse)* as the ultimate perfection of a given thing. In this respect, Aquinas moved beyond the limitations of the essentialist brand of metaphysics which dominates the anthropologies of Plato and Aristotle. In essentialist terms, existence presupposes *whatness*, and being is inseparable from stable, abiding natures.

In contrast to that somewhat static essentialist ontology, Aquinas defines existent reality as a dynamic act, with a range of operations appropriate to things of a certain kind. Such a rendering of the really real in existentialist terms has a direct bearing on the way Aquinas defines our humanness, or more precisely, our personhood. From a Thomistic perspective, a person is not merely a concept or theoretical construct with no grounding in objective reality. The distinctiveness of human beings among other beings is inextricably linked with a rationality that imparts them with a unique mode of existence—that is, a unique way of being appropriate to us as humans.

For Aquinas, there must be one principle of being from which all other existent reality derives its existence.[29] The diversity of created being points to the intentionality of God as first efficient cause. As creator, God brought things into being so that his goodness might be communicated to creatures in a manifold and variegated manner.[30] Humans assume a special standing in the scheme of creation as macrocosms of a whole encompassing both spiritual and corporeal substances. A wide-ranging investigation of the composite character of human beings is found in the first part of the *Summa Theologica* usually designated as the *Treatise on Human Nature* (ST Ia, Q. 75–89). The *Summa* neither encompasses all of what Aquinas has to say about the soul-body relationship nor provides his most detailed analysis of this topic. But it does offer a highly cohesive treatment of the main lines of his theory of psychosomatic unity. For the purposes of this discussion, our principal textual focus lies in questions 75–77 of this extended discussion.

The Status of the Soul

In Thomistic terms, "human nature" pertains to what we are as humans—not necessarily as individuals but as members of the human species. In this respect, Aquinas's *Treatise on Human Nature* addresses the traits that are fundamental to our humanity and that all human beings share in common. But while he upholds the psychosomatic unity of the human being, he remains faithful to the general thrust of mainstream Classical Greek and Christian anthropologies in considering humans in terms of the essence, power, and operation of the soul (and the body as it stands in relation to the soul). In this regard, his psychology closely follows Aristotle's methodology. For Aristotle and Aquinas alike, the proper point of departure in the science of living things is the science of the soul, as the principle of life common to them all.[31] Aquinas offers an etymological justification for linking of soul with life. "For we call living things *animate*," he observes, "and those things which have no life, *inanimate*."[32]

Aquinas's psychological analysis is closely aligned with his rebuttal of naturalism and its collapsing of any real distinction between soul and body (in favor of the body). In his reckoning, the ancient thinkers who espoused this position were bound by the limits of an imagination that could not rise above the corporeal. Consequently they viewed everything which exists (including the soul) in bodily terms. "For they asserted that only bodies were real things; and that what is not corporeal is nothing: hence they maintained that the soul is something corporeal."[33]

From the naturalistic standpoint, the fact that the soul is so closely conjoined with the bodies of living things presents a severe challenge to the immaterialist thesis. From the naturalistic perspective, the soul must be corporeal since it moves the body, and such a motive contact only occurs between bodies.[34] Accordingly, the naturalists of old assumed that the soul's ability to animate the body places it on an ontological par with what it animates. Like Augustine before him, Aquinas recognizes the soul's ontological distinctness from the body as an incorporeal, simple substance wholly immune to spatial limitations.[35]

But this sharp dichotomy between soul and body also poses a problem for one committed to hylomorphism. How can soul and body constitute a unified substance if the soul is an independent substance in its own right? Aquinas must now come to terms with the soul's involvement with the body in a way that upholds its essential integrity. He finds the means of resolving this dilemma in Aristotle's notion of the soul as the first actualizing principle of a body with the potentiality for life. From this standpoint, the matter of the body is related to life as potentiality to act, and the soul is the act whereby the body lives.[36] Indeed, the very characterization of living things as "animate" presupposes ensoulment. But not every principle of vital action is a soul; if it were, the eye (a principle of vision) would qualify as a soul (just as the heart is the principle of life in animals). As the first principle of life, the soul is not a body, but the act of a body in a potential state of becoming.[37]

But the soul is also the intellectual principle or mind. In this connection, Aquinas's distinction between soul and body parallels a later philosophical one between mind and body (including the brain). The importance of this latter distinction is immense, especially in a contemporary milieu which largely takes for granted the reduction of mind and mental activity to the function of the brain and neurophysiological processes. Because mind (as an incorporeal substance) operates independently of body, Aquinas designates it as something subsistent.[38] The notion of subsistence,

*subsistent: something that exists on its own /
in its own right*

as shall see, assumes a crucial role in Aquinas's theory of personhood. In that context, the term refers to something which exists on its own and in its own right, as an individual, particular being composed of soul and body. In the present context, however, Aquinas uses the term in a somewhat looser sense as a means of highlighting the independence of mind from body and its ability to engage in an operation per se—that is, to operate as the incorporeal knowing substance it is.[39]

Aquinas defends the soul's immateriality chiefly on epistemological grounds. The fact that humans can know the forms of things in general presupposes that the mind or intellectual principle can remain detached from them. "If the intellectual principle were corporeal," Aquinas argues, "it would be unable to know all bodies."[40] Strictly speaking, however, the proper objects of the mind's knowledge are not bodies themselves, but the universal forms which render things intelligible. Aquinas follows Aristotle in recognizing the isomorphism between knower and known: like grasps what is like itself. Thus the immaterial intellect grasps an immaterial form, the "thing in its nature absolutely."[41]

Once again, Aquinas must confront a problem rooted in the soul's intimate contact with the body and sense experience. To what extent does the soul's reliance on sense images for its understanding render it as corruptible as its corporeal data? This problem is a variation of the one Aquinas already addressed, namely, whether the fact of psychosomatic unity compromises the soul's integrity.[42] For Aquinas, corruption presupposes that contrariety which allows for generation and dissolution. But the soul admits no such contrariety; in the act of knowing, the intellectual principle grasps a subsistent form which never ceases to exist. The very mode of the intellect's knowing underscores its immateriality and incorruptibility.

> Everything naturally aspires to existence after its own manner. The intellect apprehends existence absolutely and for all time. Everything with an intellect naturally desires to exist always.[43]

The Composite Human

Aquinas has now presented two seemingly incompatible theses regarding the relationship between the soul and the body: first, that the soul constitutes the act of a living body and, second, that the soul is a substance in its own right. But such an incompatibility is only apparent if we construe these theses in dualistic terms. For Aquinas, the soul is a substantial reality, as the form of a certain kind of body.[44] The soul does not, in and of itself, constitute the human being. Humans are neither souls nor bodies alone but composites of both. This is the middle ground between the excesses of Platonic spiritualism and the materialism of the natural scientists. While such a unitary conception of the human being reflects Aquinas's commitment to Aristotle's hylomorphism, it finds a Christian precedent in Augustine's notion of humans as a "harmonious union" of soul and body.[45]

Aquinas firmly grounds his definition of humans in the tangible reality of the human being. The nature of the species is part and parcel of that definition, a definition that refers to real beings composed of form and matter.[46] This is a hallmark Thomistic realism, that the definition of the human species is not an idealistic abstraction devoid of content, but one rooted in what humans are in the concrete. "For it belongs to the notion of this particular man, "Aquinas says," to be composed of this soul, of this flesh, and of these bones."[47]

As the form of the body, the soul constitutes the principle of those operations appropriate to humans. If the soul is the act by which the body lives, it is also the principle of the body's nourishment, local motion, and sensation. But on a higher level, the human soul is the principle of understanding. Since form allows for differentiation between one class of things and another, the human soul (as intellectual principle) establishes rationality as the difference between humans and other life forms.[48] In this respect, however, Aquinas denies that rationality is an accidental property which one acquires such as gaining or losing weight. Rather, it runs to the very essence of the human being. "When we say that Socrates or Plato understands," Aquinas asserts, "it is ascribed to him as man, which is predicated of him essentially."[49] For this reason, Aquinas challenges those who would deny that the rational soul is the form of the body. Such reasoning flies in the face of the fact that the action of understanding is the action of a particular human being, who is conscious that he or she understands.[50]

But humans are sentient as well as intelligent beings. By extension, then, the body which allows for sensation is part of a being that is essentially rational. According to Aquinas, "The intellect by which Socrates understands is a part of Socrates, so that in some way it is united to the body of Socrates."[51] Indeed, one and the same individual is conscious that he or she understands and senses. But one cannot sense without a body. In this regard, Aquinas rejects the Platonic notion that we understand by virtue of the whole self, if the self in question is an intellectual soul alone.[52] He likewise resists any suggestion that the intellectual principle is only an instrumentality of the bodily apparatus, or that it is merely united to the body as a kind of "motor," whereby "intellect and body form one thing."[53]

This underscores the complexity of the relationship between soul and body, and the paradox that the same soul which animates the body and endows it with its range of operations can maintain its own integrity as an independent substance. In this connection, Aquinas adheres to the Aristotelian dictum that understanding is not possible through a corporeal medium (*De Anima* iii.4). Accordingly, Aquinas makes a key qualification: the *reason why* Socrates understands is not because he is moved by his intellect; rather, he is moved by his intellect because he understands.[54] We are reminded here of Socrates' extended discussion (*Phaedo* 96a–100e) of the soul as the ultimate cause of the body's life, and his accompanying refutation of the naturalists' claim that the soul is just another cause among physical causes.

But the recognition of the rational soul as an act of the body tells us something significant about the body as well. As Aquinas says, "It was necessary that the intellectual soul be united to a body fitted to be a convenient organ of sense."[55] Just as the rational soul is the appropriate form for the human body, the body (with its sensory powers) provides the suitable matter for the soul's actualizing power. By the same token, however, the body's dependence on the soul is absolute. In the absence of the soul, no part of the body retains its proper activity. For all practical purposes, the body deprived of the soul not only ceases to be living but ceases to be a human body.

Aquinas thus draws a sharp and unequivocal distinction between the soul as act and what is merely in a potential state of being. Accordingly, he deems it impossible for any accidental disposition to come between the soul and body or, more precisely, between a substantial form and its recipient matter. Indeed, the intellectual principle could not be united to the body through a corporeal intermediary, since the body has no qualitative or quantitative determination before it is imparted with actual existence by its form.[56] Herein lies the paradox and mystery of psychosomatic union: soul and body are inextricably bound together, as wax and the shape impressed on it; yet soul and body are distinct and separable.

> A thing is one as it is a being. The form itself makes a thing to be actual, since it is itself essentially an act; nor does it give existence by means of something else: the unity of a thing composed of matter and form is by virtue of the form itself, which is united to matter as its act.[57]

In Thomistic terms, only the presence of the intellectual principle (the form of the human being) accounts for the fact that you or I understand as the individuals we are. For this reason, Aquinas dismisses any suggestion that we could share a single intellect.[58] He demonstrates the impossibility of such a monopsychist thesis on purely logical grounds: if all people shared the same intellect, they would all have one formal principle, and therefore they would all be one. "If there is one intellect, no matter how diverse may be all those things of which the intellect makes use as instruments, in no way is it possible to say that Socrates and Plato are otherwise than one understanding man."[59]

Aquinas is also firm in the conviction that every human being has one and only one substantial form. The unity of substantial form is the sine qua non of the unity of the human being. From this standpoint, a multiplicity of souls presupposes a multiplicity of individuals. We could not be one individual if we lived by a vegetative soul, if we were animals by a sensitive soul, or if we were able to think and understand by a rational soul.[60] In this respect, Aquinas adopts the Aristotelian dictum that the powers of lower souls (i.e., the vegetative and sensitive souls) are *virtually present* in the rational soul. Life is understood in terms of an ascending hierarchy, in which lower and less perfect life forms are subsumed by and incorporated into superior and more perfect forms. For this reason, Aquinas views the substantial form as perfecting the whole, as well as each part of that whole.[61]

For all practical purposes, then, the rational, sensitive, and nutritive (or vegetative) souls are numerically one soul in humans. Because the rational soul possesses whatever belongs to the sensitive soul of brute animals and the nutritive soul of plants, the rational soul is united to an appropriate body and thereby endowed with the power of sensation and feeling.[62] A single human being can engage in reasoning, growth, and sensation simultaneously. The soul depends on the body to the extent that the body serves as its instrumentality in the world of experience, and the body depends on the soul as its principle of life and movement.

The Powers of the Soul

In addition to the intellect, the other defining faculty or power of the human composite is the will. In contrast to the sensitive appetite (which desires the particular objects of sensations), the will desires the good in general.[63] Freedom is bound up with the will and proceeds from rationality (as borne out by our ability to make unconstrained, deliberative judgments).[64] As act in relation to the potentiality of the body, the soul is separable from the body and the operations rooted in our corporeality.

> The human soul is the highest and noblest of forms. Wherefore it excels corporeal matter in its power by the fact that it has an operation and a power in which corporeal matter has no share whatever. This power is called the intellect.[65]

The composite character of human nature dictates the multiple and variegated range of the soul's powers and operations. If powers are related to the soul, it is because the soul is their cause or principle, not necessarily their subject.[66] While some operations of the soul (e.g., understanding and willing) are performed without the body (and corporeal organs), others (e.g., sensation) have the composite human being as their subject. But whether the subject of a power is the soul alone or the composite, Aquinas traces all of the soul's powers to its own essence or nature as their cause.[67] For this reason, he stresses the difference between what the soul is as act or principle and the activities it causes. God's essence, in contrast, is pure simplicity; as such, there can be no power or action in addition to God's nature as self-subsisting *esse*.[68]

But a multiplicity of powers in no way impinges on the soul's unity. Aquinas reasons that a number of things must proceed from one thing in a certain order.[69] Accordingly, he envisions an order among the powers of the soul modeled on Aristotle's comparison (*De Anima* ii.3) between the soul's powers and geometrical figures, as a pentagon contains and surpasses what is found in a tetragon. In Aquinas's adaptation of this Aristotelian motif, the dependence of one power on another is analyzed in terms of two types of order: the order of nature and the order of generation and time.[70]

In the order of nature, what is perfect is ontologically prior to what is imperfect; by extension, the powers of the intellect are prior to the sensitive powers they direct, and the sensitive powers are prior to the nutritive or vegetative powers. The order of generation and time, however, entails a reversal of relationships. In this case, a thing attains a higher degree of perfection on the basis of what is imperfect. This order reflects the ascending gradation of life forms, whereby the powers of the nutritive soul find completion in the powers of the sensitive soul, and the sensitive powers find completion in the intellectual powers of the rational soul. From this standpoint, the foundational principles of life lay the groundwork for more sophisticated psychic activities that reach their zenith in the rational soul, the substantial form of human beings.

THE FACT OF PSYCHOSOMATIC UNION

By means of his creative adaptation of Aristotelian principles, Aquinas overcame the deficiencies of earlier Christian anthropologies that displayed an excessive spiritualism or naive materialism regarding human nature. Aquinas stresses a genuinely unitary conception of human nature. Soul and body require each other: the soul depends on the body as its instrumentality in the world, and the body depends on the soul as its principle of life and activity. As the form of the body, the soul must be simultaneously present to the whole body and to each of its parts. As the intellectual principle, the rational human soul raises all of the activities of human life (including those we share in common with plants and animals) to a higher plane.

In the final analysis, the ultimate evidence of the union of soul and body is our own consciousness of self as an integral whole. Mind has an impact on our physical constitution, and conversely the body influences our mental life. Assertions like "I don't feel well" or "This is the happiest day of my life" encompass both mental and physical states. But by the same token, this sense of interaction is not always so apparent. Occasionally we can attain such levels of concentration that we seem to detach ourselves from our bodies. Likewise, a bad case of the flu can magnify an awareness of our bodies to the extent that they feel like something alien in relation to our normal sense of self.

Aquinas's anthropology addresses these seemingly paradoxical features of self-awareness. On the one hand, he localizes the nutritive and sensitive powers of the soul in the composite substance, since such powers must involve our physiological apparatus. But operations like understanding and willing do not require corporeal organs, at least not in regard to the operations themselves. This is when the soul reveals its status as a form separate from the body—that is, as a subsistent, immaterial substance. Soul assumes a causal role, as the basis of the composite's life, structure, and very being. More precisely, the rational soul is the act of an appropriate body with the capacity to exist and function in a uniquely human manner.

Aquinas's understanding of the human being as a composite of soul and body correlates with the assumption that everyone possesses a personal identity over their lifetime and beyond. But personal identity cannot be based on the continuity of self-awareness alone. For Aquinas, it is rooted in an enduring human nature that persists in the midst of the accidental changes flowing from the substantial union of soul and body. This is why humans require a metaphysical explanation that is more encompassing and penetrating than any scientific account of biological or biochemical processes. From this standpoint, what we observe regarding human nature reveals something not completely susceptible to empirical verification. Even empirical science must acknowledge that the observable features of human life require some explanatory principle capable of coordinating our growth and development for the good of the organism as a whole.

In contemporary terms, Aquinas's understanding of humans as substantial unities of soul and body implies that the soul (as an act of the human composite) cannot be confined to (or localized in) some part of the body (e.g., the brain) or bound up exclusively with physiological processes (e.g., brain wave activity, consciousness, or receptivity to feelings of pleasure or pain). For him, however, rationality (the most salient expression of the rational soul) defines the parameters of our humanity. In this regard, rationality is not viewed as a behavioral characteristic (or in

Aristotelian terms, an accidental property). Rather, it assumes a definitional significance, as a means of designating those who are spiritual and intellectual beings *by their very nature,* regardless of the quality of their rational output. Aquinas by no means views rationality in the exclusionary sense of contemporary thought, whereby one who lacks the complete use of reason is somehow barred from the moral community and emptied of intrinsic value. One cannot lose what one is by definition as a human being.

AQUINAS'S METAPHYSICS OF PERSONHOOD

The special dignity of the human being, then, is not rooted in rationality as such but in the rational soul. In contrast to material things, the rational soul possesses a special aptitude for being that it communicates to the body, as act to potency.[71] For this reason, Aquinas posits a metaphysical foundation of human beings derived from that enduring mode of subsistence rooted in the soul's own spirituality. But by acknowledging the composite character of human nature, Aquinas implicitly recognizes humans as multidimensional beings that integrate a penetrating inner life with a rich bodily existence. This integrative capacity points to the notion of humans as persons, a notion that says something significant about us on two levels. On the one hand, it affirms that we are unique beings unto ourselves, separate from other humans, even as we share a common humanity. On the other hand, it affirms that we are fundamentally relational beings, finding our fulfillment through interpersonal relationships.

Trinitarian and Christological Background

Interestingly, Aquinas's most explicit discussion of personhood in the *Summa Theologica* does not emerge in his *Treatise on Human Nature.* Rather, it unfolds in the course of his treatment of the Trinity and his analysis of the relations between the Persons of the Trinity. Aquinas adopts the major thrust of Augustine's approach to the question as to whether there are relations in God. For both thinkers, the very notion of Trinitarian processions presupposes real relations in the divine nature. As Aquinas says, "Relations exist in God really."[72]

But does the term "person" in a Trinitarian context properly speak of God or an individual member of the Trinity? The answer, of course, is both. In Aquinas's formulation, a Divine Person signifies a relation as subsisting—that is, a hypostasis subsisting in the divine nature.[73] What subsists in the divine nature, however, is the divine nature itself. In Aquinas's rendering, "relation really existing in God is really the same as his essence; and only differs in its mode of intelligibility."[74] We can say, then, that the divine nature subsists in each Person of the Trinity. "There must be real distinction in God," Aquinas affirms, "according to that which is relative."[75]

On the basis of this Trinitarian analysis, Aquinas reasons that the term "person" signifies relation. For example, the procession of the Son (the Second Person) from the Father (the First Person) places the Son in relation to the Father, and vice versa. But by the same token, Aquinas (following Boethius's formulation in *De Duabis Naturis* 4) contends that in its most general sense, person "signifies the individual substance of a rational nature."[76] We can say, then, that the divine nature subsists in each of the Divine Persons (each of which is distinct, yet one God). In this sense, the person of Christ constitutes an eternally subsisting subject that is both distinct as an individual and one with the Godhead. As such, the person of Christ also provides the nexus for the union of divinity and humanity, God and man.

"The true Divine nature is united with a true human nature," Aquinas holds, "not simply in the person, but in the ontological subject or hypostasis."[77] In this respect, his position on the Incarnation is wholly consistent with the orthodox teaching propounded by the Council of Chalcedon (A.D. 451). Any consideration of the infinite disparity between Christ's divine and human natures thus becomes a moot point, since they are conjoined in one ontological subject.[78] Aquinas, however, is careful to stress that the hypostatic union of God and man in Christ is neither in any specific nature (whether Divine or human), nor in some accidental attribute of the God-man. Aquinas opts for a third option, namely, a union "mid-way, in a subsistence or hypostasis."[79] In this context, "subsistence" or "hypostasis" is synonymous with "person." As a unified person, Christ encompasses a complete human nature (consisting of a soul and body). But this full human nature does not constitute the person of Christ in its own right; rather, the composite of soul and body is united to the person of the Word of God.[80]

Like Augustine, then, Aquinas refined his understanding of human personhood in the course of theological deliberations on the Trinity and the Incarnation. By means of these theological touchstones, Aquinas developed a refined personalism that takes into account both our relationality and our distinctness as unique individuals. In this respect, the personhood of Christ offers a perennially compelling model for coming to terms with the human person as a dynamic center of psychological and bodily experience. But whether we define our personhood in terms of our individual uniqueness or our relation to a community of other persons, a question must be addressed: what provides its metaphysical foundation? If personhood is more than a semantical or theoretical construct, then we require a viable explanation grounded in the reality of our human experience.

Subsistence and the Person

Aquinas's metaphysical analysis begins with a discussion of substance as the basis of individuality. In its broadest terms, a substance is an individual thing. On a higher level, what is particular and individual is found in rational substances capable of self-determination.[81] Such rational substances are designated as "persons." For this reason, Aquinas links the notion of individualized substance with the definition of the person, along with the qualifying phrase supplied by Boethius, "rational nature." As Aquinas contends, the term "individual" is included in the definition of the person to signify a special mode of subsistence proper to particular things or substances.[82]

Boethius's definition, as we have seen, emphasizes individuality and rationality. For Aquinas, however, that definition exhibits a potential ambiguity, since *substantia* can refer to an individual within a species or a genus or species itself. This critique reflects an understanding of the diverse meanings of substance derived from Aristotle's distinction (*Meta* V) between "the quiddity of a thing, designated by its definition" and a "subject or *suppositum*, which subsists in the genus of substance."[83] The distinction is crucial, since it underscores the difference between a mere concept and a concrete, real thing. From Aquinas's standpoint, Boethius's definition of the person as "the individual substance of a rational nature" might well refer to the definition of humans alone, rather than to the human substance in its primary sense—that is, a subsistent reality in its own right.

> What is composed of this form has the nature of . . . person. For soul, flesh, and bone belong to the nature of man; whereas this soul, this flesh, and this bone belong to the nature of this man.[84]

Accordingly, Aquinas refines Boethius's definition along these lines: "A person is a *subsistent individual* in a rational nature."[85] The designation of the individual as "subsistent" is crucial in this context, since it underscores the fact that it exists in itself and not in another (as an accidental characteristic)—that is, a subject of which characteristics and activities are attributed. "The individual substance, which is included in the definition of a person," Aquinas maintains, "implies a complete substance subsisting of itself and separate from all else."[86] From Aquinas's perspective, a rational nature encompasses an individual composed of a soul and a body with potentialities receptive to that actualizing principle. In broader metaphysical terms, however, the presence of the soul (as the formal cause of our rationality) presupposes an act of being or *esse* that constitutes the very core of our personhood, and the basis of any claim we have to individual uniqueness.

Person in any nature signifies what is distinct in that nature: thus in human nature it signifies this flesh, these bones, and this soul, which are the individuating principles of a man, and which, though not belonging to person in general, nevertheless do belong to the meaning of a particular human person.[87]

The Primacy of *Esse*

Thomistic personhood thus comprises the spiritual dimension of the rational soul, the corporeal dimension of a human body, and the metaphysical dimension of being or *esse*. By virtue of this multidimensionality, the person is the ontological center of a whole range of operations. Indeed, the rational soul not only gives rise to cognitive activity but provides for the distinct way of existing proper to us as humans on an intellectual, sensory, and nutritive level. "Unity of person requires unity of the complete and personal being," Aquinas contends, "but operation is an effect of the person by reason of a form or nature."[88]

While human personhood is bound up with a variety of actions involving mind and body alike, Aquinas' definition does not focus on any specific activity or capacity for action, but on the primacy of *esse*. In fact, human actions would have neither cause nor referent in the absence of a stable, abiding self rooted in our very mode of being. Aquinas's commitment to the primacy of *esse*, then, allows for an adequate recognition of the importance of actions in human life, while providing a means of unifying and stabilizing these behavioral features. Just as the rational soul is the formal cause whereby one is a person, *esse* is the ultimate act of a human nature in a state of potency to this higher active principle.[89] In this respect, Aquinas depicts the human person as a dynamic being that actualizes the potentiality for certain operations unique to his or her own existence.

Aquinas's theory of personhood thus presupposes the metaphysical primacy of being in any given thing. From this standpoint, our very designation as "human beings" is charged with an ontological significance. As Horst Seidl observes, both metaphysical principles (i.e., *essentia* and *esse*) fulfill a foundational role, albeit in different ways and for different reasons.

> Since *esse* is related to the nature as act to potency, and since act is prior and more perfect than potency, the highest constitutive feature of the person must be *esse*. Essence is a potential principle to *esse* which it receives from a first causal source as actuality and ultimate perfection. But essence is a real perfection in every being and can be said to cause a person's *esse*.[90]

THE PERSON AS FREE AGENT

Although human personhood is bound up with action (including consciousness of oneself and others), human actions would have neither a
cause nor a referent in the absence of a stable, abiding self that is rooted
in the person's very being. This is not to deny the relationship between
our rational nature and the actions and behavioral traits that attest to our
rationality. As already observed, Aquinas specifies self-determination
through rational choices as the mark of that exalted substance we designate as a person. Self-determination underscores the person's freedom to
act and make deliberative judgments.

Aquinas's treatment of human freedom unfolds against the background of his analysis of necessity (i.e., what must be the case) and what
impinges on the will's ability to choose. For him, free choice implies a lack
of coercion; conversely, what is coerced cannot be considered voluntary.
The necessity imposed by coercion, then, is diametrically opposed to voluntary action. But necessity arises in a number of contexts, not all of
which are relevant to the notion of freedom. On the one hand, what is necessary can be dictated by an intrinsic principle—what is part and parcel
of something's very constitution, either on a material level (whereby, for
instance, bodily things must be corruptible) or on a formal level (whereby
certain mathematical truths carry a necessity of their own).[91] But Aquinas
does not view this type of necessity as relevant to considerations of the
human will. Rather, he looks to the necessity that is dictated by something
extrinsic to the one who wills, in either the end or the agent. In the former
case, the end cannot be attained without the fulfillment of a certain condition (e.g., food is necessary to sustain life); in the latter case, a necessity
is imposed by an agent when that agent forces one to act against one's
will. Because Aquinas views such necessity by coercion as wholly at odds
with the inclination of the will, he denies the possibility of someone being
absolutely coerced and capable of voluntary action simultaneously.

Aquinas posits an extremely close link between the operations of will
and intellect that reflect his overall emphasis on psychosomatic unity. In
these defining powers of the person, he discerns a reciprocal relationship:
intellect moves the will as an end by presenting a good as the will's object; will, in turn, moves the intellect as an agent which moves all the powers of the soul to their appropriate good.[92] Still, Aquinas allows for a qualitative distinction between these defining powers of personhood based on
their respective objects. In one sense, he places intellect at a higher level,
since its objects are simpler and more absolute than those of the will. But
Aquinas also acknowledges that the will "is sometimes higher than the intellect," since the will inclines us toward a specific good that can transcend the human intellect in its excellence.[93] While the intellect grasps

truth within the parameters of its finite nature, the will is directed toward the good in things themselves.

To a certain extent, will is indistinguishable from free will for Aquinas, since they constitute different acts belonging to a common power.[94] But while he treats the will in relation to the end of human striving in general, he places free will squarely in a practical moral context, as the basis of our choice of the means to a given end (or the choice between two or more competing ends). More specifically, free will is the human capacity for rational judgment, "the principle of the act by which man judges freely."[95] This is what distinguishes us from natural objects (which respond to physical laws) and brute animals (which act in response to the dictates of natural instinct).

> Man acts from judgment, because by his apprehensive power he judges that something should be avoided or sought. But because this judgment, in the case of some particular act, is not from a natural instinct, but from some act of comparison in the reason, therefore he acts from free judgment and retains the power of being inclined to various things.[96]

The kinship between will and intellect could not be more apparent. Indeed, if an act of will is free, it is only because it involves a judgment. But judgment presupposes an ability to engage in comparative valuations about the goods to which the will is inclined and, ultimately, to opt for one good or course of action over its competitors. As an appetitive power, free will affords us the ability to approach goods in a selective manner, choosing one while rejecting others. Free will, however, is an appetitive power under rational guidance.[97]

To what extent is the will moved of necessity to its object? In regard to the exercise of its own act, we must remember, Aquinas contends that no object can necessarily move the will.[98] One may coerce another to do something at gunpoint; but one may never coerce another to do so *willingly*. As Aquinas puts it, "It is in man's power not to think of it, and thus, not to will it actually."[99] But in regard to the influence of an object on the act of willing, Aquinas reaches a different conclusion: in this case the will can be moved to an object necessarily. Such an object, however, must be compelling and desirable enough to command the will's allegiance without vitiating its integrity. "If the will is offered an object which is good universally and from every point of view," Aquinas asserts, "the will tends to it of necessity."[100]

Herein lies the dividing line between something good "universally and from every point of view" and one not so: the latter good simply cannot command the will's undivided allegiance, and thus it can be regarded as a nongood (at least in the context of a given decision). The former good, on the other hand, carries something of a paradox into the act of volition,

since it is so desirable in itself that "the will cannot not will it."[101] Aquinas
defines this unqualified good as happiness, the end to which the will necessarily adheres.[102] From Aquinas's Christian perspective, however, human happiness can only be understood in terms of a supernatural referent. Accordingly, he draws a analogy between our necessary desire for
happiness and the necessary adherence to God by the will that sees God
in his essence.[103] God alone can be the basis of our happiness, since only
God can fulfill beings that are composites of a body and a soul with a capacity for an infinite good. From this standpoint, Aquinas deems the love
of God through the will better than the knowledge of God through the intellect.[104]

The will's necessary inclination to God as the universal good points to
its status as a finite, created good. In Thomistic terms, the human will is
moved by God precisely because it is in a state of potentiality in relation
to the ultimate act of being, goodness, and every other perfection to which
we can aspire. God alone moves the will sufficiently and efficaciously to
its object.[105] First, God moves the will as its Summum Bonum, the most
desirable object of its attention. Second, God moves the will as the cause
of its very power of willing. Such a causal influence involves no constraint
but works by virtue of an interior inclination, from within the will itself,
in a manner consistent with its own free choice.[106]

Here lies the heart of Aquinas's account of human freedom: the human
will possesses a capacity for something beyond itself (and beyond the categories of being), meaning that it is not moved by any finite good of necessity.[107] Finite goods, in contrast, can always be regarded as nongoods.
Accordingly, they can be approached from various perspectives and levels of analysis. In the process, the rational agent has the freedom to assess
them in light of a greater good, namely, the happy life and the cluster of
intrinsic goods that support it. By virtue of this eudaimonistic standard,
finite goods can never motivate us of necessity.

> If the good is such that it is not found to be good in all respects, it will not
> necessarily move even with regard to determining the act, because even
> when considering it, someone can will its opposite, since perhaps that oppo-
> site good is suitable in some respect.[108]

A concrete illustration might be helpful here: an avid pipe smoker re-
linquishes what he perceived as a pleasurable activity due to a heightened
awareness of its health risks. In Thomistic terms, a judgmental process set
in, whereby the pleasures of pipe smoking were evaluated against the
greater good of health and long-range happiness. On the basis of such a
comparative assessment, the good of pipe smoking came to appear not
only as a nongood but even as something bad. The measure of our sub-

ject's freedom lay in his ability to engage in just such an assessment; by virtue of this evaluation, he demonstrated the fact that he was not bound to the particular good, no matter how appealing it was (and remained) to him. And when he was tempted to resume that practice, this standard would continue to influence his volitional power. Clearly we do not arrive at such decisions by means of a neat, step-by-step process. What Aquinas offers is something of a paradigm for the rational agent's struggle with alternative courses of action in coming to a decisive choice.[109]

In the final analysis, Aquinas's theory of human freedom reveals an intellectualist emphasis more consistent with a Platonic or Neoplatonic perspective than with an exclusively Aristotelian one. Only our rational apprehension of an unqualified good, however vague, frees us from a necessary attachment to any finite good. Aquinas's assumption that something good in every respect would necessarily move our will presupposes a prior intellectual grasp of that unqualified good conducive to an indifference of judgment toward everything falling short of this ideal.[110] From this standpoint, our will is more than just the expression of desire. According to one commentator, Aquinas finds the roots of human liberty "in man's rational nature, since his intellect knows the universal meaning of value, and cannot be determined in its judgments to limited and imperfect goods."[111] Aquinas defines the will (and more specifically the free will) as a rational appetite consistent with the rationality rooted in the human soul. For him, willing in a uniquely human way is to will under the guidance of reason toward ends we discern as good and instrumental to our ultimate end of happiness.

CONCLUSION

Aristotle's philosophy of nature and hylomorphism provided the general framework in which Aquinas came to terms with the human phenomenon in all its complexity. In this respect, he analyzes the human being in the manner of any substantial reality. For Aquinas, however, a substance (especially the human substance) is more than just an instance of intelligibility: it is an existent thing, comprising an essence composed of form and matter, and an act of *esse* which is limited according to a given nature. From this standpoint, the crucial metaphysical question is no longer What is it? but Why does it exist? Things exist because they have a potentiality for existence in relation to God, as the ultimate act of self-subsistent *esse*. This same level of metaphysical analysis is applicable to the human being. In Thomistic terms, humans enjoy a unique mode of existing that is inextricably linked with their rational nature.

While Aquinas upholds the complementarity of soul and body as the basic constituents of human nature, his anthropology is still heavily soul centered. He consistently emphasizes the independence of soul (as a subsistent reality) from body and its limitations. But if the soul is independent of the body, it is only as the body's first actualizing principle. First and foremost, the soul is the principle of intellectual activity. But even an operation which seems so remote from sense experience must still draw on the sensory apparatus for the formation of its concepts, the means to knowledge. Accordingly, rationality and sense experience work closely in conjunction.

But Aquinas's Christian commitment to the soul's immortality poses a challenge to his philosophical commitment to a unitary conception of human nature. How does he account for the continuity of personal identity once the soul is separated from the body at death? Aquinas was thus left to struggle with the nebulous notion of a "separated," disembodied soul existing in a state that can only be characterized as "unnatural" in respect to the dictates of his metaphysics and epistemology.[112] Aquinas addresses the problem along these lines. While the soul's nature always remains the same, it has one mode of existence in the body, and another mode of existence apart from it (i.e., a mode of understanding directed toward simple intelligible objects). Although it is as natural for the soul to understand by turning toward phantasms as to be conjoined with the body, it is not natural for it to exist in a separated state.

But why would God not have ordered the soul's nature so that it would be directed toward the understanding of intelligible reality on its own? Because if God had willed human souls to understand in the same way as separate substances, human knowledge would be confused and general; in order for human souls to possess perfect and proper knowledge, their nature must be united with bodies that allow for a grasp of sense realities from the realities themselves.[113] Once separated from the body, the soul no longer understands by turning to phantasms, but by turning to simple, intelligible objects. In this connection, Aquinas contrasts the knowledge of separated souls and angelic intelligences. The former only grasp the singulars to which they are determined by the knowledge they acquired in this life or by some affection, natural aptitude, or disposition of the divine order. The latter, on the other hand, know the specific nature of things as well as the singulars contained in those species.[114] Thus the knowledge acquired in this life does not remain in the separated soul in respect to the sensitive powers, but only in respect to what belongs to the intellect in the absence of the senses. The separated soul can understand what it did when embodied, but in a mode suited to its existence apart from the body.[115]

In regard to the present life, then, Aquinas emphasizes that we understand by means of the rational soul, and this intellection necessarily includes the body. From this standpoint, all psychic powers and operations (including those which rely on the body for their expression) presuppose one soul or, more precisely, one substantial form. Only the unity of substantial form ensures the unity of the self. We do not speak of a "self" in abstract or generic terms, the way we speak of "human nature" in reference to what all humans possess by virtue of their humanity. The notion of a distinct self implies personhood, based on the subsistence rooted in the rational soul. This allows for the individual uniqueness of each human being, even as we participate in a community of beings whose beginning and end is God.

While the soul is the primary metaphysical principle of the essence of human nature (as the principle of life, movement, and every other power), being or *esse* provides the constitutive element of the person and a way of being appropriate to members of the human species. Aquinas's metaphysics of *esse*, in effect, takes Aristotle's entelechism to a new ontological plane. The ascending hierarchy of living realities must be understood in terms of a broader hierarchy of existent realities, extending from God to inanimate material things. Accordingly, being itself exhibits a gradation of perfection in relation to God as the ultimate standard of being. In this case, the human person represents the zenith in the hierarchy of finite being as a substance in the most exalted sense: a rational, self-reflective being capable of self-determination through intelligent choices. For Aquinas, therefore, our rationality runs to the very core of our being, shaping and guiding everything we do as humans.

If Aquinas attributes an intrinsic value and dignity to the person, it is because his anthropology possesses a firm metaphysical grounding. From this standpoint, the person participates in a hierarchy of being in which God provides the first cause and final end of everything which exists. Persons assume a privileged status by virtue of their relation to God as creatures in his image and likeness. As the Christian philosopher par excellence, Aquinas recasts the scriptural language of "image and likeness" in the context of his notion of persons (and indeed all finite being) as analogs of their creator. A thinker as deeply versed as Aquinas in the teachings of Judeo-Christian revelation could not help being influenced by the sentiments of the Psalmist: "You have made him a little less than a god; with glory and honor you crowned him, gave him power over the works of your hand, put all things under his feet" (Ps. 8). This is why Aquinas can confidently say that "person signifies what is most perfect in all nature—that is, a subsistent individual of a rational nature."[116] Humans differ from other finite creatures to the extent that they are able to internalize reality through their intellect and even grasp something of the infinite majesty of God.

But by the same token, definitions of personhood in terms of a single attribute, activity, or capability (e.g., consciousness or reasoning) flies in the face of the multidimensionality which is part and parcel of personal being. The very attempt to do so abdicates the ontological core and center which renders human activities intelligible. Aquinas's anthropology thus provides an effective philosophical lens through which the profundity of the person comes into sharp focus. By the same token, this anthropology provides an illuminating critical referent against which we can assess the modern philosophical dichotomizing of the person in favor of mind at the expense of the body, or vice versa. In the face of such a dualistic tendency, Aquinas assists us in recapturing our appreciation of the unity of the self as an integrated, whole being.

DISCUSSION QUESTIONS

1. Discuss why Aquinas contends that humans have but one soul or substantial form.
2. Why does Aquinas teach that the notion of person refers to what is most perfect in the whole of nature?
3. Discuss the significance of Aquinas's definition of the person as a "subsistent reality in a rational nature."
4. Why does Aquinas's theory of human freedom presuppose some sense on our part of what he describes as an absolute, "unqualified" good?
5. Why does Aquinas view being *(esse)* rather than form as the core perfection in the person and in reality generally?

NOTES

This chapter draws on the following translations of Aquinas's writings: *Summa Theologica* in 3 vols., trans. Fathers of the English Dominican Province (New York: Benziger, 1947). All references to the *Summa Theologica* are abbreviated as ST. *Summa Theologica,* vol. 6 (Ia.27–32), Blackfriars ed. (New York: McGraw-Hill; London: Eyre & Spottiswoode, 1965). *An Aquinas Reader,* ed. and trans. Mary T. Clark (New York: Fordham University Press, 2000). Each citation of a specific work of Aquinas is followed by the pertinent page number of this anthology in parentheses.

1. Quoted in Josep Pieper, *The Silence of St. Thomas* (New York: Pantheon, 1957), 40.
2. For this brief biographical sketch, I draw on the account provided by Brian Davies, *The Thought of Thomas Aquinas* (Oxford: Oxford University Press, 1993), 1–10.
3. Aristotle was assimilated by the West in several stages, spanning some eight centuries. The first stage (c. fifth century) encompassed Aristotle's logical trea-

tises; the second stage (twelfth century) marked the entry of his writings on epistemology and scientific demonstration; the final stage (second half of the twelfth and early thirteenth centuries) brought his metaphysical, ethical, and psychological treatises.

4. ST Ia, Q. 2, a. 2, ad. 1.

5. ST Ia, Q. 2, a. 1, ad. 1.

6. ST Ia, Q. 1, a. 1.

7. ST Ia, Q. 1, a. 1.

8. *Commentary on Boethius' "De Trinitate"* Q. 2, a. 1, ad. 1.

9. *Summa Contra Gentiles*, trans. Anton C. Pegis (Notre Dame, Ind.: University of Notre Dame Press, 1975), I, 2–3.

10. Armand Mauer, *Introduction to Faith, Reason, and Theology: Questions I–IV of Aquinas' Commentary of the "De Trinitate" of Boethius* (Toronto: Pontifical Institute of Medieval Studies, 1987), xiv.

11. Peter Kreeft, introduction to *A Summa of the Summa* (San Francisco: Ignatius, 1990), 15.

12. *On the Power of God*, Q. 3, a. 5 (Clark, 62–63).

13. *On the Power of God*, Q. 3, a. 5 (Clark, 62–63).

14. *On Being and Essence*, c. 5 (Clark, 69–70).

15. *On Being and Essence*, c. 14 (Clark, 65).

16. *Compendium of Theology*, c. 11 (Clark, 79).

17. *Debated Questions* II, q. 2, a. 3 (Clark, 73).

18. *Summa Contra Gentiles* II, 54 (Clark, 68).

19. *On the Power of God*, q. 7, a. 2, ad. 9 (Clark, 66).

20. *Summa Contra Gentiles* I, 26 (Clark, 81).

21. *Commentary on Boethius' "Goodness of Substances"* I, 2 (Clark, 75).

22. *On Spiritual Creatures*, a. 1 (Clark, 72).

23. *On the Power of God*, q. 7, a. 2, ad. 9 (Clark, 66).

24. ST Ia, Q. 4, a. 2 (Clark, 78).

25. ST Ia, Q. 4, a. 2 (Clark, 77). Cf. Pseudo-Dionysius, *On the Divine Names* V: "God in His existence preposseses all things."

26. *On Separated Substances*, c. 3, 15–16 (Clark, 79).

27. *On the Power of God*, q. 3, a. 3, ad. 17.

28. *On the Power of God*, q. 3, a. 3, ad. 2.

29. ST Ia, Q. 65, a. 1.

30. ST Ia, Q. 47, a. 1.

31. *Commentary on the Soul* I, lec. 1. At ST Ia, Q. 18, a. 2, Aquinas designates "life" as the word used in reference to the visible attribute of self-movement; more precisely, "life" specifies a nature empowered to move itself or give itself any impulse to action.

32. ST Ia, Q. 75, a. 1.

33. ST Ia, Q. 75, a. 1.

34. ST Ia, Q. 75, a. 1, Obj. 3.

35. ST Ia, Q. 75, a. 1. Cf. St. Augustine, *De Trinitate* VI, 6.

36. *Commentary on the Soul* II, lec. 1.

37. ST Ia, 75, a. 1.

38. ST Ia, Q. 75, a. 2.

39. ST Ia, Q. 75, a. 2.

40. ST Ia, Q. 75, a. 2.

41. ST Ia, Q. 75, a. 5.

42. Cf. ST Ia, Q. 75, a. 1.

43. ST Ia, Q. 75, a. 6. Cf., *Summa Contra Gentiles* I, 19, where Aquinas inserts this creaturely aspiration to exist within the framework of his metaphysics of participation: since all things exist to the extent that they share in God's self-subsistent *esse*, all things desire to be like God as their final end. Accordingly, to become like God is the ultimate goal and completion of all things (*Summa contra Gentiles* II, 20).

44. *Commentary on the Soul* II, lec. 1.

45. ST Ia, Q. 75, a. 4. Cf. St. Augustine, *De Civitate Dei* 19.3.

46. ST Ia, Q. 75, a. 4.

47. ST Ia, Q. 75, a. 4.

48. Cf. Aristotle, *Metaphysics* viii.

49. ST Ia, Q. 76, a. 1.

50. ST Ia, Q. 76, a. 1.

51. ST Ia, Q. 76, a. 1.

52. ST Ia, Q. 76, a. 1.

53. ST Ia, Q. 76, a. 1.

54. ST Ia, Q. 76, a. 1.

55. ST Ia, Q. 76, a. 5.

56. ST Ia, Q. 76, a. 6.

57. ST Ia, Q. 76, a. 7.

58. Aristotle's *De Anima* (III.5) leaves open the question as to whether the active intellect assumes an integrity and immortality as the intellect of you or me, or whether it is merely a participant in a higher, universal intellect. During the Middle Ages, this issue became closely connected with discussions of divine illumination. The notion that the human intellect is illumined by a divine mind was a prominent feature of medieval Islamic philosophy. For Alfarabi (d. A.D. 950), for example, the human intelligence is enlightened by a cosmic intelligence, which functions as the active intellect in humans. Avicenna (A.D. 980–1037), in turn, posited a tenth intelligence which endows the human intellect with its understanding of the forms or essences.

59. ST Ia, Q. 76, a. 2.

60. ST Ia, Q. 76, a. 3.

61. ST Ia, Q. 76, a. 8.

62. ST Ia, Q. 76, a. 5.

63. ST Ia, Q. 76, a. 2.

64. ST Ia, Q. 83, a. 12. Frederick Copleston, *A History of Philosophy* (London: Search; Mahwah, N.J.: Paulist, 1950), 2:382, offers a succinct explanation of the interplay between will and reason in Aquinas' anthropology: "*Liberum arbitrium* . . . is the will, but it designates the will not absolutely, but in its relation to the reason. Judgement as such belongs to the reason, but freedom of judgment belongs immediately to the will. Still, it is true that St. Thomas's account of freedom is intellectualist in character. This intellectualism is apparent in his answer to the question whether the intellect or the will is the nobler faculty. St. Thomas answers that, absolutely speaking, the intellect is the nobler faculty, since the intellect through

cognition possesses the object, contains it in itself through mental assimilation, whereas the will tends towards the object as external, and it is more perfect to possess the perfection of the object in oneself than to tend towards it as existing outside oneself."

65. ST Ia, Q. 76, a. 1.

66. ST Ia, Q. 77, a. 2; ST Ia, Q. 77, a. 6, ad. 1.

67. ST Ia, Q. 77, a. 6.

68. ST Ia, Q. 77, a. 2.

69. ST Ia, Q. 77, a. 4.

70. ST Ia, Q. 77, a. 4. Aquinas also specifies a third type of order: the order according to the order of objects, whereby "certain sensitive powers are ordered among themselves" (e.g., sight, hearing, and smell) so that the visible naturally comes first, followed by the sound which is audible in the air, which is prior to the mingling of elements which allows for the sense of smell.

71. *The New Catholic Encyclopedia* (Washington, D.C.: Catholic University of America Press, 1967), 11:167b, s.v. "Person (in Philosophy)," by L. W. Geddes and W. A. Wallace.

72. ST Ia, Q. 28, a. 1.

73. ST Ia, Q. 29, a. 4.

74. ST Ia, Q. 28, a. 2.

75. ST Ia, Q. 28, a. 3.

76. ST Ia, Q. 29, a. 4.

77. ST IIIa, Q. 16, a. 1. In opposition to the monophysite claim that Christ possessed but a single nature in the Incarnation (the human being subsumed by the divine nature), the Council of Chalcedon taught that Jesus Christ is one person (the Word of God in a complete divine nature and a complete human nature). More explicitly, Chalcedon taught that

> the one and same only-begotten Son, Christ the Lord, must be recognized in two natures without confusion, without change, without division or separation. The difference of the natures is in no way removed by the union, but the proper characteristics of each are the more preserved thereby; they are united in one person. (Denz 302)

78. ST IIIa, Q. 16, a. 1, ad. 1.

79. ST IIIa, Q. 2, a. 6.

80. ST IIIa, Q. 2, a. 5, ad. 1. Cf. ST IIIa, Q. 2, a. 6.

81. ST Ia, Q. 29, a. 1.

82. ST Ia, Q. 29, a. 1, ad. 3.

83. ST Ia, Q. 29, a. 2. For Boethius (A.D. 480–424/5), the definition of the person as "an individual substance of a rational nature" was applicable not only to humans but to angelic beings and the Persons of the Trinity as well. In this respect, Aquinas's critique of Boethius's definition assumes a special Christological significance: does Christ's personhood encompass the substance of human nature in general or the substance of the individual that was Jesus Christ? On the basis of Boethius's emphasis on the individuality inherent in the substance of the rational being, it can be inferred that he was committed to the notion of substance in its primary sense in defining the person (even if he was not explicit enough for Aquinas).

84. ST Ia, Q. 29, a. 2, ad. 3.

85. ST Ia, Q. 29, a. 3.

86. ST Ia, Q. 29, a. 2.

87. ST Ia, Q. 29, a. 4.

88. ST IIIa, Q. 19, a. 1, ad. 4.

89. Horst Seidl, "The Concept of Person in St. Thomas Aquinas," *Thomist* 51 (1987): 439–41.

90. Seidl, "Concept of Person," 448.

91. ST Ia, Q. 82, a. 1.

92. ST Ia, Q. 82, a. 4. The exception to the will's movement of psychic powers is found in the natural powers of the vegetative or nutritive part of the soul. Our will, for example, has no bearing on hair growth or digestion.

93. ST Ia, Q. 82, a. 3.

94. ST Ia, Q. 83, a. 4, ad. 2.

95. ST Ia, Q. 83, a. 2.

96. ST Ia, Q. 83, a. 1.

97. ST Ia, Q. 83, a. 3, ad. 3.

98. ST IaIIa, Q. 10, a. 2.

99. ST IaIIa, Q. 10, a. 2.

100. ST IaIIa, Q. 10, a. 2.

101. ST IaIIa, Q. 10, a. 2.

102. ST Ia, Q. 82, a. 1.

103. ST Ia, Q. 82, a. 2.

104. ST Ia, Q. 82, a. 3.

105. ST Ia, Q. 105, a. 4.

106. ST Ia, Q. 105, a. 4, ad. 2.

107. ST Ia, Q. 82, a. 2, ad. 2.

108. *On Evil*, chap. 6 (Clark, 246).

109. Aquinas (*On Evil*, chap. 6, Clark, 246) suggests three ways in which the will may be moved to one object rather than another:

> according to the reason . . . in another way, inasmuch as he thinks of one particular circumstance and not of another . . . the third way influences through the character of men; because of whatever character a person is, so does his end seem to him.

110. Aquinas's fourth argument for the existence of God (the argument from degrees of perfection) similarly proceeds from our ability to make comparative value judgments on the basis of a standard of valuation (ST Ia, Q. 2, a. 3). This standard constitutes the exemplar of excellence in any class of things. For Aquinas, such a standard is grounded in objective reality, as something real in its own right. In this respect, claims that things are "better" or "worse" than others presuppose a maximum that constitutes the cause of everything in a given genus. Aquinas thereby argues that there is something truest, best, noblest, and highest in being that causes the being, goodness, and every other perfection of finite things.

111. Robert Edward Brennan, *Thomistic Psychology* (Toronto: Macmillan, 1969), 222.

112. Such a separation is unnatural in metaphysical terms because the soul is the form of the body; such a separation is unnatural in epistemological terms because the soul requires the instrumentality of the body for the acquisition of knowledge through sense experience.

113. ST Ia, Q. 89, a. 2.

114. ST Ia, Q. 89, a. 4. Here Aquinas presupposes the rule that what is received into anything is conditioned according to the mode of the recipient.

115. ST Ia, Q. 89, a. 6. While Aquinas contends that the souls of the dead do not know what occurs on earth by natural knowledge, he acknowledges that opinion is divided (i.e., between Augustine of Hippo and Gregory of Nyssa) as to whether the blessed are aware of earthly affairs (ST Ia, Q. 89, a. 8). He favors Gregory's position in this matter and contends that separated souls do know what happens here, since they are equal to the angels in regard to their beatitude and the scope of knowledge it imparts. At ST Ia IIae, Q. 67, a. 1, Aquinas argues that the moral virtues remain in the future life, but only in respect to the formal element, "in as much as each one's reason will have most perfect rectitude in regard to things concerning him in respect of that state of life: and his appetitive power will be moved entirely according to the order of reason." He denies, however, that the moral virtues will remain in the future life in regard to the material element, since in that state there will be no desires, pleasures, fear or daring, or distributions and commutations of things employed in this present life.

116. ST Ia, Q. 29, a. 3.

III

MINDS AND BODIES

6

René Descartes:
The Ghost in the Machine

The confidence in psychosomatic unity inspired by Aquinas wavered during the modern era in the face of challenges posed by scientific accounts of nature. The perennial tension between a teleological perspective and a mechanistic one now came into sharp focus. For philosophers confronting the all-embracing encroachments of science, this tension assumed a greater urgency than it ever could for Plato or Aristotle in the ancient world or for Aquinas in the late Middle Ages. In this dynamic milieu, nothing could be taken for granted, including the theocentrism of the medieval vision of reality and the sense that humans occupied a privileged place in the scheme of creation.

At the dawn of modernity, a thinker emerged who would radically redefine traditional anthropological presuppositions in light of the exigencies of scientific discovery and his own Christian belief system. René Descartes (1596–1650) represents a mind-set far removed from the Middle Ages. The emergence of the new physics prompted a wholesale reassessment of the ancient and medieval outlooks, as well as a revamping of the traditional scientific method and its explanatory principles. The reduction of the universe to a vast collection of quantifiable, measurable facts subject to efficient causality posed a serious threat to the exalted status of humans in the larger scheme of things. Are we special beings occupying the summit of creation or merely part of a predictable system of nature and therefore subject to the same spatiotemporal laws as everything else is? This question was the burden borne by Descartes (and modern philosophy in general) as the teleological outlook was increasingly discarded.

Chapter 6

DESCARTES AND HIS MISSION

On the night of November 10, 1619, Descartes had a series of unsettling dreams.[1] In retrospect, he interpreted these dreams as confirming the truth of a philosophical method he had been formulating during a period of seclusion from the outside world.

> I was then in Germany, attracted . . . by the wars in that country, which have not yet been brought to a termination; and as I was returning to the army from the coronation of the emperor, the setting in of winter arrested me in a locality where, as I found no society to interest me and was besides fortunately undisturbed by any cares or passions, I remained the whole day in seclusion, with full opportunity to occupy my attention with my own thoughts.[2]

This experience imbued him with an urgent sense of mission to provide a firm, unshakeable foundation for philosophy and the sciences. On the basis of one particular dream, Descartes claimed an insight into the unity of all knowledge under a single science and its overarching method. A twentieth-century biographer describes the impact of that night (and Descartes' intuition) in these terms:

> He now knew the path he must follow, the one which had been pointed out to him from on high, would lead to knowledge. With the zeal of a religiously inspired young poet, he was ready to set out on the mission of building a new scientific philosophy.[3]

Descartes' life and mission reflected the spirit of his age. Like many of his contemporaries, he experienced a sense of deep disenchantment with traditional learning, especially with what he found in scholasticism. While Descartes valued the liberal education he received at La Fleche, a Jesuit college, he would seriously question its practical value. Such a concern is distinctly modern and consistent with the assumption that knowledge can and should be applied in the interest of what is useful in improving life. Like other modern thinkers, Descartes aspired to a "fresh start" in philosophy.

But Descartes' philosophical approach by no means amounted to a complete break with the past. In its broadest terms, his philosophy reflects a rationalism which traces its origins to Parmenides and Plato and found its classic Christian expression in Augustine of Hippo and Anselm of Canterbury. From this standpoint, Descartes sought truth within the mind by means of innate a priori concepts. He found his greatest intellectual satisfaction in mathematical studies, reflecting a temperament that sought a bedrock of certitude in the midst of shifting sense experience. He also exhibited an affinity with the general thrust of the new physics and its assumption that the material universe can be understood in terms of fundamental numerical relationships. Like Galileo, he viewed the natural world as a unified system whose secrets are disclosed to those conversant in its appropriate language—mathematics.

But Descartes' desire to develop a sound scientific method represents only one aspect of his philosophical agenda. He also applied himself to the task of supporting his belief in God and the soul with arguments persuasive enough to win the support of all rational individuals, including the most ardent critics of the theistic perspective. For him, what lay in the balance was nothing less than the reconciliation of faith and reason in confronting the specter of the new physics and its materialistic accounts of the world and human nature.[4]

A BELIEVING MAN OF REASON

Descartes begins his *Meditations on First Philosophy* with a revealing dedicatory letter to the faculty of Sacred Theology at the University of Paris. While the letter underscores his own faith commitment, it leaves no doubt about his attitude toward the role of philosophizing in the theological arena. Descartes is clearly at ease within the tradition of natural theology and its rational investigation of the basic tenets of Christian belief.

> I have always been of the opinion that the two questions respecting God and the soul were the chief of those that ought to be determined by help of philosophy rather than of theology; for although to us, the faithful, it be sufficient to hold as matters of faith, that the human soul does not perish with the body, and that God exists, it yet assuredly seems impossible ever to persuade infidels of the reality of any religion, or almost even any moral virtue, unless . . . these two things be proved to them by natural reason.[5]

The fact that he eagerly submits fundamental religious teachings to philosophical demonstration says something about his overall intellectual bent. Descartes, as already observed, was rationalist to the core, and he extended his penchant for certitude into his arguments for the existence of God and the immortality of the soul. He was also motivated by practical apologetic concerns. While believers can readily accept these doctrines, nonbelievers require more compelling reasons for endorsing them. The claim that we must believe in God's existence because it is taught by Scripture (and conversely that Scripture's credibility proceeds from its divine origin) is dismissed by nonbelievers as so much circularity. From Descartes' standpoint, the only thing preventing such skeptics from believing is the lack of persuasive arguments. Accordingly, he perceived his task as one of selecting the best demonstrations and delineating them as precisely as possible.

In Descartes' view, his arguments for God's existence and the distinction between the mind and the body "shall have been brought to such a degree of perspicuity as to be esteemed exact demonstrations."[6]—so lucid, in fact, that he reckons they even surpass those found in geometry for certainty and obviousness. But as he readily acknowledges, such clarity by no means ensures their widespread acceptance. Indeed, their very length and complexity demand a freedom from prejudice in favor of sense experience and an ability to detach oneself from its influence.

For better or worse, Descartes' bifurcation of the human being into a thinking substance of mind and an extended substance of body would exert an incalculable influence on subsequent theories of human nature. Many anthropological presuppositions today reflect either a persistent attachment to Descartes' brand of dualism or a lingering Cartesian legacy embedded in our cultural heritage. Even Descartes' most ardent critics must acknowledge him as a considerable force in the history of Western philosophy. This is evident in the assessment of Descartes' greatest twentieth-century critic, Gilbert Ryle, whose attack on what he calls the "dogma of the ghost in the machine" has done so much to undermine the Cartesian distinction between mind and matter.[7] But for supporters and critics alike, Descartes' perennial ability to stimulate discussion proceeds from the engaging character of his writing. He draws us in precisely because he had a great personal stake in what he wrote. This personal dimension is nowhere more apparent than in his philosophy of mind and the sharp dichotomy he draws between our mental and physical activities. In my estimation, then, the main lines of Descartes' anthropology are best considered in an autobiographical context, through the penetrating reflections comprising his *Discourse on Method* (1637) and subsequent *Meditations* (1640). Accordingly, the following discussion draws primarily on those seminal works, with supplementary insights taken from his treatises and correspondence.

FORGING A METHOD

Descartes proceeds from the premise that common sense is universal and all people share the ability to distinguish truth from falsehood. This point of departure is consistent with his confidence in the capacity of human reasoning to arrive at true conclusions by its own unaided powers. But Descartes recognizes that the diversity of human opinion affirms that human thought follows different paths. Clearly, possessing a good mind is not enough. What is crucial is how the mind applies itself. In this respect, Descartes lays no claim to an intellect greater than others. He simply proposes an exposition of the path on which he himself has embarked as a means of expanding his knowledge, albeit on a gradual basis.[8] In roughly Socratic fashion, then, Descartes acknowledges the extent of his own ignorance. After completing his education at La Fleche, he was still filled with doubts and subject to questionable opinions. The exception was mathematics, a discipline that offered a potential foundation for solid and firm reasoning. In this respect, Descartes contrasts the firmness and persuasiveness of mathematical reasoning with those "very towering and magnificent palaces with no better foundation than sand and mud"—that is, disciplines whose teachings are always a matter of opinion and hence are open to doubt and uncertainty.[9]

Descartes' dissatisfaction with his formal studies prompted him to learn on a firsthand basis through traveling and investigating "the great book of the world."[10] By his own account, however, his subsequent wanderings yielded mixed results; the diversity of human customs prompted even more uncertainty. Accordingly, he resolved not to believe anything grounded on unstable evidence. He decided to turn within and "employ all the powers of my mind in choosing the paths I ought to follow."[11]

This introspection reached its high point during the period of solitude mentioned above. The leisure to converse freely with his own thoughts strengthened a conviction that underlies his entire method: works accomplished by a single individual contain greater perfection than those based on the opinions of the multitude.[12] In this respect, he set himself to the rigorous task of rejecting all opinions which formerly commanded his credence. Still, Descartes was reluctant to jettison all questionable opinions in a wholesale manner. He decided to proceed slowly, "like one walking alone and in the dark," in developing a true method for arriving at the knowledge of everything the mind is capable of grasping.[13]

What shape did this method assume? First and foremost, Descartes would never accept anything he did not know to be true. But what could withstand this rigorous test? In Cartesian terms, only things that remain immune to doubt—things that the mind grasps *clearly and distinctly,* in the same way it discerns mathematical truths—could withstand.[14] While these two epistemological criteria (i.e., "clear" and "distinct") are usually considered interchangeable, they actually touch on different aspects of our recognition of a thing or proposition as true. For Descartes, a clear awareness of something (e.g., the smell of smoke) does not mean that we grasp its nature, as distinct from other natures. But what is distinct is also clear, since it imposes itself on the mind in such a way that its truth is readily manifest.

Descartes' commitment to a mathematical model of knowledge is further evident in his emphasis on analysis (i.e., dividing problems into as many parts as possible), on an orderly treatment of his thoughts (i.e., beginning with the simplest things and proceeding to increasingly complex matters), and on complete enumerations.[15] In this respect, he compares the orderly arrangement of the contents of human knowledge in general to the long chains of reasoning used by geometers. The appeal of this method for him proceeded from its broad applicability: since it was not limited to one area of inquiry, he could apply it to problems pertinent to science and logic alike. For this reason, its implementation reflects a highly pragmatic stance on his part. Indeed, one who decides to rebuild his house must not only tear down the existing structure but find a place to live in the interim. This is why Descartes formulated a provisional code of morality for governing his actions as he proceeded to sort out erroneous opinions.[16] If he doubts, then, he does not doubt for the sake of doubting, in the manner of the complete skeptic. Rather, his doubt is inextricably linked with a desire for certitude that rejects as false whatever fails to dispel further doubt.

Such methodical doubt has far-reaching consequences for Descartes' attitude toward the world and the contents of his own thought. Everything he formerly took for granted must be held in abeyance. Accordingly, the application of methodic doubt immediately rules out the data of sense experience, since the senses are highly susceptible to error. But it likewise excludes the reasoning Descartes formerly accepted as demonstrations. Its truly radical nature, however, is evident in the parallel he draws between a conscious and a dreaming state. "I supposed," he affirms, "that all the objects that had ever entered into my mind when awake had in them no more truth than the illusions of my dreams."[17] How in fact do we know the difference between the contents of our dreams and our conscious experiences? Indeed, some dreams are just as vivid as actual experiences of people, things, and events (or even more so). But is their vivacity anymore sufficient to prove their reality than what we derive from sense experience in general?

AFFIRMING THE COGITO

In the face of a doubt powerful enough to collapse the distinction between the truth value of dreams and conscious experience, Descartes takes refuge in the thinking self or Cogito, the cornerstone of his rationalistic edifice. Even when he affirms that everything is false, there must be a thinker who makes this judgment.

> But immediately upon this I observed that, whilst I thus wished to think that all was false, it was absolutely necessary that I, who thus thought, should be,

. . . and as I observed that this truth, I think, therefore I am was so certain and of such evidence that no ground of doubt, however extravagant, could be alleged by the sceptics capable of shaking it, I concluded that I might . . . accept it as the first principle of the philosophy of which I was in search.[18]

In strict epistemological terms, the Cogito serves as a propositional criterion of truth and certitude. But as Descartes recognizes, the only feature of the formula "I think; therefore I am" that assures him of its truth is the fact that the mind grasps it clearly and distinctly. From this perspective, however, thinking is coextensive with being. Descartes finds definitive support for belief in his own existence in the continuity of his thought processes. He concludes that he is a thinking substance whose nature is to think.

Descartes identifies the true and essential human being with the mind, rather than any material substance (including the body and its entire physiological apparatus). "So that 'I,' that is to say, the mind by which I am what I am, is wholly distinct from the body, and is even more easily known than the latter, and . . . although the latter were not, it would still continue to be all that it is."[19] In this way, Descartes retains the classical understanding of substance as a thing which exists in its own right as a center of attributes and, in turn, is attributed to nothing whatsoever. He succinctly articulates this definition in his *Principles of Philosophy:* "By substance we can understand nothing other than a thing which exists in such a way as to depend on no other thing for its existence."[20]

The Cogito, then, assumes an anthropological significance in allowing us to differentiate what is essentially human from what is not. In Cartesian terms, this amounts to a distinction between mind (as thinking substance) and body. While he has already achieved a sense of unshakeable certitude about his own existence (as affirmed through the Cogito), everything connected with the body as an extended substance (and indeed the world of sense perception) is still open to question. But Descartes takes his methodic doubt to another level by reflecting on what it reveals about his own finitude and imperfection. Paradoxically, however, such a limited being is capable of conceiving the existence of a wholly perfect being. What is the source of such an idea in the finite mind? It clearly could not originate in a finite, imperfect, and doubting nature such as our own. By the same token, it could not be derived from what we encounter in the world, since the world is as finite and imperfect as humans. The only alternative, Descartes reasons, is that an idea of a supremely perfect nature must be derived from that nature itself.

It but remained that it had been placed in me by a nature which was in reality more perfect than mine, and which even possessed within itself all the perfections of which I could form any idea—that is to say, in a single word, which was God.[21]

THE ROLE OF GOD

If God possesses all conceivable perfections, then he must be wholly other than finite human thinkers composed of souls and bodies. God admits no imperfections whatsoever. Composition, however, attests to a radical contingency which places imperfect natures in a relationship of dependence on God for any perfection they possess, and indeed for their very being. Such things only exist by virtue of a being whose essence and existence coincide. In a manner consistent with his thoroughgoing rationalism (and Anselm's ontological argument), Descartes finds the most persuasive evidence for God's existence in the idea of God as a supremely perfect reality.[22] But certitude alone does not establish being. The certainty that a triangle must be three-sided does not guarantee the existence of any triangular object in the order of reality. In this respect, the difference between the idea of God and the idea of a triangle lies in the fact that God's nature or essence is defined on the basis of existence in its most complete sense. And while we can conceive of geometrical figures or physical bodies apart from their concrete reality, we can never conceive of God as nonexistent. For Descartes, however, God's existence is still as certain as the truth of any geometrical demonstration.

Descartes recognizes how far removed this position is from ordinary experience and widespread popular acceptance. For the majority of individuals (as well as for Descartes in his precritical days), the data of sense experience (and ideas derived from the images of external realities) are more certain than the existence of God or even their own minds. An exclusive reliance on imagination thus carries a crucial epistemological consequence, whereby people "never raise their thoughts above sensible objects and are so accustomed to consider nothing except by way of imagination."[23] But the mere fact that people generally feel more comfortable with ideas drawn from sense experience is no proof of their veracity. In this respect, Descartes contrasts a "moral assurance" about the surrounding world (which we accept on purely pragmatic grounds) with a "metaphysical certitude" that enables us to discern the truth with clarity and distinctness.[24] Indeed, the very things whose existence seems indubitably verifiable on the basis of tangible evidence (including our own bodies) are always less certain than truths the mind discovers on its own. For this reason, those who approach the ideas of God and mind by means of imagination embark on an exercise that is as flawed as using the eyes to hear sounds.[25]

But herein lies the importance of God's role in Descartes' methodology as the ultimate guarantor of truth. If truth and falsehood are determined by the mind's confirmation, what ensures that the mind itself is in touch with the really real in objective terms? This problem becomes acute when we compare the mental contents of consciousness with those of dreams. What the dreamer confronts finds a direct parallel in the world of conscious experience; what we dream has some basis in objective reality, either as images of real things or as indubitable truths. In this respect, Descartes stresses that a clear and distinct idea is as true in our dreams as it is when we are awake. "For whether I am awake or dreaming," he argues, "it remains true that two and three make five and that a square has but four sides."[26] In either case, we must be persuaded of the truth of a situation or proposition on the basis of reasoning rather than imagination alone. But in the final analysis, Descartes finds our sole rationale for accepting anything as real or true in the existence of a perfect and infinite God.[27] In the absence of God, we would have no grounds for affirming that our conscious state is more real than a dreaming one.

THE CHALLENGE OF HYPERBOLIC DOUBT

In a method governed by the norms of rationality, Descartes finds it wholly reasonable that a God of unlimited perfection should give us access to clear and distinct ideas grounded in truth. God, then, provides the ultimate criterion of truth that enables us to distinguish reality from illusion. Still, a subjective certainty that something is true provides no definitive assurance that it is objectively so. On the basis of this realization, Descartes' methodic doubt gives way to hyperbolic doubt. How, for example, do we know that the mathematical truths we discern clearly and distinctly are not really false? From this standpoint, the clear and distinct criterion no longer inspires the same confidence, since we may well be subject to a deception of cosmic proportions about the very truths the mind grasps as indubitably true.

Descartes remains secure in the belief that a supremely good God could not be guilty of such a universal deception. But in radicalizing doubt to this extent, he entertains the unsettling notion that our seemingly benevolent creator is really an "evil genius" that employs its supreme power and intelligence to mislead us about everything, including the existence of our own bodies and the order of nature.[28] Such musings are by no means conducive to a sense of intellectual serenity. Descartes admits feeling that "just as if I had fallen all of a sudden into very deep water, I am so greatly disconcerted as to be made unable either to plant my feet firmly on the bottom or sustain myself by swimming on the surface."[29] This is the anguish that accompanies the most extreme form of skepticism—corrosive doubt that accepts nothing as true other than the claim that nothing whatsoever is true.

How is this psychological impasse to be overcome? Descartes follows the dictates of his own method in discerning what is still indubitable, even in the face of the evil genius hypothesis. And what remains intact is the persistence of the thinking self, the Cogito. In actuality, someone must still be the subject of even this grandiose deception.

> I suppose, accordingly, that all the things which I see are false; I believe that none of those objects which my fallacious memory represents ever existed; I suppose that I possess no senses; I believe that body, figure, extension, motion, and place are merely fictions of my mind; what is there, then, that can be esteemed true? Perhaps this only, that there is absolutely nothing certain. But how do I know that there is not something different altogether from the objects I have now enumerated, of which it is impossible to entertain the slightest doubt? Is there not a God, or some being . . . who causes these things to arise in my mind? But there is I know not what being . . . possessed at once of the highest power and the deepest cunning, who is constantly employing all his ingenuity in deceiving me. Doubtless, then, I exist, since I am deceived; and . . . he can never bring it about that I am nothing, so long as I shall be conscious that I am something.[30]

THAT I AM, WHAT I AM

Still, the affirmation that Descartes exists as a thinking substance says nothing about what he is as a man. In attempting to define himself as a human being, he immediately rules out anything about himself that is the least bit dubitable. But what he now doubts is obviously more wide-ranging than before he adopted his rigorous method. Earlier in life, Descartes would have been content to define himself as a "man," and a "man" in turn as a "rational animal." He was also more confident that he possessed a body and physiological functions than he was about his own soul. In short, the Descartes of old uncritically assumed that he distinctly knew the body's nature.

> By body I understand all that can be terminated by a certain figure; that can be comprised in a certain place, and so fill a certain space as therefrom to exclude every other body; that can be perceived either by touch, sight, hearing, taste, or smell; that can be moved in different ways, not indeed of itself, but by something foreign to it by which it is touched.[31]

Such an assured sense of his own body was seriously undermined by the evil genius hypothesis. After Descartes entertained the possibility of a universal deception, everything he formerly took for granted regarding his body and its powers was annulled. What remains? Once again, he takes refuge in the activity of the mind; if there is anything that defines him as a human being and sets him apart from bodily substances, it lies in thinking.

> Thinking is another attribute of the soul; and here I discover what properly belongs to myself. This alone is inseparable from me. I am—I exist: this is certain; but how often? As often as I think; for perhaps it would even happen, if I should wholly cease to think, that I should at the same time altogether cease to be.[32]

The fact that the Cogito cannot be reduced to the level of imagination makes it appear less distinctly known than the body. For this reason, Descartes proposes something of a thought experiment to test the common assumption that our bodies are more distinctly known than our minds.

AN EXPERIMENT

Consider a piece of wax, fresh from the comb. The wax exhibits a variety of observable characteristics: the flavor and aroma of honey, color, size, shape, and texture. Once we melt the wax, these overt characteristics disappear, but something still remains. If we say that "wax" is present, then what was previously in the wax that we comprehended distinctly? Certainly nothing we perceived by the senses, since the observable features by which we designated it as wax have been eliminated. Descartes concludes that what we understood to be wax was nothing we can taste, smell, see, or feel. Rather, it concerns what belongs to the wax *essentially*—something extended, flexible, and changeable. Accordingly, our ability to recognize the wax for what it is does not proceed from the imagination but from the mind. In Cartesian terms, only the mind can differentiate between what is essential to the wax and what is merely extrinsic to its nature.

> But . . . the perception of it is neither an act of sight, of touch, nor of imagination, and never was either of these, though it might formerly seem so, but is simply an intuition of the mind, which may seem imperfect and confused, as it formerly was, or very clear and distinct, as it is at present.[33]

This analytical exercise, whereby Descartes reduces something to its most fundamental constituents, presupposes a distinction common among modern philosophers inspired by Galileo. In keeping with his mathematization of reality, Galileo distinguished between primary and secondary qualities. The former pertain to quantifiable properties (e.g., number, motion, rest, figure, position, size) that allow for mathematical interpretation and thus are objectively real in the things themselves; the latter refer to those properties of a thing (e.g., taste, aroma, color, sound, texture) that are purely subjective and thus allow for no quantifiability.[34]

As used by Descartes, the distinction between primary and secondary qualities assumes a crucial role in separating reality from appearances. If the secondary qualities exist, they do so only in relation to the perceiving subject. Once the secondary qualities are removed, all that remains is what is part and parcel of a body, without which it could not be a body at all. Obviously, however, Descartes' interest lies in more than the primary quality of wax. His pressing concern here is what constitutes the reality of the human being. Accordingly, the wax experiment has a direct anthropological parallel.

Consider the view we have from a high window of people walking in the street below. We readily agree that we see human beings. But is this claim based on anything we distinctly grasp about their humanity? As in the case of the wax, does it rest on anything more persuasive than observable (and highly variable) secondary qualities? As far-fetched as it may sound, perhaps what we see moving around are no more than automatons covered with coats and hats.[35] In commonsense terms, of course, there is no reason to doubt that they are really humans. But Descartes' point is that such a determination is the result of an *intellectual judgment* rather than anything we can grasp through the imagination. In this respect, he defines imagination as "a certain application of the cognitive faculty to a body which is immediately present to it, and which therefore exists."[36] In contrast to the mind's understanding (which unfolds within the mind), imagination necessarily depends on something distinct from the thinking self.

More precisely, imagination involves the mind's attention to the body, and the formation of ideas grounded in sense experience. From this standpoint, what applies to the analysis of the wax applies to our observation of the moving figures in the street as well. If we judge them to be humans, we do so through the mind, not on the basis of imagination.

> But when I distinguish wax from its exterior forms, and when, if I had stripped it of its vestments, I consider it quite naked, it is certain, although some error may still be found in my judgment, that I cannot, nevertheless, thus apprehend it without possessing a human mind.[37]

Descartes challenges the common assumption that the bodies we perceive are more distinctly known than our minds. For him, any sense experience of a physical reality involves an implicit affirmation of the existence of the mind as a thinking substance. Even if we doubt the data of sense experience (or even if we were deceived about the existence of bodies), the existence of the mind remains indubitable. Descartes, in fact, contends that our perception of bodies does not proceed from the senses but from the understanding.[38]

But if thinking is inextricably bound up with the existence of our mind, then it is the only thing about us immune to doubt and thus the only thing about us that conveys a necessary, indisputable truth. For all practical purposes, Descartes defines himself as a "thinking thing" that exhibits the full spectrum of mental activities.

> But what, then, am I? A thinking thing, it has been said. But what is a thinking thing? It is a thing that doubts, understands, affirms, denies, wills, refuses, that imagines also, and perceives. Assuredly it is not little, if all these properties belong to my nature. But why should they not belong to it? Is there also any one of these attributes that can be properly distinguished from my thought, or that can be said to be separate from myself?[39]

MIND, BODY, AND WORLD

In view of the doubt which attaches to bodily things, Descartes must confront a dilemma: how do we know that material things (including our own bodies) exist? Once again, his commitment to the existence of a good and perfect God provides his criterion of an objective truth beyond the self. More specifically, God provides a lifeline to the external world, including the bodily natures that comprise it. Descartes discerns God's providential governance at work in the world, attributing its existence and operation to divinely established laws. In his reckoning, such laws are universal in scope; they would hold in multiple worlds or in any world God chose to create.[40]

In the *Discourse on Method*, Descartes proposes a hypothesis concerning God's creation of the formless matter of a new world which he allows to act in accordance with his laws, in disposition and arrangement.[41] In this scenario, the body and its operations (like every aspect of the material world) emerge independently of the influence of mind or soul.

> I remained satisfied with the supposition that God formed the body of man wholly like one of ours, as well as in the external shape of the members as in the internal conformation of the organs, of the same matter . . . and at first placed in it no rational soul, nor any other principle. For, when I examined the kind of functions which might . . . exist in the body, I found precisely all those which may exist in us independently of all power of thinking.[42]

Descartes thus treats the body as an entity in its own right, completely independent of the mind and subject to the laws of the natural world. If thinking is the signature activity of humans, then we share with animals those functions proper to the body alone. In this connection, Descartes boldly envisions the possibility of a machine that resembles an animal in every way (both in appearance and function).[43] Because this kind of construct would replicate the functions of a living nonrational being, we would have no grounds for distinguishing them. A humanoid automaton, however, would allow for no such deception.

From Descartes' standpoint, the humanoid replica would always fall short of the genuine human being in two significant ways: on the one hand, it could never use language in a creative manner; on the other hand, it could never perform all the necessary operations of life without relying on specific organs for each task.[44] Communication demands more than the utterance of words; by the same token, rational behavior presupposes more than the presence and distribution of organs. The automaton, in short, would lack the reasoning power that coordinates diverse functions and allows us to respond to novel or unexpected circumstances through words and actions.

> For while reason is a universal instrument that is alike available on every occasion, these organs, on the contrary, need a particular arrangement for each particular action; whence it must be morally impossible that there should exist in any machine a diversity of organs sufficient to enable it to act in all the occurrences of life, in the way in which our reason enables us to act.[45]

THE BODILY MECHANISM

Descartes' two criteria of humanness (i.e., linguistic and operational) not only provide a means of distinguishing real people from machines. They also offer a basis for distinguishing humans from animals. For all practical purposes, then, Descartes views any living body without reason as a machine. This is why he rejects suggestions that the mind could have emerged from the potentiality of matter. The only alternative is that mind was expressly created by God as wholly different from matter in general and from the body specifically. By virtue of this unequivocal affirmation of the generic distinction between mind (i.e., the rational soul) and matter, Descartes finds the basis for upholding the soul's immortality.

> When we know how far they differ we much better comprehend the reasons which establish that the soul is of a nature wholly independent of the body and that consequently it is not liable to die with the latter; and finally, because no other causes are observed capable of destroying it, we are naturally led . . . to judge that it is immortal.[46]

Descartes' departure from an Aristotelian/Thomistic anthropological perspective is nowhere more apparent than in his willingness to empty the body and physiological processes of any psychic contribution. For him, the body is merely a machine, albeit one better organized and more sophisticated in its movements than any comparable man-made one. The extent to which Descartes reduces psychology to physiology (in favor of the physiological) is most apparent in his *Treatise on Man* (1632), a part of his *Treatise on the World*.[47] The title of this larger study underscores the comprehensiveness of his investigation. According to one commentator, the *Treatise on the World*

> conveys to the reader the author's intention to develop a system of cosmology founded on a physics so universal that it could apply to animal functions and to man himself, as well as to inanimate objects . . . to the world and all it contains.[48]

In keeping with this project, Descartes defines the body in purely mechanistic terms. Accordingly, he compares "the many different kinds of motions in the machine . . . made by the hands of God" with man-made machines such as clocks, mills, and artificial fountains.[49] Like these technological constructs, the bodily mechanism fashioned by God comprises the many material parts that allow it to perform its full range of functions, from digestion to heartbeat to nourishment and growth to respiration, and everything else that proceeds from the physiological apparatus. What immediately stands out in this account is the absence of any reference to the role of the soul.

> I should like you to consider that all these functions follow naturally in this machine simply from the arrangement of its organs, no more or less than the movements of a clock or other automaton follow from that of its counterweights and wheels, so that it is not at all necessary for their explanation to conceive in it any other soul, vegetative or sensitive, or any other principle of motion and life other than its blood and its spirits, set in motion by the beat of the fire that burns continually in its heart, and which is of a nature so different from all fires in inanimate bodies.[50]

MIND/BODY INTERACTION: AN UNEASY ALLIANCE

Mind and body, then, are not only distinct substances but wholly different natures. In this case, however, Descartes' dualism also presupposes a distinction between a self rooted in the mind and the composite of mind and body that constitutes the human being. Accordingly, any sense of an enduring personal identity must proceed from the mind alone, the essential part of our humanness that is immune to the change and limitations of the sense world, the sphere of bodily existence. From this standpoint, Descartes' dualism poses a severe challenge and stumbling block to the notion of psychosomatic union in any substantial sense. But by undermining psychosomatic unity, Descartes also introduces an acute and unresolvable problem of mind-body interaction.

If the mind transcends the world and physical causes, how do we explain its involvement with bodily existence in a manner that does justice to the coherence of human experience? Despite their distinctness, Descartes still recognized that mind and body are conjoined in constituting the full human being, with its full range of emotions and appetites. Mind and body are so tightly conjoined that they constitute a single reality or, in the more emphatic language of the *Discourse on Method*, the "real man."[51]

For Descartes, however, the composite entity must always exhibit an uneasy alliance of two different natures—the one incorruptible and immortal, the other corruptible.[52] This unstable union is the direct outgrowth of his dualism. Still, this does not say that mind and body must assume an adversarial relationship. Rather, Descartes finds ready confirmation of composite unity in the empirical observation of mind-body interaction on a daily basis. "Everyone feels that he is a single person with both body and thought so related by nature that the thought can move the body and feel the things that happen to it."[53] Experiences like pain, hunger, and thirst point to a symbiotic relationship between mind and body. According to Descartes, this link is especially apparent when such sensations manifest themselves in novel or wholly unexpected ways.

> The mind is aware that these sentiments do not come from itself alone, and that they cannot belong to it simply in virtue of its being a thinking thing; instead, they can belong to it only in virtue of its being joined to something other than itself which is extended and moveable . . . what we call the human body.[54]

In Cartesian terms, then, the commingling of mind and body in this manner (i.e., in the way we perceive it) is simply the product of what nature reveals.

> I know not what sensation of pain, sadness of mind should follow, and why from the sensation of pleasure joy should arise, or why this indescribable twitching of the stomach, which I call hunger, should put me in mind of taking food, and the parchedness of the throat of drink, and so in other cases, I was unable to give any explanation, unless that I was so taught by nature.[55]

The implication here is that the unity of the human being is borne out by what we naturally experience by virtue of our mental and physical components. Still, the scope of nature's "instruction" in this vein is rather circumscribed.

At most, nature "teaches" us to avoid painful things and pursue pleasurable ones.[56] But in keeping with the dictates of his rationalism, Descartes holds that any truth we grasp about external things is the result of the mind, rather than the composite of mind and body. "For it is the office of the mind alone and not of the composite whole of mind and body," he asserts, "to discern the truth in those matters."[57] This is not to say that the mind intuits such things with the same clarity and distinctness it enjoys when focusing on mathematical truths. Descartes designates sensations like hunger and thirst as no more than "confused modes of thinking" that reflect the mind's union with the body and the vagaries of sense experience.[58] Nonetheless, his affirmation of the primacy of mind over body (even in such "confused modes of thinking") reveals a fundamental tension that runs to the heart of his anthropology. He recognizes this tension in a letter to Princess Elizabeth:

> It does not seem to me that the human mind is capable of forming a very distinct conception of both the distinction between the soul and the body and the body and their union; for to do this it is necessary to conceive them as a single thing and at the same time to conceive them as two things; and this is absurd.[59]

WHERE MIND AND BODY MEET

While Descartes was confident in the fact of psychosomatic union, he was hard-pressed to demonstrate how it is possible, beyond an appeal to our direct experience of mind-body interaction. In his estimation, this experience simply attests to God's ordering of nature in a manner consistent with his goodness and perfection.

> It cannot be doubted that in each of the dictates of nature there is some truth: for by nature . . . I understand nothing more than God Himself, or the order and disposition established by God in created things; and by my nature in particular I understand the assemblage of all that God has given me. But there is nothing which that nature teaches me more expressly than that I have a body which is ill affected when I feel pain, and stands in need of food and drink when I experience the sensations of hunger and thirst . . . and . . . that I am not only lodged in my body as a pilot in a vessel, but that . . . my mind and body compose a certain unity.[60]

Because Descartes' dualism rules out a metaphysical bond between mind and body, he resorts to what amounts to a physiological account of their union. In this respect, his actual theory is less significant than the philosophical purpose it serves—that is, to show how an unextended mind can influence bodily movements and, conversely, how an extended body can affect the mind. Descartes posits this point of contact in the pineal gland in the brain.[61] On the basis of this theory, external stimuli are communicated to the mind through the senses, and the mind conveys the inclinations of the will to the bodily mechanism. Accordingly, the interaction between mind and body allows for the same kind of analysis as any other aspect of the physical world, by means of a series of efficient causes and their corresponding effects.

But while Descartes views the mind as susceptible to bodily influences, he still upholds its integrity as the basis of our free will and moral judgments. "It is a supreme perfection in man that he acts . . . freely," he asserts, "in a special way the author of his actions and deserving of praise for what he does."[62] In this respect, he posits volition or the operation of the will as one of the modes of thinking that encompasses desire, aversion, denial, and doubt. (The other mode of thinking lies in the operation of the mind itself, along with its related modes of sense experience, imagination, and understanding.) Since the will constitutes a cognitive mode in its own right, we are intuitively aware of its operation within ourselves.[63] As Descartes' method demonstrates, the will is operative in directing the mind to reflect on God and the Cogito and even in hyberbolic doubt that calls into question what was formerly viewed as indubitable. But the will not only turns us within; it also directs our attention to the body and the physical world. As the agency whereby mind influences the body to act or not to act, the will is instrumental in prompting bodily movements.[64]

ASSESSING THE CARTESIAN COMPROMISE

Descartes' recognition of the will's dual focus reflects the general thrust of his attempted reconciliation of two disparate accounts of human nature: a teleological one, which acknowledges the soul's immortality and the will's moral freedom, and a mechanistic one, which reduces all human activity (including our mental acts) to a physiological plane and thereby subjects us to the same causal influences operative throughout the natural world. Descartes' dualism reflects his desire for a compromise between the worldview promoted by the new physics and a perspective that admits the existence of immaterial reality. For Descartes, the mind thus assumes a role analogous to that of a "fountain keeper" who stands at the openings of the tubes which discharge the waters.[65] But the extent to which the Cartesian compromise succeeds is highly questionable. In the final analysis, the will's ability to influence the body depends on the mediation of a physical organ. From this standpoint, the mind depends on the body, at least to the extent that it requires the pineal gland in order to communicate its intentions to the bodily apparatus.

But recognizing a mutual interaction between mind and body does not explain psychosomatic union. Descartes contends that mind and body are united *essentially,* by their very natures. In his celebrated reply to a criticism by his disciple Regius, he argues that a human being is an *ens per se,* not an *ens per accidens.* By means of this language, Descartes affirms a real and substantial union between mind and body.[66] He thereby disavows any suggestion that the unity of mind and body is merely contingent. If Descartes views mind-body union as an *ens per se,* it is because he believes that we are not human beings at all in its absence.[67]

In Cartesian terms, however, can this union be anything but contingent? Despite his claims to the contrary, Descartes does not permit mind and body to constitute a single substantial reality in the Aristotelian/Thomistic sense. For him, the mind is an independent substance, not the first act of a body with the potential for life. He thereby severs the metaphysical link that hylomorphism presupposes between mind and body, spirit and matter. In the final analysis, there is nothing in mind or body which requires the union of one with the other. Accordingly, Descartes separates the self (rooted in the mind as the thinking substance) from the body to which it is conjoined. This is why his references to human unity must always be qualified in light of his dualism and the restrictions it necessarily imposes on his anthropology.

Descartes' anthropological model bears the clear mark of his rationalism and its emphasis on the mind's ability to grasp truth in a clear and distinct manner. The subjective turn that Descartes initiates thus exerts a decisive impact on his understanding of what it means to be human. From this standpoint, he posits the self in the mind, rather than in the composite of mind and body. In this respect, the self is affirmed on the basis of cognitive activities like thinking and doubting, rather than in the facts of our concrete experience of a larger world. Accordingly, Descartes' response to the question, What am I?, only admits of one answer: *I am a thinking substance,* or *a thing which thinks.* He arrives at this conclusion on the basis of a distillation process, whereby he distinguishes what he discerns as essentially human from what is not.

If thinking is the defining human activity, then we are identified exclusively with the mind as the thinking, unextended substance. While Descartes acknowledges that mind and body constitute the "real man," the body is wholly distinct from the mind. For all practical purposes, the body is no more than a mechanism (albeit a highly sophisticated one) completely devoid of any psychic presence. But if mind and body are distinct as substances and natures, then how can we experience their mutual influence on each other? Descartes' dualism, in effect, falsifies the very unity that interaction between mind and body presupposes.

For all practical purposes, the Cartesian self has nothing to do with the body, and thus it can be considered without reference to bodily existence.

By the same token, the Cartesian body constitutes a distinct entity in its own right, without any reference to the self or personhood. Such an assumption (whereby the body is something analyzable on its own terms, independently of the mind or any psychic principle) has exerted a tremendous influence on the way people view themselves and others, particularly in a medical context. In this respect, Descartes himself looked to medicine as a prime beneficiary of the application of his scientific method.

> If any means can ever be found to render men wiser and more ingenious . . . I believe that it is in medicine they must be sought. It is true that the science of medicine, as it now exists, contains few things whose utility is very remarkable: but without any wish to deprecate it, I am confident that there is no one, even those whose profession it is, who does not admit that all at present known in it is almost nothing in comparison of what remains to be discovered.[68]

A major legacy of Cartesian dualism lies in its influence on the relationship between the patient and physician. A significant feature of the clinical encounter in modern times has been a preoccupation with the body and physiological symptoms. Someone can be admitted to a hospital emergency room in an unconscious state, be subjected to a series of sophisticated tests, receive treatment for a life-threatening illness, and be put on the road to recovery without ever being consulted. A dualistic anthropology promoted this empirical approach and opened the way to the wonderful advantages that medicine affords us. But these advantages carry a price. According to one commentator, the dualistic model has resulted in "a *displacement* of the patient's lived relationship to his or her own body" that coincides with its *replacement* "by the physician's diagnostic relationship to that body, now conceived as an objective and scientific body."[69] Paradoxically, the patient's personal narrative is rendered all but insignificant in favor of the diagnostician's scientific analysis of the body.

A distinction, of course, must be made between Descartes' interpretation of his own dualism (and his emphasis on the interaction of mind and body) and the way in which subsequent generations of practitioners have construed that dualism.[70] By reducing the body to a value-neutral mechanism, Cartesian dualism decisively shaped modern medical interpretations of both disease and pain. Such interpretations assume a distinctly materialist thrust, as the body (rather than the mind or the mind-body composite) becomes the ultimate investigative referent. On the one hand, disease can now find its explanation on a purely physiological basis. On the other hand, pain can be understood in stark mechanistic terms, as a bodily injury's stimulation of neural impulses that are transmitted to the brain, somewhat in the manner of pulling a rope to ring a bell in the brain.[71] In recent decades, however, researchers have challenged this physicalist account of pain and, by implication, an exclusive focus on the body as indicator of what is "wrong" with the patient. This trend points to uneasiness with a rigidly mechanistic explanation of illness and an accompanying movement toward the rehabilitation of a psychosomatic understanding of the human condition.[72]

CONCLUSION

Descartes was by no means the first thinker to confront the mind-body problem and to struggle with a means of explaining their mutual interaction. At the very outset of the Western tradition, Plato was also challenged in accounting for the mind-body relation (i.e., the relation between simple and composite natures) and, in broader terms, the relation of the entire visible universe to the world of Forms. In the final analysis, Plato resorted to the somewhat nebulous notion of participation, whereby the lower world of sense experience (including the corporeal dimension of human existence) shares in a higher conceptual realm of wholly immaterial reality. His Neoplatonic successors (exhibiting the influence of Aristotelianism), in turn, introduced the theory of a "union without confusion" in coming to terms with the fact of psychosomatic union. For Greek and Christian Neoplatonists alike, the theory at least attempted to address the apparent interaction of completely different natures in a single reality, while preserving the integrity of each.

Whether this Neoplatonic model of "union without confusion" provided an adequate metaphysical explanation of the mind-body relation is not crucial here. What is significant is that the thinkers who embraced this model (including Augustine in the Christian tradition) were firmly committed to the harmonious unity of mind or soul and body in one being. The same cannot be said for Descartes, despite his claims to the contrary. Indeed, his own understanding of the mind-body composite was founded on the paradox that an unextended thinking substance is somehow conjoined with an extended corporeal one. In the words of James Collins, Descartes' version of the human composite amounts to "an unexpected melange, a disconcerting datum that remains irremediably obscure and confused within the Cartesian perspective of mental and bodily substances."[73]

The uneasy alliance between mind and body that Descartes engineered would haunt his intellectual successors as the mind-body problem became a major focus of later Cartesians' philosophical investigations. But rather than uphold the interaction thesis at the expense of Descartes' dualism, Arnold Geulincx (1625–1669) and Nicholas Malebranche (1638–1715) rejected interaction altogether.[74] In place of some questionable theory that attempts to explain how mind influences the body (and vice versa), these thinkers advocated what amounts to a psychophysical parallelism, whereby God alone is designated as the true cause of mental and physical acts that correspond in the manner of two perfectly synchronized clocks. From this standpoint, volitional commands are no more than *occasional causes* of bodily movements (i.e., the occasion on which God causes a physical response); conversely, physical activity is no more than the occasion on which God effects an conscious reaction in the mind. Accordingly, God is viewed as the only true cause of what occurs in the universe, including the interaction of mind and body which no one (including the most astute philosophers) can really explain.[75]

For Geulincx and Malebranche alike, the mere fact that we observe an apparent causal connection between my will to move and a corresponding bodily response (or physical exertion and a corresponding consciousness of fatigue) does not establish the true causes of these occurrences, or any necessary connection that links them together. In this respect, these "occasionalists" exhibit some similarities with the empiricism of David Hume, who explicitly challenged the notion of the soul as a substantial reality in its own right. This challenge would set the tone for all subsequent attempts to explain human behavior on a purely physiological basis, without further recourse to the notion of an incorruptible, immaterial mind.

DISCUSSION QUESTIONS

1. Discuss why Descartes would say that if we ceased to think we would cease to exist.
2. How does Descartes' designation of humans as "thinking substances" or "things that think" reflect his dualistic interpretation of human nature?
3. Discuss how Descartes' methodic doubt leads him to what he discerns as the indubitable truth of his own existence.
4. Discuss the role of God in Descartes' quest for metaphysical certitude, especially in dealing with the exaggerated doubt that finds expression in his evil genius hypothesis.
5. According to Descartes, how could we differentiate a humanoid machine from a real human being? What criteria does he propose for making this distinction?

NOTES

The following translations of Descartes' writings are used throughout this chapter. Citations from all works are followed by the corresponding Adam/Tannery (A/T) numbers (both volume and page numbers).

Discourse on Method and Meditations on First Philosophy, trans. John Veitch, Library of the Future, 4th ed., ver. 5.0 (World Library, 1996). The *Discourse on Method* is abbreviated as DM; the *Mediations on First Philosophy* as M.

Selected Philosophical Writings, trans. John Cottingham, Robert Stoothoff, and Dugald Murdoch (Cambridge: Cambridge University Press, 1988). For references to *Principles of Philosophy*, trans. John Cottingham, and *The Passions of the Soul*, trans. Robert Stoothoff.

The Philosophical Writings of Descartes, vol. 3, *The Correspondence*, trans. John Cottingham, Robert Stoothoff, Dugald Murdoch, and Anthony Kenny (Cambridge: Cambridge University Press, 1991).

Philosophical Essays and Correspondence, ed. Roger Ariew (Indianapolis: Hackett, 2000), for translation of chapter 18, *Treatise on Man*.

1. For a detailed discussion of these dreams, see Jack Rochford Vrooman, *René Descartes: A Biography* (New York: Putnam's, 1970), 45–67. The third dream focused on his observation of two books on a table: a dictionary and a collection of poems, which might be interpreted as symbols of the unity of the sciences and a higher form of knowledge uniting philosophy and wisdom, respectively.

2. DM II, A/T VI, 11.

3. Vrooman, *René Descartes*, 60.

4. This trend finds its most salient expression in the philosophy of Thomas Hobbes (1588–1679). Such a materialistic perspective (along with its mechanistic and deterministic presuppositions) is fully operative in Hobbes's anthropology. According to W. T. Jones, *A History of Western Philosophy*, vol. 3, *Hobbes to Hume*, 2nd ed. (New York: Harcourt, Brace & World, 1969), 128, Hobbes holds that

> each individual man is simply a certain region of the material plenum, and what distinguishes this region from other regions is only the motions occurring there . . . which are nothing but changes in the spatial relations of the parts of human bodies . . . all . . . completely determined by antecedent events in time.

5. *Letter of Dedication* to *Meditations on First Philosophy*, A/T VII, 1–2.

6. *Letter of Dedication* to *Meditations on First Philosophy*, A/T VII, 5–6.

7. Gilbert Ryle, *The Concept of Mind* (Chicago: University of Chicago Press, 1949). Ryle develops the main lines of his critique in the first chapter of this work, "Descartes' Myth."

8. DM I, A/T VI, 2–3.

9. DM I, A/T VI, 7–8.

10. DM I, A/T VI, 9.

11. DM I, A/T VI, 10–11.

12. DM I, A/T VI, 12–13.

13. DM II, A/T VI, 17.

14. DM II, A/T VI, 18.

15. DM II, A/T VI, 18–19.

16. DM III, A/T VI, 23–28.

17. DM IV, A/T VI, 32.

18. DM IV, A/T VI, 32.

19. DM IV, A/T VI, 33.

20. *Principles of Philosophy*, A/T VIII A, 51.

21. DM IV, A/T VI, 34.

22. DM IV, A/T VI, 36.

23. DM IV, A/T VI, 37.

24. DM IV, A/T VI, 37–38.

25. DM IV, A/T VI, 37.

26. M I, A/T VII, 20.

27. DM IV, A/T VI, 40.

28. M I, A/T VII, 22–23.

29. M II, A/T VII, 23–24.

30. M II, A/T VII, 24–25.

31. M II A/T VII, 26.

32. M II A/T VII, 27.

33. M II A/T VII, 31.

34. James Collins, *A History of Modern European Philosophy* (Milwaukee: Bruce, 1954), 83.

35. M II A/T VII, 32.

36. M VI A/T VII, 72.

37. M III A/T VII, 32.

38. M II A/T VII, 34.

39. M II A/T VII, 28–29.

40. DM V, A/T VI, 43.

41. DM V A/T VI, 45.

42. DM V A/T VI, 45–46.

43. DM V A/T VI, 56.

44. DM V A/T VI, 56–57.

45. DM V A/T VI, 57.

46. DM V A/T VI, 59–60.

47. *The Treatise on the World* comprises the *Treatise on Man* and the *Treatise on Light*.

48. Bernard Cohen, foreword to Descartes' *Treatise on Man* (Cambridge: Harvard University Press, 1972), xv–xvi.

49. *Treatise on Man*, chap. 18 A/T 120.

50. *Treatise on Man*, chap. 18 A/T 202.

51. DM V A/T VI, 59.

52. *To Hyperaspistes* (August 1641), 1 A/T III, 422.

53. *To Princess Elizabeth* (June 1643), A/T III, 694.

54. *Principles of Philosophy* II, 2 A/T VIII A, 41.

55. M VI A/T VII, 76. At M VI (A/T VII, 82), Descartes defines nature as "what God has bestowed on me insofar as I am composed of mind and body."

56. M VI A/T VII, 82.

57. M VI A/T VII, 83.
58. *To Regius* (January 1642) A/T III, 493.
59. *To Princess Elizabeth* (June 1643) A/T III, 693.
60. M VI A/T VII, 80–81.
61. *Passions of the Soul* I, 31 A/T XI, 352.
62. *Principles of Philosophy* I, 37 A/T VIII A, 18.
63. *Principles of Philosophy* I, 39 A/T VIII A, 19.
64. *Passions of the Soul* I, 41 A/T XI, 360.
65. *Treatise on the World,* chap. 18 A/T 131–132.
66. *To Regius* (January 1642) A/T III, 493.
67. *To Regius* (January 1642) A/T III, 508.
68. DM VI A/T 62, 35.
69. Richard M. Zaner, *Ethics and the Clinical Encounter* (Englewood Cliffs, N.J.: Prentice Hall, 1988), 104.
70. Cf. Zaner's remarks (*Ethics and the Clinical Encounter,* 120):

Descartes seems to have known quite clearly what he was doing—and it most assuredly was not what has been attributed to him by subsequent physicians or philosophers. The mind and body form a "composite whole" within daily life and clinical situations, and it is there alone that they can be properly apprehended—whether through ordinary discourse, experience, feelings, or clinical encounters. Descartes also seems to have recognized that medicine, in its clinical encounters with diseased, injured, or crippled patients, knows this "union" just as intimately—through patients' pain, pleasure, and narrowed focus on their own bodies. Therefore, even if one could speak of a dualism in Descartes' works, it is by no means the fabled mind-body dichotomy of the textbooks or that to which current physicians, philosophers, and biomedical scientists refer.

71. Atul Gawande, *Complications: A Surgeon's Notes on an Imperfect Science* (New York: Holt, 2002), 120:

The explanation of pain that has dominated much of medical history originated with René Descartes, more than three centuries ago. Descartes proposed that pain is a purely physical phenomenon—that tissue injury stimulates specific nerves that transmit an impulse to the brain, causing the mind to perceive pain. The phenomenon, he said, is like pulling on a rope to ring a bell in the brain. Twentieth-century research on pain has been devoted largely to the search for and discovery of pain-specific nerve fibers . . . and pathways. In everyday medicine, doctors see pain in Cartesian terms—as a physical process, a sign of tissue injury.

72. Gawande (*Complications,* 120–123) summarizes the results of this research and the resulting move to replace the Cartesian model of pain with the so-called Gate-Control theory and its assumption that the mind (along with factors like mood, expectations, and tolerance) can control the way we experience pain. According to Gawande (122), "Gate-Control Theory accepts Descartes' view that what you feel as pain is a signal from tissue injury transmitted by nerves to the brain, and it adds the notion that the brain controls a gateway for such an injury signal."
73. Collins, *History of Modern European Philosophy,* 185.

74. My brief consideration of the occasionalist thesis in these thinkers relies on the discussion provided by Frederick Copleston, *A History of Philosophy* (Garden City, N.Y.: Image, 1963), 6:181–210.

75. For both Geulincx and Malebranche, God's willing of the creation and conservation of things implies his willing that things should be here rather than there at any point in time. In this respect, the inclinations of creatures correspond to the divine will, and God instills in all things an orientation to the good that can only be satisfied in and through God.

7

David Hume:
A Bundle of Perceptions

Shortly before he died, David Hume (1711–1776) was visited by James Boswell, the Scottish lawyer and biographer of Samuel Johnson. Boswell asked Hume whether he believed in the possibility of an afterlife. Hume replied that he thought it was possible, just as it is possible "that a piece of coal put upon the fire would not burn."[1] This response underscores a skeptical strain that permeates Hume's entire philosophy, including his philosophical investigations into human nature. By virtue of this skepticism, Hume issued a severe challenge to classical notions of mind, soul, and substance in general. Hume brings home the full implications of a rejection of metaphysics in discussions of personhood. Humean skepticism serves as a wake-up call, not only for speculative metaphysicians of Descartes' stamp committed to the existence of an immaterial soul but to all who uncritically assume that they possess a stable, abiding self capable of surviving the body's death.

Hume did not embrace an absolute skepticism which rejected the very foundations of knowledge and truth claims. Rather, he endorsed a *mitigated skepticism* which challenged the uncritical, dogmatic claims of speculative metaphysics. In this respect, Hume philosophized in a manner consistent with the limitations of human understanding. His avowed intent was to curb the overextension of reasoning into those "distant and high enquiries" outside the scope of human experience, confining himself to "subjects as fall under daily practice and experience."[2] These goals were fully operative in Hume's analysis of human nature.

At this juncture of the history of philosophy, discussions of what it means to be human focus on investigations into the foundations of selfhood and personal identity. This individualistic preoccupation was a prominent feature of British philosophy from the late seventeenth century onward. Jerrold Seigel explains the trend in these terms:

> The impact of the new science was felt everywhere, but the combination of Baconian experimentalism and Newtonian analysis of palpable relations between things (as opposed to Cartesian deductive reasoning or the combination of mechanism and scholasticism put together by Leibniz) was a characteristically English mix.[3]

Hume's philosophy reflects the empirical orientation of the new science and the commonsense approach to philosophical problems it encouraged. This empiricist thrust received its impetus during the Renaissance with a renewed interest in the investigation of the natural world. Scientific figures like Galileo and Leonardo da Vinci believed that the world possesses a rational structure that can be understood by combining mathematical reasoning with direct observation and experimentation.

In contrast, the Continental rationalism exemplified by Descartes focused on the mathematical model of knowing, along with an emphasis on the deductive method and the analysis of reality in terms of a priori standards of truth. The British empiricism that found its greatest exponent in David Hume, however, looked to the inductive method and the gathering of observational data as a means of expanding human knowledge. Still, both sides of modern philosophy shared the conviction that the expansion of knowledge by means of the scientific method can yield practical results.[4] In this connection, British empiricism found direct antecedents in work of Francis Bacon (1561–1626), who grounded his scientific research in the facts of sense experience and the testing of hypotheses on the basis of novel experiments. For Hume, however, the dominant scientific influence proceeded from Newtonian physics.

HUME'S NEWTONIAN MODEL

At the age of twelve, Hume entered the University of Edinburgh, where he was exposed to a broad range of studies, including classics, logic, metaphysics, the Romance languages, and, most significantly, the physics of Sir Isaac Newton (1642–1727). The university had become a center of Newtonianism, and Hume internalized this theory and the vision of reality it endorsed. Newton shaped Hume's understanding of what it means to be human and defined the parameters of his psychology.[5] In this regard, Hume shared the admiration for Newtonianism that is reflected in Enlightenment thinking generally. According to one commentator, Newton was paradigmatic of the proper conduct of scientific investigation.

To the eighteenth and much of the nineteenth centuries, Newton himself became idealized as the perfect scientist: cool, objective, and never going beyond what the facts warrant to speculative hypotheses. The *Principia* become the model of scientific knowledge, a synthesis expressing the Enlightenment conception of the universe as a rationally ordered machine governed by simple mathematical laws.[6]

Like Descartes, Newton invested mathematics with great importance in scientific investigation. But Newton grounded his mathematical calculations in the observable world, and consequently mathematics assumes a descriptive rather than an explanatory role in Newton's system.[7] He dispensed with any attempt to isolate "hidden," unobservable natures or essences (or what Aristotelians designated as formal and final causality) and focused exclusively on efficient causes and the interaction of moving bodies. Newton's physics thus offers a purely mechanistic account of the natural world that proceeds inductively from the observation of bodies in motion to a positing of the "forces" of nature. According to Newton's second law of motion, the change of motion is in proportion to the force imposed on it, in the linear direction in which it was imposed.[8] In this mechanistic scheme, the forces of nature do no more than prompt changes in nature. For Newton, force is responsible for a body's acceleration, as measured by the product of its mass and acceleration.[9]

A SCIENCE OF HUMAN NATURE

If Hume understood psychology as the science of human nature, he did so within the framework of Newtonian physics. In this respect, Hume's account of personal identity is wholly consistent with the Newtonian perspective and its challenges to fundamental presuppositions about reality (at least as supported by an Aristotelian worldview and a traditional substantialist metaphysics). Humean psychology, then, is of a piece with Newton's model of the larger universe and its emphasis on a mechanistic analysis of things in motion and the limitations of one's causal claims about the observational data of sense experience.

For Hume, the success of his psychological research hinged on an incisive investigation of human nature. In his reckoning, the science of man assumes a central role in the conduct of all the sciences pertinent to human life. Like other thinkers of his time (most notably Descartes), Hume perceived his philosophical enterprise as marking a new beginning and offering a firm grounding for scientific inquiry in general.

There is no question of importance, whose decision is not compriz'd in the science of man; and there is none, which can be decided with any certainty, before we become acquainted with that science. In pretending therefore to explain the principles of human nature, we in effect propose a compleat system of the sciences, built on a foundation almost entirely new, and the only one upon which they can stand with any security.[10]

In Hume's estimation, the only means of discerning the powers and qualities of the mind lies in the experimental method. But experimentation presupposes an empirical base built on the observable effects of the mind's operation. Hume severely circumscribes the scope of reason in scientific investigation. For him, sense experience provides the context in which reason functions most fruitfully in exploring something as complex and seemingly mysterious as the mind.

And tho' we must endeavour to render all our principles as universal as possible, by tracing up our experiments to the utmost, and explaining all effects from the simplest and fewest causes, 'tis still certain we cannot go beyond sense experience.[11]

THE ORIGIN OF IDEAS

A salient Newtonian legacy in Hume's psychology lies in his emphasis on analysis—the reduction of what is complex to its simplest components. In Humean terms, mind is reduced to the fundamental constituents of thought. In this respect, Hume's psychological investigations overlap with his theory of knowledge and its account of idea formation. In keeping with his thoroughgoing empiricism, he traces the origin of ideas to a direct encounter with the data of sense experience. This empiricist criterion is a crucial component of Hume's science of human nature; notions like the soul or the self (and human nature itself) may be no more than mere ideas with no grounding in the concrete world. Hume thus divides the objects of human reasoning into relations of ideas and matters of fact.[12]

Relations of ideas encompass propositions that yield a sense of certitude on an intuitive or demonstrative basis. Accordingly, they can be understood in an a priori manner, independently of experience. The claims that "All circles are round" and "A triangle is a three-sided figure" are universally valid, necessarily true, and cannot be denied without contradiction. But such truths cannot expand our knowledge of the world in the manner of matter-of-fact statements. In contrast to relations of ideas, matters of fact are purely contingent, referring to particular people, things, or events. For this reason, they can be denied without contradiction.

The contrary of every matter of fact is still possible; because it can never imply a contradiction, and is conceived by the mind with the same facility and distinctness, as if ever so comfortable to reality. That the sun will not rise to-morrow is no less intelligible a proposition, and implies no more contradiction, than the affirmation, that it will rise.[13]

From the standpoint of Humean empiricism, however, any idea worthy of the name is ultimately traceable to sense experience and a matter-of-fact context. In this respect, Hume designates our mental contents by means of the broad category of perceptions; in turn, perceptions encompass ideas and impressions. For Hume, the only difference between ideas and impressions lies in the vivacity with which they impose themselves on the mind.[14] The fact that Hume views ideas as parasitic on impressions is part and parcel of his overall empiricist agenda. From this standpoint, every act of thinking involved in perception is no more than "a mere passive admission of the impressions thro' the organs of sensation."[15] The implication is that any idea the mind entertains (or, more precisely, any idea the mind is capable of entertaining) has an experiential base.[16] Still, Hume stresses that the distance of ideas from their empirical grounding can render them obscure. Such obscurity is the hallmark of the dogmatic, uncritical metaphysics to which his mitigated skepticism is directed.

"Our business," Hume asserts, is "to remedy that defect by keeping the idea steady and precise."[17] In this case, the "steady and precise" grasp of ideas means an attentiveness to their empirical source. For him, the failure to adhere to this task results in what amounts to a pretense to philosophical reasoning. In this respect, his philosophical goal is to empty traditional metaphysical notions of their mysterious, occult quality and lay bare their links with the impressions that produced them. Accordingly, the key question for Hume (and one that has great significance for his understanding of human nature) is, From what impression is the supposed idea derived?

While Hume emphasizes the discreteness of impressions (and the phenomenalistic character of sensation), he also holds that these primal sense experiences rarely (if ever) present themselves to us on a purely isolated basis. This issue touches on the means whereby the mind associates the ideas derived from impressions in making sense of the world and our place in it. Hume depicts this associative process as spontaneous and effortless on our part.

When the mind is once enliven'd by a present impression, it proceeds to form a more lively idea of the related objects, by a natural transition of the disposition from the one to the other. The change of the objects is so easy, that the mind is scarce sensible of it.[18]

What prompts this "natural transition" from idea to idea? Hume roots this movement in what he calls "qualities" or "relations" of perception which "produce an association among ideas, and upon the appearance of one idea naturally introduce another."[19] The first two relations are closely linked; in resemblance and contiguity in time or place, the mind responds to what is immediately present to the senses.

> We ought not to receive as reasoning any of the observations we may make concerning identity, and the relations of time and place, since in none of them the mind can go beyond what is immediately present to the senses, either to discover the real existence or the relations of objects.[20]

In resemblance, the mind links ideas of similar people or things: a photograph, for example, calls to mind the person or thing depicted by the image. Ideas associated on the basis of contiguity are based on things that are proximate in either spatial or temporal terms, as we tend to associate the smell of smoke with fire.

But the relations of resemblance and contiguity presuppose the relation of causation. For Hume, causality is the most wide-ranging of relations, providing the basis of all reasoning concerning matters of fact. "By means of that relation alone," Hume asserts, "we can go beyond the evidence of our memory and senses."[21] If, for example, one were to discover an artifact on a deserted island, we could reasonably conclude that there had been people in that locale. Despite this distance in place or time, however, the mind still discerns a connection between the facts at hand and the cause inferred. But because every effect is distinct from the cause we attribute to it, the only support for this relation lies in the accumulation of the observable data. Hume stresses that the cause-and-effect relation which binds these seemingly disparate things or events can never be discovered on a deductive basis, by means of some a priori demonstration.[22]

HUME ON CAUSALITY

A hallmark of Hume's Newtonian program is his treatment of causality. Hume's theory of causality (along with his analysis of the causal necessity between causes and effects) provides the foundation of his science of human nature. If his scientific approach to human nature is to succeed, it is vital that he address this seminal issue in a thoroughgoing manner. In keeping with the dictates of his empiricism, Hume viewed efficient causes that fall within the range of sense experience as the only causes worthy of philosophical discussion.

> All causes are of the same kind, and . . . there is no foundation for that distinction, which we sometimes make betwixt efficient causes, and causes *sine qua non;* or betwixt efficient causes, and formal, and material, and exemplary,

and final causes. For as our idea of efficiency is deriv'd from the constant conjunction of two objects, wherever this is observ'd, the cause is efficient; and where it is not, there can never be a cause of any kind.[23]

From this standpoint, there is nothing inherent in things themselves which conjoin them as causes and effects, beyond what we gather from experience.[24]

By way of analogy, if formal and final causes were likened to the glue which holds things together, what happens when this metaphysical adhesion is eliminated? How would reality appear? In Humean terms, the only recourse is to confront things and events on a one-on-one basis. Each thing or event (and on a deeper atomistic level, each individual impression that comprises our perception of those things or events) is viewed as distinct and independent from everything else. In support of this position, Hume advances the following argument:

> Let an object be presented to a man of ever so strong natural reason and abilities; if that object be entirely new to him, he will not be able, by the most accurate examination of its sensible qualities, to discover any of its causes or effects.[25]

Hume's discussion of causality is guided by the central empiricist question, From what impression (or impressions) is the idea derived? Hume, then, approaches causality (and the ancillary issue of necessary connection) on the basis of our ideas of these notions. To be philosophically meaningful, such ideas must be grounded in the concrete world among the objects of sense experience. At the outset, Hume denies that the idea of the causal relation is rooted in some quality common to all causes. Accordingly, he analyzes causality in terms of three relations that hold among objects: first, the contiguity between causes and effects, second, the temporal priority of causes over effects (i.e., that causes occur *before* the effects they generate), and third, the necessary connection we discern between cause and effect.[26]

Hume stresses that contiguity and temporal succession alone do not allow us to recognize a causal bond between things. Indeed, things may be proximate to each other or follow each other in the absence of causal significance. A true causal link can only be appreciated on the basis of repeated occurrences of events, whereby "these two relations are preserv'd in several instances."[27] For this reason, contiguity and succession must always be considered along with necessary connection, the relation at the heart of causality. The very fact that we assume a given event (i.e., an effect) *must invariably* follow another (i.e., its cause) attests to this link.

As in the case of the causal relation, Hume seeks the impression (or impressions) which provide the origin of the idea of necessary connection.

Hume adopts a heuristic approach, proceeding "like those in search of any thing conceal'd from them, and not finding it in the place they expected, beat about all the neighboring fields."[28] In this spirit, he first poses two additional guiding questions.

> First, For what reason we pronounce it necessary that every thing whose existence has a beginning, shou'd also have a cause? Secondly, Why we conclude that such particular causes must necessarily have such particular effects; and what is the nature of that inference we draw from the one to the other and of the belief we repose in it?[29]

In regard to the first question, Hume acknowledges that the maxim "Anything that begins to exist must have a cause of its existence" is so commonly accepted that no proof is required. But he denies that it is intuitively certain or demonstrable by scientific reasoning. Rather, it must be traced to observation and experience.[30] In regard to the second question, Hume again denies that causal inference is certain in intuitive or demonstrative terms. From this standpoint, nothing necessarily implies the existence of anything else. Experience is the sine qua non of any claim to causal necessity. From Hume's perspective, for example, there is nothing in the nature of "heat" and "flame" that confirms a cause/effect relation, beyond the frequency of our experiences of these objects. The very designation of "cause" and "effect" presupposes an inferential leap from one to the other.

> We remember to have had frequent instances of the existence of one species of objects and also remember that the individuals of another species of objects have always attended them and have existed in a regular order of contiguity and succession with regard to them.[31]

What, then, do we observe? Only the constant conjunction of events warrants the assumption that these events encompass a causal bond and justify the inference from one state of affairs to another. Hume simply takes this *constant conjunction* as a given of experience, with no discernible rationale, other than the fact that we tend to observe it in nature.

> We cannot penetrate into the reason of the conjunction. We only observe the thing itself and always find that from the constant conjunction the objects acquire an union in the imagination.[32]

As we have already seen, Hume attaches great importance to the role of memory in the retention of information regarding past experience. In this context, it is crucial to appreciate that occurrence B tends to follow occurrence A on a regular basis. But for Hume, repetition alone can never yield the idea of causal necessity; nothing in repeated occurrences of things or states of affairs provides its impression. In the final analysis, repeated occurrences are merely repetitions of distinct objects, with no intrinsic link to each other.[33]

If the relevant impression is not derived from what we discover in the world, it must emerge from the mind itself. But this requires qualification. Hume alternately appeals to such psychological factors as "determination," "propensity," or "internal impression" to describe the process whereby the mind moves from one object to its usual attendant under the influence of what he broadly characterizes as *custom:*

> The several instances of resembling conjunctions lead us into the notion of power and necessity. These instances are in themselves totally distinct from each other and have no union but in the mind, which observes them and collects their ideas. Necessity, then, is the effect of this observation and is nothing but an internal impression of the mind or a determination to carry our thoughts from one object to another.[34]

In Humean terms, causal necessity exists in the mind rather than in things themselves. The implication is that the weight of observable evidence induces a propensity or habit of thinking which in turn generates a belief on our part: "a strong and lively idea deriv'd from a present impression related to it."[35] On the basis of this belief, however, we are also inclined to exceed the data of experience in making inferences about things we do not directly experience. In this respect, causal inference is not merely a matter of reflecting on what has already occurred; it is also oriented toward the future. But inference can operate in two ways. On the one hand, we may infer the presence or existence of something on the basis of something else (e.g., I see people entering a building soaking wet and closing umbrellas and infer it has been raining outside); on the other hand, inference may involve a claim about what has not yet occurred on the basis of past performance.

The latter sense of inferential reasoning includes an element of expectation (e.g., if I strike a match, I expect it to ignite on the basis of observation and experience). But this expectation is only supported by an unproven assumption that what happened in the past will continue to happen in the future with the same regularity and predictability. Such claims, however, are only as credible as the evidence before us.

> The supposition, that the future resembles the past, is not founded on arguments of any kind but is deriv'd entirely from habit, by which we are determin'd to expect for the future the same train of objects to which we have been accustom'd.[36]

For Hume, then, it is no more true that fire necessarily causes heat than that the approach of a bus every morning around eight o'clock is responsible for the tolling of church bells eight times shortly thereafter.[37] In both cases, Hume would say that we are dealing with what amounts to distinct orders of events, with no intrinsic relation between fire and heat on the one hand, and the arrival of the bus and the sound of the bells on the other. According to Hume's analysis of causality and necessary connection, then, following as *a consequence* is not fundamentally different from merely *following after* something.[38] If there is any difference, it lies in the fact that one sequence of events is observed with greater frequency than another.

PERSONAL IDENTITY AND THE SELF

Hume's analysis of causality provides the basis for his discussion of personal identity and selfhood. His most detailed and sustained treatment of these topics is found in *A Treatise of Human Nature* (book 1, part 4, section 6). In a manner consistent with the principles supporting his theory of idea formation, Hume rejects any appeal to a stable, abiding self existing in its own right on a kind of rarefied level, with no reference to a changing world of sense experience. The notion of a personal identity that remains invariable over a lifetime is correlative with the uncritical sense of selfhood that Hume now challenges.

Hume lays the groundwork for this extended discussion in his incisive critique of the metaphysical theory of substance, particularly in regard to the mind. More precisely, the critique focuses on belief in the soul's immateriality. In this respect, his invective is directed toward religious metaphysicans, Cartesians, idealists, and all thinkers who uphold the existence of a stable self as a basis for arguments in favor of immortality.[39] Hume's remarks in this vein reflect his overall emphasis on the empirical origin of ideas.

> Neither by considering the first origin of ideas nor by means of a definition are we able to arrive at any satisfactory notion of substance; we have no perfect idea of any thing but of a perception. A substance is entirely different from a perception. We have, therefore, no idea of a substance.[40]

If Hume endorses the traditional definition of substance as "something which may exist by itself and not in relation to another," it is only in respect to those distinct perceptions (separable by the imagination) which provide the ultimate, irreducible constituents of sensation. In this context, the question From what impression is the supposed idea derived? assumes paramount importance. Accordingly, Hume issues his challenge in these terms:

I desire those philosophers, who pretend that we have an idea of the substance of our minds, to point out the impression that produces it, and tell distinctly after what manner that impression operates, and from what object it is deriv'd.[41]

Hume, then, rejects the traditional notion of substance as an unchanging substratum of accidental properties. Hume's position can be summed up in what amounts to a syllogism drawn from the text of the *Treatise*. "We have no perfect idea of any thing but of a perception. A substance is entirely different from a perception. We have, therefore, no idea of a substance."[42]

What Hume says about the knowability of substance applies directly to his understanding of personal identity and selfhood, and his provocative charge that we are no more than "bundles" of perceptions. This claim, as we shall see, is wholly consistent with the dictates of his epistemology. But that epistemology stands in direct continuity with the account of personal identity found in the work of an earlier British empiricist, John Locke (1632–1704). Jerrold Seigel succinctly sums up Hume's indebtedness to Locke in this particular area of his philosophy:

Such an account of identity and consciousness locates itself in the line of descent from Locke's theory of the mind as a blank tablet; the contents of such a mind are derived from the sense impressions it receives from outside.[43]

Like Hume, Locke rejects the notion of innate ideas and emphasizes the experiential origin of all objects of the mind. This empiricist principle and its assumption that the mind ultimately derives its ideas from experience is fully operative in Locke's discussion of personal identity in *An Essay Concerning Human Understanding*. For Locke, any consideration of personal identity is closely linked with a theory of the person and the selfhood it presupposes.

To find wherein personal identity consists, we must consider what *person* stands for, which, I think is a thinking intelligent being, that has reason and reflection, and can consider itself as itself, the same thinking thing, in different times and places, which it does only by that consciousness which is inseparable from thinking.[44]

Consciousness thus discloses one's existence as an independent, thinking reality and establishes the sense of spatiotemporal continuity that allows for our awareness of an enduring self.

When we see, hear, smell, taste, feel, meditate, or will anything we know that we do so. Thus it is always as to our present sensations and perceptions; and by this everyone is to himself that which he calls self . . . since consciousness always accompanies thinking . . . and in this alone consists personal identity— i.e., the sameness of a rational being.[45]

Hume's discussion of personal identity reveals the pervasive influence of Locke, even as he departs from his predecessor on some fundamental points. Like Locke, Hume emphasizes the experiential basis of personal identity and the sameness we attach to selfhood. But while Locke posits consciousness as his touchstone for affirming personal identity, Hume focuses explicitly on our perception of sense data. As Seigel further observes, "Hume was not so much rejecting his predecessor's stress on consciousness to self-existence as insisting . . . that consciousness cannot be posited by itself as the content of the self."[46] In this respect, Hume views any conscious awareness of the self as no more than the outgrowth of perception.

No Idea of Self

Hume proceeds from the observation that "some philosophers" assume we are always conscious of a self and that we are certain of its identity. Here Hume clearly has in mind Cartesians who profess an intuitive awareness of the Cogito or subjective ego and assume that nothing is certain in its absence.

> To attempt a further proof of this were to weaken its evidence, since no proof can be deriv'd from any fact of which we are so intimately conscious; nor is there any thing of which we can be certain if we doubt of this."[47]

In contrast to those thinkers, Hume boldly claims that we have no idea of a self. But in Humean terms, as we have seen, talk about the validity of a given idea demands an ability to trace its origin to an impression. The idea of the "self," however, does not proceed from any single impression but from a veritable collection of impressions and their corresponding ideas. Hume's demand for an underlying impression is only one side of his denial that the idea of the self is cognitively significant. He further requires that such an impression (if it exists) must remain the same over the course of a lifetime. From Hume's standpoint, no impressions can meet this test, since all impressions are different and independent.

> But there is no impression constant and invariable. Pain and pleasure, grief and joy, passions and sensations succeed each other, and never all exist at the same time.[48]

For Hume, then, the challenge lies in demonstrating how impressions which are distinct from each other coalesce in our conception of a unified self. But one thing is clear: we cannot divorce our sense of self from the surrounding impressions that comprise it.

Perception and the Self

If there is any discernible difference between Hume and Descartes regarding self-awareness, it lies in what each thinker posits as its basis. In contrast to Descartes, who held that the self would be annihilated in the absence of thinking, Hume asserts that "I never can catch myself at any time without a perception."[49] For him, attentiveness to the self discloses a plethora of individual perceptions. For all practical purposes, our self would be annulled in the absence of accompanying perceptions.

> When my perceptions are remov'd for any time, as by sound sleep so long am I insensible of myself, and may truly be said not to exist. And were all my perceptions remov'd by death, and cou'd I neither think, nor feel, nor see, nor love, nor hate after the dissolution of my body, I shou'd be entirely annihilated.[50]

What are we, then, and how do we account for the personal identity bound up with our notion of self? In Humean terms, we are no more than "a bundle or collection of different perceptions, which succeed each other with an inconceivable rapidity and are in perpetual flux."[51] This claim points to an atomistic understanding of reality, whereby everything we observe is reducible to so many discrete impressions. In Hume's reckoning, the mind is best likened to a theater in which a manifold of perceptions appear. But he also recognizes the limits of his theater analogy and the qualification it requires. By no means, however, does Hume wish to suggest that there is any stable mind which "contains" impressions in the manner of a structure that houses things.

> The comparison of the theatre must not mislead us. They are the successive perceptions only that constitute the mind; nor have we the most distant notion of the place where these scenes are represented or of the materials of which it is compos'd.[52]

Despite his denial that we possess a mind that exists in its own right, Hume must still explain how successive impressions are linked together to yield the objects of perception. As he did in his analysis of causality, he now speaks in terms of a tendency or, more precisely, a "propension to ascribe an identity to these successive perceptions."[53] In this context, his psychological investigation focuses on the origin of our belief in the stable identity we attribute to ourselves over the course of a lifetime. "We have a distinct idea of an object that remains invariable and uninterrupted thro' a suppos'd variation of time," Hume contends, "and this idea we call that of identity or sameness."[54]

Hume, however, does not consider such identity proper to human beings alone. Rather, he draws a telling analogy between the identity of the human self and the identity we attribute to things in general. Accordingly, his treatment of personal identity on a human level unfolds against the background of a consideration of the status of plants and natural phenomena. From Hume's perspective, the "propension to ascribe identity" to distinct impressions reflects a bias of the imagination so deeply ingrained that "we fall into it before we are aware."[55] For this reason, the relation of resemblance which allows for a sense of unity among objects is also the cause of a confusion of stable identity with objects of perception that are related but wholly distinct.

> At one instant we may consider the related succession as variable or interrupted; we are sure the next to ascribe to it a perfect identity and regard it as invariable and uninterrupted.[56]

The bias of the imagination, then, carries a crucial metaphysical consequence. This, Hume stresses, is not simply a linguistic or semantic dispute about the way we speak; rather, it generates what amounts to an elaborate fiction concerning the really real. The tendency to merge a series of discrete impressions into enduring realities finds expression in such cloudy notions as the soul, the self, and substance. In Hume's reckoning, however, such notions are merely attempts to obscure the variability of sense perception in favor of stable identities.

> Our propension to confound identity with relation is so great that we are apt to imagine something unknown and mysterious, connecting the parts, beside their relation; and this I take to be the case with regard to the identity we ascribe to plants and vegetables.[57]

Hume denies that we can perceive anything that is immutable and uninterrupted enough to justify our confidence in identity. So, how can he shake our confidence in such fictions? His strategy is to appeal to the data of everyday experience and observation and thereby demonstrate that what people assume to be invariable objects are no more than a succession of events. For Hume, identity or sameness is easily confused with a succession of different but related objects of perception. But what prompts such a blurring of the distinction between identity (and the tacit assumption that something remains unchanged over time) and the diversity of perceptions? Initially Hume attributes it to the relation of resemblance, the most common way of linking discrete impressions into a unified object of perception. In simpler terms, experiences that appear the same are conducive to a belief in stable things. "The relation facilitates the transition of the mind from one object to another," Hume contends, "and renders its passage as smooth as if it contemplated one continu'd object."[58]

In addition to the relation of resemblance, Hume adds contiguity and causation. Together, these three relations demonstrate how the objects of sense experience are no more than a succession of events linked on the basis of similar appearances (resemblance), the proximity of objects of perception in space and time (contiguity), and the observation that certain events follow other events in regular patterns (causation).

Hume is also attentive to the extent to which our sense of change is operative in our belief in identity. Gradual changes are more conducive to a belief in uninterrupted, invariable identity over time than radical ones. Likewise, changes of something immense in size are not as obvious as those which occur in something small. For this reason, Hume stresses the importance of an appreciation of a part-to-whole relationship so that "the addition or diminution of a mountain wou'd not be sufficient to produce a diversity in a planet."[59]

Likewise, we may also assume we are dealing with the same things over time on the basis of the ongoing fulfillment of a given purpose. Is the USS *Constitution* permanently docked in Boston harbor exactly the same vessel it was two centuries ago? If what we identify as that particular ship has been undergoing continual repairs, refittings, and replacements of its planking over the years, what warrants the assumption that it is exactly the *same* ship? Does anything justify it, other than the fact that we recognize it as such on the basis of its capacity to remain afloat and do what vessels are supposed to do? The common end, then, allows us to maintain a sense of continuity over time.[60]

Hume's focus on the part-to-whole relationship has special relevance in respect to organic connections in living things. The parts refer to a general purpose while exhibiting a relation to each other. We claim, for example, that a plant is a plant at any stage of its development and that "an oak, that grows from a small plant to a large tree, is still the same oak."[61] The fact that Hume extends this argument to humans as well (e.g., we assume that an infant becomes a man and acquires different characteristics without any change of identity) illustrates the degree to which he rejects any notion of a metaphysical substrate underlying change. What is significant here, it seems, is not what we do not directly observe (i.e., a full-grown plant when only a seedling is present) but how much we are willing to disregard (i.e., that the seedling looks nothing like a full-grown plant). For Hume, this is the result of a preoccupation with (1) a common purpose and (2) an organic connection of parts in relation to our sense of the whole.

> The effect of so strong a relation is . . . that in a very few years both vegetables and animals endure a total change, yet we still attribute identity to them, while their form, size, and substance are entirely alter'd.[62]

However, Hume discerns the tendency to attribute identity to certain experiences or things even in the absence of organicity of parts. A noise, for example, that is continually interrupted and resumed is construed as the *same noise*. If there is a numerical identity here, it only lies in the producing cause.[63] But what about a case where there is no constancy of parts or components? Consider, for example, a river. We designate a river as such even in the face of ceaseless change. What, indeed, constitutes the Mississippi or Nile from moment to moment? While we can localize these spans within specific geographic boundaries, the boundaries themselves are continually under alteration.[64]

Hume's illustrations of phenomena whose definitions are based on unceasing process is evocative of Heraclitus and his aphorism "No one steps in the same stream twice." For Heraclitus and Hume alike, the only constant in the universe is change. So, too, both thinkers question the assumption that what the senses report (i.e., stable entities that remain the same over time) is exactly the ways things are. This Heraclitean dimension is fully operative in Hume's account of the self. For all practical purposes, Hume places the idea of the human self on a par with our ideas of things like plants, animals, and inanimate objects in general. "The identity which we ascribe to the mind of man is only a fictitious one," Hume states, "and of a like kind with that which we ascribe to vegetables and animal bodies."[65]

The fiction of identity, then, is so wide-ranging in our experience of ourselves and the world that it can only proceed from the way we think or, in Hume's words, "from a like operation of the imagination upon like objects."[66] This is not to say that what the imagination generates has no grounding in reality. If this fiction is accepted and maintained, it proceeds from the fact that what we take to be identities are inseparable from the perceptions that provide their basis. Hume challenges anyone to deny that every perception that comes under the purview of the mind is not only distinct but "different, and distinguishable, and separable from every other perception."[67]

But what is the character of identity, and how does it relate to the operation of the imagination? In addressing this question, Hume considers two possibilities: either we grasp a real bond conjoining perceptions into unified objects, or ideas themselves give rise to the apparent bond between perceptions. Earlier in the *Treatise* (I, III, 14), he argued that the understanding never discerns any real connections linking the objects of perception. As his theory of causality (and analysis of necessary connection) discloses, the relation between cause and effect is ultimately rooted in our observation of the customary association of ideas. Hume, in effect, reduces identity to no more than a quality that we attribute to distinct perceptions, whereby unity of substance is derived from the multiplicity of sense data. He identifies these qualities, in turn, with the relations (i.e., re-semblance, contiguity, and causation) which provide the basis of identity in general.

> These are the uniting principles in the ideal world, and without them every distinct object is separable by the mind, and may be separately consider'd, and appears not to have any more connexion with any other object than if disjoin'd by the greatest difference and remoteness.[68]

In Hume's psychological analysis of idea formation, identity is not anything we discern in the midst of our perceptions. Rather, we some-how read identity into our perceptions by means of the three relations. Such relations are conducive to what Hume describes as "an easy transi-tion of ideas" that allow for a "smooth and uninterrupted progress of the thought along a train of connected ideas."[69] Accordingly, Hume consid-ers his task as a matter of isolating the precise relations operative in positing a mind or self. In this context, he confines his analysis to those relations he considers most relevant in this investigation—resemblance and causation.

Hume already considered the relation of resemblance in establishing the means the mind uses to make the transition from one object to another and lending credence to belief in stable identities. At this juncture, he deepens his psychological inquiry by considering the role of memory in preserving the past impressions that constitute the sine qua non of per-sonal identity. Hume attributes a dual role to memory as both the discov-erer and producer of identity.

> The memory not only discovers the identity but also contributes to its pro-duction by producing the relation of resemblance among the perceptions. The case is the same whether we consider ourselves or others.[70]

By way of analogy, Hume compares the mind to a republic or com-monwealth that undergoes great change but remains fundamentally the same political entity over the course of its history. A government creates a mutual commitment among its members that extends from one genera-tion to another and thereby allows for its perpetuation. The fact that we consider the United States government the same institution after more than two hundred years, with so many changes in its laws and popula-tion, attests to a belief in its enduring identity. For Hume, what applies to governments applies to humans as well. Just as the historical continuity of a government reinforces our belief that we are members of an enduring political unit, we assume we are the same individuals over the course of our own life histories.

As the same individual republic may not only change its members but also its laws and constitutions, in like manner the same person may vary his character and disposition, as well as his impressions and ideas, without losing his identity.[71]

In Hume's analysis, the causal relation assumes a special role in maintaining the fiction of personal identity. Causation links the present with the past and establishes a basis for looking to the future. Our ability to view our life as an intelligible narrative presupposes an appreciation that some occurrences tend to follow others in regular patterns. In this respect, Hume speaks of the mind as a "system of different perceptions . . . which are link'd together by the relation of cause and effect and mutually produce, destroy, influence, and modify each other."[72] This linkage, he assumes, is founded on a belief generated by the observation of a constant conjunction of happenings. If the causal relation is implicit in our sense of personal identity, it is because we are able to retain the images of past perceptions. In the absence of memory, we would have no grasp of the chain of causes and effects that comprise our sense of self. For him, memory is nothing less than the source of personal identity, since "memory alone acquaints us with the continuance and extent of this succession of perceptions."[73]

In broader terms, memory provides the framework in which we can connect even the remote past with an ongoing life history. While we may not explicitly recall each and every event that occurs throughout our lives, memory has the capacity to establish temporal referents which allow us to assume we are the same individuals, even in the face of large gaps in the story. As Hume observes, our inability to recount what we thought and did many years ago does not undermine our belief in who we are. We may rely largely on hearsay evidence for the details of our birth and early childhood. But on the basis of such background information, memory provides a means of extending the causal chain even into the most obscure regions of our background. Memory fills in the gaps and thereby allows us to assume we were born at a particular time and place that we cannot explicitly recollect.[74] But the limitation inherent in memory prompts Hume to question the extent to which it can establish personal identity in any definitive way. If our sense of self depended exclusively on memory, we would have to recall every experience in our lives. The fact that we extend our selfhood beyond what we can specifically recall attests to the power of the cause-and-effect relation on our understanding.

ASSESSING HUME ON PERSONAL IDENTITY

As we have seen, Hume's detailed analysis of personal identity stands in continuity with his account of causality. That account defines his critique of the common assumption that the self remains fundamentally the same over a lifetime. Whether he is addressing causality or personal identity, however, Hume dissociates events, at least in respect to any metaphysical bond running to their very natures. Connections between events are no more than the result of a psychological response to the observation of repeated occurrences. Accordingly, Hume draws a parallel between our belief in causal necessity and in personal identity. For Hume, both beliefs are only as firm as the experiences we gather over time. From this standpoint, human nature and the self are reduced to observable patterns of behavior and the expectations they generate.

What, then, is the referent for the self we intuit beneath the flow of perceptions? This question touches on the glaring paradox in Hume's treatment of personhood that bespeaks a fundamental inconsistency in his analysis: Hume continually speaks as if we have a stable self, even as he designates that version of selfhood an elaborate fiction. Terence M. Penulhum describes this apparent contradiction in these terms:

> Hume's readers have felt the inconsistency to come from the apparent fact that in applying his explanatory methods to the belief in the self's unity he first of all denies that unity; yet his explanatory methods require him to presuppose it.[75]

If this inconsistency is present in Hume, it also encompasses his conflicting interpretations of the debate concerning personal identity. On the one hand, he contends that this controversy "is not merely a dispute of words," since the mistake of attributing identity to changing things "is not confin'd to the expression but is commonly attended with a fiction."[76] But at the end of section 6, he draws the following conclusion:

> All the nice and subtle questions concerning personal identity can never possibly be decided and are to be regarded rather as grammatical than as philosophical difficulties. All the disputes concerning the identity of connected objects are merely verbal, except so far as the relation of parts gives rise to some fiction or imaginary principle of union.[77]

So, is the question of personal identity simply a verbal dispute about the way we speak and describe experiences, or does it assume a deeper philosophical import? Hume does not provide adequate grounds for a definitive response to this particular question. By his own admission, this topic remained a matter of deep perplexity for him, a kind of "labyrinth" which rendered him unable to correct his former opinions or even make them consistent with one another.[78] While Hume was convinced that distinct perceptions are the basis of personal identity, he was hard-pressed to explain how they are connected in relation to our sense of self. If

Descartes' major stumbling block lay in explaining mind-body interaction, Hume's obstacle proceeded from an inability to be true to the dictates of his own empiricism, an empiricism that negates the very self we require to make sense of our perceptions.

> It follows that thought alone finds personal identity, . . . but all my hopes vanish when I come to explain the principles, that unite our successive perceptions in our thought or consciousness. I cannot discover any theory which gives me satisfaction on this head.[79]

The reader of the *Treatise,* then, is left with something of an unresolved tension, since Hume seems compelled to endorse the very reality he calls into question. An analogous inconsistency is found in his appeals to the traditional theistic notion of an order of nature in coming to terms with our observation of a certain uniformity in both physical events and human behavior.[80] But Hume's empiricist program demands that any talk about the self is really talk about a flow of perceptions. If we have an idea of the self (i.e., who I am), then it must be generated by those very perceptions. Let us again consider Penulhum's remarks:

> Since the series of disconnected perceptions is all that there is, the question becomes this: how does the series come from time to time to include within it perceptions that are misinterpretations of other perceptions in the series?[81]

How can distinct perceptions, in and of themselves, provide the foundation of self-consciousness? The act of perceiving is simply not the same as an act of conscious awareness.

The fact that Hume must tacitly acknowledge what he seeks to undermine is a salient feature of his science of human nature.[82] But on the basis of the evidence, it appears that any reference to a self on Hume's part is purely a matter of expediency. As James Noxon observes, Hume's retention of the "old uncertified beliefs . . . upon which reflective men habitually act in the affairs of everyday life seemed . . . a good deal more reliable than any artificial ones the metaphysician might hope to devise."[83] Noxon's observation highlights an important facet of Hume's critical agenda. In the final analysis, a science of human nature must not only lay bare fallacious assumptions but remain faithful to our basic psychological presuppositions about the way things are, especially in regard to our sense of self. Hume is not just a thoroughgoing empiricist but a commonsense empiricist. Jettisoning the notions we require to make sense of our inner life and the surrounding world would be too high a price to pay in the interest of this empiricist commitment.[84]

Hume's most blatant appeal to the notion of a stable self is found in his discussion of the passions of pride and humility. The self in effect provides the object of these passions or, more precisely, the standard against which we measure these feelings. In Humean terms, the experience of the passions in general is inextricably bound up with self-awareness.

> 'Tis evident that pride and humility, tho' directly contrary, have yet the same object. This object is self, or that succession of related ideas and impressions of which we have an intimate memory and consciousness.[85]

Still, Hume distinguishes between the cause of these passions and their object. From this standpoint, the self does not produce the passions; it merely provides their objective correlate.

> The first idea that is presented to the mind is that of the cause or productive principle. This excites the passion, . . . and that passion when excited turns our view to another idea, which is that of self. Here then is a passion plac'd betwixt two ideas of which the one produces it and the other is produc'd by it. The first idea represents the cause, the second the object of the passion.[86]

But it is one thing to acknowledge a self that merely provides a convenient touchstone for our perceptions, passions, or emotions. It is an altogether different matter to explain what constitutes that self and the personal identity it supports. In the absence of any metaphysical understanding of a substantial reality that endures through time and remains fundamentally what it is (or more precisely *who I am*), such an explanation is ruled out from the outset. It is this absence of a metaphysical dimension that makes Hume's analysis of personal identity so compelling. Hume's science of human nature demonstrates precisely what is lost once we abdicate a metaphysical understanding of personhood grounded on an immaterial principle that philosophers and theologians designate as the soul or mind.

CONCLUSION

Hume saw his rejection of unverifiable notions like soul or mind as a great philosophical advantage, opening the prospect of a scientific psychology not impeded by such cumbersome beliefs. But this advantage only extends so far. Ultimately we must confront the probing question as to what imparts coherence to our sense of who and what we are as human beings. From a purely practical standpoint, however, it is still feasible to base personal identity on the flow of perceptual experience. As D. G. C. MacNabb has pointed out, even if the self were no more than a bundle of perceptions connected by the appropriate relations (i.e., resemblance, contiguity, and causation), it would "yet have an identity in a natural and proper sense of that word . . . as long as each of its perceptions was related to those that went before in the right sort of way it would remain the same self."[87] But in that case, we confront what amounts to an infinite-regress problem. If my personal identity or sense of self is only as secure as the sequence of perceptions, the sequence must be extended backward indefinitely; as a result, we are constantly obliged to refer each perception to its predecessors in order to establish the requisite continuity over time. What constitutes the crucial nexus of our perceptions which renders the series itself intelligible? MacNabb admits that he was "perplexed and dissatisfied" with this interpretation, since "if the self is only a relational unity of perceptions . . . that inner awareness of our own being . . . remains unaccounted for."[88]

But much more than inner self-awareness remains unexplained. Such a theory also creates a significant problem regarding our relationship with other people, specifically in the moral sphere. Moral responsibility is not rooted in perceptions alone. I cannot view myself as morally accountable in any genuine sense if there is nothing substantial from which my decisions proceed. We only impute responsibility to free, rational agents capable of making choices for which they are answerable (and thus deserving of praise or blame).

But for all the problems it generates, Hume's scientific approach to human nature raises probing questions that seriously challenge many of our fundamental anthropological assumptions. In the face of the Humean critique of the metaphysical underpinnings of the self, we can never feel completely at ease with an uncritical response to those questions. A key issue in this context (and one which provides a core of a plethora of related issues) concerns the supposed permanence of the ego. How permanent, abiding, or invariable is the self we take for granted? Experience reveals that we are constantly changing beings, engaged in a dynamic process of development, not merely over the long run but from moment to moment as well.

But must a commitment to a stable self commit us to this particular understanding of permanence? Does the assumption that we are the same persons over a lifetime mean that we must be unchanging in a static sense, in the way a rock is unchanging?[89] Hume's lack of metaphysical attunement to these issues is most telling on precisely this point. From the perspective of a substantialist metaphysics, it is possible to account for identity in the midst of change and stability in the context of ongoing process. In this respect, it would be naive to adopt a Parmenidean model of the human reality, which considers us completely immutable. But this need not commit us to the Heraclitean model Hume seems to endorse, that we are no more than aggregates of ever-changing perceptions.

In broad historical terms, Hume stands as precursor to all subsequent empiricist approaches to philosophical anthropology and psychology. By way of conclusion, it is illuminating to consider one of the most salient of these responses as it emerges in the philosophical behaviorism of Gilbert Ryle (1900–1976). Ryle exhibits a clear Humean influence that is reflected in his devastating critique of the Cartesian understanding of mind and, by extension, any metaphysical dualism between mind and body. Ryle's classic statement in this vein is found in his landmark work *The Concept of Mind* (1949). The focus of his discussion is what he terms the "official doctrine," or, alternately, the dogma of the Ghost in the Machine. While Ryle perceives Descartes as the chief exponent of this dogma, he discerns it in a wide range of theories that arose in response to the threat posed by a seventeenth-century mechanistic outlook.

> With the doubtful exceptions of idiots and infants in arms every human being has both a body and a mind. Some would prefer to say that every human being is both a body and a mind. His body and his mind are ordinarily harnessed together, but after the death of the body his mind may continue to exist and function.[90]

According to Ryle, the dogma of the Ghost in the Machine entails the teaching that we possess both a mind and a body, with events appropriate to the mind and body alike. From this standpoint, mental events are inner and private, while bodily events external and public. In Ryle's reckoning, all this amounts to two collateral histories, encompassing mind and body alike.[91] Such a distinction between the private and public spheres is correlative with one between "inner" and "outer" experience. But what might be used in a metaphorical sense can easily be construed in literal terms, whereby we assume that mind exists *inside* the body. In the official theory under scrutiny, however, this is clearly contradictory, since mind is depicted as immaterial and thus not bound by spatial categories.[92]

Ryle detects an additional assumption implicit in the official doctrine, that minds and bodies constitute two different types of existence.

> What exists or happens may have the status of physical existence or it may have the status of mental existence; . . . so, it is supposed, some existing is physical existing, other existing is mental existing.[93]

On the surface, it appears that such a polar opposition between the mental and physical demand that they be treated in completely different terms, by means of vocabularies appropriate to each. From Ryle's standpoint, however, proponents of the official doctrine resort to the mechanistic language of the body in describing the activities of a mind viewed as wholly distinct from that body and free of its physical limitations.[94]

For Ryle, the tendency to describe the mind and the mental in physicalistic terms is the result of a category mistake that generates a "double life" theory of mind-body dualism. He offers several illustrations in support of this position. For the present purposes, a consideration of one example suffices. Ryle proposes the case of a visit to Oxford or Cambridge. A foreigner is shown the various colleges, libraries, playing fields, and administration buildings of those venerable institutions. Afterward, he asks to see the "university," as if it constitutes a distinct entity in its own right, apart from the units which comprise it.[95]

According to Ryle, that visitor would be guilty of the same species of category mistake as one who conflates the difference between mental and physical events. Such an error gives rise to a great inconsistency, whereby the mental operations hidden from public scrutiny are described in relation to bodily processes, and by means of an obverse vocabulary: minds are described as neither in space, nor motions, nor modifications of matter, nor accessible to observation. "As thus represented," Ryle contends, "minds are not merely ghosts harnessed to machines; they are themselves just spectral machines."[96]

Ryle's response to the official doctrine moves on two levels. On the one hand, he wishes to eliminate any distinction between mind and matter. But he is quick to stress that the elimination of the mind-body distinction does not entail a rejection of mental processes or any reduction of mind to matter (or matter to mind). Rather, he merely seeks to lay bare what he perceives as the logically absurd corollaries proceeding from the same category mistakes on which the official theory rests.[97] This strategy provides the segue for a more radical agenda, whereby almost every assertion about mental activity can be described on the basis of observable behavior, whether it be an act of knowing, understanding, willing, imagining, or feeling. For all practical purposes, then, Ryle dispenses with the need for any reference to a mind at all. In this respect, his overall project stands in continuity with that of Hume. In both thinkers we find the suggestion that difficulties which arise in discussions of human nature (specifically the mind-body problem) are resolvable by addressing the grammatical and linguistic problems that accompany such discussions.

But the clearest point of contact between Hume and Ryle lies in their respective uses of observable criteria in dealing with different aspects of the inner life. In Hume's case, the criteria are perceptual; for Ryle, they are behavioral. Hume exerted a tremendous influence in highlighting the extent to which our sense of self is bound up with experience so that "I never can catch myself at any time without a perception."[98] But where does one go from here? After disclosing the obvious empirical dimension attached to self-awareness, Hume must still come to terms with the depth of the self and the fact that we come to an increasingly refined awareness of our identities over the course of our life's journey.

After Hume, however, we find a growing conviction that even the richness of our inner life is ultimately explicable on a purely empirical basis.

This trend has a special applicability to contemporary discussions of the meaning of personhood. In a postmodernist context, a person is defined principally on the basis of overt behavioral characteristics, rather than in terms of what one is, by virtue of a uniquely human nature or distinctive mode of being. The presupposition that personhood is a matter of how one behaves opens the way to a bold assumption that not every human being necessarily qualifies as a person or, more radically, that members of the human species have no monopolistic claim on personhood at all.

DISCUSSION QUESTIONS

1. What does Hume mean when he defines personal identity (i.e., our sense of self) in terms of a bundle of perceptions?
2. Discuss the Newtonian background of Hume's empiricist analysis of causality and its significance for his attempt to develop a "science" of human nature.
3. In what sense (according to Hume) are the relations of resemblance, contiguity, and causality important components of our belief in a stable, enduring self?
4. Discuss the implications of Hume's key question "From what impression is the supposed idea derived?" for his interpretation of metaphysical notions like God, the soul, and the self.
5. What role does Hume attribute to memory in respect to our sense of personal identity?

NOTES

All references to Hume's *A Treatise of Human Nature* are drawn from www.class .uidaho.edu/michelsen/texts/Hume%20Treatise. Citations of this work refer to *Treatise*, followed by the appropriate book, part, and section. References to Hume's *Enquiries Concerning Human Understanding* are drawn from the third edition, revised by P. H. Nidditch (Oxford: Clarendon, 1978). Citations of this work refer to *Enquiries*, followed by the section, part, marginal, and page numbers of the edition (e.g., *Enquiries* IV, I, 20, p. 25).

1. Quote from the private papers of James Boswell, ed. G. Scott and F. A. Pottle (Mt. Vernon, N.Y.: Rudge, 1928–1934), 12: 227–232, in W. T. Jones, *A History of Philosophy (Hobbes to Hume)*, 2nd ed. (New York: Harcourt Brace & World, 1969), 297 n. 1.
2. *Enquiries* XII, III, 130, p. 162.
3. Jerrold Seigel, *The Idea of the Self: Thought and Experience in Western Europe since the Seventeenth Century* (Cambridge: Cambridge University Press, 2005), 87.

4. James Noxon, *Hume's Philosophical Development: A Study of his Method* (Oxford: Clarendon, 1973), 9, stresses both the common ground shared by Descartes and Hume and the differences in their respective approaches:

> Although Hume's philosophy develops in opposition to Descartes' at almost every point, the *animus* of its ruthless questioning of assumptions, beliefs, and principles is indelibly Cartesian. Beneath the differences in style, there is in Descartes and Hume the same sense of obligation to test the power of reason. There is no doubt in my mind that it was Hume who pressed the questions harder, far beyond the point where reason could reestablish itself by claiming intuitive certainty of an existential truth.

5. Noxon (*Hume's Philosophical Development*, 30) qualifies this Newtonian influence:

> Newton's scientific work has been widely recognized as a formative influence upon the development of Hume's, especially that of his method. What Hume scholars call the "Newtonian method" was not the invention of Newton; it was the resolutive/compositive (or analytic/synthetic) method which had its fifteenth-century origin in the University of Padua and had been perfected by the mathematical and experimental genius of Galileo. The most important discovery of the early modern scientists was the discovery of science itself (i.e. of the scientific method).

6. Paul Edwards, ed., *Encyclopedia of Philosophy* (New York: Macmillan, 1972), 5:491a, s.v. "Newton, Isaac," by Dudley Shapere.

7. R. S. Westfall, "Newton," in *New Catholic Encyclopedia*, 10:428a.

8. *Encyclopedia of Philosophy*, 491b, s.v. "Newtonian Mechanics and Mechanical Explanation," by Dudley Shapere.

9. *New Catholic Encyclopedia* (Washington, D.C.: Catholic University of America Press, 1967), 10: 427a, s.v. "Newton, Sir Isaac," by R. S. Westfall.

10. *Treatise*, introduction.

11. *Treatise*, introduction.

12. *Enquiries* IV, I, 20–21, 25.

13. *Enquiries* IV, I, 21, 25–26.

14. *Enquiries* I, I, I, 1.

15. *Treatise* I, I, II.

16. Hume cites one exception to this rule (*Treatise* I, I, I) in a case where someone encounters a new shade of the color blue:

> Let all the different shades of that colour, except that single one, be plac'd before him, descending gradually from the deepest to the lightest; 'tis plain, that he will perceive a blank, where that shade is wanting, and will be sensible, that there is a greater distance in that place betwixt the contiguous colors, than in any other.

17. *Treatise* I, III, I.

18. *Treatise* I, III, VIII.

19. *Treatise* I, I, IV.

20. *Treatise* I, III, II.

21. *Enquiries* IV, I, 22, 26.

22. *Enquiries* IV, I, 23.

23. *Treatise* I, III, XIV.

24. *Treatise* I, III, II.

25. *Enquiries* IV, I, 23, 27. For purposes of illustration (*Enquiries* IV, I, 24, 28), Hume proposes the following scenario:

> Present two smooth pieces of marble to a man who has no tincture of natural philosophy; he will never discover that they will adhere together in such a manner as to require great force to separate them in a direct line, while they make so small a resistance to a lateral pressure.

26. *Treatise* I, III, II. Hume's discussion of contiguity in this context requires clarification. He does not mean that causality only encompasses cause-and-effect relationships that are close to each other in space and time. Accordingly, he by no means wishes to suggest that causality only involves proximate causes and effects. He wants to stress the common view of causality operative in the majority of people's attitudes toward the world.

27. *Treatise* I, III, VI.

28. *Treatise* I, III, II.

29. *Treatise* I, III, II.

30. *Treatise* I, III, II.

31. *Treatise* I, III, VI.

32. *Treatise* I, III, VI.

33. *Treatise* I, III, XII.

34. *Treatise* I, III, XII.

35. *Treatise* I, III, VIII. Cf. the remarks of John Valdimir Price, *David Hume* (New York: Twayne, 1968), 41:

> Hume affirms that subjective, individually-experienced custom is the unifying power or agent between cause and effect, that the contiguity and the constant conjunction of two events impose upon our minds so strong a sense of permanent relation that we cannot dissociate them.

36. *Treatise* I, III, XII.

37. Here I draw on the example provided by Justus Hartnack in *Kant's Theory of Knowledge*, trans. M. Holmes Hartshorne (New York: Harcourt, Brace & World, 1967), 8.

38. Hartnack (*Kant's Theory of Knowledge*, 8) provides these additional comments regarding this dimension of Hume's causal theory:

> No sense impression exists that can show us the difference between merely following after another event temporally and following as a consequence of the event. In other words, to follow as a consequence is not, according to Hume, something that is essentially different from merely following after. It means simply that one is accustomed to seeing a certain kind of event succeeded always by a certain other kind of event, whereby one is led to the view that this is something that necessarily must happen.

Similarly, James Collins, *A History of Modern European Philosophy* (Milwaukee: Bruce, 1954), 409, highlights the relationship between Hume's skepticism toward metaphysics and his psychological method:

> Once we become reconciled to foregoing any ultimate ontological principles, we are free to observe the uniformities within our experience, identify and demarcate the

powers at work, and render our principles of explanation as general as possible within empirical bounds.

39. Seigel, *Idea of the Self,* 126.
40. *Treatise* I, IV, V.
41. *Treatise* I, IV, V.
42. *Treatise* I, IV, V.
43. Seigel, *Idea of the Self,* 126.
44. John Locke, *An Essay Concerning Human Understanding,* ed. A. D. Woozley (New York: New American Library, 1964), 2:27, 9.
45. Locke, *An Essay Concerning Human Understanding,* 2:27, 9, 211.
46. Seigel, *Idea of the Self,* 127.
47. *Treatise* I, IV, VI.
48. *Treatise* I, IV, VI.
49. *Treatise* I, IV, VI.
50. *Treatise* I, IV, VI.
51. *Treatise,* I, IV, VI.
52. *Treatise* I, IV, VI.
53. *Treatise* I, IV, VI.
54. *Treatise* I, IV, VI.
55. *Treatise* I, IV, VI.
56. *Treatise* I, IV, VI.
57. *Treatise* I, IV, VI.
58. *Treatise* I, IV, VI.
59. *Treatise* I, IV, VI.
60. *Treatise* I, IV, VI.
61. *Treatise* I, IV, VI.
62. *Treatise* I, IV, VI.
63. *Treatise* I, IV, VI. Hume proposes an additional analogy, involving the replacement of one building by another. Even if the form and the materials of the new structure are different, people assume it is the same on the basis of its relation to the inhabitants.
64. *Treatise* I, IV, VI.
65. *Treatise* I, IV, VI.
66. *Treatise* I, IV, VI.
67. *Treatise* I, IV, VI.
68. *Treatise* I, IV, VI.
69. *Treatise* I, IV, VI.
70. *Treatise* I, IV, VI.
71. *Treatise* I, IV, VI.
72. *Treatise* I, IV, VI.
73. *Treatise* I, IV, VI.
74. *Treatise* I, IV, VI.
75. Terence M. Penulhum, "The Self in Hume's Philosophy," in *David Hume: Many-Sided Genius,* ed. Kenneth R. Merrill and Robert W. Shahan (Norman: University of Oklahoma Press, 1976), 13.
76. *Treatise* I, IV, VI.
77. *Treatise* I, IV, VI.

78. *Treatise*, appendix.

79. *Treatise*, appendix.

80. *Treatise* II, III, I. Similarly, the *Enquiry* (V, II, 44) refers to a "preestablished harmony" that Hume links with the custom that is instrumental in our belief in the necessary connection between regular patterns of perceptions.

81. Terence Penulhum, "Hume's Theory of the Self Revisited," *Dialogue* 14 (1975): 406. In a later work, *David Hume: An Introduction to his Philosophical System* (West Lafayette, Ind.: Purdue University Press, 1992), 62, Penulhum casts the problem in these terms: "Hume at first denies the reality of any self beyond the perceptions one has, but then proceeds to explain how it is that we manage to evolve the firm belief that there is a self."

82. Penulhum ("Self in Hume's Philosophy," 15) offers this suggestion for coming to terms with this apparent impasse in Hume's psychology: "Hume could . . . hold that among the ideas that the series that is the self contains, there comes to be the idea of that series, and the ideas that constitute the mistaken judgments about the identity the series manifests." But this interpretation leaves us with little more than a vicious circle, in which a series of perceptions gives rise to an idea of that series, along with an erroneous idea of identity that is itself rooted in the same perceptions on which these ideas are based.

83. Noxon, *Hume's Philosophical Development*, 9–10.

84. Conversely, D. Garrett, "Hume's Self-doubts about Personal Identity," *Philosophical Review* 90 (1981): 337–58, attributes any inconsistency in Hume's account of personal identity to a failure to adhere rigidly to the dictates of his own empiricism. According to Garrett (358),

> It is his empiricism that prevents him from permitting real connections of inherence or necessary connection that could help him, [but] it might be more accurate to say that given his empiricist views of personal identity and causation, his problem is caused by a view of the mental that is not empiricist enough.

85. *Treatise* II, I, II.

86. *Treatise* II, I, II.

87. D. G. C. MacNabb, *David Hume: His Theory of Knowledge and Morality*, 2d ed. (Hamden, Conn.: Archon, 1966), 151.

88. MacNabb, *David Hume*, 151.

89. This analogy must be qualified, since even rocks are subject to the same changes we observe throughout the natural world. I use the analogy anyway, however, since we tend to identify rocks with permanence (or at least as much permanence as we can find in nature).

90. Gilbert Ryle, *The Concept of Mind* (Chicago: University of Chicago Press, 1949), 11.

91. Ryle, *Concept of Mind*, 11–12.

92. Ryle, *Concept of Mind*, 12.

93. Ryle, *Concept of Mind*, 13.

94. Ryle, *Concept of Mind*, 18.

95. Ryle, *Concept of Mind*, 16.

96. Ryle, *Concept of Mind*, 20.

97. Ryle, *Concept of Mind*, 22.

98. *Treatise* I, IV, VI.

IV

HUMANITY
AND PERSONHOOD

8

Postmodernism: Humans, Persons, and Nonpersons

The 1982 film *E.T. the Extra-Terrestrial* (ranked twenty-fifth on the American Film Institute's list of greatest movies) concerns the friendship between three children and a space alien. The alien, E.T., does not look human at all. But as the story unfolds, we see that E.T. possesses human qualities and exhibits a degree of empathy that allows him to forge a clear emotional bond with the characters and viewing audience alike. Does E.T.'s otherworldly appearance render him any less human than the earthlings he encounters, at least in his capacity for interpersonal relationships? From the outset, it becomes apparent that this is no mere science fiction movie. On a deeper level, it raises thought-provoking questions about the parameters of personhood and fundamental presuppositions about its meaning in a contemporary context.

Is personhood limited to the human species? For that matter, are there human beings who do not qualify as persons? While such questions would be viewed as startling from a traditional anthropological perspective, they assume a genuine relevance at the beginning of the new millennium within that philosophical outlook loosely designated as postmodernism. The assumption that every human being is a person simply by virtue of his or her humanity is severely challenged by postmodern philosophers. Indeed, these thinkers press the envelope of our anthropological presuppositions to the limit and beyond.

POSTMODERN PHILOSOPHY: A BROAD OVERVIEW

Postmodern philosophy embraces a distinctive outlook that touches on a variety of disciplines. In this respect, postmodernism is a blanket term that covers a wide range of themes and ideas. Like other intellectual movements (e.g., existentialism), it is so broad in scope that it eludes succinct characterization. At the very least, however, we can try to isolate some common features which any thinker or position labeled as "postmodern" may share and/or endorse.

In its most general sense, postmodernism is decidedly antifoundational in character, challenging any claim to objectivity regarding truth, knowledge, or meaning. This antifoundationalist agenda is implicit in the term "postmodern" itself. In historical terms, postmodernism comes after or succeeds the modern period (beginning in the seventeenth century) but not merely as a sequel to what precedes it. Postmodernism assumes a polemical connotation as a perspective that stands against modernity (especially Enlightenment ways of thinking) and its optimistic commitment to a universal rationality. In the words of one commentator, "Postmodern philosophy typically opposes foundationalism, essentialism, and realism."[1] Accordingly, postmodern philosophers exhibit a marked skepticism toward the capacity of reason to resolve the fundamental problems that permeate the Western tradition as a whole. This critique represents an indictment of the disinterested use of reason in every branch of philosophical investigation, especially in the moral sphere.

In an intellectual milieu characterized by tremendous pluralism and a fragmentation of belief systems, we encounter the widespread assumption that basic moral norms cannot be justified through rational argumentation. From this standpoint, moral values are viewed as by-products of nonrational decisions, based on the instincts of the heart rather than the dictates of discursive reasoning and the shared values of a culture or society. This antirationalist stance is closely aligned with a rejection of the universal validity of moral standards. The upshot of this dual critique (i.e., a critique of the capacity of reason to resolve or adjudicate disputes and a critique of the objectivity of moral judgments) is a thoroughgoing relativism which reduces moral truths to the diverse perspectives of their adherents.

Postmodern philosophers issue a severe challenge to moral objectivity precisely because they reject any suggestion of a common standard for moral evaluations which allow for a theory-neutral assessment of what is right or wrong.[2] But in the absence of a firm foundation for our moral claims, to what can we appeal? Postmodern philosophy endorses a key feature of twentieth-century linguistic analysis in assuming that intellectual systems operate like languages and that linguistic signs function in a self-reflective manner rather than a referential one.³ This premise stands in direct opposition to a classical correspondence theory of truth and the notion that truth claims are based on a conformity or an isomorphism between what is in our minds and what is "out there"—that is, a stable reality beyond the self. From the postmodern perspective, truth becomes largely a matter of coherence, whereby the truth value of our statements is measured in terms of the extent to which they cohere with or fit into a conceptual framework or web of beliefs.

Such a relativizing of moral judgments has a clear bearing on postmodern interpretations of human nature and ultimately any conception of personhood which these interpretations support. In this respect, a particular focus of postmodern critiques is the notion of an ahistorical human nature transcending time and culture. For Richard Rorty, that notion is inextricably bound up with a specific understanding of the philosophical enterprise itself. From his standpoint, the search for universal agreement and objectivity is linked with an understanding of humans in wholly objective terms. In place of a model of philosophy as a confrontational (i.e., a systematic) discipline aimed at discerning "the truth," Rorty emphasizes the importance of sustaining the conversation of humankind in a mutually edifying way. This alternate model of philosophy issues a clear challenge to the idea of a stable, abiding human nature. For Rorty, the assumption that we can reduce ourselves to a single descriptive vocabulary linked to a nature or an essence (capable of accurate description) serves to treat human beings as objects rather than true subjects.⁴

In lieu of a fixed human essence or nature, on what are determinations of our humanness based? Biological criteria, for example, are readily established and thus easily verifiable in empirical terms. So, even in the absence of an appeal to a metaphysical foundation of our humanness, we can still establish who is a human being on purely scientific grounds. The real casuality, however, in the postmodern denial of a human nature is the notion of human personhood. Once the objectivity of human nature is called into question, the objectivity of personhood easily falls by the wayside as well.

A more radical question, then, is, Does biological humanness, in and of itself, provide a sufficient guarantee of personhood? Postmodern philosophers unanimously answer in the negative. For them, an individual may not qualify as a person because he or she has not yet acquired the fundamental attributes of persons or, conversely, because that individual has lost those attributes. Accordingly, someone may be designated as a human being in strictly biological terms but be excluded from a moral community of persons with rights and responsibilities to oneself and others. From this standpoint, not every human being necessarily assumes a moral standing simply because that individual is human. Postmodernist philosophers, in short, draw an explicit distinction between humanity and personhood. In so doing, they offer a critical reassessment of basic presuppositions about what it means to be human and, conversely, what it means to be a person. As defined by Roland Puccetti, a person is not just a living human organism but a conscious entity with a range of experiences that substantiate its claim to a right to life.[5]

THE CONSCIOUSNESS CRITERION OF PERSONHOOD

In its classical interpretation (as exemplified by Aquinas), personhood is a unique participation in the rational nature of each human being. Such rationality is the mark of membership in the human species, as reflected in the capacities and very being of individual persons. But as Puccetti's definition indicates, the assumption that every human being is a person (simply by virtue of his or her humanity) is severely challenged in a postmodernist context. On the one hand, the distinction between human nature (based on membership in the human species) and moral personhood is wholly consistent with the sharp dichotomy between mind and body drawn by Descartes. But as observed in the previous chapter, the former distinction (i.e., between humanness and personhood) finds a more explicit inspiration in the empiricism of John Locke.

For Locke, personhood presupposes conscious awareness of *self as self*. Locke's definition holds that a person constitutes "a thinking, intelligent being that has reason and reflection and can consider itself as itself, the same thinking thing in different times and places."[6] In Lockean terms, then, only the connected flow of conscious experience provides a foundation of personal identity and consequently a basis for attributing moral responsibility to individuals for their actions.[7] By implication, Locke establishes the consciousness criterion of personhood which assumes a central role in postmodernist discussions. For him, consciousness is essential to thinking, since it is "impossible for anyone to perceive without perceiving that he does perceive."[8]

But if consciousness is bound up with thinking, it is also the crucial component of selfhood and the sense of permanence we attach to our very sense of self. Locke's assumption here is that personal identity presupposes the "sameness" of a rational being, and only this continuity with the past allows us to affirm that we are the same selves now as before.[9] For Locke, then, the key issue is the persistence of personal identity over time, not the endurance of a single, identical human substance. In Lockean terms, what counts is the uninterrupted flow of conscious experience that allows one to be a self to oneself at all.[10]

From this standpoint, any talk about what humans are is reducible to a consideration of their capability of thinking or feeling. After Locke's criterion of consciousness is pushed to its logical conclusion, personhood becomes a superogatory attribute that some individuals possess and some do not, depending on the quality of their conscious experience. For those who proceed from this premise, consciousness (in the words of one commentator) is nothing less than "the most important characteristic that distinguishes humans from other forms of animal life."[11]

But what constitutes "conscious experience," and what behavioral characteristics does it encompass? Clearly the consciousness in question cannot be purely sensory, since such a criterion would extend personhood to animal life in general. This particular consideration poses a special challenge to postmodernist accounts of personhood, since a wide-ranging criterion like consciousness lends to a broad application of the term "person" to human and nonhuman species alike. Can any living creature capable of sensory awareness be designated a person? According to one assessment, members of other species may be viewed as persons if they possess properties or characteristics (e.g., intelligence and a receptivity to pain or distress) that render them similar to humans in "morally relevant" ways.[12]

But as postmodern thinkers acknowledge, such characteristics may be shared in common by human and nonhuman species. Indeed, how flexible is the notion of personhood before it loses its meaning altogether? Charles Taylor offers a more precise determination in this vein. From Taylor's standpoint, the consciousness in question is not simply the ability to represent objects but, more significantly, the capacity for concern.[13] In Taylor's reckoning, a person must be capable of responding but not merely to sensory stimuli. Rather, personal status presupposes the ability to respond on a one-on-one basis. Taylor designates this kind of being a person, "a being who can be addressed, and who can reply"—that is, as a *respondent*.[14]

The underlying assumption here is that in the absence of self-consciousness (and, by extension, consciousness of others) one does not qualify as a member of the moral community. In this regard, moral standing presupposes the social interaction of beings who enjoy a rich inner life that allows them to enter a web of relationships carrying personal rights and generating corresponding duties to others.[15] Such an assumption reveals a marked neo-Kantian dimension in postmodernism that acquires a pivotal role regarding the definitions and limits of personhood. In classical Kantian terms, humans occupy a unique role as the mediators between the phenomenal and noumenal orders, the sensible and suprasensible worlds respectively. On a phenomenal level, humans are subject to the same spatiotemporal laws as anything else in the universe. Morally, however, humans are related to the noumenal realm as free agents. Free agency thus points to a spiritual status which is the mark of persons alone. Accordingly, personhood implies freedom, self-consciousness, and an accompanying awareness of duty to oneself and others. In Kantian terms, personality presupposes a subject of duty.[16]

By virtue of their duty consciousness, Kant defines humans as noumenal realities because they are not things but persons. In this way, rationality is inextricably bound up with Kant's understanding of personhood, since persons qualify as ends in themselves rather than mere means to ends.[17] Strictly speaking, then, only persons deserve respect, precisely because persons can never be used as a means to achieve another end. From this standpoint, only the person has the capacity to appreciate the moral law and its demands.

But if defining personhood in terms of consciousness alone is susceptible to an overextension of the notion to all living things, then defining persons on the basis of moral agency may well justify the inclusion of nonhumans who qualify as moral agents, including robots. Oswald Hanfling pointedly asks what would prevent extending personhood to machines resembling ourselves.[18] Can robots achieve the kind of moral status that allows them to respect others and be respected in turn? Can humanoid mechanisms participate in a community of persons on any level? If so, then perhaps determinations of who (or what) is a person proceed from nothing more than people's attitudes toward the being in question, rather than from its intrinsic properties. R. G. A. Dolby grounds these attitudes in the background assumptions and expectations generated by cultural membership. For Dolby, what qualifies a being as a person has nothing to do with inner processes but with what we are led to see on the basis of cultural influences.[19] The pertinent consideration is whether people would be *willing* to accept robots as persons, not whether they lack human nature. In the absence of a firm metaphysical grounding in the order of being, personhood can be whatever we wish it to be, provided that our definitions meet certain behavioral criteria that allow for a broad consensus. As William Stephens observes, "The core meaning of 'person' is neither intensively nor extensively coincident with the concept 'human being' and thus is in no way . . . limited to earthlings."[20]

From the postmodernist standpoint, however, the difficulty of defining the person is an outgrowth of the extent to which this notion is heavily laden with subjective and ideological presuppositions. For these thinkers, such diversity and variability of meaning support the thesis that personhood is a matter of interpretation or, more precisely, the interpretation which reflects current societal values and practices. Richard Rorty, for one, acknowledges a "metaphysical longing" for one unifying concept of personhood which allows us to attribute moral liability to a specific subject. But in A. O. Rorty's estimation, a fundamental error is that regionalized functions are subsumed in a structured concept.[21] From this standpoint, it makes little difference whether the concept of the person assumes diverse functions or whether a foundational concept of personhood even exists. In the final analysis, she views any appeal to the notion of personhood as no more than a rhetorical device convenient in expanding political rights or curtailing the exercise of political power.[22]

If definitions of personhood are not grounded on something metaphysically substantial, then what lends them intelligibility? Daniel Dennett proposes six conditions which any person worthy of the name must fulfill: rationality, intentionality, an attitude or stance toward intentionality, reciprocity, verbal communication, and consciousness in some special way (e.g., self-consciousness).[23] Some observations are in order here. First, it is evident that postmodernist philosophers heavily emphasize overt characteristics as criteria of personhood. Even the traits that focus on something intrinsic to the individual (i.e., qualities of an inner life such as self-consciousness) are closely linked with their observable behavioral manifestations. This observation prompts a second one: the lists of "conditions" or "properties" which these philosophers specify as their criteria of personhood can be extremely random. Dennett acknowledges as much when he argues that humans "can only aspire to . . . approximations of the ideal, and there can be no way to set a 'passing grade' that is not arbitrary."[24] What constitutes the definitive list of characteristics a person must possess in order to qualify as such? Postmodern assessments of personhood are ultimately based on how one is perceived by others in a public forum, rather than on what one is by virtue of a nature, essence, or substantial form.

THE BIOETHICAL DIMENSION

The postmodern distinction between humanity and personhood acquires a pivotal role in many contemporary bioethical debates regarding end-of-life decisions and the right to life of those deprived of higher consciousness. In a bioethical context, postmodernists share the conviction that personhood is determined on the basis of empirically observable traits. From this perspective, the loss of rational capacity, autonomy, and conscious experience presupposes a corresponding loss of moral agency and the personhood on which moral agency depends. This dichotomization of human nature and personhood coincides with an emphasis on the diversity of moral visions and differing accounts of obligations, rights, and values. In this respect, postmodernists critique the Enlightenment project of establishing what H. Tristram Engelhardt Jr. characterizes as a "universal content-full ethics."[25] For him, such a failed project is rooted in basic Western philosophical assumptions about reason's capacity to resolve the moral problems we confront in a contemporary setting.

Engelhardt offers an interesting referent for examining the main lines of a postmodernist bioethics and the theory of personhood shaped by postmodern ways of thinking. He draws a crucial distinction between those he characterizes as *moral friends* and *moral strangers,* respectively. *Moral friends* are those who share enough of our content-full morality that they can acknowledge the resolution of moral conflicts on the basis of (1) sound moral arguments or (2) a mutual appeal to a jointly recognized authority. *Moral strangers,* on the other hand, are those who (1) do not share sufficient moral premises or rules which enable them to resolve conflicts by sound rational agreement or (2) have no mutual agreement as to which moral authorities are capable of resolving such conflicts.[26]

What prospects do we have for achieving a genuine moral consensus if the very people with whom we enter into conflicts are moral strangers? Most moral debates (especially those regarding life-and-death matters) appear completely irreconcilable. "Rational argument does not quiet moral controversies," Engelhardt contends, "when one encounters moral strangers, people of different moral visions."[27] If opponents do not endorse each other's fundamental principles, then attempting to resolve moral controversies by rational argumentation is futile. In Engelhardt's assessment, the failure of the Enlightenment project (the assumption that reason can resolve all disputes and solve all problems) is paradigmatic for the failure to fashion a general secular bioethics based on a canonical set of moral teachings. The recognition of this failure reveals the postmodernist crisis and its "irremedial plurality" of moral viewpoints.[28]

In response, Engelhardt proposes a purely secular means of coming to terms with the apparent chaos and diversity of postmodernity. But a secular ethics, devoid of universal moral principles, offers little substantive guidance. In the absence of universally binding moral norms, precisely how are "moral strangers" to reach agreement, especially in a society which extols the virtues of democracy and religious pluralism? For that matter, how does one cross the divide separating individuals who possess radically different viewpoints regarding what is right or wrong, or the scope and extent of moral responsibility? In confronting such questions, Engelhardt supplants the Enlightenment emphasis on the principle of autonomy with an emphasis on the principle of permission. For him, the principle of permission underscores those situations in which people do not belong to a unified, closely knit community. A secularly justifiable moral authority proceeds neither from God nor from the moral vision of a particular community, nor even from reason, but from the permission of individuals alone.[29] Accordingly, if the moral authority binding moral strangers cannot be derived from reason, it can at least proceed from the permission of those who choose to collaborate. From this standpoint, we can never discover whether something like experimentation on human embryos is wrong per se. Rather, we can only affirm the necessity of obtaining the consent of those who control the embryos.

Engelhardt's postmodernist challenge to the Enlightenment project is fully operative in his discussion of personhood. He stipulates that secular morality imparts a special status to persons rather than to human beings as such. "A human body that can only function biologically, without an inward mental life," he contends, "does not sustain a moral agent."[30] For this reason, only persons are viewed as members of the secular moral community, since only those capable of entering into agreements and engaging in collaborative projects can lay claim to personhood.[31] Conversely, anyone incapable of choosing, making agreements, or possessing a consciousness of what he or she does cannot be designated as a moral agent and therefore can never be included in that group of humans we designate as "persons" in the strict sense as moral agents.[32] Like other postmodernist thinkers, Engelhardt thus coordinates personhood with a moral agency whereby individuals are able to appreciate the blameworthiness or praiseworthiness of their actions, understand their choices, resolve moral controversies by agreement, and give or withhold moral permission.[33]

Such a circumscribed understanding of personhood carries an uncompromising distinction between those who qualify as persons and those who do not. Like other postmodernists, Engelhardt finds no apparent contradiction in speaking of such "human nonpersons" as fetuses, infants, the profoundly mentally retarded, the hopelessly comatose, and anyone lacking moral autonomy.[34] But while he unequivocally excludes those he designates as "human nonpersons" from the moral sphere, he easily includes those he characterizes as "nonhuman persons" under this protective umbrella.

> Although failing to treat a fetus or an infant as a person in the strict sense shows no disrespect in general secular terms to that fetus or infant, to fail to treat a peaceable extra-terrestrial moral agent without such respect would be to act immorally in a fundamental fashion.[35]

Engelhardt, then, fully endorses the postmodernist distinction between human *personal* life and human *biological* life. Still, he is quick to stress that the general secular bioethics he envisions does not necessarily deny traditional views regarding the soul's existence or its relation to the body, nor does it question the intrinsic value of human life as it emerges in specific religious frameworks. But in a manner consistent with the narrow parameters of secular morality, a comparable secular bioethics can only make judgments about things in which "moral strangers" can find mutual agreement. In certain instances, for example, personhood is imputed in a social sense when individuals are accorded nearly the full rights of moral agents.[36]

But what is the rationale for protecting these individuals at all in secular moral terms? For Engelhardt, it lies in justifying a social sense of the person in terms of the utility of treating these individuals as hypothetical persons—that is, treating them *as if they were persons.* If such a practice is justifiable, he reasons, a social sense of personhood is desirable on purely consequentialist grounds. While the social sense of personhood has no real standing in a secular context, Engelhardt contends that secular morality can recognize that certain social roles are legitimized on the basis of agreements geared to the promotion of such virtuous behavior as sympathy, care for human life, protection of people during periods of incompetence, and child rearing, whereby humans develop into persons in the full moral sense.[37] But when push comes to shove, the rights of these persons in a social sense are only as secure as their granting communities allow them to be. Those who fail to meet mutually agreed criteria of personhood stand on extremely shaky moral ground.

If mental life is the mark of personhood, then the locus and sustainer of that mental life is the brain. As Roland Puccetti succinctly puts it, "Where the brain goes, the person goes."[38] Accordingly, the body becomes a necessary but ancillary mechanism that has no bearing on the person's moral status. For Engelhardt, brain transplantation (if such a procedure were possible) would amount to the transplanting of the person from one body to another.[39] In this connection, he defines the death of the person as the cessation of a being capable of making promises, entering into agreements, and upholding moral responsibilities. The implications of this position for patients deprived of consciousness are readily apparent. Since a body with whole-brain death (or even the death of the lower brain) cannot support mental life, it cannot support the life of a person.[40]

In this context, the higher brain or cerebrum determines the life of the person (or conversely, the person's death in its absence). Since the bodies of the permanently unconscious no longer embody persons or even minds (in general postmodernist terms, at least), they can only qualify as "biologically living corpses."[41] Implicit in this claim is the assumption that personhood depends exclusively on the higher brain as the seat of consciousness. While Engelhardt identifies the embodied entity (the entity incarnate in the world) with the person, he only does so to the extent that this embodied entity retains "the capacities that are the physical substrata of moral agents."[42]

POSTMODERNISM AND INCOMMENSURABILITY

Postmodernist theories of personhood pose a challenge to those who identify with a traditional metaphysical account of the soul-body relation and the tacit assumption that human beings have an inherent claim to the status of persons simply by virtue of their humanness. In postmodernist terms, as we have seen, criteria of personhood are inclusive enough to admit machines, hypothetical extraterrestrial beings, or highly developed primates like chimpanzees and dolphins. But those same criteria are narrow enough to exclude human infants, the comatose, the senile, the insane, and those in a persistent vegetative state from the ballpark of personhood and membership in the moral community. But, intuitively speaking, something is not quite right with this kind of assessment. While I readily acknowledge that humans and animals (particularly more highly developed animals) have much in common, and that an extraterrestrial being (if we ever were to encounter one) might well exhibit personal qualities worthy of respect, I am not prepared to deny personhood to my fellow humans who fail to "measure up" to arbitrary behavioral criteria.

But how does one defend this claim (i.e., that every human being is a person) in a pluralistic society like our own? Do we really enjoy the luxury of taking for granted the legitimacy of any anthropological presupposition on a broad scale? In this regard, the real challenge of critiquing a postmodernist anthropology lies in its seeming unassailability from a rational perspective. Indeed, the postmodernist position represents more than a rejection of a traditional metaphysical approach to personhood along the empiricist lines of David Hume. For classical empiricists like Hume, the falsity of metaphysics was still demonstrable on rational grounds, once such obscure notions as soul, human nature, and personal identity were subjected to critical analysis. But for postmodernist thinkers, even reason must be rejected as an arbiter in debates regarding the meaning of human nature, personhood, and end-of-life decisions. To what extent, then, can a traditional metaphysical account of personhood (as exemplified in the Aristotelian/Thomistic model) be taken as seriously among "moral strangers" as among one's "moral friends"?

Indeed, how does one respond to the postmodernist understanding of what it means to be human in a manner that is both cogent and persuasive to a broad-based, secular audience? It would be naive to ignore the tremendous gulf separating people of different ideological and religious outlooks. But does such a disparity of viewpoints necessarily rule out the possibility of forging a meaningful consensus allowing for at least a tentative resolution of these issues? If this happens to be the case, then we are left with a situation in which moral perspectives are only intelligible and compelling to their own supporters, and moral principles are always

relative to a given conceptual framework. In this situation, rival morali-
ties confront the problem of incommensurability and the impasse it creates for sustaining any genuine dialogue between opponents.

The notion of incommensurability is a commonplace in current discussions involving seemingly incompatible viewpoints. While the term
emerges in a variety of contexts which address the difficulty of dialogue
between disparate outlooks, it is ultimately rooted in the philosophy of
science. In this respect, "incommensurability" assumes a prominent role
in Thomas Kuhn's analysis of scientific change in terms of a series of paradigm shifts in which a constellation of beliefs, values, and techniques
shared by members of one community of practitioners is completely supplanted by another.[43]

Postmodernist philosophers share with Kuhn the tacit assumption that
the claims of competing paradigms (in Engelhardt's parlance, "moral
communities") are so incompatible that transparadigmatic communication becomes impossible. But as Larry Lauden points out, a central flaw
inherent in this new version of the Tower of Babel story is "the presump-
tion that rational choice can be made between theories only if those theories can be translated into one another's language or into a third 'theory-
neutral language.'"[44] Postmodernist philosophers succumb to this flaw in
two ways: first, by relegating moral principles to mere outgrowths of
moral communities (and, conversely, denying their validity in a broader
secular context) and, second, by rejecting the possibility of meaningful dialogue between such communities in the absence of overarching principles that allow for the resolution of moral conflicts.

Kuhn's notions of paradigm shift and incommensurability are applied
to revolutionary change in various fields ranging from politics to music to
art history to morals. As Richard Noonan observes, the idea of incommensurability has been borrowed by moral philosophers to express the
position that moral dilemmas may be irresolvable in the midst of a plurality of values.[45] But ethicist Alasdair C. MacIntyre has initiated and implemented what amounts to a profound refocusing of moral inquiry in a
manner that confronts the difficulties posed by the incommensurability
thesis implicitly endorsed by postmodernist bioethicists like Tooley, Puccetti, or Engelhardt. MacIntyre offers an insightful diagnosis of the problem and a bold strategy for overcoming the impasses plaguing contemporary ethical debates. In MacIntyre's project, we find an ongoing attempt
to come to grips with the fragmentation of moral conversation by means
of a teleological understanding of human nature rooted in Aristotelianism
and, in broader terms, in the Thomistic tradition of inquiry. From this
standpoint, MacIntyre's response to the postmodernist problem of moral
incommensurability provides an ideal segue for a critical response to
postmodernist theories of personhood.

MacIntyre's seminal work *After Virtue* offers a perceptive assessment of the current state of moral discourse.

> The most striking feature of contemporary moral utterance is that so much of it is used to express disagreements; and the most striking feature of the debates . . . is their interminable character. There seems to be no rational way of securing moral agreement in our culture.[46]

From the standpoint of postmodernism, the situation which MacIntyre describes is indicative of the stalemate accompanying the confrontation of incommensurable viewpoints. According to MacIntyre, what postmodernists view as a state of moral incommensurability assumes that every argument advanced by the competing viewpoints is logically valid (or can be expanded to be made so), but that we possess no rational basis for evaluating the claims of rival arguments.[47] Paradoxically, however, each argument still claims to represent a rational position of its own.

But as thinkers like Engelhardt demonstrate, the very possibility of rational debate becomes a moot point if each tradition tries to adjudicate debates on the basis of standards peculiar to itself. As MacIntyre recognizes in his later work *Whose Justice? Which Rationality?* a world comprised solely of rival traditions would undermine any attempt to justify one's claims outside of one's own tradition of inquiry.

> Given that each tradition will form its own standpoint in terms of its own idiosyncratic concepts, and given that no fundamental correction of its conceptual scheme from some external standpoint is possible, it may appear that each tradition must develop its own scheme in a way which is liable to preclude even translation from one tradition to another. So it may appear that communication between traditions will at certain crucial points be too inadequate for each even to understand the other fully.[48]

MacIntyre, in contrast, firmly rejects the claim that what is said within one tradition can never be grasped by rival traditions. In this regard, he finds flaws in relativism and perspectivism alike and their respective theses (1) that rational choice among rival traditions is not feasible (in the absence of a "rationality as such") and (2) that truth claims can never even be made within any one tradition (since truth or falsity is no more than a matter of one's vantage point). For MacIntyre, if relativism and perspectivism wield any persuasive power, it only proceeds from an inversion of certain Enlightenment positions regarding truth and rationality. In this respect, he depicts post-Enlightenment relativism and perspectivism as the negative counterparts of the Enlightenment tradition's insistence on a truth and rationality guaranteed by an appeal to principles which any rational agent must endorse.[49] From this standpoint, the failure of relativists and perspectivists alike lies in their viewing the world through a narrow lens which yields a distorted vision of things. Because they assume that an appeal to rationality must be framed in the terms prescribed by the Enlightenment, they rule out its possibility altogether. Accordingly, they assume they offer the only viable alternatives once Enlightenment conceptions of truth and rationality are proven untenable.

MacIntyre's critique of contemporary relativism and perspectivism provides the basis for a tailor-made response to postmodern thinkers like Engelhardt who interpret rationality in distinctly Enlightenment terms, as an abstract standard of adjudication to which all rational persons can appeal. The assumption that rationality must be understood exclusively in such terms fails to recognize the extent to which rationality itself is bound up with tradition.

> It is . . . not surprising that what was invisible to the thinkers of the Enlightenment should be equally invisible to those postmodernist relativists and perspectivists who take themselves to be enemies of the Enlightenment, while in fact being to a large and unacknowledged degree its heirs. What neither was or is able to recognize is the kind of rationality possessed by traditions.[50]

In the absence of a teleological anthropology, we are left with the notion of an untutored human nature, or a set of injunctions deprived of any context. If the moral project of the Enlightenment philosophers failed, it was because they drew on the scattered fragments of a coherent scheme of thought and praxis. From this standpoint, the apparent problems of modern moral theory are the by-products of the Enlightenment failure on two levels: on the one hand, in the freeing of the moral agent from the constraints of hierarchy (and the elevation of the self to the status of moral sovereign), and, on the other hand, in the fact that old rules of morality require a new standing without any teleological grounding.[51] For these reasons, the contemporary participant in moral discourse is confronted with a dilemma: either our appeal to those rules must find rational support, or such an appeal will be based on no more than individual preferences.

MacIntyre's emphasis on the importance of a teleological understanding of human nature is but one component of his strategy for overcoming the problem of incommensurability. This position is closely aligned with his contention that rationality is inextricably bound up with traditions of inquiry. From this standpoint, the claim that one tradition of inquiry is rationally superior to its rivals can only emerge from *within a tradition* already engaged in dialectical conversation with its opponents.

> The person outside all traditions lacks sufficient rational resources for enquiry and *a fortiori* for enquiry into what tradition is to be rationally pre-

ferred. To be outside all traditions is to be a stranger to enquiry; it is to be in a state of intellectual and moral destitution.[52]

Does any particular tradition of inquiry exhibit a rational superiority over its rivals so that it can respond to the questions they generate in a way that bridges the gap between seemingly incommensurable viewpoints? MacIntyre finds a compelling candidate for this role in the Thomistic tradition. In his reckoning, Thomism constitutes nothing less than a project for constructing a form of moral narrative that can speak to rival narratives, not merely to individual theories. In this respect, the narrative which prevails over its rivals is not one which merely retells their stories as so many episodes within its own narrative but tells the story of "the telling of their stories as such episodes."[53] For MacIntyre, any success which Thomism has displayed and continues to display in relation to its rivals must be measured on the basis of the quality of its responses to their questions.

 Aquinas's theology and philosophy, in fact, were the outgrowths of a conflict between the distinct and apparently incompatible traditions of Augustinianism and Aristotelianism. Augustinianism confronted what amounted to an epistemological crisis in its encounter with Aristotelianism at the University of Paris. This crisis severely tested the truths of its own doctrines, as well as its capacity to address and integrate ideas from a different outlook. Philosophy assigned the natural sciences a content and importance completely foreign to Augustinianism, and Aristotelians resorted to standards of explanation and judgment wholly different from their Augustinian opponents.[54]

In the minds of many thirteenth-century thinkers, the conflict between these schools of thought could only be perceived as irresolvable—incommensurable in contemporary parlance. MacIntyre, however, stresses that genuine incommensurability can only be recognized by someone capable of "inhabiting" rival schemes and thereby capable of functioning as a native speaker in those frameworks.[55] Yet the ability to function as a native speaker obviates the need for translation and the accompanying sense of distance between rivals. In MacIntyre's estimation, Aquinas was just such a thinker, since he was able to insert himself imaginatively into what could easily have been viewed as an impenetrable viewpoint. By virtue of this flexibility, Aquinas effected a bold synthesis of competing schools of thought.

Aquinas integrated both rival schemes of concepts and beliefs in such a way as both to correct in each that which he took[by its own standards]could be shown to be defective or unsound and to remove from each, in a way justified by that correction, that which barred them from reconciliation.[56]

According to MacIntyre, the strength of Thomism lies in the fact that Aquinas never succumbed to the current belief in the unattainability of any rational resolution of seemingly incommensurable disputes. Instead, Aquinas exploited the competing standards before him for his own purposes by working with the schemes in which those standards were operative.[57] Implicit in this strategy is a means of determining the rational superiority of one tradition over its rivals. This method proceeds from the capacity to identify its rivals' deficiencies by their own standards and explanatory methods and, conversely, by an inability of the rival traditions to launch a corresponding critique of their own.[58]

CONCLUSION

At a time when it is tempting to take refuge in one's own ideological camp, MacIntyre provides an insightful assessment of such partisanship and offers an effective means of reestablishing lines of communication with seemingly alien ways of thinking (between those Engelhardt characterizes as moral strangers). But the success of this approach must be qualified. MacIntyre himself is as much a product of the epistemological turn in the history of philosophy as the Enlightenment and post-Enlightenment thinkers he criticizes. Such thinkers tend to reduce philosophical problems to questions regarding the scope and extent of human knowledge and the grounds for justifying one's truth claims.

By the same token, MacIntyre's appeal to Thomism provides another case in point of this general trend. While he displays a competent grasp of Aquinas's moral theory (and its value as a touchstone in moral debates), he still treats Thomism as but one tradition among others. And although he acknowledges Thomism as rationally superior to its competitors, this accolade is tentative. "No one at any stage," he argues, "can ever rule out the future possibility of their present beliefs and judgments being shown to be inadequate in a variety of ways."[59]

While MacIntyre astutely recognizes that inquiry is always embodied in traditions, this insight carries us only so far before we must come to terms with the deeper ontological dimension of our truth claims. It is one thing to say that my assertions are only justifiable within the context of a given tradition (i.e., my own tradition or the one I learn to inhabit as a "native speaker"). But it is quite another thing to say that my assertions are true because they connect with *what is the case*. What MacIntyre calls a correspondence theory of truth differs radically from its traditional interpretation as the mind's conformity to a reality beyond it. For him, truth is a matter of *corroboration*, based on a tradition's ability to weather sustained criticism.[60]

Nonetheless, MacIntyre effectively demonstrates the extent to which Thomism is capable of entering into meaningful dialogue with competing traditions and how its insights provide a means of resolving the conflicts which arise in contemporary moral debates. In the next and concluding chapter, I reassess the Thomistic anthropology in light of its relevance for understanding the meaning of personhood in a contemporary setting. This reassessment is not directed toward a specific refutation of any postmodern thinker or postmodern theories of personhood in general. The very notion of refutation can become something of a moot point for those who neither accept nor acknowledge the truth claims of the refuting tradition. Accordingly, I simply present what might be viewed as an alternate anthropological vision that does greater justice to the depth of our humanity and the profundity of our personhood than postmodern accounts offer.

DISCUSSION QUESTIONS

1. Define the postmodern distinction between biological humanity (and membership in the human species) and moral personhood, and discuss the anthropological implications of this distinction.
2. From a postmodern perspective, what is the significance of the category "human nonpersons," particularly in a bioethical context?
3. Define the consciousness criterion of personhood, and discuss what this criterion presupposes about the meaning of personhood.
4. In what sense did the empiricist philosopher John Locke link personhood with a conscious awareness of self?
5. In what sense could robots or extraterrestrials be said to qualify as persons?

NOTES

1. Robert Audi, ed., *The Cambridge Dictionary of Philosophy*, 2nd ed. (Cambridge: Cambridge University Press, 1999), 725a, s.v. "Postmodern," by Bernd Magnus.
2. *Concise Routledge Encyclopedia of Philosophy* (London: Routledge, 2000), 700a, s.v. "Postmodernism," by Elizabeth Deeds Ermath.
3. "Postmodernism," 700a.
4. Richard Rorty, *Philosophy and the Mirror of Nature* (Princeton, N.J.: Princeton University Press, 1980), 378.
5. Roland Puccetti, "The Life of a Person," in W. B. Bondeson et al., eds., *Abortion and the Status of the Fetus* (Dordrecht, Holland: Kluwer Academic, 1983), 169–82; William O. Stephens, ed., *The Person: Readings in Human Nature* (Upper Saddle River, N.J.: Pearson Prentice-Hall, 2006), 293b. In subsequent references to

this anthology, I list the author, the title of the article, and the complete original citation in brackets, followed by "Stephens" and the appropriate page number(s).

6. John Locke, *An Essay Concerning Human Understanding*, ed. A .D. Woozley (New York: New American Library, 1964), 2:27(9), 211.

7. Locke, *Essay Concerning Human Understanding*, 2:27(9), 211.

8. Locke, *Essay Concerning Human Understanding*, 2:27(9), 211.

9. Locke, *Essay Concerning Human Understanding*, 2:27(9), 212.

10. Locke, *Essay Concerning Human Understanding*, 2:27(10), 213.

11. Ronald E. Cranford and David Randolph Smith, "Consciousness: The Most Critical Moral (Constitutional) Standard for Human Personhood," *American Journal of Law and Medicine* 13, no. 2–3 (1987): 233.

12. Boyd Group, "The Moral Status of Non-human Primates: Are Apes Persons?" www.boydgroup.demon.co.uk/Paper3.pdf, in Stephens, 411a.

13. Charles Taylor, "The Concept of a Person," *Social Theory as Practice*, B. N. Ganguli Memoral Lectures, 1981 (Delhi: Oxford University Press, 1983), 48–67, in Stephens, 280a.

14. Taylor, "Concept of a Person," 276a.

15. In this context, note the observations of Oswald Hanfling, "Machines as Persons?" *Human Beings*, Royal Institute of Philosophy Supplement 29, ed. David Cockburn (Cambridge: Cambridge University Press, 1999), 25–34, in Stephens, 382b, who stresses that persons are beings we respect and expect to respect us in return, as participants in moral networks encompassing rights and duties and the inner life which sustains these relationships.

16. Immanuel Kant, *The Metaphysics of Morals*, introduction, translation, and notes by Mary Gregor (Cambridge: Cambridge University Press, 1991), 422.

17. Immanuel Kant, *Critique of Practical Reason*, trans. and ed. Lewis White Beck (Chicago: University of Chicago Press, 1949), sec. 2, IV, 428 (pp. 86–87).

18. Hanfling, "Machines as Persons?" in Stephens, 382b.

19. R. G. A. Dolby, "The Possibility of Computers Becoming Persons," *Social Epistemology* 3, no. 4 (1989): 321–64, in Stephens, 263b.

20. William O. Stephens, "Masks, Androids, and Primates: The Evolution of the Concept 'Person,'" *Etica & Animali* 9, special issue on Nonhuman Personhood, ed. Paula Cavalieri (1998), 111–27, in Stephens, 404a.

21. A. O. Rorty, "Persons and Personae," in *Mind in Action*, ed. Amelie Oksenberg Rorty (Boston: Beacon, 1988), 27–46, in Stephens, 349b.

22. Rorty, "Persons and Personae," 349b.

23. Daniel C. Dennett, "Conditions of Personhood," in *The Identities of Persons*, ed. Amelie O. Rorty (Berkeley: University of California Press, 1976), 175–96, in Stephens, 228b–229a. Michael Tooley, "Personhood," in *A Companion to Bioethics*, ed. Helga Kuhse and Peter Singer (Oxford: Blackwell, 1998), 120, on the other hand, proposes seventeen properties generally cited by philosophers as sufficient features of personhood. Tooley's broad catalog of properties encompasses consciousness, preferences, conscious desires, feelings, the ability to experience pleasure and pain, the ability to think, the capacity for self-consciousness and rationality, a temporal awareness, memory of past actions and mental events, the ability to plan a future for oneself, nonmomentary interests, the unification of desires over time, rational deliberation, the ability to choose between alternative courses

of action based on moral considerations, character traits that change in a nonchaotic manner, and the ability for social interaction and communication with others.

24. Dennett, "Conditions of Personhood," in Stephens, 238a.

25. H. Tristram Engelhardt Jr., *The Foundations of Bioethics*, 2nd ed. (New York: Oxford University Press, 1996), viii. Hereafter referred to as Engelhardt.

26. Engelhardt, 7.

27. Engelhardt, 8.

28. Engelhardt, 9.

29. Engelhardt, xi.

30. Engelhardt, 242.

31. Engelhardt, 136. Cf. Engelhardt's remarks in "Foundations, Persons, and the Battle for the Millennium," *Journal of Medicine and Philosophy*, November 1988, 387:

> Peaceable negotiation, as the last resort for resolving moral controversies in a way that maintains a sense of moral blameworthiness and of moral authority when reason fails, places persons as possible negotiators at the core of moral considerations. It is only persons who can provide moral authority and participate in negotiations. It is only if one acts against persons without their consent . . . that one rejects peaceable negotiation as such and therefore the moral project in its core.

32. Engelhardt, 239. Cf. Engelhardt's remarks in "Brain, Life, Brain Death, Fetal Parts," *Journal of Medicine and Philosophy* (February 1989): 2:

> Being a person alive and present in the world must at least include being able to sense and feel the environment and respond in an integrated fashion, not simply react in a reflex way. Human life that cannot meet those criteria cannot yet be alive as a person. If there is not sensation or action, the person is no longer present in the world.

33. Engelhardt, 136. Elsewhere he proposes (139) self-consciousness, rationality, moral sense, and freedom as criteria of personhood.

34. Engelhardt, 139.

35. Engelhardt, 139.

36. Engelhardt, 149.

37. Engelhardt, 149. As examples of such virtues, Engelhardt cites sympathy, the care for human life, and the protection of people during periods of incompetence, as well as the promotion of child rearing (whereby humans develop as persons in the full moral sense).

38. Roland Puccetti, "Brain Transplantation and Personal Identity," *Analysis* 29 (1989): 65.

39. Engelhardt, 243. Engelhardt endorses the position of Roland Puccetti, "Brain Transplantation and Personal Identity," that "where the brain goes, the person goes." In a manner consistent with this position, Engelhardt proposes the following scenario (247):

> Imagine that one consults one's neurologist and is diagnosed as suffering from a serious neurological disease. The bad news is that it will destroy one's whole brain. The good news is that due to the advances in medicine a normal life expectancy can still be assured. If one's reaction to this information is not simply that such a life would be of

no use to oneself but that one would *not be there* for the life to be either useful or use-less, one has embraced a whole-brain-oriented concept of death. The step toward a neo-cortically oriented (or more precisely, a higher-brain-centers-oriented) definition of death is taken when the physician returns the next day, stating that the bad news is not that bad. Though the patient will lose the entire cerebrum, the lower brain stem, pons, and cerebellum will be able to be preserved. The patient will be able to continue nor-mal breathing unsustained by a respirator. However, there will no sentience, no expe-rience of the world; the patient will be permanently comatose. If one still concludes that one would not be there, . . . one has taken the further step toward a higher-brain-centers-oriented concept of death.

40. Engelhardt, 243. Cf. Engelhardt's remarks in "The Patient as Person: An Empty Phrase," *Texas Medicine* (September 1975): 59a:

> The brain-oriented definition [of death] presupposes that being a person involves hav-ing, in a least some minimal sense, a mind. It further presupposes that minds are lo-cated more in one part of the body than in others and that that part must be an organ capable of complex sensory-motor integration. In short, the brain-oriented concept of death presupposes that being a person involves having a mind, and that minds are fairly precisely embodied, namely, in brains.

41. Engelhardt, 248.
42. Engelhardt, 153.
43. Thomas S. Kuhn, *The Structure of Scientific Revolutions,* 2nd ed. (Chicago: University of Chicago Press, 1970).
44. Larry Laudan, *Progress and Its Problems: Toward a Theory of Scientific Growth* (Berkeley: University of California Press, 1977), 142.
45. Ted Honerich, ed., *The Oxford Companion to Philosophy* (Oxford: Oxford Uni-versity Press, 1995), 397b, s.v. "Moral Incommensurability," by Richard Noonan.
46. Alasdair MacIntyre, *After Virtue* (Notre Dame, Ind.: University of Notre Dame Press, 1981), 6.
47. MacIntyre, *After Virtue,* 23.
48. Alasdair MacIntyre, *Whose Justice? Which Rationality?* (Notre Dame, Ind.: University of Notre Dame Press, 1988), 348.
49. MacIntyre, *Whose Justice?* 353.
50. MacIntyre, *Whose Justice?* 353.
51. MacIntyre, *Whose Justice?* 62.
52. MacIntyre, *Whose Justice?* 367.
53. Alasdair C. MacIntyre, *Three Rival Versions of Moral Enquiry: Encyclopedia, Geneology, and Tradition* (Notre Dame, Ind.: University of Notre Dame Press, 1990), 80–81.
54. MacIntyre, *Three Rival Versions,* 67. In the same work, MacIntyre (109) rec-ognizes three areas of conflict between Augustinians and Aristotelians: (1) an epis-temological conflict between the Augustinian notion of the mind as contingent on a reality outside the self and the Aristotelian view of the intellect as potentiality for further actualization, (2) a conflict between the Aristotelian notion of truth as the mind's relation to its objects and the Augustinian notion of truth as a recogni-tion of things as they really are, and (3) a conflict between the Augustinian attri-

bution of error to the will and the Aristotelian notion that the intellect is self-sufficient in its pursuit of theoretical and practical knowledge.

55. MacIntyre, *Three Rival Versions*, 144.

56. MacIntyre, *Three Rival Versions*, 123.

57. MacIntyre, *Three Rival Versions*, 173:

> The questions and problems which Aquinas posed about Augustinianism to Augustinians and about Aristotelianism to Aristotelians are each initially framed in terms internal to the system of thought and enquiry which was being put in question. Aquinas's strategy . . . was to enable Augustinians to understand how, by their own standards, they confronted problems for the adequate treatment of which . . . they lacked the necessary resources; and in a parallel way to provide the same kind of understanding for Averroistic Aristotelians.

58. MacIntyre, *Three Rival Versions*, 181.

59. MacIntyre, *Whose Justice?* 361.

60. This criterion of truth finds its clearest articulation in Karl Popper's philosophy of science. For a survey of Popper's falsifiability criterion, see Paul Edwards, ed., *The Encyclopedia of Philosophy* (New York: Macmillan, 1972), 5:399, s.v. "Karl Raimund Popper," by Anthony Quinton. For Popper, the development of a hypothesis always represents a creative act by the imagination rather than a passive response to the observation of regularities in nature, and even observation presupposes some anticipatory theory on the part of the observer. In this respect, falsifiability by observation replaces verifiability by induction as the criterion of the scientific character of a given theory. Popper, then, maintains that a genuine scientific test requires falsifying instances; the more falsifiable the hypothesis (i.e., one that has a greater prospect of refutation because it excludes more), the less probable it is; by excluding more, it says more about the world and possesses more empirical content. From this standpoint, a hypothesis only proves its worth after it survives repeated attempts at falsification. The upshot, however, is that a theory never allows for definitive proof. The most falsification provides is corroboration. Cf. Karl Popper, *The Logic of Scientific Discovery* (London, 1959), chap. 10, sec. 85:

> Science is not a system of certain, or well-established, statements, . . . our science is not knowledge *(episteme)*; it can never claim to have attained truth, or even a substitute for it, such as probability . . . we do not know: we can only guess.

Ask how much Wojtyla is in this chapter-
phenomenology?

9

Our Interpersonal Journey

Protisis

If Thomism offers a viable alternative to postmodern anthropologies (and a claim to a rational superiority over its rivals), its value cannot merely rest on its dialectical resources or facility for challenging other viewpoints. It must also tell us something that rings true about personhood, and this account must resonate with our own experience of psychosomatic unity and a sense of personal identity on its deepest level. But this does not mean that we must approach these issues in the adversarial terms of some debate. This is why I place special emphasis on the phrase "viable alternative." If the Thomistic response is judged superior to other anthropological theories, it will be because it speaks to a contemporary audience with greater cogency than its rivals do. Herein lies the perceptiveness of MacIntyre's analysis of Thomism as a tradition of inquiry. As we saw in the preceding chapter, that analysis is highly attuned to the fragmentation in moral outlooks that characterizes the present age.

MacIntyre makes an excellent case for viewing Thomism as a tradition that is rationally superior to its competitors, not as a detached judge but as an active interlocutor. This rational superiority is rooted in the resilience and perennial relevance that allows Thomism to enter into conversation with its rivals and expose their weaknesses from within their own conceptual frameworks. MacIntyre's interpretation, then, provides an illuminating point of departure for recasting the Thomistic vision of personhood in a contemporary idiom, not only among one's moral "friends," but among moral "strangers" as well.[1] At the outset, then, let us reconsider MacIntyre's contention that the best response to moral pluralism lies in a teleologically grounded narrative of human nature shaped by the Thomistic tradition of inquiry.

A TELEOLOGICAL MODEL

According to MacIntyre, moral conflicts always presuppose certain assumptions about personal identity through time and the maintenance of a continuity between past, present, and future.[2] In this interpretation, personal identity encompasses the notions that (1) one is the same person throughout a single bodily life, (2) one is able to account for one's actions and convictions to those within the same community, and (3) one's life is understood as a unity ordered toward a definite end, with the sense of continuity that a lifelong project requires. Such a continuity presupposes that our selfhood rests on something enduring that allows for the integrity, wholeness, and intelligibility of our personal narrative history.

> From this tradition-informed Thomistic point of view every claim has to be understood in its context as the work of someone who has made him or herself accountable by his or her utterance in some community whose history has produced a highly determinate shared set of capacities for understanding, evaluating, and responding to that utterance.[3]

MacIntyre explicitly addresses these issues in the context of a discussion of the parameters of polemical discussions and how participants in these conflicts understand the personal identities of their interlocutors. He assesses what he perceives as the impoverishment of the contemporary moral terrain on the basis of a scheme whose basic structure is outlined in Aristotle's *Nicomachean Ethics*. In that particular framework, he discovers an outlook which presupposes a contrast between humans as they *happen to be* and as they *could be*, if they were able to realize their essential human nature. For MacIntyre, ethics constitutes the science that allows us to understand how we make the transition from a potential state of becoming fully human to an actualized version of our ideal as persons.[4] Accordingly, this type of ethics must incorporate accounts of our nature as rational animals and our final end as humans, as well as provide a means of ordering desires and emotions.

MacIntyre's account of the virtues raises a key question: in view of the vast differences and incompatibilities between the various virtue theories of history, what grounds do we have for assuming that their representatives are even discussing the same thing? Only a unitary conception of virtue can free us from this malaise. But hope for such a solution is illusory in the absence of a notion of a *telos* encompassing human life in its entirety as an integral unity.[5] For MacIntyre, the failure to posit such a *telos* can only result in the arbitrariness of moral judgments which dominates the contemporary scene. By extension, the abdication of a unitary conception of human nature finds expression in the modern tendency to divorce the individual from his or her social roles. This, he further suggests, results in a rejection of the Aristotelian understanding of virtue as a disposition which is operative in many different settings.[6] Indeed, any attempt to provide an intelligible account of what one is doing at any given time demands that we situate that episode in a set of narrative histories encompassing the individuals involved and the settings in which they act. In this way, human action is inextricably bound up with historical contexts and the narratives describing them.

MacIntyre perceives an intimate and mutual relationship between personal identity on the one hand and notions of intelligibility and accountability on the other. "We render the actions of others intelligible," he contends, "because action itself has a basically historical character."[7] For him, a human being is a storytelling animal through the histories which localize human acts and render them coherent in light of an overall pattern of development.

> I am forever whatever I have been at any time for others . . . no matter how changed I may be now. There is no way of founding my identity . . . on the psychological continuity or discontinuity of the self. The self inhabits a character whose unity is given as the unity of a character.[8]

In this context, MacIntyre draws on the medieval notion of the quest and the conviction that it presupposes some sense of a final end or *telos* from the outset. From this standpoint, the unity of an individual human life can be said to assist in developing that unity of a narrative which is embodied in the life of an individual or, more succinctly, the unity of a "narrative quest."[9] Accordingly, a grasp of the good for humans qua humans can only proceed from the questions that allow us to transcend a theory of virtue grounded in praxis alone. Only a sense of such an overarching good allows for an ordering of those other goods instrumental in human fulfillment.[10]

Paradoxically, however, this conception of the human good or *telos* is by no means defined completely at the outset. "A quest," MacIntyre asserts, "is always an education both as to the character of that which is sought and in self-knowledge."[11] That education must involve a prolonged process of encounter with the varied range of episodes conducive to an understanding of our *telos* once it has been attained.

MacIntyre views the virtues as dispositions which refine practices and the goods they presuppose, and sustain us in the struggles surrounding

our larger lifetime quest. But this understanding of virtue must be qualified in light of the modern individualist dictum that we are exclusively
what we choose to be. In the final analysis, we cannot seek the good or
practice virtue on a purely individual basis, even if the meaning of the
good life varies according to the circumstances in which we find ourselves.[12] In opposition to an individualistic interpretation of the virtuous
life, MacIntyre inserts the life story of any person in that of the community. "I find myself part of a history," he contends, "and that is generally
to say . . . one of the bearers of a tradition."[13]

For MacIntyre, the flaws inherent in the Enlightenment conception of
rationality were rooted in its naive assumption that an adequate response
to the challenge of skepticism demanded a theory-neutral framework of
rational inquiry which subjected all disciplines (including theology and
philosophy) to its supposedly universal standard of judgment. This position stands opposed to what MacIntyre describes as a conception of philosophy as "the master of master crafts" (encompassing the philosophical
tradition extending from Socrates to Aquinas in the High Middle Ages)
and its conviction that an embodied mind conforms to its objects or subject matter under the guidance of those habits of judgment and action we
designate as "virtues."[14] This historical perspective underscores the importance of membership in a community that appeals to an authority beyond the self as the necessary condition for rational inquiry.

At the beginning of the twenty-first century, we cannot expect the
same unanimity (or near unanimity) of opinion regarding human personhood that existed in the premodern era. Indeed, a contemporary
Thomistic anthropology must address moral pluralism and the challenges posed by current versions of mechanistic or naturalistic anthropological theories. But disagreement is by no means an insurmountable
obstacle in the search for truth, especially the truth of what it means to be
a person. In responding to the antifoundational assumption that no anthropological theory can be objectively true (in the absence of some common denominator of rationality that compels universal assent), what
shape should such a viable alternative assume? If this account is to command any credibility amid the great divergence of viewpoints, it must
build on features that are so fundamental and irreducible as to demand
a consensus, at least among those who are intellectually honest. In this
respect, our viable alternative begins with an appeal to our common humanity, a humanity to which everyone can relate in light of certain universal aspirations and commitments.[15]

There are indisputable facts about our humanity that transcend ideological lines and that all reasonable people must acknowledge as true.
From this writer's standpoint, however, these anthropological givens are
not established by means of empirical investigation alone or by an appeal

to our biological requirements for survival. Rather, they presuppose a more penetrating metaphysical explanation that runs to the core of our being as humans and as unique individuals in our own right. Such a metaphysics of the person is a hallmark of Thomism and the broader teleological perspective that traces its origins to the wellsprings of the Western intellectual tradition. In the following discussion, I draw on that perspective as a critical touchstone and inspiration for crafting the main lines of a viable alternative to postmodernist theories of personhood (and by implication to any anthropology shaped by a mechanistic or naturalistic outlook).

AN INFINITE HORIZON

Greek mythology recounts the story of Sisyphus, a man who cheated death and received a unique punishment for his presumptuousness. Sisyphus was condemned to roll a huge boulder up a hill only to see it roll it down again, for all eternity. In this tale, the French existentialist Albert Camus found a poignant commentary on the absurdity of human existence as a treadmill of striving for nothingness.

> You have already grasped that Sisyphus is the absurd hero. He *is* as much through his passions as through his torture. His scorn of the gods, his hatred of death, and his passion for life won him that unspeakable penalty in which the whole being is exerted toward accomplishing nothing. This is the price that must be paid for the passions of this earth. I see that man going back down with a heavy yet measured step toward the torment of which he will never know the end. That hour like a breathing space which returns as surely as his suffering, that is the hour of consciousness. At each of those moments when he leaves the heights and gradually sinks toward the lairs of the gods, he is superior to his fate. He is stronger than rock.[16]

In a vicious circle of unremitting striving, is there any basis for happiness, other than a courageous resignation to one's unalterable fate and the capacity to endure? According to Camus, "the struggle itself toward the heights is enough to fill a man's heart."[17]

But does a sense of unfulfilled struggle necessarily affirm the absurdity and meaningless of the human condition? In my estimation, our experience of life and its possibilities may well yield a different conclusion. A Thomistic perspective readily acknowledges that we can never derive complete happiness from finite things. None of those things, no matter how desirable, are capable of satisfying the hunger of the human spirit for increasingly greater levels of fulfillment. But does this render the pursuit meaningless? This is precisely where an Aquinas differs so radically from a Camus. In Thomistic terms, the very open-endedness of our striving for finite goods points to something which completely transcends us, namely, an infinite ground of being and goodness that we identify with God. Taken on its own, our earthly life may seem as absurd as the proverbial "tale told by an idiot, full of sound and fury, signifying nothing."[18] But viewed in terms of an inexhaustible reality, it assumes a bold new trajectory that manifests itself at every stage of life's ongoing quest.

We are confronted, then, with an either/or option, a challenge for a decisive choice between competing visions of the human endeavor. On the one hand, we may assume that any meaning we derive from this life must ultimately be found in the natural world itself. Or we may be bold enough to embark on what Socrates called a "noble risk," opening ourselves to a source of intelligibility that wholly transcends the world and its limited values.[19] From a purely practical standpoint, the choice of one vision over the other arguably might not have a radical impact on the way we live. Indeed, many people who invest their hopes and dreams in this world alone do succeed, flourish, and find some measure of happiness in this life, however fleeting. But a question must still be addressed: does a mechanistic or naturalistic interpretation (and the assumption that all our efforts are oriented toward a finite world) really explain the dynamism inherent in our humanity, a dynamism that can take us to the most sublime heights of religious, intellectual, moral, and cultural expression? In these instances (as in every instance of human striving), we glimpse a window to the infinite in the movements of our intellect and will, those defining drives of our humanity.

KNOWING AND WILLING

These deeply rooted drives manifest themselves as the desire to know truth simply for the sake of knowing and the desire for the good implicit in every act of willing. Any attempt to confine these affectivities to a finite range of objects is falsified by the reach of human aspirations. Our desire to know cannot be restricted; its very limitlessness bespeaks our openness to an infinite horizon of being. Our desire for the good is likewise unrestricted in scope; the motivation toward this end undergirds every intentional action on our part. For these reasons, we cannot derive a sense of genuine fulfillment from counterfeit claims to knowing and willing.

On the one hand, the quest for knowledge is not prompted by a frivolous curiosity that finds momentary delight in novel items of information. Since knowing for its own sake is fundamental to our constitution as humans, it must be motivated by something that reflects our orientation toward the infinite. In its broadest terms, then, our desire to know arises from a sense of wonder or awe at the mystery of being. In this respect, the very dynamics of knowing reflects the kind of beings we are: rational agents with a dynamic orientation toward the truth of being itself. By reflecting on ourselves as knowers, we come to appreciate that we are oriented toward God as the ultimate ground of meaning and intelligibility. By the same token, the human will can never rest content with limited goods alone. Our own experience reveals that every good we seek opens the way to another and so on, ad infinitem. Augustine's famous prayer (at the beginning of the *Confessions*) that "our hearts are restless until they rest in you" underscores the fact that the human will finds its ultimate referent in an absolutely unqualified Good that sets the standard for all acts of volition.

The philosopher Bernard Lonergan offers a succinct statement regarding the rich multidimensional character of mind and will which shapes our lives as humans.

> To inquire and understand, to reflect and judge, to deliberate and choose are as much an exigence of human nature as waking and sleeping, eating and drinking, talking and loving. Nor is there any escape from the universe of being and its intelligible order by devising some particular type of metaphysics or counter-metaphysics. For the universe of being is whatever is intelligently grasped and reasonably affirmed; by its definition it includes an intelligible order; and to set up as a philosopher of any school whatever, one has to claim to understand and pretend to be reasonable.[20]

We neither know nor will in a vacuum. Our intellectual and volitional acts are directed toward ends beyond ourselves that are knowable and good in themselves. Accordingly, their knowability and goodness are not the products of our own interpretation. Such traits are part and parcel of the things we seek. Only this can account for the passion with which we pursue them, a passion rooted in our recognition of something real and substantial beyond ourselves that is worthy of our commitment. This realism, which presupposes the existence of a truth and goodness beyond the mind and its constructs, is consistent with a metaphysical vision of reality as a whole in which the person assumes a privileged status.

A PARTICIPATION SCHEME

In Thomistic terms, persons find their appropriate place within a scheme that encompasses not only the physical universe but the entire universe of being. Thomism depicts the macrocosm of existent things as a vast participation system in which what is finite and limited in being shares or participates in what exists in the fullest sense—Being Itself. The scheme just outlined was the fruit of Aquinas's synthesis of insights drawn from Judeo-Christian revelation, Aristotelianism, and the Neoplatonic tradition. His achievement lay in his ability to link his religious appreciation of creatures' dependence on God for their existence with Aristotle's key metaphysical distinction between act and potency and the Neoplatonic interpretation of participation as a sharing of lower orders of reality in higher ones (or in broader terms, a sharing of the many in a principle of absolute unity). In Neoplatonic terms, participation presupposes an infinite source of unlimited power, limited participants, and the latter's dependent relation on the former.

Aquinas's theory of metaphysical participation thus proceeds from the assumption that when many distinct beings share a common perfection, that points to a common origin of the perfection that cannot be derived from any of those beings themselves.

> If in a number of things we find something that is common to all, we must conclude that this something was the effect of some one cause: for it is not possible that to each one by reason of itself this common something belong, since each one by itself is different from the others: and diversity of causes produces a diversity of effects. Seeing then that being is found to be common to all things, which are by themselves distinct from one another, it follows by necessity that they must come into being not by themselves, but by the action of some cause.[21]

In Aquinas's synthesis, God provides the pure Act of Being in which beings share in varying degrees. The notion of participation on this scale presupposes a teleological framework, wherein everything has its appropriate place and function in relation to a greater whole. But this relation of absolute existential dependence by no means obscures or negates the integrity of beings. Indeed, Aquinas's theory of participation presupposes that finite things participate in God's Act of Being according to the potentialities inherent in their own natures. In this respect, the potentiality of each nature for existence shapes or limits the Act of Being in a manner consistent with its capacity to receive it. Aquinas's participation metaphysics thus establishes the extent to which being presupposes a sharing in something other: in the broadest metaphysical sense, in the wider community of being that proceeds from God; in a personalistic sense, in a community of other persons. In this latter sense of participation, we are not so many atomistic, self-enclosed entities. Each of us, in our own distinctive way, not only shares in the totality of being but shares personal being with others through a communicability that emanates from the sheer fact of our existence.

THE BEING OF PERSONS

In Aquinas's existentialist metaphysics, we find the tools for a compelling account of the dynamic character inherent in our personhood. Any attempt to depict us as mere intellectual constructs or instantiations of a universal human nature fails to capture the active dimension of being on a personal level. Aquinas's affirmation *agere sequitur esse* ("action follows [or accompanies] being") underscores not only that the ultimate perfection of a given reality lies in its act of being but that our very existence implies an openness to the other. If being a person is to be in act, then action lies at the core of our personhood. In this context, however, such terminology does not mean that only those capable of physical activity are deemed persons. Rather, "act" is used here in a technical metaphysical sense, in reference to the principle *by which* something exists, or that which brings something in a potential state of existence to actualization.

Like every other reality, human beings exist in the context of a great participation network of radical dependence. Each of us (as the unique individuals we are) provides an analog of the really real, from the lowest to the highest on the ontological spectrum, from the material universe to which our bodies are organically related to the Creator whose image and likeness we bear as rational creatures. In this respect, the universe of being is charged with the creative efficacy that ultimately flows from God. An adequate understanding of personhood, then, must presuppose this deeper metaphysical dimension.

SUBSISTENCE AND SELFHOOD

A watershed in the development of the philosophy of the person proceeds from Aquinas's characterization of the person as a subsistent reality. In this way, he highlights what he considers the mark of personhood—individuality in the most unequivocal sense. His use of the term "subsistence" in this personalistic context represents an impressive adaptation of Aristotelian tools for his own philosophical purposes. In Aquinas's hands, Aristotle's notion of primary substance provides an effective means of accentuating the fact that individuality finds its fullest and richest expression in persons. The upshot of this development is an interpretation of personhood grounded on something real and substantial enough to support and sustain it over a lifetime.

Designating the person as a subsistent being also serves to distinguish personhood from human nature, even while affirming their inextricable connection. Human nature concerns what we all possess as humans—our fundamental psychosomatic structure, with all the drives and abilities we identify with humans. Accordingly, when we refer to our human nature, we refer to "what" we are. In this respect, the postmodern tendency to separate human nature from moral personhood bespeaks a failure to grasp what is metaphysically at stake in our humanness. Such a tendency reflects an exclusivistic focus on overt, observable criteria and the value we impart to them in ourselves and others. In contrast, the claim that every human being is a person (simply by virtue of that humanness) rests on the assumption that the ultimate explanation of what we are as humans and who we are as persons concerns our very mode of being, as individuals in our own right.

We often hear others described as "wonderful persons," and we readily assume that they possess characteristics worthy of our respect and emulation. But such a statement must be qualified. On the surface, it might suggest that personhood is a superogatory trait that is acquired or earned on the basis of certain qualities (e.g., compassion or kindness), and that some of us are more complete persons than others. I do not reject this qualitative interpretation of personhood, since it can play a crucial role in recognizing and promoting virtuous behavior conducive to the common good. But defining personhood solely on the basis of personality traits overlooks the foundation that ultimately allows for personal qualities at all. In the final analysis, a qualitative sense of personhood must rest on a fundamental metaphysical one, as the core of our humanity and individuality. In the absence of this metaphysical grounding, our basic anthropological notions are highly susceptible to the subjective (and often arbitrary) interpretations endemic in postmodern accounts.

SUBSTANTIALITY AND RELATIONALITY

Critics have suggested that Aquinas's model of the person (and the classical model of personhood in general) emphasizes the notion of subsistence to the detriment of relationality. From this standpoint, an excessive focus on subsistence and substantiality promotes an isolated, ontologically impoverished conception of the person. For such critics, this interpretation can only be offset by a greater attentiveness to the active and communicative dimensions of personal existence.[22] In a similar vein, Horst Seidl considers the charge that the classical definition of the person as a "subsistent being" presupposes a corresponding definition of human nature in terms of the universal feature of rationality.[23] In the face of an emphasis on rationality as the key criterion of personhood, what room is there for an appreciation of humans as unique individuals, not in regard to self-consciousness alone, but freedom and relationality as well? For Seidl, however, the conflicting responses to this issue touch on a more fundamental metaphysical conflict concerning the distinction between nature (or essence) and existence *(esse)*.[24] Since existence embraces all that the person is and all that the person can do, the subsistence of the individual need not be divorced from relationality. Accordingly, Seidl contends that Aquinas's understanding of personhood (which upholds an unequivocal distinction between *esse* and essence) provides a compelling response to contemporary charges that the classical interpretations neglect the relational status of the person altogether.

For a commentator like Seidl, the notion of self-subsistence affords human actions a communicability and openness to the world. He argues that any perceived tension between human self-subsistence or substantiality and self-consciousness rests on a false dichotomy, since the classical understanding of substantial being is a sine qua non for a proper understanding of person and personal identity.[25] Similarly, W. Norris Clarke considers substantiality and relationality as distinct but inseparable modes of the human reality.

> Substance is the primary mode, in that all else, including relations, depend on it as their ground. But since "every substance exists for the sake of its operations," as St. Thomas has . . . told us, being as substance, as existing *in itself*, naturally flows over into being as relational, turned *towards others* by its self-communicating action. To be is to be *substance-in-relation*.[26]

In order to appreciate other selves for who and what they are, we must be a self in our own right. But this presupposes an inextricable bond between the human substance (i.e., a subsistent being in a rational nature) and the relationality whereby we bridge the gap between self and world, and more specifically, between self and other persons. In Clarke's interpretation, Aquinas's emphasis on the dynamic and relational character of being itself is closely linked with "the indissoluble complementarity of substantiality, the *in-itself* dimension of being, and relationality, the *towards-others-aspect*."[27]

The substantiality of personhood is indispensable to the communicability whereby we enter into interpersonal relationships, those person-to-person encounters in which there is a mutual revelation of personal being. While personhood is relational to the core, however, there must still be a "core" principle which allows for relationality and all the richness that persons offer each other. One cannot give what one does not have. This familiar adage touches on something vital to human personhood and the metaphysics of being it must presuppose. We can enter into interpersonal relations with others only because we are already something substantial as persons.

In this vein, Kenneth Schmitz draws an illuminating distinction between "person" and "personality": in contrast to the hidden depth of personhood, personality pertains to surface impressions and one's public image.[28] The preoccupation with personality, Schmitz contends, is an outgrowth of the eighteenth-century emphasis on individuality defined in terms of autonomy and privacy. The modern notion of the isolated individual was closely linked with a subjectivistic emphasis on the self as the ultimate referent for judging the really real. By extension, such a presupposition supported the conviction that only self-consciousness provides a means of validating claims to personhood and membership in a community of free moral agents capable of exercising responsibilities and worthy of rights.

In contrast to such an atomistic conception (whereby one is a person by being set apart from others as a privatized entity), Schmitz focuses on an intimacy which allows for interpersonal relationships. From this perspective, intimacy is only possible through genuine self-disclosure and the sharing of self-disclosure that allows for a true knowledge of the other.[29] For Schmitz, such a revealing of one's inner self transcends any specific attributes or any overt capacities the individual might possess.

> But this self-disclosure brings persons together in a closeness that reaches beyond formalities. So that intimacy is not rooted ultimately in the formal features we can identify about persons: their charm or intelligence, their culture or learning, their physical strength and looks, their achievements, social status or influence.[30]

Schmitz, in turn, traces intimacy to a unique act of presencing by which we reveal our being as persons for what it is, or more specifically, for who I am.

> Strictly speaking, we do not learn anything *about* another person through intimacy . . . rather, we simply acknowledge our attunement with another personal presence; and the self we come to know in and through intimacy is just this presencing. In knowing this presencing we come to the root of the person, to *personal existence* as such.[31]

Schmitz's use of the term "presencing" calls to mind the dynamic character of being in its broadest terms, especially the mode of being peculiar to substances of a rational nature. In this context, presencing is easily linked with substance or *ousia* as the inner reality of a thing—that is, what constitutes a given thing and defines its range of potentialities.

The act of presencing proceeds from a dynamic and luminous center of being that makes a difference and consequently demands a recognition of its ontological integrity. Human persons "presence" by manifesting what

presencing:

is otherwise hidden from public view, or what is wholly inaccessible to scientific scrutiny. This is the mystery inherent in our own act of being, a mystery that only begins to be revealed by entering into the experience of the other as person. In the face of such a mystery, a metaphysical explanation alone suffices, not just an epistemological theory of meaning that confines itself to what is observable through sense perception. Intimacy, then, discloses a level of being that transcends any distinctive properties an individual may possess. Because intimacy has a capacity to reveal being, it places us in touch with the core of personhood. "Metaphysically speaking, intimacy is not grounded in the recognition of this or that characteristic a person *has*," Schmitz asserts, "but rather in the simple unqualified presence the person *is*."[32]

Intimacy must be understood in relational terms. On the one hand, we reveal our personhood by communicating our inner self through the act of presencing. On the other hand, however, intimacy presupposes a receptivity to the presencing of the other, and the disclosure of being that the other renders possible. This can only happen if we open ourselves to the other's *esse* in the fullest sense, not merely to behavioral characteristics alone. This is a crucial consideration in the rough-and-tumble world of bioethics, where the value and dignity of people are often assessed on the basis of what they can do, rather than on the basis of what they are in metaphysical terms—subsistent beings with a rational nature that permeates their being as humans.

EMBODIED SPIRITS

A compelling feature of Thomistic anthropology lies in its attempt to mediate between the extremes of excessive spiritualism (which defines us exclusively in terms of the soul or mind and mental acts) and a thoroughgoing materialism (which reduces mind or soul to body and all our acts to the physiological level). Only such a middle ground does justice to our experience of psychosomatic unity and the wholeness of our personhood. But by the same token, our lives unfold within the context of a changing world of potential realities. In this way, our defining drives of intellect and will continually reveal our openness and receptivity to an infinite horizon of being and goodness.

Reason can establish on its own the necessity of an ultimate causal principle of the being shared in common by everything which exists. Reason can also establish that such a cause must possess (in the fullest possible way) all of the perfections that we discern in limited beings like ourselves, including goodness. Reason finds its limitation, however, in its inability to link this ultimate causal principle with a personal and loving Creator. This is a presupposition that only proceeds from Revelation, a presupposition that carries important consequences for understanding ourselves and others. In this lies the real point of divergence between theistic and nontheistic accounts of human personhood. In the absence of an understanding of persons as beings created in the image of a good, loving, and benevolent Godhead, any account of human dignity must rest on variable naturalistic factors alone. From a theistic perspective, persons are viewed as assuming a certain exaltedness in the scheme of things by virtue of an intellect and free will, the marks of their rationality. Such an assumption also entails a commitment to the thesis that every human is a person, simply because he or she possesses an intellect or soul, the basis of our subsistence as rational beings.

Appeals to divine Revelation in the name of philosophical anthropology raise a plethora of problems. First and foremost, such appeals only persuade those with a faith commitment to Revelation. Can the notion of creation in God's image carry any cash value for a secular audience? Perhaps not. Still, the fact remains that many of the presuppositions we take for granted about human dignity and the privileged status of human life in Western culture are ultimately rooted in the Judeo-Christian tradition. Indeed, if secular postmodernist thinkers can draw inspiration from empirical science in coming to terms with the mind-body problem (and thereby reducing us to bodily beings), why cannot a Thomistically inspired anthropology draw its inspiration from revelatory wisdom in coming to terms with our spiritual dimension? Revelation raises the bar of our understanding of what it means to be human and thereby provides a higher standard of human striving on every level. So, even those who do not explicitly endorse such a theology of creation (and all it says about our privileged status) can find compelling insights for new philosophical reflection on human nature and personhood. As Clarke so aptly puts it,

> the light from Revelation does not operate strictly as the premise for philosophical argument . . . but operates as opening up for reflection a new possibility in the nature and meaning of what we might never have thought of ourselves from our limited human experience.[33]

Human nature = what
Personhood = Who

THE UNITY OF SELF

If human nature pertains to what I am, personhood encompasses *who I am*, someone with a specific history and a capacity to recognize it as such. On a simple biological level, we are directly in touch with our own bodies in simple physiological terms. But genuine self-awareness encompasses more than an awareness of the bodily dimension of my life. I can also direct my intellectual gaze within, in self-reflective acts. I not only

'Unicity of substantial form' = key to individuality & selfhood / free will

know a world outside my own mind, but I know that I know and I recognize myself as a knowing subject. In so doing, however, I am not aware of myself as some anonymous member of the species. Self-awareness amounts to awareness of the distinct individual I am. Distinctness in this sense by no means implies separation or isolation from a larger community of persons. Rather, it pertains to the completeness of nature and subsistence that renders us unique beings in our own right. For this reason, a person is not whatever we want it to be, or however we wish to define it. Personhood is rooted in something real and substantial that runs to our very nature.

But if personhood presupposes a rational nature, then this entails more than an ability to act in a rational way. A highly developed primate (with the proper training) can do this, or in time, high-tech robots. Such surface rationality (i.e., the appearance of acting rationally) is not the same as a rational nature which defines a manner of being appropriate to our own humanness. Our rational nature defines that being, not just as members of the human species but as the distinct individuals we are. This is why the classical arguments (as developed by thinkers like Aristotle and Aquinas) in favor of the unicity of substantial form are so cogent and compelling. In the absence of such a unifying principle, we have no claim to individuality and selfhood. For all practical purposes, a plurality of substantial forms or defining principles would amount to the paradox of many selves in one individual.

A unicity of substantial form not only allows for a unified sense of self and the intelligibility it imparts to my thought processes. It also supports any claim on my part to a free will and the recognition of personal responsibility that accrues to moral agents. As succinctly stated by Karol Wojtyla (later Pope John Paul II), the person who can assert himself as somebody "shows himself as having the special ability and power of self-governance which allows him to have the experience of himself as a free being."[34] In the final analysis, our ability to accept the fact that each of us is responsible for the choices we make and how we act on them compellingly attests to our own selfhood and the unity of self in the integrated existence of an embodied spirit. Augustine puts it so memorably,

> I knew just as surely that I had a will as that I was alive. I was absolutely certain when I willed or refused to will it that it was I alone who willed or refused to will.[35]

Our status as free agents proceeds from the interplay of will and intellect, the defining faculties of our human nature. In a manner consistent with the psychosomatic unity of the self, the human will operates in conjunction with the dictates of reason and our capacity to act according to motives established on the basis of an intellectual discernment of alternative courses of action. Such choices presuppose a deeply rooted sense of an unqualified Good as the ultimate standard against which we judge the limited goods we confront in a practical decision-making context. This is something that materialists and behavioralists can neither acknowledge nor appreciate. From their standpoint, an act of choice is a purely instinctive response. But how can the will be genuinely free if it acts without a rational motive? I am free not merely because I can act without constraint, or because I can do anything I want to do. My freedom lies in my ability to remain indifferent to certain goods for the sake of other goods that I recognize as conducive to a genuinely happy life, not just on an immediate basis but in the long run.

An affirmation of the unity of the self, then, cannot be based on the mind or mental life alone, without any reference to the body and the impressive contribution our physicality imparts to our individuality and uniqueness. Once we appreciate our status as embodied spirits (and how this status is revealed in the way we think and will), then the credibility of a radically dualistic model is severely undermined. The mystery inherent in our human nature and personhood lies in the fact that such a multidimensional reality constitutes an inseparable unity—that is, an integration of inner and outer dimensions that is firmly rooted in the material world, even while transcending it. Persons are beings in the world but not completely of the world. This paradox is characteristic of embodied spirits—beings who mirror the totality of things and consequently represent the point of intersection between what is spiritual and material, not as divided selves but as unified wholes.

A MORAL COSMOS

From a Thomistic perspective, the universe of created being can be viewed as an analog of the divine nature. This analogical relationship, in which creatures mirror God's *esse* in their own finite natures, finds its perfection in human persons, who image God in their capacity to know and to will as free agents. Knowing and willing in this realist sense presuppose a connaturality of the intellect for being and the will for the good. But our attunement to the really real and the value we attach to it presupposes an attunement to an order that is part and parcel of things. This cosmic vision defines reality in terms of a part-to-whole relationship, wherein the parts enhance the greater whole in which they share in varying degrees. Like the stones in a great mosaic (to use a classic Augustinian motif), finite beings complete that whole, with all their variety and diversity. Accordingly, order on the universal scale of creation dovetails with a moral order revealed in our intuition of the fundamental goodness of things and our appreciation of the beauty and fittingness of its components.

But this aesthetic sensibility is not just receptivity to what is pleasing or desirable on a purely sensory level. In broader terms, it encompasses a moral consciousness that is intimately bound up with our awareness of who we are and the unity we attach to our own life story. In his work *Sources of the Self*, Charles Taylor draws an important connection between our selfhood and what he terms our "orientation to the good," that is, "some sense of qualitative discrimination, of the incomparably higher . . . woven into my understanding of my life as an unfolding story . . . that we grasp . . . in a narrative."[36] Taylor's contention carries an unmistakable Thomistic ring. The assumption here is that each of us possesses a deeply ingrained attunement to the good that allows us to make sense of self and personal identity.

> A self or person . . . is not like an object in the usually understood sense. We are not selves in the way that we are organisms, or we don't have selves in the way we have hearts and livers. We are living beings with these organs quite independently of our self-understandings or-interpretations, or the meanings things have for us. But we are selves insofar as . . . we seek and find an orientation to the good.[37]

Our orientation toward (and aptitude for) the good finds one of its richest expressions through artistic endeavors. In such pursuits, we imitate the creative efficacy of God, as far as this is possible for finite creatures like ourselves. In his Nobel Prize acceptance speech, William Faulkner poignantly described his life's work in terms of "the agony and sweat of the human spirit . . . to create out of the materials of the human spirit something which did not exist before."[38] We cannot, of course, create in the absolute and unequivocal sense of *creatio ex nihilo*. This is reserved for God alone. Human art, in contrast, must rely on what nature provides. But the artist is one who can produce something new and in turn move other embodied spirits to a vision of what is good, true, and beautiful. In this way, the artist becomes a participant in God's own creative activity, albeit with materials already at hand. In Jacques Maritain's classic rendering, the artist is "an associate of God in the making of works of beauty . . . by developing the faculties which the Creator has endowed . . . and making use of created matter."[39]

But this demands an attentiveness to the existing order of things and consequently a revealing of the forms embedded in nature. As Maritain puts it, the artist is one "who sees more deeply . . . and discovers in reality spiritual radiations which others are unable to discern."[40] If moral living is cast in terms of an aesthetic model, then our task as persons is to mirror the order of reality in the choices we make and the manner in which we pursue those goods that fall under our contemplative and volitional purview. When Augustine defines the virtuous life as "rightly

be for patterns sensitive to others.

ordered love," he affirms the coincidence of the created cosmos with a moral one in which humans occupy the crucial role of mediating between what is higher and lower in the scheme of things. Accordingly, the life which is most conducive to long-term happiness is consistent with how things are, in all their created magnificence.

Like a work of art, moral persons exhibit a right relationship between their constitutive parts, not just as physical beings but as embodied spirits that observe the same hierarchical arrangement on a personal level that is operative in reality as a whole. From a theistic perspective, we assume that crucial midrank between the noetic and corporeal realms. In concrete terms, existence in the "middle" of things encompasses a mode of being capable of integrating the inner and outer dimensions of our existence—that is, the life of the spirit and the life of the body, respectively. The way we think and act reflects our place in an intelligible universe that finds its grounding in God.

LIFE AS QUEST

Being fully human, then, presupposes an openness to the change and growth we experience as bodily beings. But beyond change of a purely empirical character, the depth of our inner life affirms an ongoing developmental process measured in terms of an end that transcends this world and its finite goods. Each of us has a personal history that can be recounted by means of an extended narrative. But the rest of the story, so to speak, of our personal being can only be appreciated in relation to a future, supernatural destiny that lends intelligibility and purpose to our striving here and now. This is where a theistic perspective becomes crucial, since it opens the possibility of a supernatural end above and beyond whatever we might achieve in the present life.

At the beginning of this chapter, I drew on Alasdair MacIntyre's appeal to the medieval notion of life as a quest and its compatibility with a teleological understanding of moral virtue. When human life is depicted in such peregrine terms, it must have a destination (however vague it may seem at the outset), if it is to be one infused with meaning. In contrast, some would say that the journey itself is important, rather than its goal or even an implicit awareness of that goal. But a perpetual life "on the road" without a sense of a definitive *telos* is no more than a vagabond existence which condemns us (like the hapless Sisyphus) to a perpetual cycle of aimless drifting. Indeed, our very ability to raise the teleological question Why? says something significant about us and our relation to everything which exists. This question represents more than a search for intelligibility on some abstract level. It presupposes a personal search for meaning that is implicitly a search for God as the final end of the restless heart.

If the open-endedness of our striving underscores our dynamic orientation toward God, then our life's journey as a whole affirms an implicit search for ultimate meaning that only God can offer rational creatures with insatiable drives toward being and goodness. In this connection, the psychologist Viktor Frankl makes a compelling case for the centrality of a "will to meaning" as the primary motivational force in humans. As Frankl astutely observes, however, the meaning we seek cannot be the product of our own interpretation or imaginings alone.

> If the meaning that is waiting to be fulfilled by man were really nothing but a mere expression of self, or no more than a projection of . . . wishful thinking, it would immediately lose its demanding and challenging character; it could no longer call man forth or summon him.[41]

According to Frankl, life's meaning is not a matter of invention but one of discovery, by means of a free decision on our part for moral living. In this context moral living entails more than just another way of living that yields a positive sense of self. When one decides to behave morally, Frankl suggests, he does so "for the sake of a cause to which he commits himself, or for a person whom he loves, or for the sake of his God."[42] And in this kind of endeavor, each individual must come to terms with the meaning question, in light of his or her calling as a person. Is this not wholly consistent with Aquinas's moral vision, which proceeds from the premise that the "vocation" or final end of all things is to become like God? Aquinas's depiction of created reality in terms of two complementary movements (i.e., *exitus* and *redditus*) provides the context in which we can situate this journey and, more specifically, the life of the person.

Since we are relational beings to the core, this journey is necessarily an interpersonal one that must take into account the social dimension of our humanity. Paradoxically, we become attuned to the profundity inherent in our selfhood only through interpersonal relationships. In this context, I by no means interpret "self" in the individualistic, privatized sense of modern philosophy. Persons neither exist in isolation from each other nor on a solitary basis. This is not to deny that some people in fact live that way, either through choice or the circumstances in which they find themselves. But this does not refute the claim that we are fundamentally relational beings who find optimal personal fulfillment in communion with others. In the absence of such person-to-person contact, our sense of our own capacity to give would be severely diminished or even nullified.

People give of themselves in many ways and for many different reasons. In Joseph Conrad's novel *Lord Jim*, the main character receives the following advice on the meaning of life from a wise man of the world: *to the destructive element submit yourself.*[43] The suggestion here is that one can only derive fulfillment from some all-consuming endeavor. But to hurl ourselves into life headlong, without something truly ultimate at stake and worthy of our complete devotion, amounts to no more than a meaningless drive toward death. For rational beings like ourselves, our capacity to give finds its fullest outlet in disinterested love, losing ourselves for the sake of the other. Because genuine love presupposes self-giving, it stands directly opposed to the isolation of an egoism that cuts us off from every mode of participation in which we engage as persons, from a metaphysical participation in being to the various levels of social participation we experience in the context of human communities.

We embark and proceed, then, on our journey to the God in whom *we live and move and have our being* on an interpersonal basis. The human community is inextricably bound up with the larger community of being that finds its beginning and end in our creator. But if this journey is interpersonal in its dynamics, it is also historically grounded. In the final analysis, our teleological progress as embodied spirits relies on our material bodies and unfolds in an historical context. Each of us possesses a personal history encompassing the totality of our finite existence. This personal history, in turn, participates in and reflects the broader temporal framework in which we localize that extended narrative. None of us chooses the time of our birth and the period in which our life unfolds. There is certainly, as Heidegger contends, an "essential thrownness into the world" that characterizes the sheer facticity of our being, "in each case already delivered over to existence."[44] But by the same token, free agents are never prisoners of their historicity. Freedom of will implies the capacity to assume a decisive role in shaping our identities, or as W. Norris Clarke puts it, "the ability freely to make his own history as he journeys through time."[45]

As embodied spirits, we are not completely subservient to the vagaries of evolutionary processes and natural change. Our ability to transcend our external environment through our fundamental noetic orientation allows us to put our own unique stamp on the world in which we find ourselves. Initially, we may be thrown into that world, but by no means as so many extras in the epic film of our life. We are very much the actors who have a direct hand in the composition of our script, despite the many extraneous factors involved in the overall production process. In this sense, life can be viewed as an artistic enterprise in which the creative agent assumes the responsibility of crafting his or her own vision of what it means to be human, albeit with the materials at hand. In keeping with Frankl's emphasis on the "will to meaning," persons assume the responsibility of "making" themselves, and thereby, shaping their world and the lives of others as well.

The recognition of the historicity of our human journey (and of our very humanness) opens an area of discussion that is extremely fertile territory for what a contemporary Thomist like Clarke describes as a "creative retrieval and completion of St. Thomas's own thought on the metaphysics of the person."[46] Aquinas does not explicitly develop the notion of historicity and its bearing on our self-understanding in his anthropological deliberations. But his rich account of the *exitus/redditus* structure of finite being offers ample space in which to develop this theme in a contemporary setting. In this regard, a receptivity to the historicity of our personal journey need not commit us to historicism or a relativization of human nature. It merely affirms the creativity inherent in our humanness while maintaining a healthy respect for what remains metaphysically stable and enduring in that nature. Such a stance is wholly consistent with the Thomistic vision of personhood and the dynamism that drives us to our final end. From this standpoint, human nature is not whatever we wish it to be, without any adherence to the dictates of metaphysical laws. Rather, human nature provides the fixed parameters in which our creativity as free agents finds expression.[47]

CONCLUSION

If we are, as MacIntyre suggests, storytelling animals, it is because we have a significant story to tell that assumes the character of an extended and cohesive personal narrative encompassing our teleological journey in its entirety. As the creative source of being, God provides the ultimate origin of this journey and, more specifically, of beings with minds capable of discerning the really real and free will capable of pursuing the good in a morally accountable manner. If God's creative efficacy is responsible for the emergence of being, then our task is the search for our final end by means of all the resources our human nature affords us, especially our religious and moral inclinations. From this standpoint, we can view the human quest as an ongoing heuristic endeavor in which we penetrate the mystery of being in all its depth. In this great metaphysical and epistemological learning experience, we trace our steps back to God, our Summum Bonum and the ultimate object of human striving on every level. This quest is the vocation of *embodied spirits*, beings that stand on the periphery of spirit and matter and encapsulate within themselves the totality of things. Accordingly, the human journey is a voyage of discovery whereby we confront the universe as rational actors who think and know, will and choose, contemplate and love their God, and in so doing, enter into interpersonal relationships with other humans.

The person is indeed more than the sum of its constitutive parts. The very sophistication of the human organism (as demonstrated by contemporary scientific investigation) underscores the necessity of such an organizing principle. But in this case, we must be able to appeal to some irreducible sphere of our humanness which simply cannot be explained away on the basis of what scientific discovery discloses. This was Descartes' dilemma, namely, how to be receptive to scientific advances and what they reveal about us while remaining true to the deeper spiritual dimension of our humanity. But Descartes' dualistic solution need not be our own in confronting this dilemma. In this chapter, I have attempted to provide the main lines of a viable alternative to such dualism (which radically separates mind and our inner life from the body and our physicality) or, for that matter, to any anthropological theory which would undermine the unity of the personal self.

The notion of humans as embodied spirits provides the basis of a robust conception of what it means to be human and, by extension, of what it means to be a person. This conception presupposes a metaphysical account that defines persons as subsistent beings sharing in human nature in a unique way appropriate to them as true individuals. Such a theory of personhood is broad and comprehensive enough to do justice to the depth of our mental life and the biochemical complexity of our bodily existence, along with our immediate awareness of mind/body interaction. In this respect, the designation of humans as embodied spirits is no mere cliché gleaned uncritically from the philosophical tradition. On the contrary, it finds grounding in a nature that can perform a range of activities that draw on the physical apparatus of the body and the senses but also point to an immaterial principle responsible for coordinating these diverse activities for the good of our whole being.

DISCUSSION QUESTIONS

1. Explore the significance of Alasdair MacIntyre's characterization of humans as storytelling animals, and consider how this motif is linked with his notion of life as a narrative quest in pursuit of our end as humans.

2. Consider the myth of Sisyphus as recounted by Camus. Contrast two divergent responses to Sisyphus's fate (i.e., existential atheism and Thomism), and explain their implications for the way we understand the seeming open-endedness of human striving.

3. In what sense would a Thomist maintain that we know against the background of an infinite horizon of being and that we exercise our acts of willing against the background of an infinite horizon of goodness?

4. Why does the definition of the person as a "subsistent individual" suggest a potential tension between the notion of persons as "sub-

stantial" and "relational"? In Thomistic terms, how might this tension be resolved?

5. How do artistic endeavors affirm our status as embodied spirits, as borne out by our capacity for creative pursuits?

NOTES

1. As noted in the preceding chapter, H. Tristram Engelhardt Jr. makes this distinction in *The Foundations of Bioethics*, 2nd ed. (New York: Oxford University Press, 1996), 7. He complements this distinction with an additional one between (1) communities (i.e., groups of people bound together by common moral principles and behavior that center upon a mutual vision of the good life allowing for agreement as "moral friends") and (2) societies (i.e., associations of individuals of diverse communities capable of cooperating with people outside the community with which they identify.

2. Alasdair C. MacIntyre, *Three Rival Versions of Moral Enquiry: Encyclopedia, Genealogy, and Tradition* (Notre Dame, Ind.: University of Notre Dame Press, 1990), 196.

3. MacIntyre, *Three Rival Versions*, 202–3.

4. Alasdair C. MacIntyre, *After Virtue* (Notre Dame, Ind.: University of Notre Dame Press, 1984), 25.

5. MacIntyre, *After Virtue*, 30.

6. MacIntyre, *After Virtue*, 191.

7. MacIntyre, *After Virtue*, 197.

8. MacIntyre, *After Virtue*, 202.

9. MacIntyre, *After Virtue*, 203.

10. MacIntyre, *After Virtue*, 204.

11. MacIntyre, *After Virtue*, 204.

12. MacIntyre, *After Virtue*, 204.

13. MacIntyre, *After Virtue*, 206.

14. MacIntyre, *Three Rival Versions*, 51. MacIntyre's interpretation draws on the interpretation of Joseph Kleutgen, *Die Philosophie der Vorzeit Verteidigt*, 4 vols. (Munich, 1853–1860).

15. I am prompted to recall a statement by President John F. Kennedy in a speech delivered during the height of the cold war, when tensions between the superpowers were strained and a thaw in relations seemed wholly beyond reach (address at American University, June 9, 1963; quoted from an audio recording): "For in the final analysis, our most basic common link is that we all inhabit this small planet, we all breathe the same air, we all cherish our children's future, and we are all mortal."

16. www.nyu.edu/classes/keefer/hell/camus.html, 1.

17. www.nyu.edu/classes/keefer/hell/camus.html, 2.

18. Shakespeare, *Macbeth* 5.5.

19. Plato, *Phaedo* 114d.

20. Bernard J. F. Lonergan, *Insight* (New York: Harper & Row, 1978), 474.

21. Thomas Aquinas, *On the Power of God (Quaestiones Disputatae De Potentia Dei)*, Q. 3, art. 5. Translated by the English Dominican Fathers (London: Burns Oates & Washbourne, 1932).

22. John S. Grabowski, "Person: Substance and Relation," *Communio: International Catholic Review* (Spring 1995): 152.

23. Horst Seidl, "The Concept of Person in St. Thomas Aquinas," *Thomist* 51 (1987): 451.

24. Seidl, "Concept of Person," 440.

25. Seidl, "Concept of Person," 458.

26. W. Norris Clarke, "Person, Being, and St. Thomas," *Communio: International Catholic Review* (Winter 1992): 607.

27. W. Norris Clarke, *Person and Being* (Milwaukee, Wis.: Marquette University Press, 1993), 5. The Aquinas Lecture, 1993.

28. Kenneth L. Schmitz, "The Geography of the Human Person," *Communio: International Catholic Review* (Spring 1986): 27.

29. Schmitz, "Geography of the Human Person," 41.

30. Schmitz, "Geography of the Human Person," 41.

31. Schmitz, "Geography of the Human Person," 43.

32. Schmitz, "Geography of the Human Person," 44.

33. Clarke, *Person and Being*, 87.

34. Karol Wojtyla, *The Acting Person*, trans. Andrzej Potocki (Dordrecht: Reidel, 1979), 180.

35. Augustine, *Confessiones* VII, 3(5).

36. Charles Taylor, *Sources of the Self: The Making of the Modern Identity* (Cambridge: Harvard University Press, 1989), 47.

37. Taylor, *Sources of the Self*, 34.

38. William Faulkner, Nobel acceptance speech 1949, www.literatureawards .com/william_faulkner_nobel_speech_htm.

39. Jacques Maritain, *Art and Scholasticism with Other Essays*, trans. J. F. Scanlan (New York: Scribner's, 1962), 49.

40. Maritain, *Art and Scholasticism*, 49.

41. Viktor E. Frankl, *Man's Search for Meaning: An Introduction to Logotherapy* (New York: Pocket Books, 1963), 156.

42. Frankl, *Man's Search for Meaning*, 158.

43. Joseph Conrad, *Lord Jim* (New York: Harper & Row, 1965), 152.

44. Martin Heidegger, *Being and Time*, trans. John Macquarrie and Edward Robinson (New York: Harper & Row, 1962), 236, 321.

45. Clarke, *Person and Being*, 39.

46. Clarke, *Person and Being*, 1.

47. Consider Clarke's assessment of the importance of the historical dimension of human nature (*Person and Being*, 40):

> The Thomistic understanding of human nature as embodied spirit . . . does not imply a static structure, rigidly determined . . . but rather a dynamic center of free, self-conscious action on two levels (material and spiritual), whose outside limits of develop-

ment are set *a priori* only as those of a spirit united to a material body. This leaves an immense open field for unpredictable development within these broad parameters, telling us nothing a priori about what the bodily instrument of the soul is going to look like at a given time or for how long, or what kind of environment, inner and outer, this free creative spirit will produce through its instruments.

Epilogue: In Search of an Irreducible Self

In 1637 (the year his *Discourse on Method* was first published), René Descartes considered the prospect of machines capable of imitating human actions in a convincing manner. As we saw in chapter 7 above, Descartes proposed two tests for distinguishing real humans from their technological impostors: a facility for language and a multidimensional range of activities that require more than bodily parts for their implementation.

> Of these the first is that they could never use words or other signs arranged in such a manner as is competent to us in order to declare our thoughts to others; for we may easily conceive a machine to be so constructed that it emits vocables . . . but not that it should arrange them . . . so as reply to what is said in its presence. The second test is, that although such machines might execute many things with equal or perhaps greater perfection than any of us, they would . . . fail in certain others from which it could be discovered that they did not act from knowledge but solely from the disposition of their organs.[1]

But how well do Descartes' tests hold up in a contemporary context? Can we be as confident in the twenty-first century as Descartes was in the seventeenth that humans enjoy a special status, as reflected in our linguistic and operational capacities? Is the possibility of humanoid machines that can replicate language and rational behavior so far-fetched? Descartes' prophecy highlights the widespread contemporary skepticism about our uniqueness grounded on a conception of an irreducible self immune to a thoroughgoing empirical account. In the centuries separating us from Descartes, of course, much has transpired that accentuates the perennial tension between the teleological and the mechanistic perspectives. For the vast majority of philosophers and scientists, the teleological perspective (and its appeal to an immaterial mind or soul) has been supplanted by reductionism (or, more precisely, eliminative materialism or epiphenomenalism)—the position that what was formerly attributed to a spiritual dimension of our humanness is "nothing but" or "no more than" physical states and neurophysiological functions. This reductionist emphasis is a hallmark of cognitive science and neuroscience, and these relatively new disciplines' focus on conscious experience as the primary indicator of selfhood. In this connection, we must also confront increasingly successful attempts to simulate human intelligence by means of computer technology.

THE CHALLENGE OF REDUCTIONISM

But do these applications of artificial intelligence (which can equal or surpass their human counterparts in problem-solving effectiveness) place us on a par with machines, with no need for what philosophers and theologians have traditionally designated as the soul or intellect? Such attempts at demystifying the self find further support in sophisticated imagining technology (e.g., computed tomography, positron emission tomography, magnetic resonance imaging) that opens new windows to our understanding of the brain, including an ability to map regions responsible for different conscious experiences. The upshot of these bold new investigations is the widespread assumption of the triumph of reductionism and the claim that the inner self is a matter of neuronal circuitry and its supporting biochemistry alone. Francis Crick succinctly defines this hypothesis in these terms:

> The Astonishing Hypothesis is that "You," your joys and your sorrows, your memories and your ambitions, your sense of personal identity and free will, are in fact no more than the behavior of a vast assembly of nerve cells and their associated molecules.[2]

Among contemporary thinkers, the principal target of the reductionist hypothesis is the dualistic model of Descartes, along with the belief that some mysterious entity called a "mind" directs or orchestrates the contents of conscious awareness. This is what Daniel Dennett dismisses as "our old nemesis, the Audience in the Cartesian Theater."[3] For Dennett, the debunking of the image of consciousness as occurring in a kind of theater is comparable to penetrating the "secrets" of magic tricks and coming to realize that there is no difference between what occurs "onstage" (i.e., conscious experience) and "backstage" (i.e., brain activity). In the process, the traditional mind/body problem dissolves as well. From this standpoint, reductionism obviates any need for an irreconcilable gulf between mind and body.

> Once we take a serious look backstage, we discover that we didn't actually see what we thought we saw onstage; . . . there is no Cartesian Theater; the very distinction between onstage experiences and backstage processes loses its appeal. We still have plenty of amazing phenomena to explain, but a few of the most mind-boggling special effects just don't exist at all and hence require no explanation.[4]

Dennett's remarks reveal the common postmodern assumption that any reference to a mind or irreducible self must be framed in Cartesian terms. In his zeal to insulate the mind from the encroachments of empirical science, Descartes rendered the mind a nonextended substance wholly different from the extended bodily substance. In a contemporary context, however, we also encounter a growing suspicion that the inner life of the self does not allow for an exhaustive reductionist explanation. Representatives of this trend acknowledge the persistent mystery surrounding consciousness, despite their rejection of an unbridgeable Cartesian gap between mind and body.

The philosopher John Searle, for one, stresses that conscious experience presupposes a subjective element not reducible to the objective data of neuron firings alone. In the absence of a first-person description of a phenomenon like pain, Searle contends, what is essential to pain would be missed altogether.[5] This is not to say that Searle accepts the notion of mind as some occult reality operative behind the scenes of consciousness. But by the same token, he argues that consciousness still lies beyond the scope of reduction, at least according to present standards of reductionism.

> Pretheoretically, consciousness, like solidity, is a surface feature of certain physical systems. But unlike solidity, consciousness cannot be redefined in terms of an underlying microstructure, and the surface features then treated as mere effects of real consciousness, without losing the point of having the concept of consciousness in the first place.[6]

Searle's emphasis on the subjectivity inherent in consciousness points to another dimension of current critiques of reductionist treatments of mind. In this connection, David Chalmers draws an intriguing parallel between the laws governing physical and experiential phenomena.

> All sorts of microscopic physical phenomena can be explained in terms of underlying physical laws; similarly, we might expect that all sorts of "macroscopic" experiential phenomena might be explained by the psychophysical laws in a theory of consciousness.[7]

But what shape can such a psychophysical theory assume? We find a compelling model of consciousness in quantum physics and its attempt to synthesize an account of the subatomic structure of the physical universe with an explanation of mental life and the role of the human observer in determining the really real. In this respect, quantum theory poses a direct challenge to the classical modern assumption (rooted in the ideas of Galileo, Descartes, and Newton) that the universe constitutes a mechanical system whose processes conform to certain invariable laws. This classical modern model is a dualistic one, drawing a sharp distinction between mind and matter, and positing matter alone (or, in anthropological terms, the body alone) as pertinent to scientific investigation. But this dualistic point of departure leaves us with the seemingly unresolvable problem as to how mind can causally influence the body and the physiological domain. The modern model renders human thought and conscious awareness either wholly irrelevant to physics or completely reducible to matter and biochemical processes. Such an eliminative materialism (whereby the mind is reduced to the brain) thus assumes the appealing feature of obviating the unequivocal dualism inherent in Cartesianism.

A QUANTUM THEORY OF CONSCIOUSNESS

For our purposes, the importance of the quantum model lies in its impact on current theories of consciousness and the prospects they offer for coming to grips with the specter of mind-body dualism and the problem it generates for an understanding of the wholeness of the self. My discussion here draws on insights derived from two key contributors to a quantum-based approach: Henry P. Stapp and Evan Harris Walker.[8] These thinkers propose an intriguing alternative to the dualistic restrictiveness of classical modern physics. Quantum theory, in effect, opens the possibility of achieving a fully integrated scientific account of the mind-body relation.

Historically, quantum physics is a twentieth-century phenomenon, traceable to the groundbreaking work of Max Planck and brought to completion by figures like Heisenberg, Bohr, Pauli, Dirac, Schrodinger, and Born in the 1920s.[9] In contrast to the determinism that characterizes classical modern physics, quantum theory stresses the statistical probability of the links between empirical observations. But this subjectivist emphasis results in an abdication of a realist commitment to the search for the truth of physical reality. While quantum theory exhibits a development from its earlier to later interpretations, Stapp finds an enduring theme in its ongoing affirmation that the world must be understood in informational terms.

The "tiny bits of matter" that classical physics had assumed the world to be built out of are replaced by spread-out nonmaterial structures that combine to form a new kind of physical reality.[10]

In quantum theory, the brain's experience of consciousness amounts to a passage from a potential to an actual state, as expressed through the firing of synapses. Consciousness is thus bound up with the creation of possibilities and the selection of a state through observation. Walker specifies the observer's role in this process.

> In the development of quantum theory, the observer emerges as a co-equal in the foundry of creation. Just as the clock tender is implied by the clock's turning hands, so the quantum view of matter requires the presence of an observer . . . that . . . interacts with matter. Consciousness, the substance of this new-found reality that defines the observer has fundamental existence. It is the quantum mind that is the basic reality.[11]

From this quantum perspective, consciousness can never assume the role of a passive spectator imposed by the classical model. Rather, consciousness assumes an active role, since each quantum event qualifies as a "choice" that selects an actual event out of all available potentialities.

> The new conception of the universe emphasizes an intricate and profound global wholeness and it gives man's consciousness a creative, dynamical, and integrating role in the intrinsically global process that forms the world around us.[12]

The very observation of a given quantum state thereby suggests an act of will on the part of the observer. As Walker characterizes this "volitional" act, consciousness "brings into being the one state that actually occurs from the realm of the possible."[13]

For all practical purposes, the universe of quantum physics is constituted by the potentialities and probabilities of quantum events. Accordingly, the basic matter of the universe is not substantial but purely eidetic, what Stapp designates "idealike in character rather than matterlike, apart from its conformity to mathematical laws."[14] From this standpoint, the deeper we penetrate into the nature of reality, the less materiality we encounter. The potentiality inherent in these subatomic structures allows for what Stapp characterizes as a "nonlocal" action of subjective experience on the physical world, whereby a decision to do something in one place can immediately exert an influence on what occurs at a distance in the brain or another part of the body.[15] Such a notion, of course, is a conceptual world apart from the classical "billiard ball" model of causal interaction. In this respect, Walker perceives a link between quantum mechanical tunneling (the process through which subatomic particles move between points separated by what would normally be viewed as impenetrable barriers) and the spreading of monads of conscious being over the mechanism of the brain.[16]

By recognizing the causal efficacy of consciousness, quantum theory corroborates our commonsense intuition that thought has a genuine impact on the things we do. Since it links consciousness inextricably to the physical world, this model provides a means of harmonizing the physical and the psychological in a manner otherwise lacking in the dualistic framework of the classical model. In this way, quantum theory connects its principles with human experience through what Stapp describes as "part of the essential dynamical structure," a structure that requires intentionality and choice on the part of the conscious observer.[17] But intentionality, choice, and consciousness must have a referent in something enduring in the flux of quantum events. In this respect, Walker finds a basis of personal identity in the sameness of quantum mechanical states in the brain and the corresponding continuity of consciousness over time.

> Something changes when the brain undergoes the transition to this new mode of functioning that lies outside the capabilities of all present computing machines. When this happens, we acquire our identity—an identity that exists in and as that consciousness state. Individual identity resides in the continuity of this quantum mechanical process.[18]

In response to reductionist claims that mind and consciousness are "no more than" or "nothing but" brain processes, quantum physics makes a compelling scientific case for affirming quite the opposite, namely, that mind and conscious experience involve much more than outgrowths of physical systems. This identification of mind with the most fundamental, subatomic level of things supports the notion of mind as intellect or rational soul and its contribution to the fullness of personhood. Herein lies that "added ingredient," that "something more" that underscores our status as knowers and willers in an efficacious sense, as dynamic centers of the really real.

THE CAUSAL ROLE OF MIND

The quantum-based model of consciousness clearly requires much more development and refinement to provide a persuasive account of the causal role of the mind in human thought and rational behavior. First and foremost, it confronts the challenge of linking its physical theory with the concrete facts of our experience. It is no easy task to grasp how activities as complex as knowing and volition are associated with quantum events that represent mere tendencies or potentialities for future events. Likewise, some call into question the efficacy of consciousness itself in quantum theory. According to one critic, the quantum observer's role is not an active one but a "pure and blind sentience" in which a worm might have the same effects on electrons as humans.[19] In this respect, it might be argued that a quantum theory of consciousness makes as little distinction between mind and matter as does classical physics. From this standpoint, consciousness can be viewed as no more than an epiphenomenal by-product of the interaction of subatomic particles.[20]

But as already observed, current trends among cognitive researchers, neuroscientists, and philosophers of mind reveal a growing uneasiness with a materialism that would reduce our mental life to quantifiable brain function. A quantum-based model of consciousness offers an alternative scientific response to the contemporary search for the irreducible self. As this model strongly suggests, an affirmation of the causal efficacy of mind does not demand an uncritical commitment to static dualism of the Cartesian variety. The Aristotelian/Thomistic anthropology, in contrast, upholds our psychosomatic unity, even as it distinguishes mind and body as substantial form in relation to matter and its range of potentialities in need of actualization. This is where an Aquinas can speak in a cogent philosophical manner to the general thrust of a quantum interpretation of consciousness and what it discloses about our humanness.

In Thomism, our status as "embodied spirits" presupposes an inextricable connectedness between mind and body in which mind (as rational soul) assumes a causal role in both intentional and volitional terms. If the rational soul is the substantial form of a body with the potential for life, this psychic principle cannot merely be some added attribute; it qualifies as nothing less than the defining principle of our entire being. Accordingly, Aquinas resists what Stump designates as the two main problems endemic in Cartesian dualism: "it cannot explain . . . causal interaction between soul and body, and . . . it divides cognitive functions into those . . . implemented only in the soul and those . . . implemented only in the body."[21] Once we define ourselves as embodied spirits, the insolubility of the modern mind-body problem is effectively neutralized. In Thomistic terms, the reciprocal relationship between soul as substantial form and body as its matter sustains the living human being. The human being as embodied spirit is not a divided being but an integrated whole that bridges the gap between spirit and matter in its unique mode of existence.

If humans are unique in their ability to know and to act, it is because they make sense of the facts at hand and can anticipate what is not yet realized in making causal judgments. We do this constantly in solving complex problems and in meeting all the unexpected contingencies that arise in the most commonplace circumstances. As Roger Penrose observes, there is something about conscious thinking that is markedly different from the algorithmic simulations of intelligence by computers.

> In themselves, algorithms can never ascertain truth; one needs external insights in order to decide the validity of an algorithm: it is this ability to divine or intuit truth from falsity and beauty from ugliness in appropriate circumstances that is the hallmark of consciousness.[22]

But the considerable research developments in artificial intelligence carry a promissory note on the future. Even if computers cannot replicate human thinking and conscious awareness right now (the argument might run), they will do so in due course. Penrose suggests a scenario in which a computer program is formulated by a master program. In that case, however, we would confront what amounts to a contemporary expression of the classical infinite regress problem (but in the realm of artificial intelligence rather than cosmology per se). This version of the problem proceeds from the possibility of an ongoing series of programmed computer programs. Could the series itself become self-generating? In Penrose's reckoning, "The validity and the very conception of the program would have ultimately been the responsibility of (at least) one human consciousness."[23] In the final analysis, we must confront the causal role of the human mind. No matter how dependent on technology we become (as useful as it is) or insulated from our own humanness by its benefits (as wonderful as they are), we simply cannot evade the efficacy of human thought and the accountability that follows upon our possession of a free will. In a practical context, the self that reductionists dismiss as "elusive" is not all that elusive; we affirm it whenever we think or choose.

In my estimation, the notion of humans as embodied spirits provides a useful standard against which the claims of artificial intelligence (and the reductionist assumptions it reflects) can be meaningfully assessed. Despite impressive evidence that computers can reproduce what we do on many cognitive levels, my remain obstinate in my conviction that we enjoy a privileged sphere of humanness that remains irreducible to thoroughgoing materialistic explanation. Even if a machine does replicate cognitive activity or rational behavior, does such "intelligent" output constitute knowing and rationality in a true human sense? In this context, I understand "knowing" and "rationality" in terms of a dual capacity that is part and parcel of what we are as human beings and who we are as persons: the capacity for creativity and the capacity for free and purposeful action directed toward ends we discern as intrinsically good, and conducive to the realization of our highest aspirations.

In short, we are able to dream, not just of things that are but of things that never were, in a genuinely imaginative way. This is the mark of what

Aristotle and Aquinas recognize as the active dimension of the mind: a noetic power by which we are able to transcend the raw data of sense experience in achieving a coherent vision of reality, as expressed through universal concepts, the symbolic representations of the really real. From this standpoint, knowing and rationality involve more than processing information or crunching numbers, however impressive the results.

HUMAN AND ANIMAL INTELLIGENCE

The materialist claim that the human mind is analyzable exclusively in terms of brain function (and that brain function can be replicated by machines) is but one side of the reductionist critique. A more naturalistic version of reductionism holds that we are no more than animals, albeit highly complex ones. While there is something counterintuitive about the claim that humans are on a par with machines, the suggestion that we are sophisticated animals finds more appeal in a postmodern culture that increasingly blurs the distinction between natures or species. Current research in animal intelligence presents a real challenge to those of us who wish to uphold the uniqueness of human beings, even as we readily acknowledge the kinship between humans and animals on many levels. As Alasdair MacIntyre puts it, "In transcending the limitations of animals, we never separate ourselves entirely from what we share with them."[24]

But recognizing this kinship is not the same as endorsing the thesis that "we are all animal and the brain is our soul."[25] I am unwilling to forfeit my commitment to our uniqueness so easily. I assert this with an awareness of the compelling evidence that various animal species can behave in highly human ways, from chimpanzees who make tools and pass on such techniques to their young, to life-saving, nurturing canines, to dolphins who display impressive communication skills. From my standpoint, the crucial consideration is not what such animals occasionally do, but what we as humans do so well on a continual basis.

Many contemporary thinkers would also scoff at the suggestion that membership in the human species carries a privileged status or special dignity. From a postmodern perspective, any attempt to impart a special dignity to humans (by virtue of an immaterial mind or soul, the basis of God's image in us) is guilty of "specieism," the unwarranted elevation of the human species over other species in the name of rational superiority or a certain sacrosanctness which renders human rights preeminent over the rights of other living things. Peter Singer, for example, challenges extending a privileged status to humans on the basis of some theological rationale.

The doctrine of the sanctity of human life, as it is normally understood, has at its core a discrimination on the basis of species and nothing else. Those who espouse the doctrine make no distinction, in their opposition to killing, between normal humans who have developed to a point at which they surpass anything that other animals can achieve, or humans in a condition of hopeless senility, or human fetuses, infant humans, or severely brain-damaged humans.[26]

But does a recognition of the dignity and exaltedness of the person necessarily imply that we impose our will on animal life and the environment with an arrogant sense of impunity? The very notion of creation in God's image that Singer implicitly challenges is wholly consistent with a teleological vision in which humans assume the role of stewards within a hierarchy of goods exhibiting all the richness inherent in a vast participation system of being. As I perceive it, the difficulty here is steering a subtle middle course between viewing ourselves as animals alone and dissociating ourselves completely from our biological links with all living things. It is between these two extremes, I believe, that we find a basis for affirming our uniqueness as human beings and ultimately our uniqueness as individual persons. That basis is found in the very notion of rationality as the criterion for separating humans from members of other species, including higher primates.

In this context, I assume a critical difference between rational behavior (which some animals may imitate or some machines may replicate) from a rationality rooted in a rational soul that runs to our very nature and shapes our special mode of existence. Aquinas is helpful here, distinguishing between an imperfect and a perfect voluntariness.[27] Aquinas attributes perfect voluntariness (which knows the end under the aspect of the end and the relationship of the means to that end) only to beings of a rational nature like ourselves. But he concedes that animals possess an *imperfect voluntariness,* since they are capable of apprehending the end (but without knowing it as end or the relationship between an act and the desired end). In this way, he strikes a healthy balance between a recognition of the distinctiveness of human rationality and an acknowledgment of the behavioral complexity that now finds increasing support in contemporary research in animal intelligence.

On what do people ultimately base claims of animal intelligence, conscious awareness, or rationality? Such claims, it would seem, are made by reference to an anthropomorphic model that looks to human behavior as paradigmatic of those kinds of traits. In this respect, Stephen Budiansky observes that "what makes an animal worthy of consideration . . . is how closely its behavior resembles that of a human."[28] But how else could we interpret it? Given the fact that we cannot enter into the experience of animals and approach the world from their perspective, we can only use our own experience as a touchstone and a standard. In the final analysis, we not only act but we possess reasons for our actions, and those reasons are intimately connected with our involvement in a larger community of persons engaged in constant interaction and the give-and-take of communication.

MacIntyre reckons that "humans go beyond the reasoning characteristic of dolphins when they become able to reflect on and to pass judgment on the reasons by which they have been guided."[29] This a Thomistic way of considering whether animals possess intelligence. Aquinas shows the importance of separating an intelligent activity proper to humans alone (e.g., voluntariness) and those resemblances of human activity that can be attributed to members of other species. From this standpoint, we need not completely deny intelligent capacity or conscious awareness to animals. Anyone (like myself) who has long observed the behavior of a pet (a family cat of eighteen years) could easily draw the conclusion that this wonderful creature enjoyed some impressive analytical skills and a level of awareness that often seemed human. And such behavioral characteristics are magnified in higher primates like chimpanzees. But it would do animals a great disservice to expect them to conform to a human model of intelligence. Is that not another dimension of specieism, namely, the assumption of an anthropocentric standard in evaluating what animals are able to do in an extremely well-adapted manner as animals? By the same token, it would do us a great disservice to abdicate the uniqueness of our own cognitive life, along with the moral responsibility that our rationality encompasses. When push comes to shove, none of us can evade our innate ability to seek reasons for what we do and, more significantly, the ability to find reasons for those reasons. MacIntyre puts it in this way:

> For when I take myself to have good reasons for acting in this way rather than that, I or someone else may always find good reasons to raise the question of whether what I take to be good reasons really are good reasons.[30]

EMBODIED SPIRITS AND OUR WORLD

So where has this assessment led us? Is there an irreducible self? Or is Peter Watson's conclusion the correct one?

> There *is* no inner self. Looking "in," we have found nothing . . . stable, . . . nothing enduring, nothing we can all agree upon, nothing conclusive— *because there is nothing to find.* We human beings are part of nature and therefore we are more likely to find out about our "inner" nature, to understand ourselves, by looking outside ourselves, at our role and place as animals.[31]

By now, the reader can surmise that I vehemently disagree. There *is an inner, irreducible self* that is revealed in the uniquely human range of operations and activities. If someone retorts that this range of operations and activities is not all that special (at least not special enough to presuppose some spiritual dimension), then perhaps we have reached an irreconcilable impasse. But I refuse to succumb to the sense of futility that accompanies the incommensurability thesis. I can only hope that critics will be honest enough to acknowledge the facts of our humanness, specifically, the open-endedness of human thought and the unrestricted character of free will. These features of human nature have been evident since the initial appearance of *Homo sapiens* and the explosion of consciousness that coincided with their emergence.

When I gaze on reproductions of the Paleolithic cave paintings found at places like Chauvet, Lascaux, and Altamira, I admire their sheer beauty and technical sophistication. I am inspired by the arduous conditions under which they were produced, and the fact that early human beings chose to make this incredible effort to produce art, whatever it was that motivated them. But I am absolutely amazed at what this endeavor says about our relationship to the larger world. It affirms nothing less than our inherent capacity to internalize our environment and translate it into symbolic depictions that transcend the very realities they represent. This is the mark of a creative intellect that can effect the transition from the particular aspects of our experience to the universal concepts that facilitate our ongoing quest for intelligibility. A major component of this quest lies in our ability to learn language.

In her powerful account of the breakthrough that opened the way to her ability to communicate, Helen Keller (who had been rendered deaf and blind as a result of an illness during her nineteenth month) highlights the inextricable link between thought and the acquisition of linguistic skills.

> Someone was drawing water, and my teacher placed my hand under the spout. As the cool water gushed over one hand she spelled into the other the word water. Suddenly I felt a misty consciousness as of something forgotten—a thrill of returning thought; and somehow the mystery of language was revealed to me. I knew then that "w-a-t-e-r" meant the wonderful cool something that was flowing over my hand. Everything had a name, and each name gave birth to a new thought.[32]

We are clearly more than language users or communicators. We are language acquirers, and that skill presupposes a process which can move from a raw stimulus response to an attunement to meaning and intelligibility. In Keller's words, it encompasses a gradual advance from naming objects "until we have traversed the vast distance between our first stammered syllable and the sweep of thought in a line of Shakespeare."[33]

Can this great developmental process find its explanation on the basis of behavioralist or functionalist criteria alone? I return here to the Thomistic dictum that *action follows being (actio sequitur esse)*. What we are able to do points to what we are and the mode of being appropriate to us as humans. We are the beings that carry within ourselves an aptitude for the totality of things and a dynamism to self-transcendence. If we are defined exclusively as animals, that definition must still come to terms with our trajectory toward the infinite as knowers and willers. If we are animals, then we are metaphysically oriented animals that can raise the question of our own being and its ground. And in my estimation, that is tantamount to saying that we are embodied spirits.

From this standpoint, denying the uniqueness of the human species and the special dignity of the person is tantamount to denying what we do in the most spontaneous and sustained manner: we think, we reflect on our options, we make choices, and we even reflect on our reflections. If we were no more than machines or animals, would we be able to engage in the full range of cognitive and volitional acts that we in fact perform? For that matter, would we even be able to appreciate the differences between what we do and what machines or animals clearly do not? If we cannot explain everything humans do on the basis of organizational or evolutionary complexity alone, then our only alternative is to appeal to an immaterial principle which Western thinkers traditionally designate as the soul or mind.

But our humanness is not just revealed in our ability to internalize and render intelligible what is "out there," beyond the self. It's also affirmed in our ability to give something of ourselves back to the world, specifically, to other persons. The fullest expression of this kind of giving proceeds from the human capacity for an unselfish love that finds its perfection in the surrender of self for the sake of the other. *Greater love than this no one has than to lay down one's life for one's friends.* Only a person can make such an act of self-surrender, even when he or she knows that no one cares, or that this sacrifice might gain nothing but contempt. We can do this because we appreciate other persons as deserving of our selflessness. This is the perfection of our intellectual and volitional drives: a free choice directed toward the good of the other for his or her own sake. This kind of decision, which brings to bear the complete harmonization of heart and mind, can only be made by beings that encapsulate spiritual and bodily dimensions in their very constitution. In this writer's estimation, then, the best evidence for the image of God in humans lies in those instances of disinterested giving in which we attain a genuine self-transcendence on behalf of other persons, or in the name of ideals we deem worthy of all we have to give. These acts reveal that we are far more than animal, indeed, at a great ontological remove, or in the words of the Psalmist, *a little less than a god.*

DISCUSSION QUESTIONS

1. Define reductionism in relation to philosophical explanations of mind and mental activity.
2. Why is Descartes' dualism a special target of contemporary reductionist critiques of classical theories of mind?
3. What is the role of the subjective observer in a quantum-based theory of consciousness?

NOTES

1. René Descartes, *Discourse on Method* V, A/T 56–57 (pp. 23–24), trans. John Veitch, Library of the Future, 4th ed., ver. 5.0 (World Library, 1996).

2. Francis Crick, *The Astonishing Hypothesis: The Scientific Search for the Soul* (New York: Scribner's, 1994), 3.

3. Daniel C. Dennett, *Consciousness Explained* (Boston: Little, Brown, 1991), 445.

4. Dennett, *Consciousness Explained*, 434.

5. John R. Searle, *The Rediscovery of the Mind* (Cambridge, Mass.: MIT Press, 1992), 117.

6. Searle, *Rediscovery of the Mind*, 122–23. But by the same token, Searle (124) affirms the feasibility of a reductionist account in the future: "No one can rule out a priori the possibility of a major intellectual revolution that would give us a new—and at present unimaginable—conception of reduction, according to which consciousness would be reducible."

7. David J. Chalmers, *The Conscious Mind: In Search of a Fundamental Theory* (New York: Oxford University Press, 1996), 214.

8. Henry P. Stapp, *Mind, Matter, and Quantum Mechanics,* 2d ed. (New York: Springer-Verlag, 2004); Evan Harris Walker, *The Physics of Consciousness: Quantum Minds and the Meaning of Life* (New York: Basic, 2000).

9. Stapp, *Mind, Matter, and Quantum Mechanics,* 265.

10. Stapp, *Mind, Matter, and Quantum Mechanics,* 268. Stapp (267) delineates this development in terms of "Copenhagen" and "post-Copenhagen" interpretations of quantum theory. Stapp describes the former as an "essentially subjective approach" (promulgated by Bohr) that involved a "retreat to the position of being satisfied with . . . statistical predictions about connections between their empirical observations, renouncing all claims to understanding what was going on." Stapp describes the latter interpretation (which he links with von Neumann and Wigner) as one that accepts "as real the subjective elements of experience . . . and relates them to an equally real, but nonmaterial, objective physical universe."

11. Walker, *Physics of Consciousness*, 330.

12. Stapp, *Mind, Matter, and Quantum Mechanics,* 216.

13. Walker, *Physics of Consciousness*, 258.

14. Stapp, *Mind, Matter, and Quantum Mechanics,* 223.

15. Stapp, *Mind, Matter, and Quantum Mechanics,* 268.

16. Walker, *Physics of Consciousness*, 217.

17. Stapp, *Mind, Matter, and Quantum Mechanics*, 241.

18. Walker, *Physics of Consciousness*, 253–54.

19. Roger S. Jones, *Physics for the Rest of Us: Ten Basic Ideas of Twentieth-Century Physics That Everyone Should Know and How They Have Shaped Our Culture and Consciousness* (Chicago: Contemporary Books, 1992), 215.

20. Chalmers (*Conscious Mind*, 121) questions whether any physical account of conscious experience will succeed in its reductionist efforts:

> Even such "revolutionary" developments as the invocation of connectionist networks, nonlinear dynamics, artificial life, and quantum mechanics will provide only more powerful functional explanations . . . but the mystery of consciousness will not be removed.

21. Eleonore Stump, *Aquinas* (London: Routledge, 2005), 210.

22. Roger Penrose, *The Emperor's New Mind: Concerning Computers, Minds, and the Laws of Physics* (New York: Oxford University Press, 1989), 412.

23. Penrose, *Emperor's New Mind*, 414.

24. Alasdair MacIntyre, *Dependent Rational Animals: Why Human Beings Need the Virtues* (LaSalle, Ill.: Open Court, 1999), 8.

25. Owen Flanagan, *The Problem of the Soul: Two Visions of the Mind and How to Reconcile Them* (New York: Basic, 2002), xv.

26. Peter Singer, *Unsanctifying Human Life*, ed. Helga Kuhse (Malden, Mass.: Blackwell, 2002), 228.

27. Thomas Aquinas, ST Ia, IIae, Q. 6, a. 2.

28. Stephen Budiansky, *If a Lion Could Talk: Animal Intelligence and the Evolution of Consciousness* (New York: Free Press, 1998), xiii.

29. MacIntyre, *Dependent Rational Animals*, 57.

30. MacIntyre, *Dependent Rational Animals*, 157.

31. Peter Watson, *Ideas: A History of Thought and Invention, from Fire to Freud* (New York: HarperCollins, 2005), 746.

32. Helen Keller, *The Story of My Life* (Cutchogue, N.Y.: Buccaneer, 1976), 36.

33. Keller, *Story of My Life*, 39–40.

Bibliography

This bibliography is confined to secondary sources. Bibliographic entries to all major primary sources are cited in the chapter endnotes.

Armstrong, A. H. *The Cambridge History of Later Greek and Early Medieval Philosophy*. Cambridge: Cambridge University Press, 1970.

Brehier, Emile. *The History of Philosophy: The Hellenic Age*. Translated by Joseph Thomas. Chicago: University of Chicago Press, 1963.

Brennan, Robert Edward. *Thomistic Psychology*. Toronto: Macmillan, 1969.

Budiansky, Stephen. *If a Lion Could Talk: Animal Intelligence and the Evolution of Consciousness*. New York: Free Press, 1998.

Cahall, Perry J. "Saint Augustine on Marriage and the Trinity." *Josephinum Journal of Theology* n.s. (Winter-Spring 2004): 82–97.

Chalmers, David J. *The Conscious Mind: In Search of a Fundamental Theory*. New York: Oxford University Press, 1996.

Clarke, W. Norris. "Person, Being, and St. Thomas." *Communio: International Catholic Review* (Winter 1992): 601–618.

———. *Person and Being*. The Aquinas Lecture, 1993. Milwaukee, Wis.: Marquette University Press, 1993.

Collins, James. *A History of Modern European Philosophy*. Milwaukee, Wis.: Bruce, 1954.

Copleston, Frederick W. *A History of Philosophy*. Vol. 1, pt. 1. Garden City, N.Y.: Image, 1962.

Cranford, Ronald E., and David Randolph Smith. "Consciousness: The Most Critical Moral (Constitutional) Standard for Human Personhood." *American Journal of Law and Medicine* 13, no. 2–3 (1987): 233–48.

Crick, Francis. *The Astonishing Hypothesis: The Scientific Search for the Soul*. New York: Scribner's, 1994.

Davies, Brian. *The Thought of Thomas Aquinas.* Oxford: Oxford University Press, 1993.

Dennett, Daniel C. *Consciousness Explained.* Boston: Little, Brown, 1991.

Dodds, E. R. *The Greeks and the Irrational.* Berkeley: University of California Press, 1973.

Ehrlich, Paul R. *Human Natures, Genes, Cultures, and the Human Prospect.* Harmondsworth, U.K.: Penguin, 2000.

Engelhardt, H. Tristram, Jr. "Brain, Life, Brain Death, Fetal Parts." *Journal of Medicine and Philosophy* (February 1989): 1–3.

———. "Foundations, Persons, and the Battle for the Millennium." *Journal of Medicine and Philosophy* (November 1988): 387–91.

———. "The Patient as Person: An Empty Phrase." *Texas Medicine* (September 1975): 57–63.

Ermath, Elizabeth Deeds. "Postmodernism." In *Concise Routledge Encyclopedia of Philosophy.* London: Routledge, 2000.

Flanagan, Owen. *The Problem of the Soul: Two Visions of the Mind and How to Reconcile Them.* New York: Basic, 2002.

Frankl, Viktor E. *Man's Search for Meaning: An Introduction to Logotherapy.* New York: Pocket Books, 1963.

Garrett, D. "Hume's Self-Doubts about Personal Identity." *Philosophical Review* 90 (1981): 337–58.

Gawande, Atul. *Complications: A Surgeon's Notes on an Imperfect Science.* New York: Holt, 2002.

Geddes, L. W., and W. A. Wallace. "Person (in Philosophy)." In *The New Catholic Encyclopedia,* vol. 11. Washington, D.C.: Catholic University of America Press, 1967.

Gilson, Etienne. *The Spirit of Medieval Philosophy.* New York: Scribners, 1936.

Grabowski, John S. "Person: Substance and Relation." *Communio: International Catholic Review* (Spring 1995): 139–63.

Guthrie, W. C. K. *The Greek Philosophers from Thales to Aristotle.* New York: Harper Torchbooks, 1975.

Hadot, Pierre. *What Is Ancient Philosophy?* Translated by Michael Chase. Cambridge, Mass.: Belknap Press, Harvard University Press, 2002.

Hartnack, Justus. *Kant's Theory of Knowledge.* Translated by M. Holmes Hartshorne. New York: Harcourt, Brace & World, 1967.

Heidegger, Martin. *Being and Time.* Translated by John Macquarrie and Edward Robinson. New York: Harper & Row, 1962.

Jaeger, Werner. *Aristotle: Fundamentals of the History of His Development.* Translated by R. Robinson. Oxford: Clarendon, 1948.

Jones, Roger S. *Physics for the Rest of Us: Ten Basic Ideas of Twentieth-Century Physics That Everyone Should Know and How They Have Shaped Our Culture and Consciousness.* Chicago: Contemporary, 1992.

Jones, W. T. *A History of Western Philosophy.* Vol. 3, *Hobbes to Hume.* 2d ed. New York: Harcourt, Brace & World, 1969.

Keller, Helen. *The Story of My Life.* Cutchogue, N.Y.: Buccaneer, 1976.

Kreeft, Peter. Introduction to *A Summa of the Summa.* San Francisco: Ignatius, 1990.

Kuhn, Thomas S. *The Structure of Scientific Revolutions.* 2nd ed. Chicago: University of Chicago Press, 1970.

Kuhse, Helga, and Peter Singer, eds. *A Companion to Bioethics.* Oxford: Blackwell, 1998.

Laudan, Larry. *Progress and Its Problems: Toward a Theory of Scientific Growth.* Berkeley: University of California Press, 1977.

Lauder, Robert E. "Augustine: Illumination, Mysticism, and Person." In *Collectanea Augustiniana. Augustine: Mystic and Mystagogue,* edited by Frederick Van Fleteren, Joseph C. Schnaubelt, and Joseph Reino. New York: Lang, 1994.

Lloyd, A. C. "On Augustine's Concept of a Person." In *Augustine: A Collection of Critical Essays,* edited by R. A. Markus. Garden City, N.Y.: Anchor/Doubleday, 1972.

Lonergan, Bernard J. F. *Insight.* New York: Harper & Row, 1978.

MacIntyre, Alasdair. *After Virtue.* Notre Dame, Ind.: University of Notre Dame Press, 1981.

———. *Dependent Rational Animals: Why Human Beings Need the Virtues.* La Salle, Ill.: Open Court, 1999.

———. *Three Rival Versions of Moral Enquiry: Encyclopedia, Genealogy, and Tradition.* Notre Dame, Ind.: University of Notre Dame Press, 1990.

———. *Whose Justice? Which Rationality?* Notre Dame, Ind.: University of Notre Dame Press, 1988.

MacNabb, D. G. C. *David Hume: His Theory of Knowledge and Morality.* 2nd ed. Hamden, Conn.: Archon, 1966.

Magnus, Bernd. "Postmodern." In *The Cambridge Dictionary of Philosophy,* edited by Robert Audi. 2d ed. Cambridge: Cambridge University Press, 1999.

Maritain, Jacques. *Art and Scholasticism with Other Essays.* Translated by J. F. Scanlan. New York: Scribners, 1962.

Mauer, Armand. *Introduction to Faith, Reason, and Theology: Questions I–IV of Aquinas' Commentary of the "De Trinitate" of Boethius.* Toronto: Pontifical Institute of Medieval Studies, 1987.

McLean, George F., and Patrick Aspell. *Ancient Western Philosophy: The Hellenic Emergence.* New York: Appleton-Century Crofts, 1974.

Merrill, Kenneth R., and Robert W. Shahan, eds. *David Hume: Many-Sided Genius.* Norman: University of Oklahoma Press, 1976.

Noonan, Richard. "Moral Incommensurability." In *The Oxford Companion to Philosophy,* edited by Ted Honerich. Oxford: Oxford University Press, 1995.

Noxon, James. *Hume's Philosophical Development: A Study of His Method.* Oxford: Clarendon, 1973.

Nuland, Sherwin B. *Doctors: The Biography of Medicine.* New York: Vintage, 1995.

Pasnau, Robert. *Thomas Aquinas on Human Nature.* Cambridge: Cambridge University Press, 2002.

Penrose, Roger. *The Emperor's Mind: Concerning Computers, Minds, and the Laws of Physics.* New York: Oxford University Press, 1989.

Penulhum, Terence. *David Hume: An Introduction to His Philosophical System.* West Lafayette, Ind.: Purdue University Press, 1992.

Pieper, Josep. *The Silence of St. Thomas.* New York: Pantheon, 1957.

Porter, Roy. *Flesh in the Age of Reason.* New York: Norton, 2003.

Price, John Valdimir. *David Hume.* New York: Twayne, 1968.

Puccetti, Roland. "The Life of a Person." In *Abortion and the Status of the Fetus,* edited by W. B. Bondeson et al. Dordrecht, Holland: Kluwer Academic, 1983.

Quasten, Johannes. *Patrology.* Vol. 3. Allen, Tex.: Christian Classics, 1995.

Quinton, Anthony. "Karl Raimund Popper." In *The Encyclopedia of Philosophy,* vol. 6, edited by Paul Edwards. New York: Macmillan, 1972.

Rich, Ben A. "Postmodern Personhood: A Matter of Consciousness." *Bioethics* 11, no. 3–4 (1997): 206–16.

Robinson, Cyril E. *History of Greece.* London: Crowell, 1929.

Rorty, Richard. *Philosophy and the Mirror of Nature.* Princeton, N.J.: Princeton University Press, 1980.

Schmitz, Kenneth L. "The Geography of the Human Person." *Communio* (Spring 1986): 27–48.

Searle, John R. *The Rediscovery of the Mind.* Cambridge, Mass.: MIT Press, 1992.

Seidl, Horst. "The Concept of Person in St. Thomas Aquinas." *Thomist* 51 (1987): 439–41.

Seigel, Jerrold. *The Idea of the Self: Thought and Experience in Western Europe since the Seventeenth Century.* Cambridge: Cambridge University Press, 2005.

Shapere, Dudley. "Newton, Isaac." In *Encyclopedia of Philosophy,* vol. 5, edited by Paul Edwards. New York: Macmillan, 1972.

———. "Newtonian Mechanics and Mechanical Explanation." In *Encyclopedia of Philosophy,* vol. 5. New York: Macmillan, 1972.

Singer, Peter. *Unsanctifying Human Life.* Edited by Helga Kuhse. Malden, Mass.: Blackwell, 2002.

Stapp, Henry P. *Mind, Matter, and Quantum Mechanics.* 2d ed. New York: Springer-Verlag, 2004.

Starr, Chester G. *The Ancient Greeks.* New York: Oxford University Press, 1971.

Stephens, William O., ed. *The Person: Readings in Human Nature.* Upper Saddle River, N.J.: Pearson Prentice Hall, 2006.

Stevens, Wallace. *Opus Posthumous.* New York: Knopf, 1957.

Stump, Eleonore. *Aquinas.* London: Routledge, 2005.

Tattersall, Ian. *Becoming Human: Evolution and Human Uniqueness.* New York: Harcourt Brace, 1998.

———. *The Fossil Trail: How We Know What We Think We Know about Human Evolution.* New York: Oxford University Press, 1996.

Taylor, Charles. *Sources of the Self: The Making of the Modern Identity.* Cambridge: Harvard University Press, 1989.

Thompson, Mel. *Teach Yourself Philosophy of Mind.* London: Hodder Headline, 2003.

Thucydides. *History of the Peloponnesian War.* Translated by Rex Warner. London: Penguin, 1972.

Tolson, Jay. "Is There Room for the Soul? New Challenges to Our Most Cherished Beliefs about Self and the Human Spirit." *U.S. News & World Report* (October 23, 2006): 57–63.

Torchia, N. Joseph. "Incommensurability and Moral Conflicts: A Critical Assessment of the Response of Alasdair C. MacIntyre." *Providence: Studies in Western Civilization* (Fall–Winter 2003): 40–68.

————. "Postmodernism and the Persistent Vegetative State." *National Catholic Bioethics Quarterly* (Summer 2002): 257–75.

Trigg, Roger. *Ideas of Human Nature: An Historical Introduction.* 2d ed. Oxford: Blackwell, 2000.

Uttal, William R. *Neural Theories of Mind: Why the Mind-Brain Problem May Never Be Solved.* Mahwah, N.J.: Erlbaum, 2005.

Vrooman, Jack Rochford. *René Descartes: A Biography.* New York: Putnam, 1970.

Walker, Evan Harris. *The Physics of Consciousness: Quantum Minds and the Meaning of Life.* New York: Basic, 2000.

Watson, Peter. *Ideas: A History of Thought and Invention, from Fire to Freud.* New York: HarperCollins, 2005.

Westfall, R. S. "Newton." In *The New Catholic Encyclopedia,* vol. 10. Washington, D.C.: Catholic University of America Press, 1967.

Whitehead, Alfred North. *Process and Reality.* New York: Free Press, 1979.

Wojtyla, Karol. *The Acting Person.* Translated by Andrzej Potocki. Dordrecht, Holland: Reidel, 1979.

Zaner, Richard M. *Ethics and the Clinical Encounter.* Englewood Cliffs, N.J.: Prentice Hall, 1988.

Zeller, Eduard. *Outlines of the History of Greek Philosophy.* New York: Dover, 1980.

Zimmer, Carl. *Soul Made Flesh: The Discovery of the Brain and How It Changed the World.* New York: Free Press, 2004.

Index

About the Author

Joseph Torchia, O.P., is an associate professor of Philosophy at Providence College and the Editor-in-Chief of *The Thomist*. He holds doctorates in Philosophy (Fordham University) and in Early Christian Studies (The Catholic University of America). His wide-ranging publications in philosophy, historical theology, and bioethics include the books *Plotinus, Tolma, and the Descent of Being: An Exposition and Analysis* (1993) and *Creatio ex nihilo and the Theology of St. Augustine: The Anti-Manichaean Polemic and Beyond* (1999).